The Greatest Batman® Stories Ever Told

Batman created by Bob Kane

DC®

THE GREATEST BATMAN STORIES EVER TOLD

WARNER COMMUNICATIONS COMPANY
666 FIFTH AVENUE, NEW YORK, NY 10103

A WARNER COMMUNICATIONS COMPANY
PRINTED IN CANADA.

10 9 8 7 6 5 4 3 2 1

COVER ILLUSTRATION BY *WALTER SIMONSON.*
BOOK DESIGN BY *KEITH WILSON.*

TO BOB KANE

AND BILL FINGER,

AND TO THE DOZENS

OF TALENTED MEN AND WOMEN

WHOSE CREATIVE CONTRIBUTIONS

OVER THE PAST FIFTY YEARS

HAVE MADE THE BATMAN

ONE OF THE MOST ENDURING

LITERARY LEGENDS

OF OUR TIME.

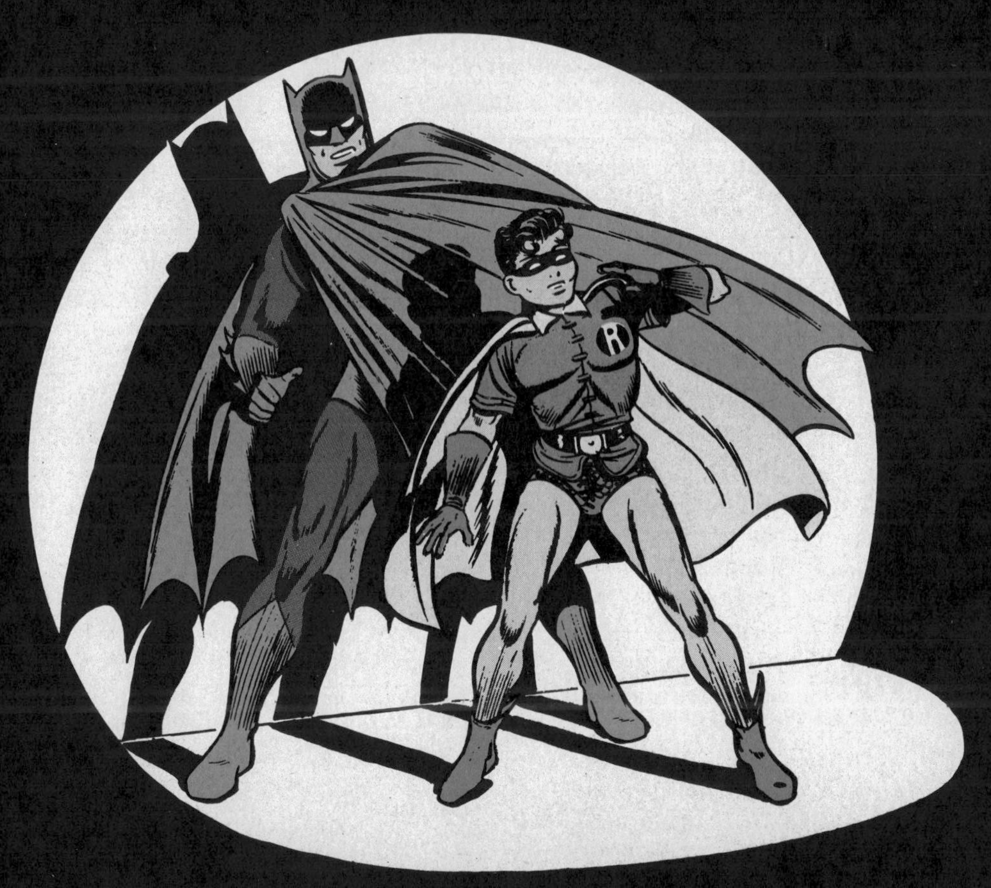

TABLE OF CONTENTS

Growing Up With The Greatest

Introduction By Dick Giordano

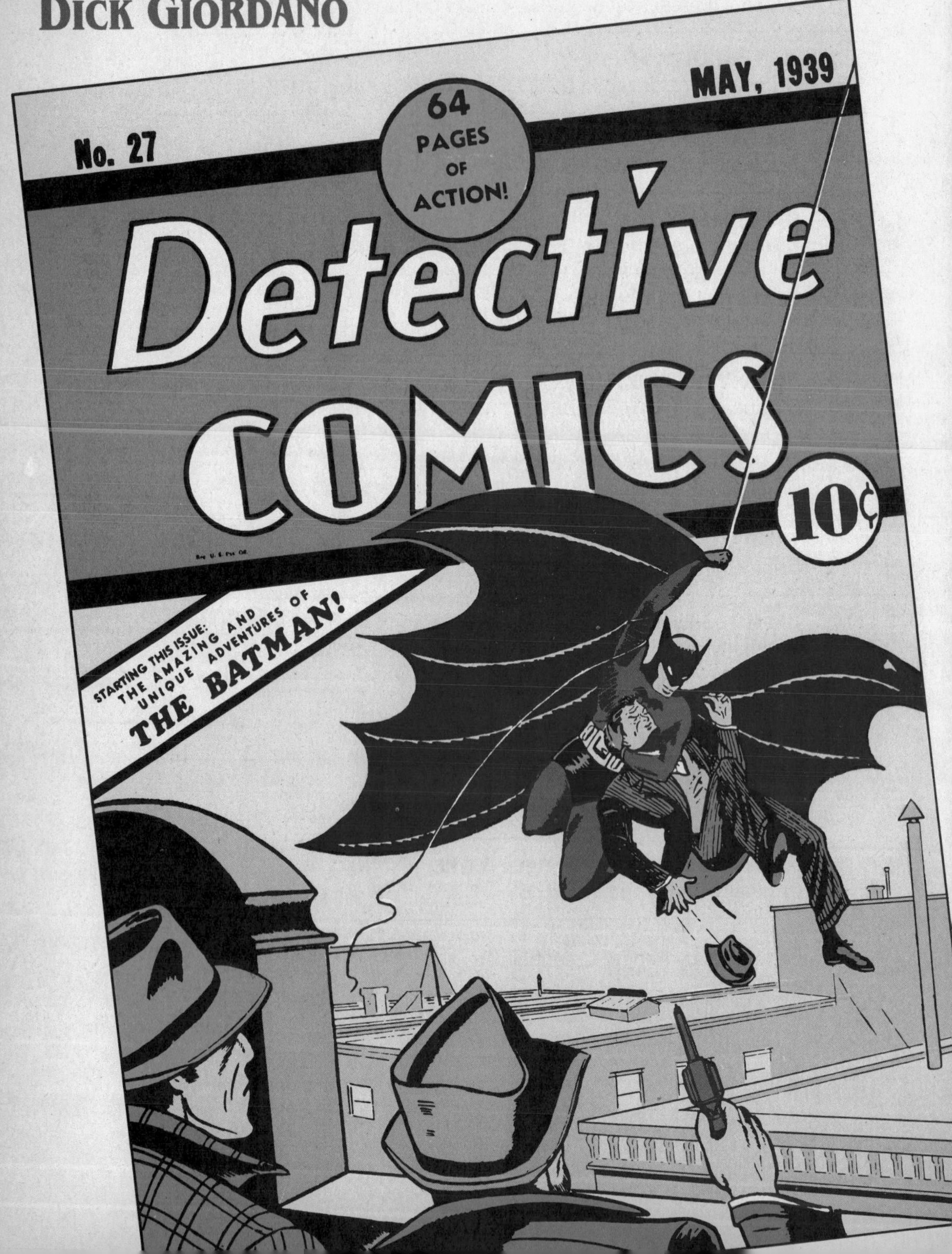

INTRODUCTION BY DICK GIORDANO

"Here. Dick, I picked up a couple of new comics for you." The paper bag containing the eagerly-awaited goodies plopped onto my bed. My father knew I loved to read comics. He'd been buying them for me regularly since *Famous Funnies* first hit the newsstands. Reading comics helped me while away the days and weeks spent in bed as a child, a victim of severe asthma attacks. They also were my passport to a fantasy wonderland where I could forget my unwelcome confinement and where the good guys always prevailed (some wearing nifty outfits and capes, even) over the bad guys.

Anyway, I flipped through the handful of comics in the bag, trying to decide which one to read first. One of them was DETECTIVE COMICS, a title I'd read before and enjoyed. DETECTIVE COMICS usually had several stories, all featuring the adventures and exploits of various crimefighter or detective types. Good reading as a rule, but nothing special.

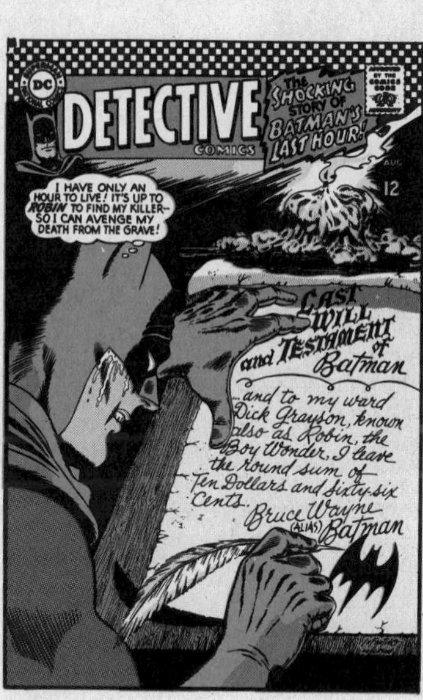

Until now.

The comic book I held in my hand *was* special. It contained a story about a crimefighter I'd never seen before, one with a cape and a mask and a dark look to him, not at all like Superman or any of the other super-heroes I had read.

It was my very first exposure to The Batman. It was a special day in my life, although I surely didn't realize how special at the time. I don't remember the cover on that issue of DETECTIVE COMICS or the story that it contained. It *could* have been DETECTIVE #27, the first appearance of Batman ever, but I recall it was the first time *I'd* ever seen and read a Batman story. No matter—I was hooked... for life, as it turned out.

Time went by and I never missed an issue of DETECTIVE COMICS, featuring my favorite hero, The Batman. Later, I added BATMAN COMICS to my must-buy list and eventually WORLD'S FINEST COMICS, the first anthology book in which Superman and Batman both appeared regularly (in separate stories at first, though their adventures as a team started in the early 1950's, thereby creating the first regularly published crossover series in U.S. comics).

Young cartoonist Bob Kane, aided and abetted by writer Bill Finger and artist Jerry Robinson (one artist couldn't possibly produce all that work), knew the secrets of keeping a series fresh, exciting and creative: never rest on the oars, never let up, and never become predictable.

With those creative minds fired up, a long list of exciting villains, supporting players, environments, vehicles, and scientifically plausible contraptions were created, most of which still exist today. These characters and characteristics helped define The Batman *and* his series and made both unique in comics hero annals.

Over a period of only a few years, we were introduced to the Batcave, the Joker, Alfred the butler, Commissioner Gordon, the Batmobile, Wayne Mansion (with its secret places), Robin the Boy Wonder, the Penguin, the Batplane, Catwoman, the utility belt, Batwoman, two different Batgirls, the Batarang, Gotham City... and the best and most believable origin story ever created for a comic book hero.

An impressive list. Is it any wonder that I found the by-line "by Bob Kane" (I didn't know about Finger and Robinson at that time) a beacon for fun reading?

But, wait. Let's talk about Batman's origin and why I believe it is intrinsic to his believability, popularity, and longevity.

The Batman was born in a few, brief, violent moments in which a young Bruce Wayne was forced to

Opposite: DETECTIVE COMICS #27, May, 1939—The Batman's first appearance.

Left: Carmine Infantino and Murphy Anderson's classic cover from DETECTIVE #366 (1967).

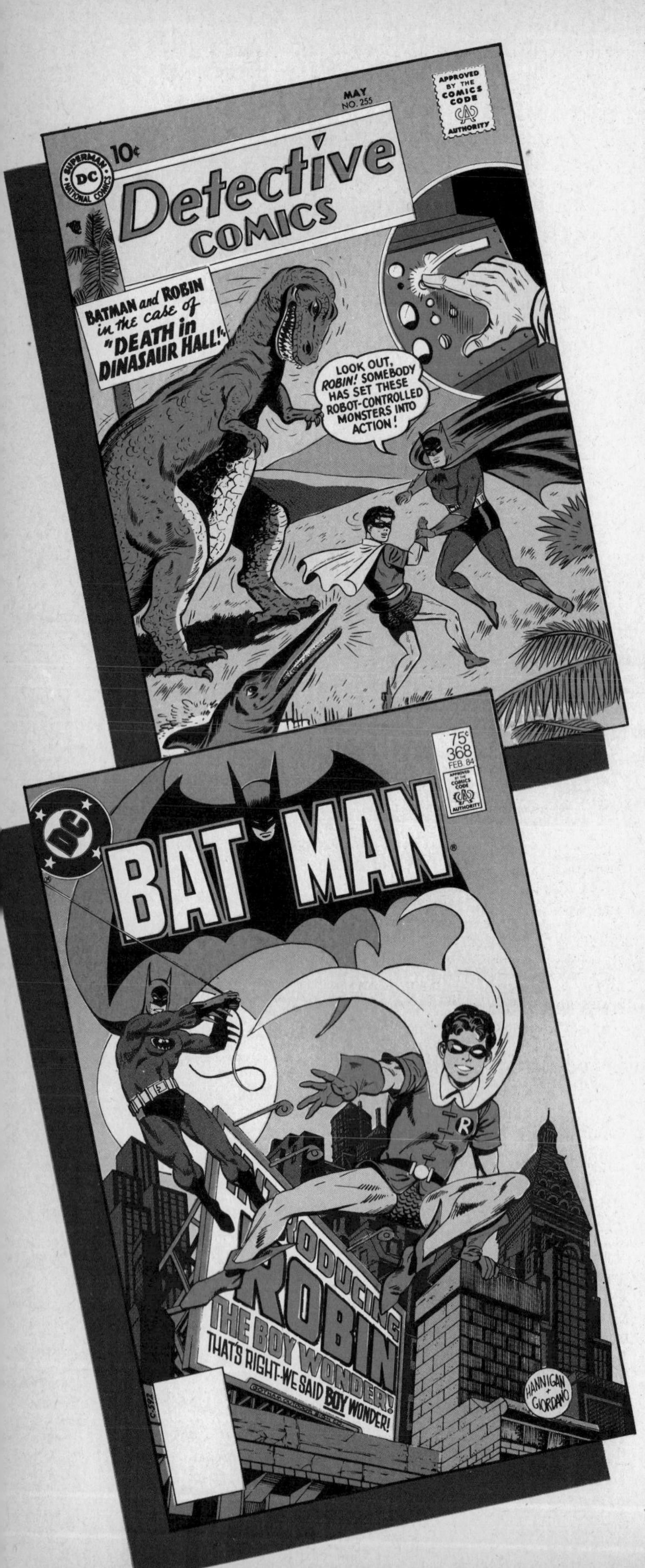

watch the brutal murder of his parents at the hands of a street thief. At that moment of immense and intense grief, young Bruce commits himself to a life dedicated to making criminals pay for their deeds. His obsession guides and motivates him to accomplish feats that we are all, theoretically at least, capable of accomplishing... if only we were similarly motivated.

We all can understand Bruce's grief, we can all understand his frustration at having to watch helplessly as the lives of the most important people in his young life are taken uselessly, and we all can understand his need to do something to avenge the deaths of his parents. The origin of The Batman is grounded, therefore, in emotion. An emotion that is primal and timeless and dark.

The Batman does what he does for himself, for *his* needs. That society gains from his actions is incidental, an added value... but *not* the primary reason for his activities. And even when we're (perhaps ever so slightly) feeling unsettled by the dark side of the Batman's nature, we still understand. We're not sure we wouldn't try to do the same thing as The Batman does, if we watched our parents being murdered.

Of course, I didn't think of it exactly that way at the time. I was only six or seven years old and incapable of thought process at that level. To me, The Batman was a neat-looking crime fighter with acrobatic skills who was very strong and very smart, but with no superpowers. He was just an ordinary guy who learned how to do a lot of nifty things, like swinging from place to place on his bat-rope (that I never knew what the rope was attached to or how Batman attached it never really bothered me).

I knew that I could aspire to be Batman but I couldn't aspire to be Superman. No way could I get powers like Superman... I would have had to be born somewhere else for that... but I *could*, if I started young enough, train myself the way young Bruce Wayne did and maybe some day be just like Batman.

Well, I never started training and so remained ordinary, but I knew I *could* have, and that was a good portion of the character's appeal to the kids who read Batman.

Of course, there were many other elements that added to the basic appeal of the character—his alter ego Bruce Wayne being rich and pretending to be an ineffectual playboy was part of the fun. I felt like an "insider" when I saw Bruce acting silly at a party because *I* knew he was The Batman and before too long he would put aside his foppish ways, don cape and cowl and bring the bad guys to justice, returning to the role of useless playboy before the story ended. No one in the story knew, but I knew!

I also enjoyed the father/son relationship Bruce had with his ward, Dick Grayson (a.k.a. Robin the Boy Wonder); the faithfulness of Bruce's butler, Alfred; and the very special and unstated relationship between Commissioner Gordon and Batman—they both knew they were more effective working together but that it could never be official and that certain questions not pertaining to the case at hand could never be asked.

As I grew older, I continued to read and enjoy Batman stories. Many of the trappings of the series took on different meanings as I matured but they all remained valid nevertheless.

Sometime during those years I decided that I couldn't leave my childhood joys entirely behind and by the age of 13 I decided that I wanted to become a cartoonist. I had been drawing ever since I could remember and my experience in reading those early Batman stories convinced me that I wanted to use my meager talents to try to entertain people as I had been entertained.

Having made that decision, I then focused my energies on that goal and never thought of doing anything else with my life. So in a very real sense, that first contact with The Batman in my formative years played a very important role in my ultimate career choice and has been a factor in my remaining in this field for 36 years.

I became a working professional in the comics industry in March of 1952. I did a lot of "stuff" for 15 years. Then, my training period over, I came to work for DC Comics in 1967 (it was then called National Periodical Publications, a name that disguised its main activity of publishing comics). Although my "day job" of editing several of DC's popular titles was very satisfying, my real satisfaction came from spending my "spare" time at home at a drawing board inking stories for the other editors. Everyone seemed to like my work and after a spell, they gave me a Batman story to ink.

They gave *me* a Batman story to ink!

It was as if I had died and gone to heaven.

As I read the story I was given to ink and looked at the drawings, I was immediately transported back to that day many years before when, as a child, I removed a batch of comics from a paper bag and caught my first glimpse of the grim visage of The Batman. My reaction was: I'm back home again! I've gone full circle!

The rush was breathtaking. Words could not express how much pure joy I felt at being allowed to make a creative contribution to the continuing legend of a character that I loved and was widely acclaimed as one of the greatest fictional heroes of our time. I simply could not have been happier.

That was the start of my rekindled relationship with the Darknight Detective, but by no means the end. I've been fortunate enough to often be in the right place at the right time during the 20 or so years that have elapsed since that first Batman assignment and have benefited from being able to work with the most talented people in this business when opportunities to pencil and/or ink or edit the Batman presented themselves.

I've been lucky, too, in that I've gotten more than my fair share of important Batman stories to work on, several of which are presented again in this volume.

Which pretty much brings me to the reason for this lengthy (and sometimes windy) dissertation: Why did we cull these particular Batman stories out of the thousands that DC has published and call them THE GREATEST BATMAN STORIES EVER TOLD? Did we use completely objective criteria or did serendipity rule?

Well, maybe a bit of both, but we (Mike Gold, Bob Greenberger, Brian Augustyn and myself) tried

Opposite, above: Batman and Robin battle a misspelled Thunder Lizard courtesy Sheldon Moldoff (1958).

Opposite, below: Artists Ed Hannigan and Dick Giordano help Batman introduce his new partner—Jason (Robin) Todd (1984).

to put aside personal bias and choose important, pivotal stories in the Batman *mythos*: stories that introduced new characters or villains; origins of one kind or another; important events; or stories that in some way or another, illuminated some important aspect of the Batman mythos. We also tried to present a good cross-section of the creative people who have helped to shape the Batman's fortunes and guided him through the five decades that have elapsed since Bob Kane created him.

It is our fond hope that the stories we present here could, taken as a whole, be considered a definitive history of our Caped Crusader and provide the uninitiated reader (wherever he lurks) with all he needs to know to join the horde of those of us who worship at the shrine.

Failing that, we hoped that it would be a pretty good read. Incidentally, "we" were chosen to be "we" because between us we had probably read and/or owned and *could* read all of the hundreds (thousands?) of Batman stories published by DC Comics.

We met at Mike Gold's house and during the brainstorming session that followed, when one of us would mention a particular Batman story that might be appropriate, Bob Greenberger would appear to look heavenward for inspiration and then, trance-like, say something like "hmmm, that story appeared in BATMAN somewhere around issue number 235/240." We would then go through the bound volumes piled in front of us or Mike would jump up, dash to his bookcase and return with the appropriate volume. Bob was on the money most, if not all, of the time. His photographic memory made our day go faster and we finished with a great list. Alas, we had too much good material and had to trim enough to keep this book from being priced as high as a mint copy of BATMAN #1. Some pretty good stories didn't make the cut. Some went into our companion volume, THE GREATEST JOKER STORIES EVER TOLD. Others . . . well, maybe next time.

We are certain that you will agree that the stories in this edition are significant enough to have been included. We also know that many of you will feel that we were dumb not to include your personal favorite. Maybe you're right...or maybe The Batman is such a special hero that each of us has a highly personal view of who The Batman is and tend to favor those stories that reinforce our view.

I do know that various and radically different interpretations of The Batman can coexist. On occasion, we have published two or more Batman projects simultaneously that have presented different takes on the then-current Batman character or that might have slightly altered our continuity and have found that readers are *reasonably* comfortable with these personal and divergent views. How many fictional heroes, comic book or otherwise, could survive and even prosper with that kind of tinkering? That Batman can exist comfortably in such circumstances speaks volumes for the strength and lasting appeal of the character that although he celebrates his 50th birthday this year, seems as young as he did that day many years ago when he leaped out of the pages of DETECTIVE COMICS and caused young hearts to beat faster at that sight.

Happy Birthday, Batman!

Thank you, Bob Kane....And good afternoon.

(One of the most respected artists and editors in the field, Dick Giordano presently is Vice-President/Executive Editor of DC Comics Inc.)

Opposite, above: A rare Bat-cover by Joe Kubert (1966).

Opposite, below: Neal Adams brings The Batman into a new decade with a classic look (1970).

Left: The Guardian of Gotham, once more courtesy of Neal Adams (1972).

Our Darkest Knight

Foreword by Mike Gold

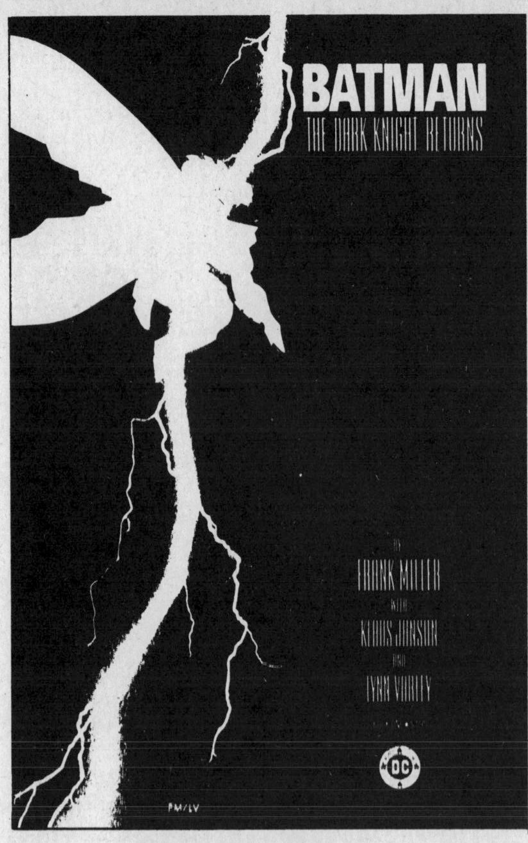

Those of us who are in the communications business—be it book writing, music singing, and/or picture drawing—live within the confines of a bone-chilling axiom: popular culture is a transient thing. What is popular today will be forgotten tomorrow, only to be rediscovered as "nostalgia" a few weeks later.

It's hard to determine exactly why The Batman has prevailed for fifty years while most of its inspirations have fallen by the wayside. Certainly, Dick Tracy has endured, with its gory villains and police procedural storytelling techniques. Yet, The Shadow has flickered in and out of existence: the radio show that gave birth to the character has been gone for more than three decades, the pulp magazine that put flesh on the cloaked crimefighter was cancelled back when most Americans were still saving up for their first television set.

Zorro has all but disappeared from our popular culture, leaving behind some classic movies during this century's first several decades and an adequate television series some thirty years ago. And, of course, only film historians and literature majors recall Mary Robert Rinehart's The Bat.

These classic characters—Tracy, The Shadow, Zorro, The Bat, and a handful of others—may have served as the inspirational background for The Batman, but such a pedigree does not, in and of itself, insure enduring success.

The vitality of The Batman lies in its primary storytelling medium: the graphic story, the so-called "comic book." A collaborative art form, comics stories come into existence due to the combined efforts of a variety of creative talent: writers, artists, colorists, letterers, and editors. But unlike that *other* great American collaborative medium, movies, the comic book is a periodical: it renews itself each and every month.

The youthful artist/writer team of Bob Kane and Bill Finger—both barely in their twenties at the time—was joined or succeeded by a legion of legendary talents over the next fifty years: Jerry Robinson, Gardner Fox, Mort Weisinger, Dick Sprang, Jack Schiff, Bill Woolfolk, Otto Binder, Bob Brown, Sheldon Moldoff, Carmine Infantino, Julius Schwartz, Dennis O'Neil, Frank Robbins, Neal Adams, Dick Giordano, Jim Aparo, Steve Englehart, Marshall Rogers, Len Wein, Irv Novick, Walter Simonson, Frank Miller, and Alan Moore . . . to name but a *few*. With this sort of pure talent on the guy's team, enduring success was hard to miss: each creator added his own sense of vitality to The Batman. The character did not merely change—he *grew*.

Yet the combination of inspiration and talent are only two of the three elements that have led to The Batman's success. The third element is *accessibility*.

At a very early age, each and every one of us realized that we probably were not born on Krypton, we were unlikely to get bitten by a radioactive spider, and we were not the spawn of mud touched by the gods. We knew, however, that if given the proper motivations, we could *become* The Batman. More important, we knew that if we had to endure those motivations, becoming The Batman probably was the *proper* thing to do.

The Batman was the combination of two different beings locked up in our souls: the shining knight . . . and Mr. Hyde.

THE GREATEST BATMAN STORIES EVER TOLD is the chronicle of the efforts of a number of the finest comics creators who ever lived, and their work on the most important comic book hero who ever lived: important because there is at least a little bit of him in every one of us.

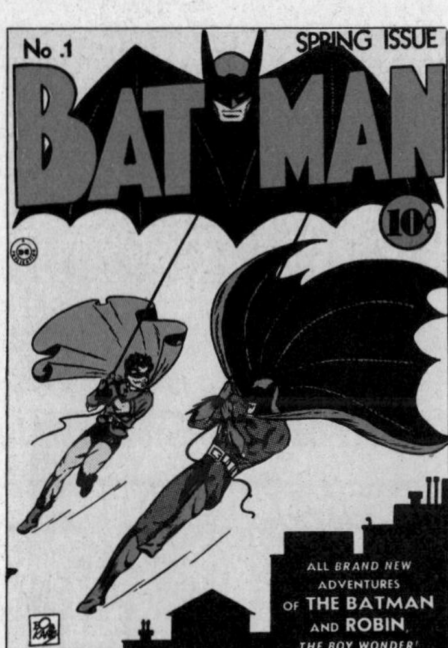

The Nominating Process

Get fifteen Batman fans together and ask each of them to select the greatest Batman stories, and you will get *at least* fifteen different lists. But if you ask fifteen people to nominate the greatest Batman stories according to established criteria, you will achieve a diversity of opinion.

We asked a number of Batman writers and artists, historians, and fans to be members of our nominating committee. We then gathered these nominations and sorted them out according to those criteria.

In selecting our committee members, we started with *Bob Kane*, the artist who came up with the idea of The Batman and who guided his destiny through the first half of his career to date (Bill Finger, Kane's collaborator, passed away in 1974). *Dick Sprang* was the predominant Batman artist from the mid-1940's through the early 1960's; it was Dick who made those huge gadgets and preposterous buildings look realistic and not silly.

Jack Schiff wrote a great many of the Batman stories published in comic books and newspaper strips between 1942 and 1964, and served as Batman editor during that same period. Jack also served as consultant to the 1949 Batman movie serial. And, rounding out our cadre of Batman writers and artists, *Dennis O'Neil* is regarded as one of the (if not *the*) leading Batman writers of the post-television period, whose work did much to establish the "darknight detective" characterization dominant for the past twenty years. Today, Dennis is the primary Batman editor and has resumed writing the character for other editors at DC.

Our team of comics historians consists of *Jerry Bails*, one of the founders of comics fandom; *Gene Reed*, who, along with Jerry and others, energetically catalogs the careers of comics talent and characters alike; and *Michael Fleisher*, himself a comics writer and the author of *The Encyclopedia of Comic Book Heroes*, the first volume of which chronicles the first three decades of The Batman.

Two of our Batman fans come from the world of advertising. The one who doesn't, *Jenette Kahn*, is president and publisher of DC Comics Inc. and an avowed life-long enthusiast of the character. *Rick Stasi* is an art director for a large Kansas City-based building supplies company; himself an occasional comics artist, Rick's enthusiasm for the character knows no bounds. *Joe Desris*, who is associated with a Wisconsin advertising agency, might very well be America's foremost Batman collector, with a gathering of original art, comic books, and memorabilia that is second to none.

Opposite: Frank Miller and Lynn Varley introduce a Dark Knight embarking on his greatest—and final—case (1986).

Left: Batman and Robin swing from the pages of DETECTIVE into their own comic book (1940).

Almost rounding out our team of nominators are those editors who worked on this book: coordinating editor Robert Greenberger, associate editors Mark Waid and Brian Augustyn, and myself.

Which leaves *Dick Giordano*, executive editor at DC Comics, former editor of Batman, and once and no doubt future Batman artist (pencils and/or inks . . . not to mention the cover to this very book). If you've read this book in order, you've already read Dick's thoughts concerning the Darknight Detective. Quite frankly, *if* there is anybody on the face of this planet who is a bigger Batman fan than Jenette, it's Dick. Since Jenette is Dick's boss, and Dick is mine, I'll let those two fight it out.

Nominating Criteria

Our process for selecting the stories included in this volume is the same one used in last year's tome, THE GREATEST SUPERMAN STORIES EVER TOLD. First, we determined several balances that must be struck.

The past fifty years of Batman stories could be divided into at least five distinct eras: the earliest days—the creation of the series through the World War II years; the larger-than-life days of big clocks and surrealistic yet existential buildings; the monster days of aliens, gimmick costumes, and weirdos; the short-lived "new-look" Batman that stressed the more detective-like aspects of the character; the regrettable and, as far as the comic books were concerned, equally short-lived television era; and the Darknight Detective era which, oddly, has been the longest and most enduring of them all. All these eras are represented in this project, although some are largely seen in the cover art reproductions illustrating the text features and the end papers.

We wanted to include as many of the truly significant stories as possible: those that introduced major characters or concepts. Of course, many of these stories have been reprinted several times each, and we did not want to have a book consisting of duplications of that which already was in most collectors' libraries.

Additionally, whereas these stories were truly seminal, many could hardly be thought of as the greatest. A few stories—fewer than anticipated, though—did not "date well." Some might even have been memorable solely out of childhood nostalgia: as a young comics fan, I thought "The Gorilla Boss of Gotham City" was among the greatest comics stories ever. I was prepared to hold my breath until I turned blue to insure its inclusion in this volume—until Dick Giordano suggested I reread it.

Similarly, we wanted to include as many of the significant characters as possible. Some, like Robin, Commissioner Gordon, and Alfred the butler, were in the majority of stories and would be represented

Right: Batman meets one of his deadliest foes—crime lord R'as al Ghul (1971).

whether we wanted them or not. Most—but not all—of the villains had to be represented as well, as did the various aspects of the Batman mythos: the Batcave, the various Batmobiles, the Batplane, and so on.

Once we looked at these considerations, we wanted to make certain we established a representative cross-section of talent: the aforementioned writers and artists, and others whose works were the fibre of The Batman's existence.

That's pretty tough to squeeze into one volume—even if that volume was longer than THE GREATEST SUPERMAN STORIES EVER TOLD.

Our choices were limited by availability of reprint material. DC's files of negatives go back only to the early 1950's, although negatives of certain earlier stories were painstakingly created from published material over the years and we were able to avail ourselves of quite a number of them.

(For the record, it should be noted that the techniques of reproducing from published material are improving, and with computer enhancement soon to be cost-effective, within the next several years a whole slew of spectacular stories from the 1930's and 1940's will be available to us. Previous attempts to recreate reproducible material from published comic books involved fading and/or bleaching copies of those books and touching up the artwork by hand—a process that can involve a great deal of redrawing.)

Further, we excluded recent stories that were quite long and are still in print in hardcover or trade paperback formats. In other words, *some* of the greatest Batman stories ever told are still to be found at most comic book specialty stores.

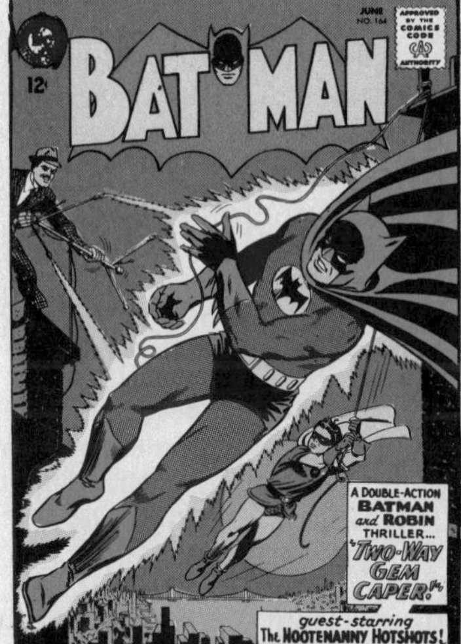

Left: After battling a long string of extraterrestrial menaces, Batman gets a "new look" (1964).

Even so, we had too much to fit into one volume, so we did the logical thing: we separated THE GREATEST BATMAN STORIES EVER TOLD into *two* books, the second entitled THE GREATEST *JOKER* STORIES EVER TOLD.

After all, the Joker *did* appear in a great many stories nominated for inclusion, and he *has* been around *consistently* for forty-nine years . . . longer than virtually every other comic book character with the exception of Superman, Batman, and Robin. We kept one Joker story in this book in the belief that many short-sighted libraries, and a few short-funded enthusiasts, might acquire only THE GREATEST BATMAN STORIES EVER TOLD and not its sequel.

Our nominators selected their stories based upon these criteria, tempered by the breadth of their own experience. As noted in the introduction, the final selections were made by Dick Giordano, Robert Greenberger, Brian Augustyn and myself at a lengthy donut-and-water-filled meeting at my home, surrounded by dozens of bound volumes and sundry other reference material.

A Note As To Credits

Unfortunately, the writers and/or artists of a number of the stories included in this book have been lost to the ages. It's a shame not to be able to give these talented people their due credit, and a number of people, including Joe Desris, long-time Batman fan Bill J. White, and numerous people on DC's staff, have attempted to nail down a number of these credits. Art styles are fairly easy to identify, but we included these credits only when the entire group was satisfied we were accurate. Those records that survived from the early years are spotty and mistakes did happen, and we apologize to those talented

individuals whose work remains uncredited.

The Next Fifty

That Batman remains vital is attributable to a number of factors: BATMAN and DETECTIVE COMICS remain among DC's best-sellers; there has been a constant flow of merchandising items—more than enough to fill a large warehouse; he has been the subject of two 1940's movie serials and the upcoming fiftieth anniversary major motion picture from Warner Bros.; his mid-1960's television series remains in syndication and is viewed by tens of millions of people worldwide *each week*, and his cartoon adventures have endured on television and in home video for twenty years.

But that is the stuff that keeps corporate officers and stockholders happy. Those of us who have eagerly haunted the racks since that fateful day in 1939 know that Batman is the *strength* of the comic book medium: the symbol of just how good comic books can be. It is no surprise to us that The Batman has been the most wanted character for use in the new Prestige Format, or that Frank Miller's *The Dark Knight* has brought in more retail dollars than any other single comic book story ever.

In looking back over the past fifty years, we might be intrigued by how both the character and the medium have grown, but we're not really surprised.

Batman has done well at age fifty. He has not shown his age, and if the quality of upcoming artistic talent I've seen lusting after the character at comic book conventions is any indication, Batman's second fifty will be just as exciting.

(*Mike Gold is Senior Editor/ Director of Development for DC Comics.*)

From top to bottom, three interpretations of the Darknight Detective, by Dick Giordano; Sheldon Moldoff; Gene Colan and Giordano.

BATMAN
THE BATMAN-WEIRD MENACE TO ALL CRIME-AT LAST MEETS AN OPPONENT WORTHY OF HIS METTLE. A STRANGE CREATURE, COWLED LIKE A MONK, BUT POSSESSING THE POWERS OF A SATAN! A MAN WHOSE POWERS ARE UNCANNY, WHOSE BRAIN IS THE PRODUCT OF YEARS OF INTENSE STUDY AND SECLUSION!
BY BOB KANE

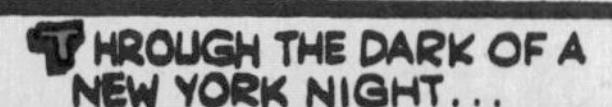

THROUGH THE DARK OF A NEW YORK NIGHT...

SOON NOW, AND I SHALL KNOW.

DISTANCE KNOWS NO BOUNDS BY WHICH TO HOLD THE EERIE FIGURE.

HE SIGHTS HIS QUARRY!

I HAVE BEEN SENT TO YOU BY THE MASTER MONK!
I... HELP.. HELP!!

AS IF IN ANSWER TO THE DOOMED MAN...

Story by Gardner Fox/Art by Bob Kane/Coloring by Tom Ziuko

WHO... WHO ARE YOU?
REMAIN UNTIL I GIVE YOU LEAVE TO GO!!

THE BATMAN RECOGNIZES HIS FIANCEE, JULIE MADISON.
JULIE.. YOU!

WHA-WHAT AM I DOING HERE? WHO ARE YOU?

BUT...IF YOU ARE TAKING ME HOME...HOW DO YOU KNOW WHERE I LIVE? WHY WON'T YOU TALK? YOU WON'T TELL ME A THING!

BUT...WON'T YOU TELL ME WHO YOU ARE?
TELL YOUR FIANCE, BRUCE WAYNE, ALL THAT HAPPENED! G'NIGHT!

THE NEXT MORNING, BRUCE WAYNE IS CALLED TO HIS FIANCEE'S HOME!

BRUCE, THERE IS SOMETHING I MUST TELL YOU. A MAN DRESSED AS AN ENORMOUS BAT FOUND ME LAST NIGHT ON THE STREET ABOUT TO KILL A MAN!

GOOD LORD, JULIE - SUPPOSE YOU HAD! WE'D BETTER SEE DR. TRENT RIGHT AWAY!

AND SCARCELY TWO HOURS LATER.

YOUNG LADY, I'VE SEEN VICTIMS OF AN EXPERT HYPNOTIST EXHIBIT YOUR SYMPTOMS! DON'T YOU RECALL ANYTHING THAT WOULD SUGGEST SOMETHING LIKE THAT? I ADVISE AN OCEAN VOYAGE!

YET, AS DOCTOR TRENT TALKS, BRUCE WAYNE NOTICES HIS STARING EYES AND WONDERS . . .
YES, YES_AN OCEAN VOYAGE TO PARIS . . AND PERHAPS, LATER, TO HUNGARY_THE LAND OF HISTORY AND WEREWOLVES.

ONE TICKET TO PARIS, PLEASE. PORT CABIN.
LUNAR LINES

I DON'T LIKE THE CRACK THE DOCTOR MADE ABOUT WEREWOLVES, JULIE. AND HE SEEMED HYPNOTIZED HIMSELF, WHEN HE GAVE YOU THAT ADVICE. BUT MAYBE I'M IMAGINING THINGS.
OF COURSE YOU ARE! I'VE WORRIED YOU. BUT I'LL BE GOOD, I PROMISE.

BUT BACK AT THE WAYNE MANSION . . .
JULIE WOULD BE SUPRISED TO KNOW HER BATMAN IS HER FUTURE HUSBAND.

AND IN A SECRET HANGAR KNOWN ONLY TO HIMSELF . . .
TWO NEW WEAPONS. MY BATGYRO, IN WHICH TO FOLLOW JULIE, AND . . .

THE FLYING BATERANG - MODELED AFTER THE AUSTRALIAN BUSHMAN'S BOOMERANG!

THE END OF THE WORLD! WE ARE ATTACKED BY MARTIANS!
LOOK!
A BAT!

AND OUT TO SEA...

WHILE ON BOARD THE LUNAR LADY..
A MONSTER BAT! FLYING OVER THE OCEAN.

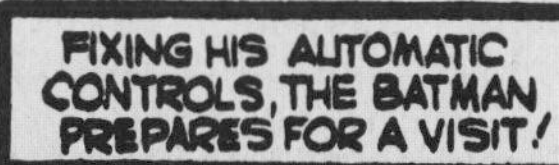
FIXING HIS AUTOMATIC CONTROLS, THE BATMAN PREPARES FOR A VISIT!

YOU... HERE!!

JULIE EXPLAINS HER PLIGHT TO THE BATMAN.
..AND SO THAT'S WHY I'M HERE. IF...LOOKOUT!

THE EYES OF THE GAUNT FIGURE SEEM TO BURN. HE IS THE ARCH-CRIMINAL KNOWN AS THE MONK!

THAT MAN HAS UNCANNY POWERS. I SEEM TO BE HYPNOTIZED. IT IS HARDER AND HARDER TO MOVE.

BY A TREMENDOUS EFFORT OF WILL, THE BATMAN LEAPS INTO ACTION.

THE SPELL IS BROKEN! ... THE MONK EVADES THE BATERANG.
SWISH

THE BATMAN LEAPS FOR THE ROPE LADDER!
SWISH

THE BATMAN, ANXIOUS TO GET TO THE BOTTOM OF THE MYSTERY, FOLLOWS THE SHIP, AND THE MONK - TO PARIS...
PARIS AT LAST!

THE SEARCH BEGINS...

THE TRAIL LEADS EVERYWHERE.

HELP! THE DEVIL HIMSELF.
CAB

THE WEIRD FIGURE IS SEEN ALL OVER PARIS, UNTIL, ONE NIGHT —
JULIE... AT LAST!

BUT A WARM RECEPTION HAS BEEN PREPARED FOR HIM!

THE BATMAN NIMBLY DODGES THE HUGE APE, ONLY TO FLY THROUGH A SLIDING DOOR...

...AND TUMBLES DOWN, DOWN, DOWN, INTO A GIGANTIC NET.

CAUGHT LIKE A RAT IN A TRAP, AS THE NET CLOSES ABOUT HIM . . .

THE BATMAN ONCE AGAIN FACES THE DIABOLICAL MASTER MONK!
RASH MORTAL... TO DARE FACE THE POWER OF THE MONK... LOOK BELOW YOU AT YOUR FATE! WHEN I PULL THIS LEVER—HEH! HEH!!

THE NET BEGINS TO DROP SLOWLY INTO THE DEN OF SNAKES.

IN A FLASH, THE BATMAN FLIPS HIS BATERANG.

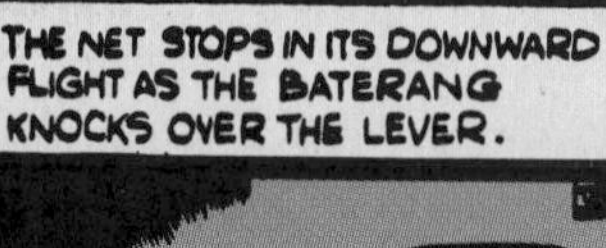
THE NET STOPS IN ITS DOWNWARD FLIGHT AS THE BATERANG KNOCKS OVER THE LEVER.

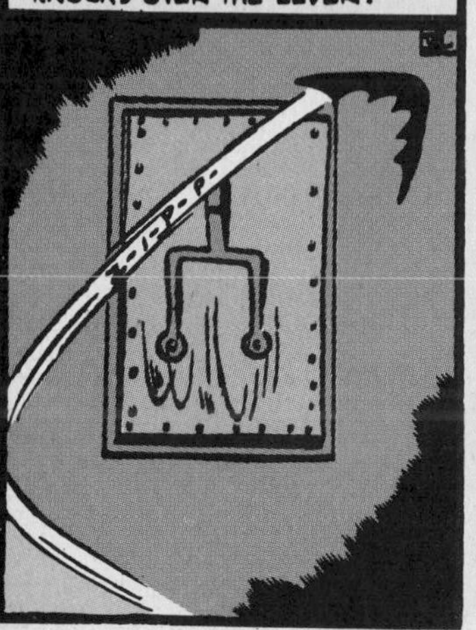

CONTINUING ON ITS UPWARD SWEEP, IT CRASHES INTO A GLASS CHANDELIER.
ZING

THE BATMAN GRASPS THE BATERANG AND THE BROKEN GLASS!

A HEROIC GESTURE, BUT A FUTILE ONE. THE LEVER WILL REMAIN DOWN THIS TIME!

WORKING AGAINST TIME, THE BAT-MAN SEVERS STRAND AFTER STRAND.

FREEING HIMSELF NONE TOO SOON..

THE BATMAN, IN FULL PURSUIT OF THE FLEEING MONK...

SUDDENLY, A BARRED DOOR DROPS BETWEEN THE BATMAN AND THE MONK...
DIE HERE, YOU FOOL, WHILE I SEND THE GIRL, JULIE, ON TO MY CASTLE IN HUNGARY, TO FEED MY WEREWOLVES!

THE GIGANTIC GORILLA IS LOWERED, AS THE BAT-MAN IS CAGED BY BARS ALL ABOUT HIM.

THE BATMAN MAKES A DESPERATE LEAP FOR THE ROPE THAT LOWERED THE GORILLA...

... AS HE CLIMBS HAND OVER HAND UP THE ROPE - HE SIGHTS THE GUARD ABOUT TO DRAW A GUN...

THE BATERANG HITS ITS MARK!
SOCK!

THE IDLING BAT-PLANE HOVERS ABOVE THE BATMAN!

AS A POWERFUL CAR RACES TOWARDS HUNGARY, THE SHADOW OF THE BAT FOLLOWS IT!

THE BATMAN PREPARES TO BOARD THE CAR FROM THE AIR!

A GLASS PELLET FILLED WITH GAS IS THROWN INTO THE CAR...

THE CAR SWERVES INTO A TREE...
THE MONK KNEW BETTER THAN TO COME —BUT I CAN SAVE JULIE!

THE BATMAN MAKES A VALIANT LEAP FOR THE LADDER OF HIS BAT-PLANE!

WITH JULIE SAFE, THE BATMAN PLANS ON VENGEANCE...
POOR KID!

...AND SETS HIS AUTOMATIC CONTROLS FOR HUNGARY—HOME OF THE VICIOUS MONK AND HIS WEREWOLVES!

Continue THE THRILLING ADVENTURES OF THE BATMAN AND HIS COMBAT AGAINST THE MYSTERIOUS MONK! WHAT PLANS HAS THE MONK IN MIND? WHY DOES HE WANT JULIE?
See THE NEXT EPISODE OF THE
BATMAN

BATMAN

BY BOB KANE

—FOLLOWING HIS FIANCEE, THE BATMAN, IN REALITY BRUCE WAYNE, HAS TRAILED A SINISTER FIGURE, COWLED LIKE A MONK, INTO HUNGARY ...

LIKE AN ANIMAL OF PREY.. THE BATMAN WATCHES HIS QUARRY.

ON THE END OF A SILKEN CORD, THE BATMAN RACES OVERHEAD...

...AND DROPS LIKE A HUGE BAT -

ONTO A SPEEDING CARRIAGE.

Story by Gardner Fox/Art by Bob Kane/Coloring by Tom Ziuko

HE WHIPS OUT A GLASS PELLET OF CHOKING GAS AND...

THE FUMES OVERCOME THE OCCUPANT OF THE CAB!

INSTEAD OF HIS QUARRY, THE MONK, THE BATMAN FINDS...
WHAT..?

THE EERIE FIGURE RETURNS TO HIS BATPLANE.
I DON'T KNOW WHO SHE IS, BUT I HAVE A FEELING I'LL SOON FIND OUT.

STRANGE FOR ANYONE TO BE TRAVELING ALONE WAY OUT HERE...AND YET THE MONK... I WONDER?

THE BATMAN ARRIVES AT HIS HOTEL, EMBEDDED DEEP IN THE CARLATHAN MOUNTAINS IN HUNGARY...
AH, SHE'S COMING TO! I HOPE JULIE IS SAFE.

WHO... WHO ARE YOU?
MY NAME IS DALA. I SEEM TO HAVE BEEN KIDNAPPED BY YOUR FRIEND HERE.

THAT NIGHT, THE BATMAN SAFEGUARDS HIS FIANCEE AND THE STRANGER.

DURING THE NIGHT, THE BATMAN HEARS SOBBING MOANS!

THROUGH THE OPEN DOOR COMES THE WOMAN, DALA!!

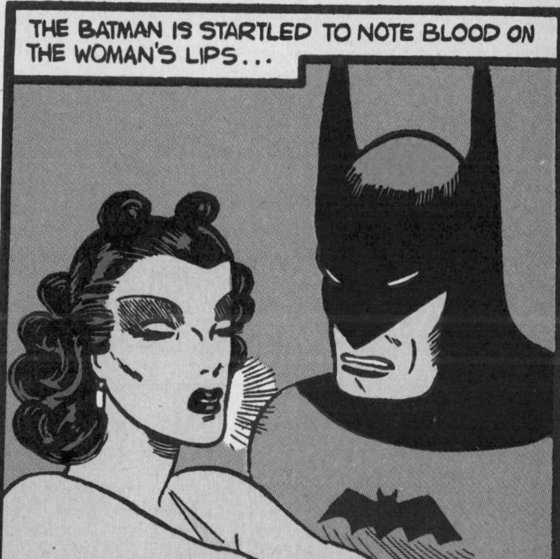
THE BATMAN IS STARTLED TO NOTE BLOOD ON THE WOMAN'S LIPS...

AND FEARS FOR JULIE'S SAFETY.

SUDDENLY, DALA SNAPS OUT OF HER TRANCE, GRABS A STATUETTE AND...

THE BATMAN IS STUNNED MOMENTARILY, ALLOWING THE STRANGE WOMAN TO ESCAPE.

THE BATMAN RETURNS TO JULIE, WHOSE THROAT SHOWS TWO RED SPOTS... MARKS OF THE VAMPIRE!

I SHOULD HAVE KNOWN. NEVER SHOULD HAVE TRUSTED HER.

SHE WON'T GET FAR.

LIKE A PLUMMET, THE BATMAN OVER-TAKES HIS PREY.

YOU SHALL TALK NOW, DALA, YOU WITCH! I THOUGHT YOU AN ACCOMPLICE OF YOUR EVIL MASTER WHO CALLS HIMSELF THE MONK. SO YOU ARE VAMPIRES!!

YOU WANT TO KNOW WHERE THE MONK IS? YOU FEAR HIM - WELL, I DO, TOO. I'LL TELL YOU WHERE YOU MAY FIND HIM IF YOU PROMISE TO KILL HIM!

I'LL BE JUDGE OF THAT! WHERE DOES THE MONK HIDE?

IN THE LOST MOUNTAINS OF CATHALA BY THE TURBULENT RIVER DESS. I SHALL GUIDE YOU.

THIS MONEY WILL SAFE GUARD YOU. I AM GOING. YOU MUST FIGHT AGAINST THE POWER THAT CALLS YOU TO THIS MONK!

OH - I WILL FIGHT. I WILL ... BUT I AM SO AFRAID WITHOUT YOU!!

AND SO THE BATMAN AND DALA DEPART ON THEIR WEIRD MISSION...

TOWARD THE STRONGHOLD OF THE 'MONK' WINGS THE EERIE BATPLANE...

SUDDENLY, THE BATMAN SEES...

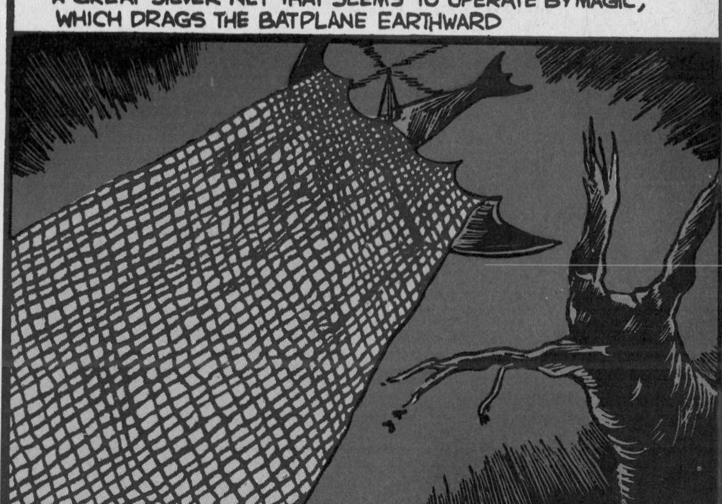
A GREAT SILVER NET THAT SEEMS TO OPERATE BY MAGIC, WHICH DRAGS THE BATPLANE EARTHWARD

YOU FOOL! PITTING YOUR PUNY BODY AGAINST THE MIGHTY MONK.

MY FRIEND, THE BATMAN! SO YOU ARE STILL ALIVE! AH...DALA..WELCOME.

BY HIS MARVELOUS HYPNOTIC POWERS, THE MONK SLOWLY OVERPOWERS THE BATMAN _

YOU MUST GET RID OF THIS BATMAN.
I THINK A TASTE OF THE WERE WOLF DEN WOULD HELP.

WAIT...YOUR VENGEANCE MUST BE PERFECT.

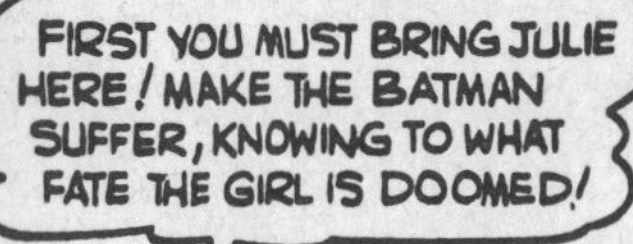
FIRST YOU MUST BRING JULIE HERE! MAKE THE BATMAN SUFFER, KNOWING TO WHAT FATE THE GIRL IS DOOMED!

BY A TREMENDOUS CONCENTRATION OF WILL, THE MONK FORCES HIS POWER THROUGH SPACE.

THE 'MONK'S' MIND FASTENS ON JULIE'S WILL, COMPELLING HER TO COME TO HIM!

THE HELPLESS BATMAN SEES HIS FIANCEE DRAWN INTO THE MONK'S TRAP!
SOON YOUR JULIE WILL BE AS WE ARE - WEREWOLVES TO RAVISH ON ALL LIVING MEN - AND YOU SHALL BE DEAD. HELPLESS TO AVENGE HER!

THE BATMAN IS FORCED TO SUFFER IN SILENCE.
YOU HAVE DONE SOMETHING TO HIM. HIS EYES ARE SUFFERING, BUT HE CANNOT MOVE! OH_YOU FIEND!

INTO THAT DEN OF WOLVES WHICH I SHALL CALL FROM THE FOREST YOU SHALL BE CAST TO DIE BY THEIR THIRSTY FANGS!

BEFORE THE BATMAN'S HORRIFIED EYES, THE MONK BEGINS TO CHANGE...

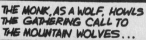

THE MONK, AS A WOLF, HOWLS THE GATHERING CALL TO THE MOUNTAIN WOLVES...

-AND FROM THE SURROUNDING MOUNTAINS, THE WOLVES GATHER.

YOU SHALL BE THROWN INTO THE ARENA BELOW, TO DIE AT THEIR RENDING FANGS.. AS YOU ARE SCREAMING IN DEATH—REMEMBER THAT JULIE WILL BE A WEREWOLF HERSELF IN TIME! TO RUN WITH THE PACK ON MOONLIGHT NIGHTS!

AS HE IS PUSHED FORWARD, THE BATMAN'S SENSES SUDDENLY RETURN TO THEIR FULL POWER.

HE TWISTS IN MID-AIR AND TRIES A DESPERATE THROW WITH HIS SILKEN ROPE.

- HIS CAST FAILS!

-AND HE FALLS INTO THE WOLF DEN.

THE BATMAN SWIFTLY EXTRACTS A GLASS PELLET FROM HIS BELT!!

THE GAS IN THE EXPLODING PELLET OVERCOMES THE WOLVES..

I CAN HOLD THE WOLVES OFF ONLY AS LONG AS MY GAS PELLETS LAST- THEN IT'S OVER!

THE LIGHT BUT STRONG ROPE FAILS TO CARRY TO THE PIT'S EDGE.

TOWARD DAWN, THE WOLVES AWAKE..

FLASHING FANGS AGAIN MENACE THE BATMAN!

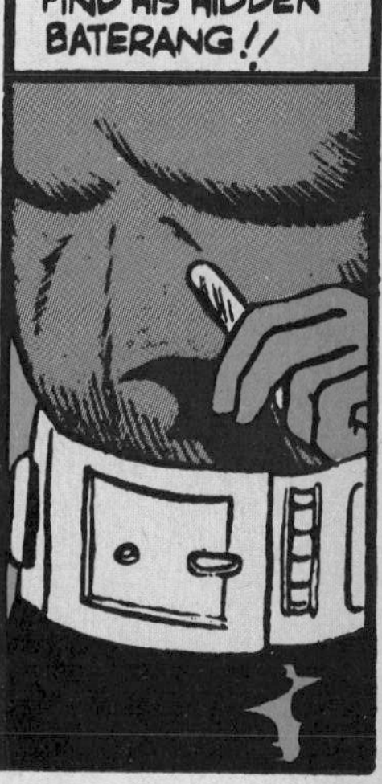
THE BATMAN'S FINGERS FIND HIS HIDDEN BATERANG!!

ONE STRONG CAST WILL WIN ME FREEDOM.

THE BATERANG SLIPS PAST A STONE POST AND THE ROPE HOLDS.

THE BATMAN CLIMBS TO SAFETY!

AND THEN SEEKS HIS VENGEANCE...

SAFE SO FAR-
NOW FOR THE OTHERS!

A SILVER STATUE! WHILE THE VAMPIRES SLEEP, DURING THE DAYTIME, I SHALL MELT THIS STATUE AND MAKE TWO SILVER BULLETS- ONE FOR DALA AND ONE FOR THE MONK!

ONLY A SILVER BULLET MAY KILL A VAMPIRE!

NOW TO FIND THE OPEN TOMB IN WHICH THESE VAMPIRES SLEEP AND BRING THEM DEATH THAT WILL RELEASE JULIE!

THE BATMAN PAUSES BEFORE THE OPEN TOMBS OF THE VAMPIRES...

NEVER AGAIN WILL YOU HARM ANY MORTAL BEING!

THE SPELL IS BROKEN... AND LIFE RETURNS ONCE AGAIN TO JULIE!
I DON'T KNOW WHO YOU ARE, BUT YOU SAVED MY LIFE AND I SHALL BE FOREVER GRATEFUL!
BOB KANE

FINIS
A NEW INTRIGUING
BATMAN
STORY EVERY MONTH IN
DETECTIVE COMICS

BATMAN

BY BOB KANE

ALREADY AN ALMOST LEGENDARY FIGURE, THE COWLED SHADOW OF THE **BATMAN** PROWLS THROUGH THE NIGHT PREYING UPON THE CRIMINAL PARASITE, LIKE THE WINGED CREATURE WHOSE NAME HE HAD ADOPTED

WHILE AN INNOCENT METROPOLIS SLEEPS, LITTLE DOES IT REALIZE THAT HUGE, TERRIFYING MAN-MONSTERS SHALL SOON STALK THE STREETS AND BRING TO THEM HAVOC AND DESTRUCTION: AND LITTLE DOES BRUCE WAYNE SUSPECT THAT FATE SHALL TOUCH HIS SHOULDER AND SINGLE HIM OUT AS THE ONE TO DO BATTLE WITH THESE MONSTERS, AS HE GOES FORTH CLAD IN THE GARB OF THE WEIRD AND MENACING.... **BATMAN!**

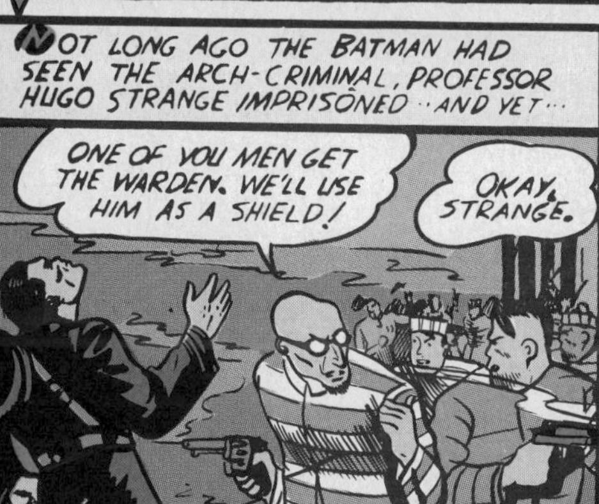

NOT LONG AGO THE BATMAN HAD SEEN THE ARCH-CRIMINAL, PROFESSOR HUGO STRANGE IMPRISONED ··AND YET···
ONE OF YOU MEN GET THE WARDEN. WE'LL USE HIM AS A SHIELD!
OKAY, STRANGE.

ONCE MORE PROFESSOR HUGO STRANGE IS FREE TO CARRY OUT THE NEXT OF HIS DIABOLICAL SCHEMES.
WUXTRY! PROFESSOR STRANGE ESCAPES IN PRISON BREAK!

THE NEXT NIGHT···· THE METROPOLIS INSANE ASYLUM.
GET THEM OUT QUICKLY!
C'MON NUTS!
GOODY! GOODY!
OH GOO!

Story by Bill Finger/Art by Bob Kane/Coloring by Nansi Hoolahan

THAT NIGHT ... THE HOME OF BRUCE WAYNE
— FLASH — A GUARD IDENTIFIED PROFESSOR STRANGE AS THE LEADER OF THE MEN WHO FREED FIVE INSANE PATIENTS FROM THE CITY INSANE ASYLUM.
INSANE MEN?

CRIMINALS, MANIACS, AND STRANGE CAN ONLY ADD UP TO ONE THING ... SOMETHING NEW IN CRIME ... SOMETHING FANTASTIC AND TERRIBLE VERY TERRIBLE !!

A MONTH LATER ... A CROWDED STREET IN LOWER MANHATTAN

SUDDENLY A WOMAN STOPS AND SCREAMS IN FRIGHT!
AA..AA.AH! LOOK!
HELP!
WHAT IS IT? IT ISN'T HUMAN!

TOWERING UP A FULL FIFTEEN FEET, A GIGANTIC HULK LOOMS ABOVE THEM, HUGE AND TERRIBLE!!
BIJOU
HELP!
A MONSTER!
WE'LL ALL BE KILLED!

THE HORRIBLE CREATURE BEGINS ITS WAVE OF DESTRUCTION ...
HELP!
W-WHAT IS IT?
YAA-A-A-A

BULLETS THUD INTO THE BEAST BUT THIS ONLY MADDENS HIM!
LOOK! BULLETS DON'T STOP HIM ... HE'S STILL LIVING!

THE ENRAGED BEAST SEEMS TO GO MAD!

THE PEOPLE ARE PANIC-STRICKEN!
HELP!
RUN FOR YOUR LIVES!!

AS MORE POLICE RUN UP, THE MONSTER RIPS UP A LAMP POST...

THE MONSTER WIELDS THE WEAPON WITH TERRIBLE EFFECT!

SUDDENLY AS POLICE CARS APPEAR, THE MONSTER LUMBERS TOWARD A TRUCK IDLING NEARBY
THERE HE GOES TOWARDS THE TRUCK! STEP ON IT!!

THE POLICE CAR STARTS IN PURSUIT!

AS THE POLICE DRAW NEAR, THE MONSTER HURLS SOMETHING AT THE CAR ...

THERE IS A SHATTERING ROAR AS THE OBJECT HITS THE POLICE CAR!
BOOM!

THAT NIGHT...
AND THE MONSTER MADE GOOD HIS ESCAPE BY BOMBING THE POLICE CAR THE PEOPLE...
IT COULD BE THE WORK OF ONLY ONE MAN... STRANGE

IF I KNOW PROFESSOR STRANGE THERE WILL BE MORE OF THEM TO COME. I MUST STOP HIM... HMMM...

AGAIN THE NEXT DAY, THE MONSTER APPEARS!
HELP!! IT'S TEARING DOWN THE "EL" THEY'LL ALL BE KILLED!!
AS POLICE AGAIN PURSUE, THEY MEET THE SAME FATE AS THOSE THE DAY BEFORE.!!
BOOM!

BUT HIGH ABOVE....
THAT TRUCK SHOULD LEAD ME STRAIGHT TO THE HIDEOUT OF HUGO STRANGE!

WELL, IT LOOKS LIKE THE END OF MY SEARCH!

A FEW MINUTES LATER...

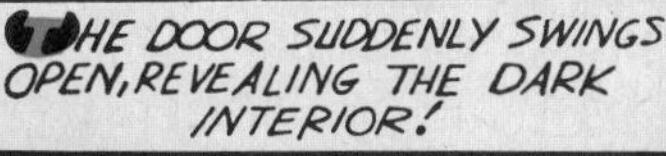
THE DOOR SUDDENLY SWINGS OPEN, REVEALING THE DARK INTERIOR!

WHAT TH', IT LOOKS LIKE A TRAP BUT I'VE GOT TO CHANCE IT!
1
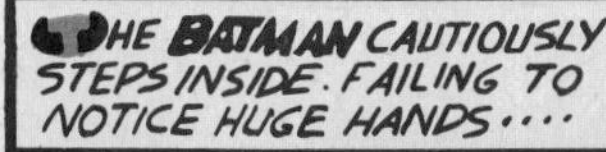
THE BATMAN CAUTIOUSLY STEPS INSIDE. FAILING TO NOTICE HUGE HANDS....

2

SUDDENLY THE LIGHT FLASHES ON! THE BATMAN IS IN THE HANDS OF THE MONSTERS!!

ER.. GOOD EVENING, GENTLEMEN!
3
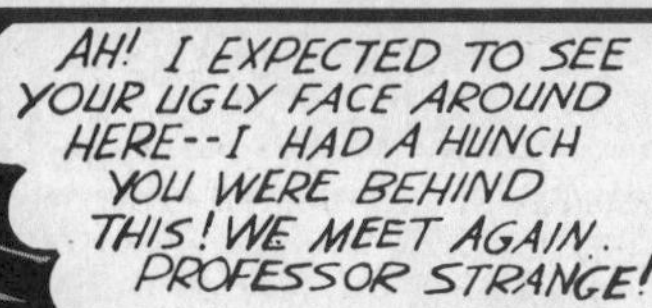
AH! I EXPECTED TO SEE YOUR UGLY FACE AROUND HERE--I HAD A HUNCH YOU WERE BEHIND THIS! WE MEET AGAIN. PROFESSOR STRANGE!

THEN... A VOICE!
CAUGHT! AND VERY NEATLY, TOO!
4

NOW THAT YOU'VE GOT ME, I DON'T SUPPOSE I'LL LIVE VERY LONG. GRANT ME A DYING MAN'S REQUEST AND TELL ME HOW YOU'VE CREATED THESE MONSTERS, AND WHY?
WITH THE GREATEST OF PLEASURE, MY DEAR BATMAN. IF YOU WILL LOOK CLOSELY YOU WILL RECOGNIZE THEIR PICTURES IN THE PAPERS. THEY ARE THE ESCAPED LUNATICS....
5

...AND THESE ARE MONSTERS. I MADE THEM, SO! I DISCOVERED AN EXTRACT THAT SPEEDS UP THE GROWTH GLANDS. I INJECT THIS FLUID INTO A NORMAL MAN. THE SUDDEN GROWTH NOT ONLY DISTORTS THE BODY BUT ALSO THE BRAIN--AND SOON HE IS A MONSTER!!
5.

I HAVE SENT OUT A MONSTER IN CLOTHES OF BULLET PROOF MATERIAL SO THAT THE PUBLIC AND THE POLICE MAY BE--ER--ACQUAINTED WITH HIM TOMORROW I SHALL SEND OUT TWO MONSTERS AND WHILE THE POLICE ARE CONCERNED WITH THEM MY MEN WILL LOOT THE BANKS. CLEVER ISN'T IT? YOU KNOW, AT TIMES I AM AMAZED AT MY OWN GENIUS!
AN EVIL GENIUS, STRANGE!

REMOVE HIS BELT OF GAS CAPSULES...I WANT NO ESCAPE--I AM GOING TO INJECT THIS FLUID INTO YOU! YOU, DEAR BATMAN, ARE TO BE A MONSTER! A MONSTER! HA-HA-HA

THE BATMAN STRUGGLES MIGHTILY, BUT THE MONSTERS HOLD HIM FIRM!
YOU FIEND!!
THAT IS NO WAY TO TALK TO YOUR MASTER! SOON YOU WILL BE A MONSTER AND OBEY ME AS THEY DO! PREPARE TO MEET YOUR FATE!

THE DEADLY NEEDLE PLUNGES DEEP INTO THE ARM OF THE BATMAN!
DONE!!

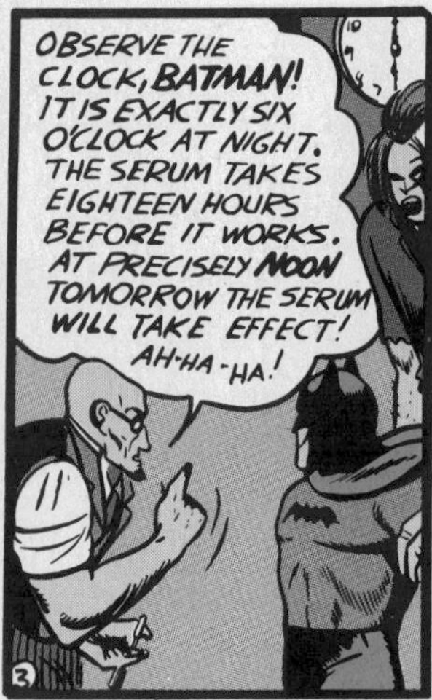
OBSERVE THE CLOCK, BATMAN! IT IS EXACTLY SIX O'CLOCK AT NIGHT. THE SERUM TAKES EIGHTEEN HOURS BEFORE IT WORKS. AT PRECISELY NOON TOMORROW THE SERUM WILL TAKE EFFECT! AH-HA-HA!

A MASSIVE FIST CRASHES AGAINST THE BATMAN'S JAW-- THEN BLACKNESS

HOURS LATER
WOW! WHAT HIT ME! THE CLOCK! IT SAYS ALMOST A QUARTER TO TWELVE I'VE BEEN UNCONSIOUS ALMOST EIGHTEEN HOURS... AND IT'S ALMOST TIME FOR THE SERUM TO WORK!

THEN THE BATMAN SEES...
NOW REMEMBER! THREE MEN TAKE A MONSTER, ONE TRUCK WILL GO BY DALY AVENUE AND THE OTHER BY THE POST ROAD NOW, GET GOING.. AND NO SLIP UPS!
DON'T WORRY, STRANGE! THOSE BANKS ARE AS GOOD AS OPENED RIGHT NOW!

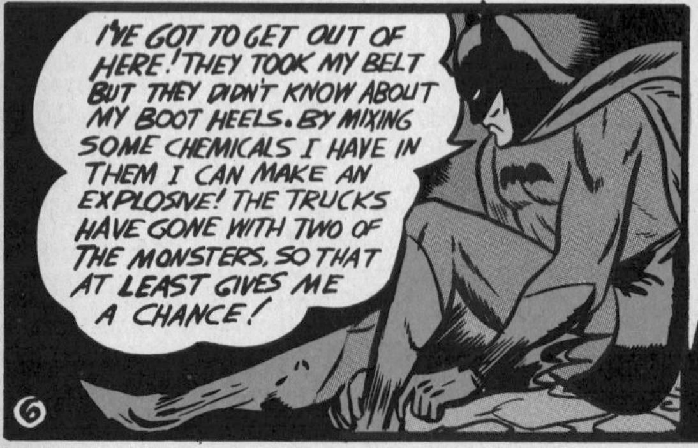
I'VE GOT TO GET OUT OF HERE! THEY TOOK MY BELT BUT THEY DIDN'T KNOW ABOUT MY BOOT HEELS. BY MIXING SOME CHEMICALS I HAVE IN THEM I CAN MAKE AN EXPLOSIVE! THE TRUCKS HAVE GONE WITH TWO OF THE MONSTERS, SO THAT AT LEAST GIVES ME A CHANCE!

A MOMENT LATER...
THAT DOES IT!
BOOM!

WHAT... YOU... OUT!!
YES...

AND SO ARE YOU!

THE POWERFUL BLOW SENDS STRANGE OUT-TO FALL TO MURKY WATERS BELOW...

I WONDER IF THIS REALLY IS THE END OF PROFESSOR HUGO STRANGE? ? ? MEANWHILE, TIME IS FLYING - IT MUST BE ALMOST TIME FOR THE SERUM TO WORK! I'VE GOT TO STOP IT!

SUDDENLY A DOOR OPENS... AND THERE... THREE MONSTERS!!
THE REST OF THE MONSTERS!!

THE BATMAN SPIES THE LONG POLE USED TO OPEN THE SKYLIGHT...
THERE'S STILL A CHANCE!

ALTHOUGH YOUR BULLET-PROOF CLOTHING PROTECTS YOU FROM BULLETS - IT DOESN'T FROM THIS!!

THE BATMAN TRIES FOR THE KNOB ON THE SKYLIGHT!
IF THIS DOESN'T CATCH, THEN I'LL CATCH IT FROM THE MONSTERS!
1.

THE HOOK CATCHES AND...
BIG BOY, HERE I COME!
2

I BET YOU'RE SURPRISED!
?
3

AS THE ENRAGED COLOSSUS LUMBERS FORWARD, THE BATMAN DEFTLY THRUSTS THE POLE BETWEEN HIS LEGS...
4.

...AND PULLS HARD!!
I HOPE THIS WORKS!
5

AS THE MONSTERS COLLIDE, THEY IMMEDIATELY BECOME ENRAGED AND STARE AT EACH OTHER WITH HATE IN THEIR EYES!
6

ALL THOUGHTS OF THE BATMAN ARE FORGOTTEN AS THE MADDENED BEASTS FIERCELY ENGAGE IN HEATED BATTLE!

IT WORKED! AND NOW I'VE GOT TO WORK FAST TO STOP THE SERUM ... I'VE JUST GOT FIVE MINUTES!

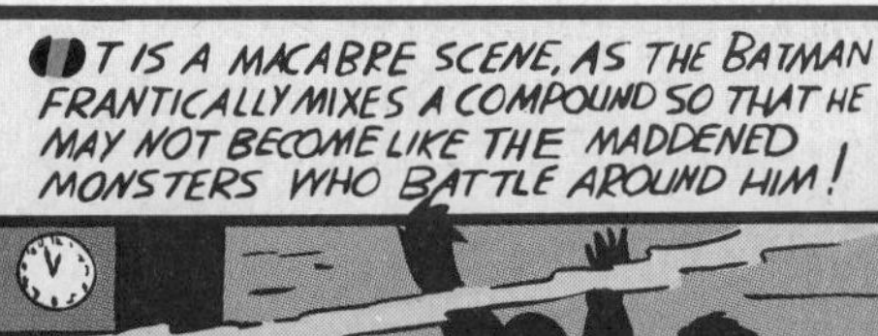
IT IS A MACABRE SCENE, AS THE BATMAN FRANTICALLY MIXES A COMPOUND SO THAT HE MAY NOT BECOME LIKE THE MADDENED MONSTERS WHO BATTLE AROUND HIM!

THIS COMPOUND WILL ACT AS AN ANTIDOTE AND STOP ANY EXCESS ACTION FROM THE GROWTH GLANDS... THERE! IT'S IN! I'VE BEATEN HUGO STRANGE BY A SINGLE MINUTE!!

THEY'VE KILLED EACH OTHER AS I HOPED THEY WOULD! THEY ARE NOW DEAD! TWO STILL LIVE. THEY'RE IN THOSE TRUCKS. ONE IS ON DALY AVENUE AND THE OTHER ON POST ROAD I CAN STILL CATCH THEM..

A MOMENT LATER.. THE BATPLANE RISES INTO THE AIR!
THE POST ROAD FIRST!

ON THE POST ROAD...
IT WONT BE LONG NOW!
WHAT A CINCH! THE MONKEY IN THE BACK STARTS A RIOT, KILLS A FEW PEOPLE AND WE CRACK A BANK! A SWEET RACKET!
9.

BUT OUT OF THE SKY, SPITTING DEATH AT THE BATMAN!
RAT-TAT-TAT-TAT-TAT..

MUCH AS I HATE TO TAKE HUMAN LIFE, I'M AFRAID THIS TIME IT'S NECESSARY!
RAT-TAT-TAT-TAT-TAT

THE BULLETS TAKE THEIR TOLL.. THE TRUCK CRASHES INTO A TREE!

AS THE MONSTER RISES, THE STEEL-LIKE ROPE OF THE BATMAN LOOPS ABOUT HIS NECK!

THE RISING BATPLANE JERKS THE MONSTER FROM THE GROUND
I'VE ROPED STEERS BEFORE, BUT YOU'RE MUCH MORE DEADLY!

THE GIANT TRIES TO BREAK THE EVER-TIGHTENING ROPE!

A FEW MOMENTS LATER...
HE'S PROBABLY BETTER OFF THIS WAY.

NOW I'LL CUT THIS FELLOW DOWN AND THEN GO TO DALY AVENUE ... FOR THE LAST MONSTER!

I'M IN TIME!! THERE'S THE TRUCK NOW!!
TAT-- TAT. TAT...

FROM THE BACK OF THE TRUCK!
HELP! THE MONSTER IS BACK!

AS THE MONSTER GAZES UP AT THE BATPLANE HE SEEMS TO REALIZE IT MEANT TO DO HIM HARM. HE MUST GET UP TO DO IT BATTLE

THE CRAZED BEAST, SEEING THE BUILDING REAR HIGH IN THE AIR, THINKS HE CAN REACH THE BATPLANE THAT WAY

THE INSANE MONSTER STARTS TO CLIMB THE TOWER
...AND FINALLY THE TOP!

UP... UP.. HE CLIMBS...

THE BULLET PROOF CLOTHES PROTECT THE MONSTER...
IF BULLETS DON'T STOP HIM - I KNOW WHAT WILL!

THIS TIME FROM THE BATPLANE GAS PELLETS!!

AS THE GAS TAKES EFFECT THE MONSTER ONCE MORE SEES THE BATPLANE... SHAKES HIS HANDS DEFIANTLY---

...AND THEN TOPPLES OFF TO HIS DOOM!!

THERE GOES THE LAST OF THE MONSTERS... YET I HAVE A FEELING THAT THE BIGGEST MONSTER OF THEM ALL, PROFESSOR HUGO STRANGE, STILL 'LIVES!' PERHAPS WE SHALL MEET AGAIN... PERHAPS!!
BOB KANE

THE BATMAN
APPEARING EVERY MONTH IN DETECTIVE COMICS

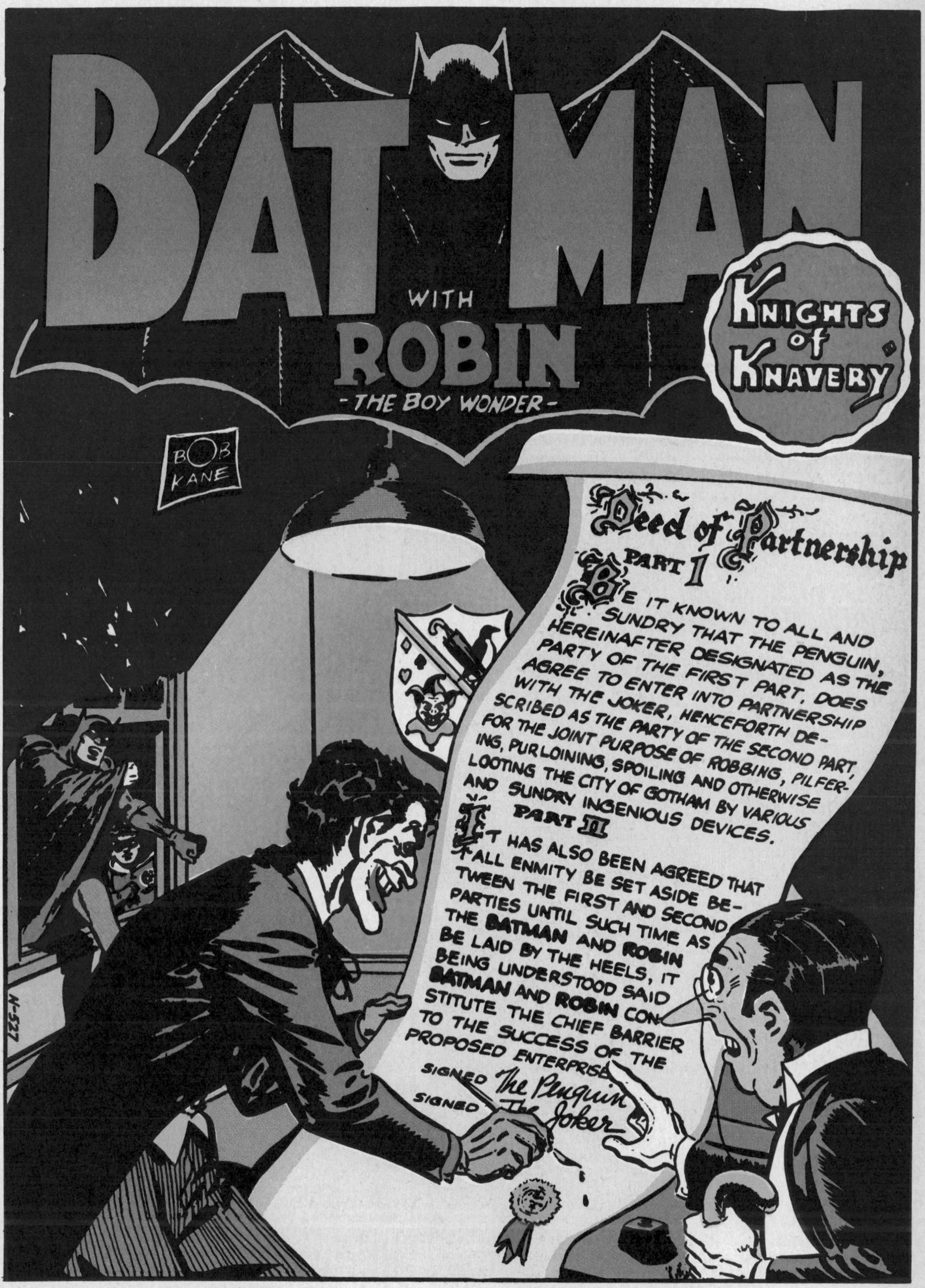

Art by Jerry Robinson & George Roussos/Coloring by Anthony Tollin

NESTLED AMONGST THE ROLLING SLOPES OF GOTHAM'S SUBURBS LIES THE HOME OF THE RICHEST WOMAN IN TOWN, MRS. VAN LANDORPF...
WHAT A SERENE AND TRANQUIL PICTURE ---

BUT WAIT--!
DEAR ME -- TO THINK THAT ONE OF MY INTELLECT SHOULD WALK INTO SUCH A TRAP. HASTE IS MY ONLY RESOURCE NOW!

NO-YOU ARE NOT DECEIVED. IT IS INDEED THE PENGUIN, THAT GROTESQUE BIRD OF ILL-OMEN!
THE BATMAN AND ROBIN! WILL THOSE TWO NEVER CEASE TO HAUNT MY WAKING MOMENTS?
HE CAN'T GET AWAY FROM US NOW, BATMAN!

QUICK AS A WINK, WE'LL HAVE YOU IN THE CLINK!
BUT I'LL BE OUT MUCH SOONER THAN YOU THINK!

A SHORT WHILE LATER, AT GOTHAM PENITENTIARY --
WELL, PENGUIN -- HOW DOES IT FEEL TO BE HOME AGAIN?
TERRIBLE! BUT WAIT AND SEE IF I DON'T BEGIN TO ROAM AGAIN.

-- TO BE DOGGED BY SUCH ILL-FORTUNE! HOW COULD I HAVE KNOWN THAT THEY WERE WAITING FOR ME TO STEAL THE VAN LANDORPF EMERALD? THAT THIS SHOULD HAPPEN TO ME -- THE SMARTEST CROOK IN TOWN!
2

HA-HA! HO-HO-HO! LOOK WHO CALLS HIMSELF THE SMARTEST CROOK IN TOWN!
HUH? WHY THIS RAUCOUS OUT-BURST OF MIRTH, MY LAUGHING HYENA?

THOSE SPINE-CHILLING CHUCKLES! THAT SATANIC VOICE! WHERE HAVE WE HEARD THEM BEFORE?
ALLOW ME TO INTRODUCE YOU TO THE SMART-EST CROOK IN TOWN -- MY CARD!
J
THE JOKER! THAT LEERING MONSTER OF MENACE! WHAT STRANGE TWIST OF FATE HAS PLACED HIM IN THE SAME CELL AS THE PENGUIN? WHAT IMPISH IRONY HAS BROUGHT THESE TWINS IN TRANSGRESSION FACE TO FACE? CAN PRISON WALLS CONTAIN THIS COMBINA-TION OF CRAFT AND CUNNING?

POOF--THE JOKER! I READ HOW **BATMAN** CAUGHT YOU TRYING TO LIFT THE VAN LAN-DORPF EMERALD LAST WEEK. YOU OUGHT TO HIDE YOUR SILLY, GRINN-ING FACE IN SHAME. ***I'M*** THE KING OF CRIME IN THESE PARTS.
IS THAT SO? LISTEN, YOU PUFFED CANARY-- IF YOU'RE SO GOOD, HOW IS IT ***YOU*** DIDN'T GET THE EMERALD?
ER- WE WON'T GO INTO THAT, YOU GIGGLING GHOUL. WHY, YOU COULDN'T PICK A BLIND MAN'S POCKET ON A FOGGY NIGHT!
NOW, LOOK HERE, YOU UMBRELLA-TOTING UNDERWORLD UPSTART-THIS TOWN ISN'T BIG ENOUGH FOR BOTH OF US TO OPER-ATE IN! WE'VE GOT TO SETTLE WHO GOES AND WHO STAYS!
THAT'S ALL RIGHT WITH ME. HOW ABOUT A LITTLE CON-TEST? WE'RE BOTH AFTER THE VAN LANDORPF EMERALD-- SHALL WE SAY THAT WHOEVER GETS IT FIRST WINS EXCLUSIVE CON-TROL OF THE GOTHAM CITY TERRITORY?
THAT SUITS ME FINE! NOW TO GET OUT OF THIS ESTABLISHMENT AND SHOW YOU UP!

LATER, THE TWO KNIGHTS OF KNAVERY BEGIN A FEARFUL CLAMOR IN THE CELL BLOCK...
WE DEMAND A CLEAN CELL! THIS PLACE IS A PIG-STY!
THE FLOOR HASN'T BEEN SWEPT IN A MONTH!

IF YOU NOISY STIR-NUTS WANT A CLEAN CELL, TRY CLEANING IT YOURSELVES!
THE SERVICE IN THIS JAIL IS WORSE THAN ALL THE OTHERS I'VE EVER BEEN IN!

BUT AS SOON AS THE GUARD LEAVES THEM WITH THE BROOM--
TAKING OFF THIS WIRE THAT BINDS THE BROOM'S STRAWS TOGETHER WAS QUITE A BRIGHT IDEA OF MINE!
NOT QUITE AS BRIGHT AS MY IDEA OF FASHIONING IT INTO A LONG HOOK!
HO-HUM--WHAT A DULL JOB THIS IS -- PLAYING NURSE TO A COLLECTION OF CROOKS. NOTHING EVER HAPPENS AROUND HERE...
GUESS I'LL GO SEE WHETHER THOSE TWO PUNKS HAVE SWEPT THEIR CELL YET--
OOGH!
THANKS FOR THE BROOM, DIM-WIT. HERE'S WHERE WE SWEEP YOU OFF YOUR FEET-- HA-HA!
CLUNK
AND BRIEF MINUTES LATER, TWO FLEEING FIENDS REGAIN THEIR FREEDOM--AS PRISON SIRENS BELATEDLY SOUND THE ALARM!
WELL, HERE'S WHERE WE SEPARATE. AND DON'T FORGET OUR AGREEMENT!
EEEEEEEEEEE
DON'T YOU FORGET IT! WHEN I GET THAT EMERALD, IT'S GOING TO BE GOOD-BYE, GOTHAM FOR YOU!
THAT EVENING, AT THE HOME OF BRUCE WAYNE--
WITH THOSE TWO ON THE LOOSE, GOTHAM IS GOING TO BE TURNED UPSIDE-DOWN!
THE JOKER AND PENGUIN BOTH! IT WAS BAD ENOUGH WHEN WE HAD TO WORRY ABOUT ONE OF THEM AT A TIME. WE CAN'T AFFORD TO LOSE A MOMENT!
GOTHAM NEWS
JOKER AND PENGUIN MAKE SENSATIONAL ESCAPE FROM PENITENTIARY!
SCANT SECONDS ELAPSE BEFORE THE ANXIOUS PAIR IS TRANSFORMED INTO THAT DOUBLE-BARRELLED BLIGHT OF EVIL, THE BATMAN AND ROBIN--
WHAT'S OUR FIRST MOVE, BATMAN?
THE JOKER AND THE PENGUIN HAVE BOTH BEEN AFTER THE VAN LANDORPF EMERALD FOR A LONG TIME. THEY'RE SURE TO STRIKE AGAIN-- AND WHEN THEY DO, WE WANT TO BE THERE!
BUT THEY'RE NOT GOING TO WALK INTO A TRAP TWICE. THEY'RE TOO SMART FOR THAT.
NO--BUT I THINK WE MIGHT BE ABLE TO USE THEIR OWN SMARTNESS AGAINST THEM. I'LL NEED MRS. VAN LANDORPF'S COOPERATION...
4

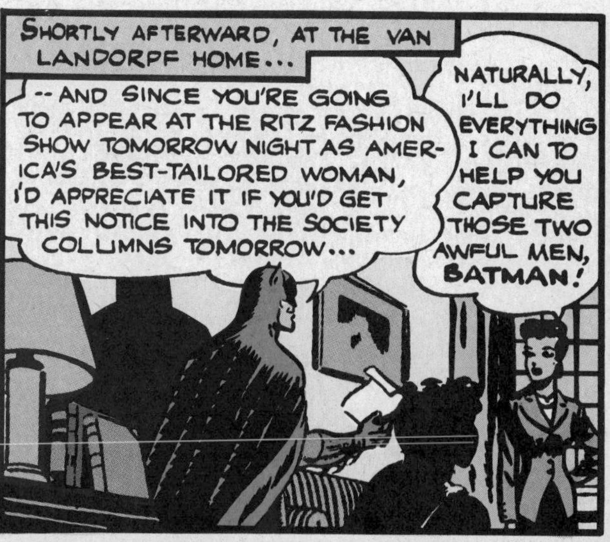
SHORTLY AFTERWARD, AT THE VAN LANDORPF HOME...
--AND SINCE YOU'RE GOING TO APPEAR AT THE RITZ FASHION SHOW TOMORROW NIGHT AS AMERICA'S BEST-TAILORED WOMAN, I'D APPRECIATE IT IF YOU'D GET THIS NOTICE INTO THE SOCIETY COLUMNS TOMORROW...
NATURALLY, I'LL DO EVERYTHING I CAN TO HELP YOU CAPTURE THOSE TWO AWFUL MEN, BATMAN!

--OH, YOU WANT ME TO SAY THAT I'LL BE WEARING THE EMERALD TOMORROW NIGHT! BUT I COULDN'T POSSIBLY!
I QUITE UNDERSTAND. I INSERTED THAT DELIBERATELY. YOU WON'T HAVE TO WEAR THE EMERALD. ROBIN AND I WILL TAKE CARE OF THAT!

YOU MAY BE SURE I'LL ARRANGE TO HAVE THE NOTICE INSERTED. AND I LEAVE THE EMERALD IN YOUR CARE. I DO HOPE IT WILL BE SAFE!
IT WILL BE.. NEVER FEAR!

I CAN'T IMAGINE ANYTHING DULLER THAN A FASHION SHOW, BUT I'M WILLING TO GO AS LONG AS YOU EXPECT TO LURE THE PENGUIN AND THE JOKER THERE!
YOU'RE WRONG, ROBIN--WE'RE NOT GOING TO THE FASHION SHOW!

YOU SEE, THE JOKER AND THE PENGUIN ARE MUCH TOO CLEVER TO BE FOOLED BY THAT NOTICE. THEY'LL SMELL A TRAP IMMEDIATELY. THAT'S EXACTLY WHAT I WANT THEM TO DO. MY IDEA IS TO USE THEIR OWN CLEVERNESS AGAINST THEM!

LET'S PAY A VISIT TO THE HEADQUARTERS OF THE WILY PENGUIN AS HE SCANS THE PAPERS ON THE FOLLOWING AFTERNOON--
HMM--HERE'S AN INTERESTING LITTLE PIECE IN THE SOCIETY COLUMN. JUST WHAT I'VE BEEN WAITING FOR!
LET'S SEE, BOSS. TEAR IT OUT!
GOTHAM NEWS

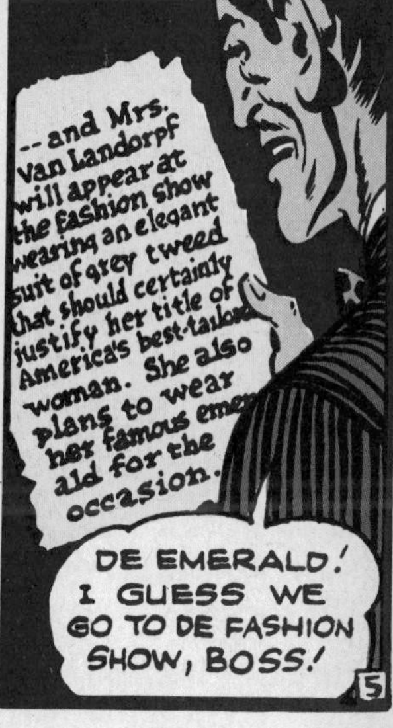
--and Mrs. van Landorpf will appear at the fashion show wearing an elegant suit of grey tweed that should certainly justify her title of America's best-tailored woman. She also plans to wear her famous emerald for the occasion.
DE EMERALD! I GUESS WE GO TO DE FASHION SHOW, BOSS!
5

SUCH STUPIDITY! DON'T YOU KNOW THAT ONE DOESN'T WEAR COURT EMERALDS WITH TAILORED CLOTHES? IT SIMPLY ISN'T DONE. MY GUESS IS THAT THE **BATMAN** HAD THIS NOTICE INSERTED--

BUT WHAT'S HIS ANGLE?

HE KNOWS I'M AFTER THE EMERALD, SO HE PLANS TO LURE ME TO THE FASHION SHOW, WHERE HE'LL BE WAITING FOR ME! BUT I'M A LITTLE TOO SMART FOR HIM...

SINCE EMERALDS AREN'T WORN WITH TAILORED THINGS, IT'LL BE IN THE **SAFE** AT THE LANDORPF HOME! AND WHILE **BATMAN** IS EXPECTING ME AT THE SHOW, WE'LL BE TAKING THE EMERALD OUT OF THE UN-GUARDED HOUSE!

GEE, PENGUIN-WHAT A BRAIN!

AND THAT NIGHT, AT THE VAN LANDORPF HOME...

I HEAR FOOT-STEPS OUTSIDE, **ROBIN**. WE'D BETTER HIDE!

THEY AREN'T EVEN TAKING THE TROUBLE TO SNEAK IN QUIETLY, THEY'RE SO SURE WE'RE EXPECT-ING THEM AT THE FASHION SHOW!

SEE-NOT A SOUL ABOUT. AND THEY DIDN'T EVEN BOTHER TO LOCK THE DOOR. BUT THE FUNNIEST PART OF ALL THIS IS THAT THE JOKER IS PROBABLY WALKING RIGHT INTO THE **BAT-MAN'S** TRAP! I ALMOST FEEL SORRY FOR HIM—

DERE'S DE SAFE!

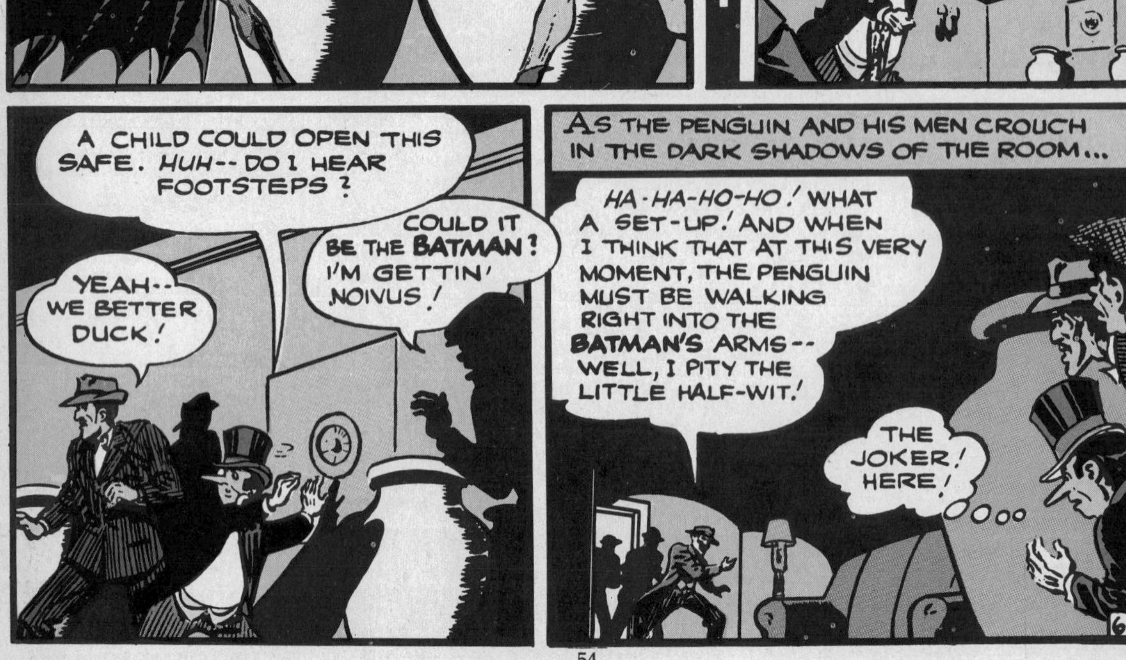
A CHILD COULD OPEN THIS SAFE. *HUH*-- DO I HEAR FOOTSTEPS?
COULD IT BE THE **BATMAN**? I'M GETTIN' NOIVUS!
YEAH-- WE BETTER DUCK!
AS THE PENGUIN AND HIS MEN CROUCH IN THE DARK SHADOWS OF THE ROOM...
HA-HA-HO-HO! WHAT A SET-UP! AND WHEN I THINK THAT AT THIS VERY MOMENT, THE PENGUIN MUST BE WALKING RIGHT INTO THE **BATMAN'S** ARMS-- WELL, I PITY THE LITTLE HALF-WIT!
THE JOKER! HERE!
6

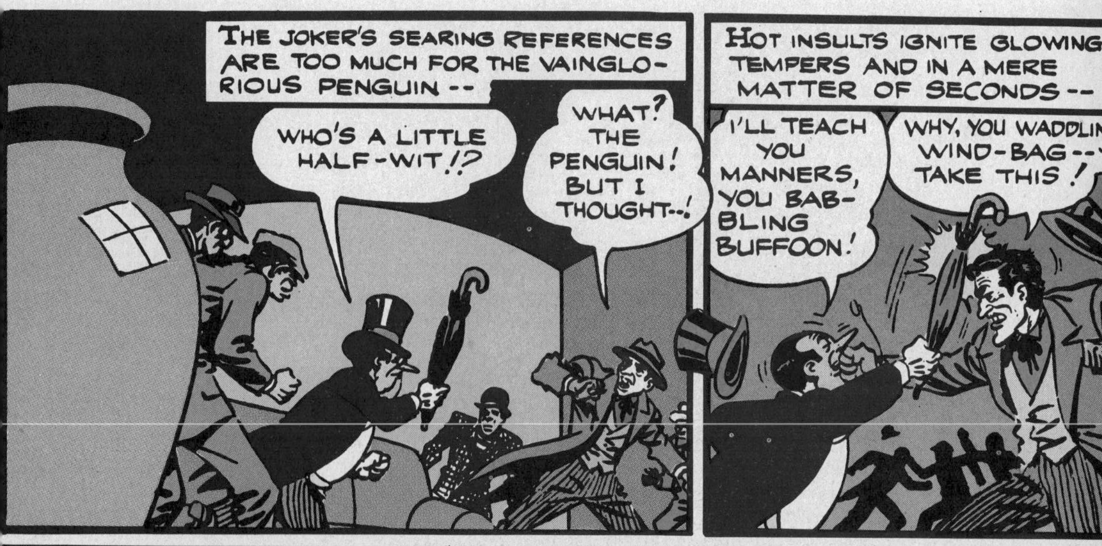
THE JOKER'S SEARING REFERENCES ARE TOO MUCH FOR THE VAINGLORIOUS PENGUIN --
WHO'S A LITTLE HALF-WIT!?
WHAT? THE PENGUIN! BUT I THOUGHT--!
HOT INSULTS IGNITE GLOWING TEMPERS AND IN A MERE MATTER OF SECONDS --
I'LL TEACH YOU MANNERS, YOU BABBLING BUFFOON!
WHY, YOU WADDLING WIND-BAG--TAKE THIS!

BUT WHEN THIEVES FALL OUT, TWO CAPED FIGURES SUDDENLY ENTER THE FRAY--
KEEP UP THE GOOD WORK, BOYS -- I'LL HELP YOU IN A SECOND!
WHA--THE BATMAN!
ROBIN!
THIS TIME THE JOKE'S ON YOU, JOKER!
MY UMBRELLA'S ALWAYS READY TO MAKE BATMAN UNSTEADY!

THIS SMOKE BOMB SHOULD CLOUD THE ISSUE!
OH, NO, YOU DON'T, PENGUIN!

WHERE ARE YOU, BATMAN? I CAN'T SEE A THING!
RIGHT OVER HERE--I'VE GOT ONE OF 'EM, BUT I CAN'T SEE WHO IT IS!
7

AND WHEN THE SMOKE LIFTS...
THE JOKER AND THE PENGUIN! THEY'RE GONE!
WE CAUGHT THE SMALL FRY WHILE THE BIG FISH GOT AWAY!
WHA--? NEEDLES--IT'S YOU!

IN THE MEAN-TIME--
WE DIDN'T GET THE EMERALD, BUT THEY DIDN'T GET US--HA-HA!
WE MIGHT HAVE SUCCEEDED IN GETTING THE EMERALD IF WE HAD WORKED TOGETHER. AFTER ALL, BATMAN IS OUR REAL ENEMY!

YOU'RE RIGHT! FROM NOW ON, LET BYGONES BE BYGONES! WE'RE PARTNERS!
TOGETHER WE CAN PICK GOTHAM CITY CLEAN! HERE'S TO CRIME--MAY IT PROVIDE US WITH GOLD AND THE BATMAN WITH GLOOM!

SO IS BORN A PERNICIOUS PARTNERSHIP UNITING THE JOCULAR GENIUS OF THE JOKER WITH THE PREDATORY PROFICIENCY OF THE PENGUIN! AND NOT MANY HOURS PASS BEFORE THIS UNHOLY UNION OF MASTER-MINDS STRIKES WITH SWIFT, EVIL EFFICIENCY!

THE HOME OF BRUCE WAYNE ON THE EVENING OF THE FOLLOWING DAY--

THOSE TWO ARE RUNNING WILD, BRUCE. WHAT ARE WE GOING TO DO ABOUT IT?

TO BEGIN WITH--WE HAVE AN APPOINTMENT WITH COMMISSIONER GORDON THIS AFTERNOON! HE NEEDS MORAL SUPPORT--ALTHOUGH I DON'T KNOW WHAT TO TELL HIM..

GOTHAM GAZETTE
DARING CRIME DUO SNATCH PAYROLL
PENGUIN PILFERS PEARLS AS JOKER JIMMIES JEWELRY FROM SAFE

GOTHAM NEWS
JOKER AND PENGUIN STEAL FORTUNE IN GEMS FROM HERRING HEIRESS!

SOME TIME LATER, AT THE POLICE COMMISSIONER'S OFFICE...
--AND MY MEN ARE ABSOLUTELY STYMIED IN SPITE OF DOUBLE PATROLS EVERYWHERE.
THEY'RE TOO WISE TO FALL FOR ANOTHER TRAP. WE'LL HAVE TO GO OUT AND HUNT FOR THEM!

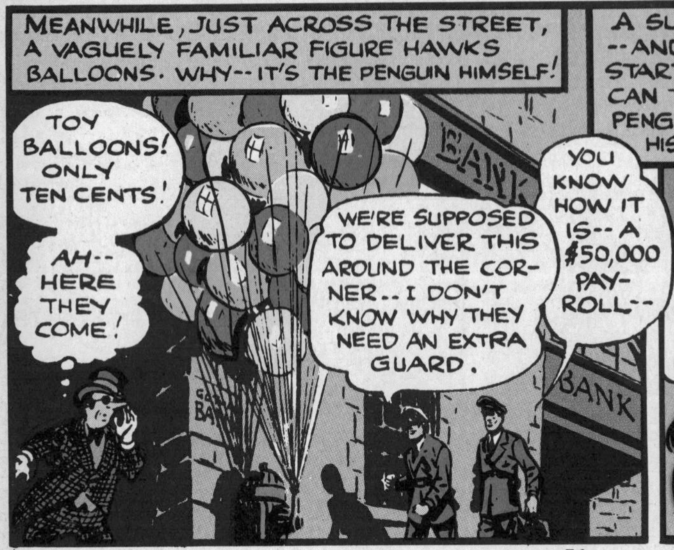

MEANWHILE, JUST ACROSS THE STREET, A VAGUELY FAMILIAR FIGURE HAWKS BALLOONS. WHY--IT'S THE PENGUIN HIMSELF!
TOY BALLOONS! ONLY TEN CENTS!
AH--HERE THEY COME!
WE'RE SUPPOSED TO DELIVER THIS AROUND THE COR-NER..I DON'T KNOW WHY THEY NEED AN EXTRA GUARD.
YOU KNOW HOW IT IS--A $50,000 PAY-ROLL--
BANK
BANK

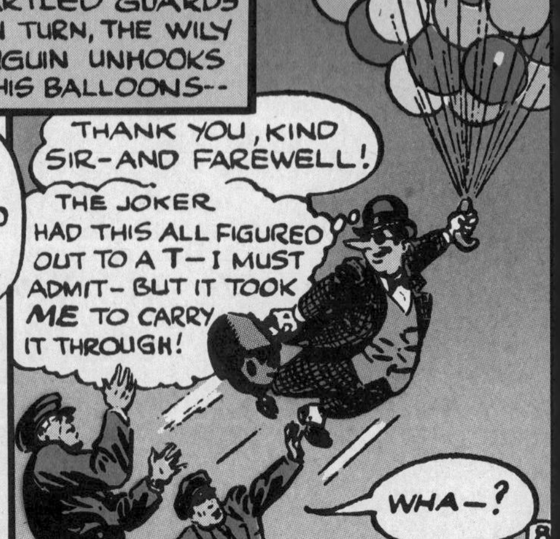

A SUDDEN SNATCH--AND BEFORE THE STARTLED GUARDS CAN TURN, THE WILY PENGUIN UNHOOKS HIS BALLOONS--
THANK YOU, KIND SIR-AND FAREWELL!
THE JOKER HAD THIS ALL FIGURED OUT TO A T-I MUST ADMIT-BUT IT TOOK ME TO CARRY IT THROUGH!
WHA-?
8

AS THE BALLOONS STREAK SKYWARD, THE WIND CARRIES THE PENGUIN PAST COMMISSIONER GORDON'S WINDOW--
WHA--? BATMAN-- LOOK!
THE PENGUIN! I'D RECOGNIZE HIM ANYWHERE!
TWO CAPED FIGURES MAKE A DESPERATE PLUNGE---
MAYBE OUR COMBINED WEIGHT'LL BRING HIM DOWN!
EITHER THAT--OR WE GO ALONG FOR THE RIDE!
ULP! STOWAWAYS!
YOU'VE SLOWED ME UP, BUT YOU HAVEN'T BROUGHT ME DOWN! AND WHEN WE DO LAND -- THERE'LL BE A NICE SURPRISE FOR YOU - IF THE WIND STAYS RIGHT!
I DON'T LIKE THE WAY HE SAYS THAT!
WELL, THERE'S NOTHING WE CAN DO ABOUT IT NOW! WE CAN'T LET GO!
ON A HIGHWAY SEVERAL MILES AWAY-- THE PENGUIN'S JOCUND PARTNER --
HERE HE COMES NOW! WHA--? HE HAS BATMAN AND ROBIN WITH HIM! GET THE NET READY, BOYS--AND PREPARE FOR ACTION!
WE'RE ALL SET!
THE BARK OF A SHOT-GUN FROM BELOW, AND--
AH-- MY PARTNER'S ON THE JOB!
WE'RE FALLING!
IF THE PENGUIN LANDS SAFELY-- SO WILL WE!
BANG BANG
WHOOMP! HERE I COME-- WITH THE BOODLE AND THE BATMAN!
THUMP!
HA-HA--SO THEY TRIED TO NAB YOU AND WE NABBED THEM! QUICK--LET'S GET THEM TO THE HIDEOUT!
THEY REALLY DID ME A FAVOR! THERE WAS TOO MUCH GAS IN THE BALLOONS AND WITHOUT THEIR HOLDING ON, I'D HAVE RISEN OUT OF SHOT-GUN RANGE!
9

NOW THAT WE'VE CAUGHT THEM, THE THING TO DO IS FINISH THEM OFF IN A FITTING MANNER. HOW ABOUT THE WATER TREATMENT-- A DROP AT A TIME ON THE FOREHEAD TILL THEY GO MAD?
LATER, AT ROGUE'S ROOST, THE PALATIAL SANCTUARY OF THE SINISTER PAIR...
NO-- LET'S USE AN OVERDOSE OF LAUGHING GAS!

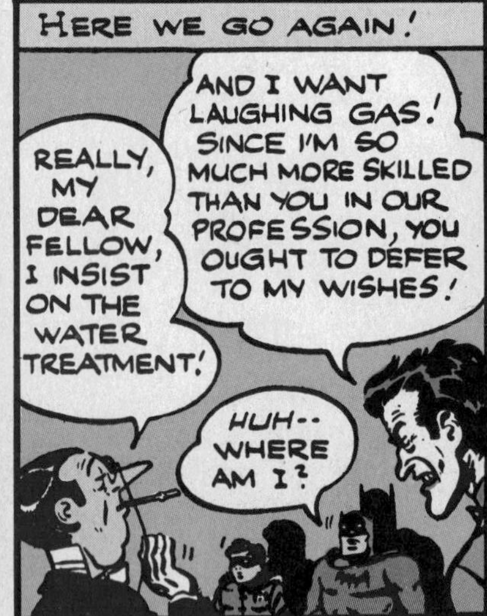
HERE WE GO AGAIN!
REALLY, MY DEAR FELLOW, I INSIST ON THE WATER TREATMENT!
AND I WANT LAUGHING GAS! SINCE I'M SO MUCH MORE SKILLED THAN YOU IN OUR PROFESSION, YOU OUGHT TO DEFER TO MY WISHES!
HUH-- WHERE AM I?

YOU A BETTER CROOK THAN ME? WHY, YOU CHORTLING CHUMP, IF IT WEREN'T FOR ME, YOU'D BE IN THE CLINK NOW!
AND IF I WEREN'T YOUR PARTNER, YOU FOUL-FEATHERED FOWL, YOU'D PROBABLY BE SNATCHING PURSES FROM OLD LADIES!
THEY SEEM TO BE HAVING A DISAGREEMENT!
ALL RIGHT- LET'S ASK THE BATMAN WHICH OF US HE THINKS IS THE SMARTEST CROOK IN GOTHAM. HE SHOULD KNOW!
HOW ABOUT IT, BATMAN?
WELL, THE TRUTH IS, I DON'T THINK EITHER OF YOU MERITS THAT TITLE -
WHAT?
THERE WAS ONCE A CROOK NAMED STUTTERING SAM WHO COULD SHOOT AN OBJECT TWICE THE SIZE OF ONE OF THESE VASES OFF MY HEAD AT FIFTY YARDS. YOU'RE JUST A COUPLE OF MUGGS COMPARED TO HIM!

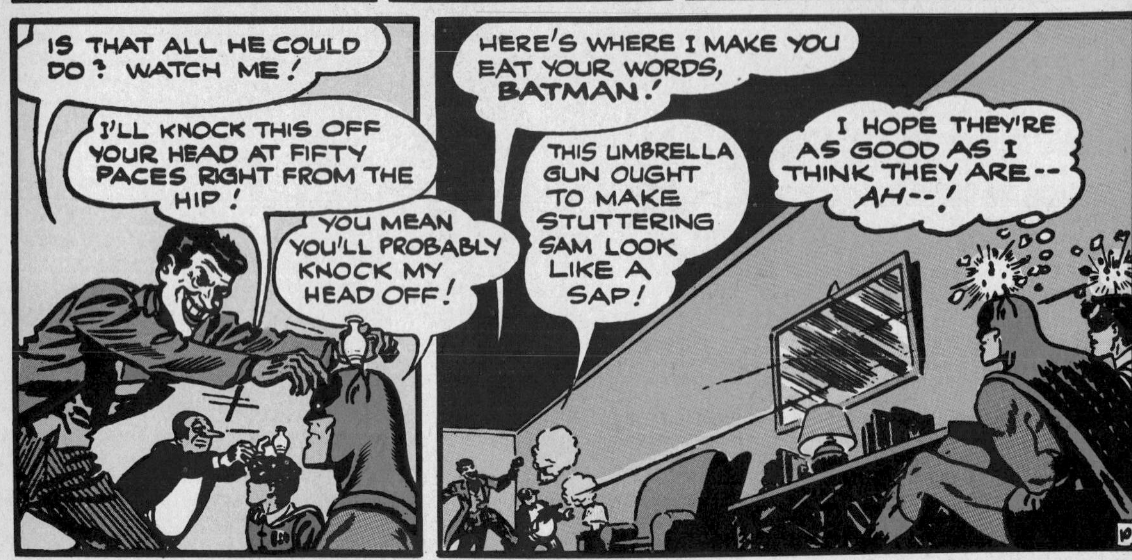
IS THAT ALL HE COULD DO? WATCH ME!
I'LL KNOCK THIS OFF YOUR HEAD AT FIFTY PACES RIGHT FROM THE HIP!
YOU MEAN YOU'LL PROBABLY KNOCK MY HEAD OFF!
HERE'S WHERE I MAKE YOU EAT YOUR WORDS, BATMAN!
THIS UMBRELLA GUN OUGHT TO MAKE STUTTERING SAM LOOK LIKE A SAP!
I HOPE THEY'RE AS GOOD AS I THINK THEY ARE-- AH--!
10

NOW-- WHAT ABOUT YOUR STUTTERING SAM? AM I OR AM I NOT THE MOST DANGEROUS CROOK IN GOTHAM?
I'LL HAVE TO ADMIT THE JOKER'S SHOT WAS TRUE, BUT, REMEMBER, I SHOT FROM THE HIP--
I NEVER THOUGHT YOU TWO HAD IT IN YOU!

AS THE BOASTING BANDITS SWAGGER FORWARD, THE **BATMAN** FURTIVELY SAWS HIS BONDS WITH A JAGGED SPLINTER OF THE SHATTERED VASE!

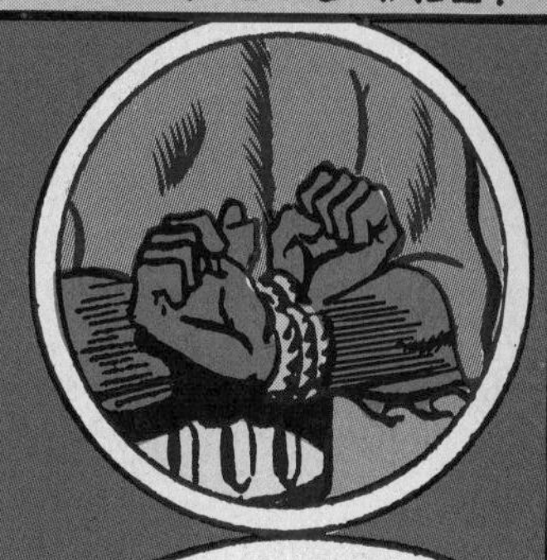

AND **ROBIN** IS NOT FAR BEHIND!

WELL-- IN MY OPINION, THE PENGUIN HAS IT ALL OVER THE JOKER!
WRONG, ROBIN-- I'D SAY THE JOKER WAS FAR SUPERIOR!
OF COURSE, I KNOW YOU'LL SAY ROBIN'S ONLY A KID, BUT--
-HE'S NO ORDINARY KID, REMEMBER THAT! HE'S AS GOOD AS BATMAN ANY TIME!

LISTEN-- WE'LL BE ARGUING ALL DAY! I'M IN FAVOR OF A COMPROMISE. NO LAUGHING GAS-- NO WATER TREATMENT! LET'S FINISH THEM OFF RIGHT AWAY!

WELL, IF YOU PUT IT THAT WAY- ALL RIGHT! LET'S GET RID OF THEM NOW! WE'VE GOT IMPORTANT THINGS TO STEAL!

ANYWAY, I THINK **BATMAN** TRIED TO PROLONG THE ARGUMENT TO GAIN TIME. BUT NOW HIS TIME IS UP!

A SPLIT SECOND REMAINS AS HAMMERS CLICK BACK FOR THE SHOTS THAT WILL SEND **BATMAN** AND **ROBIN** CRASHING INTO OBLIVION--AND THEN--!

I'M FREE! BUT YOU WON'T BE!

MY BONDS ARE LOOSE! HERE'S WHERE I COOK YOUR GOOSE!

WE'VE BEEN TRICKED-- AGH!
I HATE TO UPSET YOU, BUT I PROMISED TO GET YOU!

I'M STARTING A VICTORY GARDEN... DO YOU MIND IF I PLANT MY FIST?
OOF-- MY UMBRELLAS!

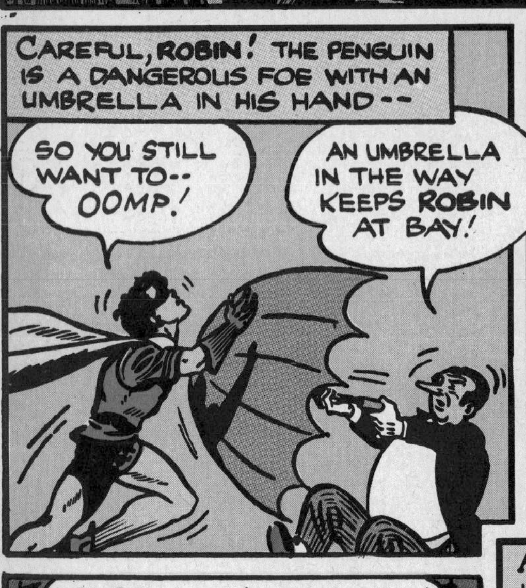

CAREFUL, ROBIN! THE PENGUIN IS A DANGEROUS FOE WITH AN UMBRELLA IN HIS HAND--
SO YOU STILL WANT TO-- OOMP!
AN UMBRELLA IN THE WAY KEEPS ROBIN AT BAY!

I'LL SEE YOU SOON, I HOPE-- NOT!
HURRY-- WE'VE GOT TO STOP HIM!
AND HERE'S THE WAY WE'LL DROP HIM!

OOPS--I CAN'T JUMP NOW!
WE'VE GOT HIM NOW. HE CAN'T JUMP DOWN TEN STORIES WITHOUT HIS UMBRELLA!

AND SO A UNIQUE PARTNERSHIP IS OFFICIALLY DISSOLVED WHILE ALL AWAIT THE ARRIVAL OF THE POLICE--

A FINE PARTNER YOU TURNED OUT TO BE! IF YOU HADN'T BEEN SO VAIN, WE'D NEVER HAVE BEEN CAUGHT!

AND I SUPPOSE YOU HAD NOTHING TO DO WITH IT! WELL, FROM NOW ON, I'M OPERATING ALONE!

RIGHT, PENGUIN--YOU'LL BOTH GET SEPARATE CELLS THIS TIME!

LATER--

--AND FROM THE LIST FOUND IN THE HIDEOUT, THE POLICE MADE SHORT WORK OF ROUNDING UP THE REST OF THE GANG! WHICH MEANS THAT GOTHAM OUGHT TO BE QUIET FOR A WHILE!

Art by Jack Burnley & Charles Paris/Coloring by Anthony Tollin

BATMAN
AND
ROBIN
by BOB KANE
BATMAN AND ROBIN HAVE JUST CAPTURED THEIR FAMED FOE, THE PENGUIN—"MAN OF A THOUSAND UMBRELLAS"—WHO HAS JUST FILCHED FROM THE LOCAL POST OFFICE A MYSTERIOUS CARD ADDRESSED TO...
COPYRIGHT 1946 BY DETECTIVE COMICS, INC.

OSWALD CHESTERFIELD COBBLEPOT! IS IT A NAME OR A PUBLICITY STUNT?
I'LL NEVER TELL YOU THAT, BATMAN. AND WHAT'S MORE-
POST OFFICE

—I'LL HAVE MY POST CARD BACK!
HUH! HE'S GOT MORE UMBRELLAS!

WAIT, PENGUIN! YOU FORGOT YOUR OTHER UMBRELLA!

NOW—LET'S SEE WHAT'S ON THIS POST CARD!
NO! NO!

Dear Oswald:
Congratulations again on your birthday. I'm happy to learn you're doing so well in the umbrella business. Your success only proves that honesty is always the best policy. And now for my surprise..

THE UMBRELLA BUSINESS, EH? WHY, PENGUIN-THEN YOU MUST BE—
YES! I AM OSWALD CHESTERFIELD COBBLEPOT! AND NO CRACKS!

OH—THIS IS AWFUL! DEAR AUNT MIRANDA! TO HAVE BROUGHT ME UP AND BELIEVED IN ME ALL THESE YEARS! THE DISGRACE WILL KILL HER!
WHAT'S WRONG?

HIS AUNT MIRANDA WHO HASN'T SEEN HIM IN TEN YEARS IS COMING TO VISIT HIM. HE'S SUPPOSED TO MEET HER ON THE AFTERNOON TRAIN!

BUT I WON'T BE THERE! I'LL BE IN JAIL! OH, BATMAN-I'M A HEEL, BUT YOU CAN'T BREAK THAT DEAR OLD LADY'S HEART! YOU'VE GOT TO DO SOMETHING!

ONE HOUR LATER AT THE RAILROAD TERMINAL...
ONE MOMENT, YOUNG MAN! IF YOU WERE NEVER TAUGHT THAT LADIES COME FIRST, I'LL TEACH YOU RIGHT NOW!

OSWALD!
AUNTIE-MEET MY VERY DEAR FRIENDS, BATMAN AND ROBIN!

COPYRIGHT 1946 BY DETECTIVE COMICS, INC.
BATMAN AND ROBIN
THE OLD LADY'S NICE, BATMAN.
TOO NICE TO LEARN THAT HER NEPHEW'S A CROOK. BY TAKING THEM AROUND IN THE BATMOBILE, IT'LL BE EASIER TO WATCH THE PENGUIN AND PREVENT HIS ESCAPING.
TO SPARE THE FEELINGS OF THE ELDERLY AUNT WHO REARED THE PENGUIN, BATMAN AND ROBIN HAVE DECIDED NOT TO ARREST THE PENGUIN UNTIL HER VISIT IS OVER...
121
2-24

SORRY–BUT AUNTIE ABSOLUTELY INSISTS ON SEEING THE TOWN FROM AN OPEN BUS.
WHAT A HEADACHE! WELL–ALL RIGHT! BUT LET ME WARN YOU! DON'T TRY TO ESCAPE, PENGUIN!

SHORTLY AFTER...
I DIDN'T KNOW YOU HAD SUCH DISTINGUISHED FRIENDS, OSWALD.
THE BATMAN? OH, YES. THIS IS A FINE UMBRELLA, AUNTIE. MAY I SEE IT?
KEEP YOUR EYE ON HIM, ROBIN.

BATMAN AND ROBIN! AND LOOK AT THE PENGUIN!
OSWALD! DID YOU HEAR THAT FRESH COUPLE? THEY CALLED ME A PENGUIN!
ER–AH–THEY'RE JUST IGNORANT, AUNTIE. PAY NO ATTENTION.
CO.

DID YOU HEAR THAT?
THAT'S REALLY FUNNY. SHE DOESN'T REALIZE HER NEPHEW IS KNOWN AS THE PENGUIN, THE MOST NOTORIOUS CROOK IN TOWN.

EXCUSE ME, AUNTIE, BUT I'LL SEE YOU LATER.
HE'S DONE IT!
OSWALD! COME RIGHT BACK HERE AND STOP SHOWING OFF!
457
5 FIFTH AVE

I'LL HAVE TO USE THE ROPE TRICK!
OOPS! I SHOULD HAVE LOOKED BEFORE I LEAPED!
5 FIFTH AVE

GOT HIM! AND SAVED HIS WORTHLESS LIFE AT THE SAME TIME!

PRESENTLY...
OSWALD! WON'T YOU EVER GROW UP? I'VE A GOOD MIND TO TAKE YOU ACROSS MY KNEE!
YOU LITTLE RAT! IF IT WEREN'T FOR YOUR AUNT–!

MEANWHILE, ELSEWHERE IN TOWN...
BOSS! BOSS! WE GOTTA DO SOMETHIN'! THE PENGUIN'S TURNED STOOL PIGEON! I JUST SEEN HIM PALLING AROUND WIT' THE BATMAN!!

BATMAN AND ROBIN
122
AFTER ALL YOUR LETTERS, OSWALD, ABOUT YOUR THRIVING UMBRELLA BUSINESS, I SIMPLY MUST SEE YOUR UMBRELLA SHOP!
GRACIOUS! HOW CAN I TAKE HER THERE WITHOUT BATMAN DISCOVERING MY HIDEOUT?
BUS STOP
BOB KANE
FOR THE SAKE OF THE PENGUIN'S VISITING AUNT WHO DOESN'T KNOW HE'S A CROOK, BATMAN HAS DEFERRED ARRESTING THE PENGUIN UNTIL AFTER HER VISIT. UNTIL THEN, HE MUST KEEP THE PENGUIN FROM ESCAPING...
3/3
COPYRIGHT 1946 BY DETECTIVE COMICS, INC.

AUNTIE—I—I MUST CONFESS. THE WHOLE PLACE JUST BURNED DOWN.
WHY, OSWALD, OLD PAL. YOU KNOW THAT'S NOT TRUE. YOU DON'T HAVE TO HIDE YOUR BUSINESS SECRETS FROM YOUR DEAR AUNT MIRANDA!

NOT FROM YOU, AUNTIE. BUT, WELL—FRIENDSHIP AND BUSINESS DON'T MIX. I DON'T THINK BATMAN SHOULD SEE IT.
I DECLARE! BATMAN JUST SAVED YOUR LIFE! WHAT INGRATITUDE! LEAD ON NOW, OSWALD, OR I'LL GIVE YOU SOMETHING TO REMEMBER!

SHORTLY AFTER...
IS THIS IT? BUT THAT SIGN DOESN'T MAKE SENSE. I THOUGHT YOU WERE IN THE UMBRELLA BUSINESS.
ER—MY UMBRELLAS ARE SO GOOD I HAVE TO CAMOUFLAGE THE PLACE TO KEEP THE MOBS AWAY!
ICE-COAL
CLOSED FOR WINTER

A FINELY EQUIPPED SHOP LIKE THIS AND I'LL BET YOU HAVEN'T HAD A CUSTOMER IN MONTHS! OSWALD, I ALWAYS SAID YOU HAD NO HEAD FOR BUSINESS!
BUT, AUNTIE—!

WELL—I'M DETERMINED TO HELP YOU! WE'LL START WITH A BIG ADVERTISED SALE AND GET RID OF ALL THIS OLD STOCK!
NO! DON'T TOUCH THAT UMBRELLA!

GOODNESS GRACIOUS! IT'S FULL OF BULLETS!
DON'T YOU KNOW IT'S BAD LUCK TO OPEN AN UMBRELLA INDOORS? CLOSE IT—QUICK!

OSWALD! WHAT KIND OF BUSINESS ARE YOU RUNNING HERE?
WHY—ER—AUNTIE—THAT UMBRELLA HAPPENS TO BE A NEW SECRET WEAPON I'M DEVELOPING FOR THE ARMY!

MEANWHILE, ELSEWHERE IN GOTHAM...
I TELL YOU, STONEHEAD, I'M POSITIVE! I SEEN THE PENGUIN GOING AROUND WITH BATMAN IN BROAD DAYLIGHT. HE MUSTA TURNED STOOL PIGEON!

IT'S HARD TO BELIEVE ME OLD PAL WOULD TURN STOOLIE. BUT—THIS AIN'T NO TIME FOR SENTIMENT!
To my dear cell-mate, Stonehead. The Penguin

ROUND UP THE BOYS! WE GOT BUSINESS AT THE PENGUIN'S UMBRELLA SHOP!

BATMAN AND ROBIN
BOB KANE
123
BECAUSE BATMAN HAS DEFERRED ARRESTING THE PENGUIN UNTIL HIS AUNT MIRANDA'S VISIT ENDS, CERTAIN CROOKS SEEING THEM TOGETHER HAVE ASSUMED THAT THE PENGUIN HAS TURNED STOOL PIGEON!
3-10
COPYRIGHT 1946 BY DETECTIVE COMICS, INC.
DA PENGUIN A STOOL PIGEON! (SIGH) WHAT A SHAME!
YEAH! I WISH I WAS WRONG, STONEHEAD!

LOOK! HE'S ALREADY GAWN OUTA BUSINESS!
WHAT DID YOU CALL ME, YOUNG MAN?
COME OUTA THEM SKIRTS, PENGUIN! WE KNOW YA!
BIG SALE
UMBRELL

I'LL TEACH YOU TO RESPECT A LADY, YOU FLANNEL-MOUTHED BABOON! CALL ME A PENGUIN, INDEED!
HE'S GETTIN' TOUGH! LET HIM HAVE IT, GUYS!
UMBRELLAS

MY OWN BUDDIES PICKING ON MY AUNT MIRANDA! THIS IS TOO MUCH!
I'M SEEIN' DOUBLE! IT MUST BE A DOUBLE-CROSS!
THE BATMAN! I-I THINK I GOT AN IMPORTANT APPOINTMENT IN CHINA!
SALE
BRELLAS

NET PROFIT FOR THE DAY-ONE BULLY OF OLD LADIES!
OSWALD-DON'T YOU DARE CALL ME AN OLD LADY!
NOT BAD, THESE PENGUIN UMBRELLAS- WHEN THEY'RE ON OUR SIDE!

AFTER THE SMOKE OF BATTLE HAS CLEARED...
WELL-LOTS OF EXCITEMENT IN THE BIG CITY, BUT DEAR ME-I'VE BARELY TIME TO CATCH MY TRAIN FOR HOME! OSWALD-COME HERE!
ER-YES-AUNTIE!

GOOD-BYE, OSWALD. BEHAVE YOURSELF. REMEMBER TO EAT LOTS OF FRESH VEGETABLES. AND-OH, YES-HELP YOUR FRIEND BATMAN TAKE THESE HOODLUMS WHERE THEY BELONG.
DON'T WORRY, MISS COBBLEPOT. HE'S COMING ALONG.

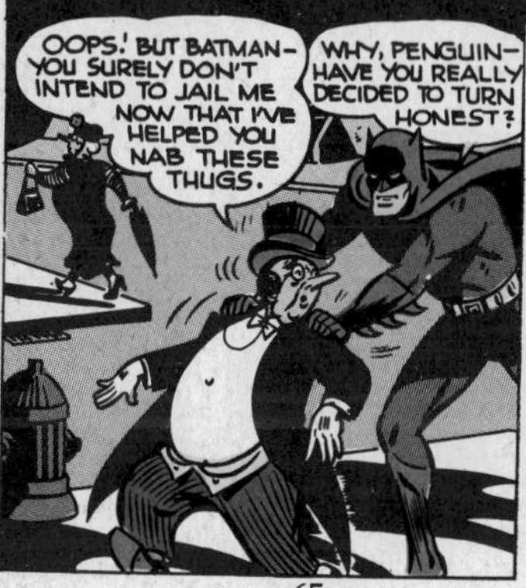
OOPS! BUT BATMAN-YOU SURELY DON'T INTEND TO JAIL ME NOW THAT I'VE HELPED YOU NAB THESE THUGS.
WHY, PENGUIN-HAVE YOU REALLY DECIDED TO TURN HONEST?

HONEST? ME? NOT A CHANCE! THERE ARE STILL 237 WAYS OF ESCAPING FROM JAIL I HAVEN'T TRIED OUT YET!
DON'T WORRY, OSWALD-ER-PARDON-PENGUIN! YOU'LL GET YOUR CHANCE TO TEST THEM!
THE END

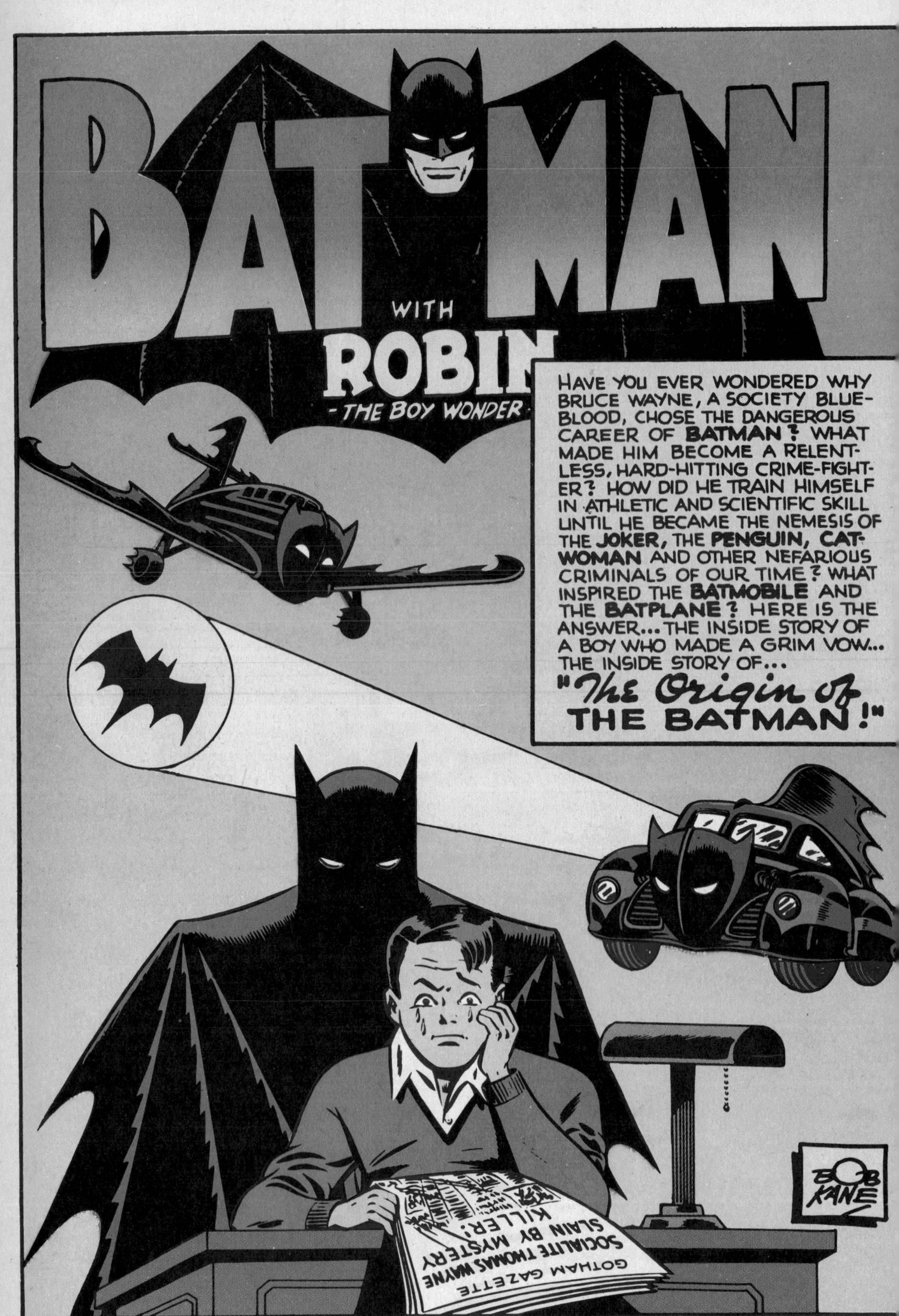

Art by Bob Kane & Lou Schwartz/Coloring by Adrienne Roy

BONG! BONG!
MIDNIGHT OUTSIDE GOTHAM CITY, AND AS A TRANSPORT TRUCK ROARS OVER THE HIGHWAY, A SUDDEN BLOWOUT SPELLS DOOM!
CRASH!!!

VITNESSES TO THE DISASTER ARE BATMAN AND ROBIN, THE BOY WONDER, HOMEWARD BOUND IN THEIR STREAMLINED BATMOBILE, AFTER AN EVENING OF CRIME-SMASHING...
IT LOOKS BAD, ROBIN! THAT TRUCK FOLDED UP LIKE A CHUNK OF TINFOIL!

THE DRIVER'S DEAD. HE WAS KILLED INSTANTLY!

BATMAN ... LOOK! A SECRET DOOR N THE TRUCK'S SIDE... THERE'S A MAN COMING OUT!
OOHH... MY HEAD...

AS ROBIN ADVANCES TOWARD THE STUMBLING MAN TO HELP HIM...
YOU OKAY, MISTER...? UHHH!
ROBIN! YOU AIN'T TAKIN' ME IN!

YOU MUST HAVE A GOOD REASON FOR FLASHING THAT GUN! BETTER TELL IT—FAST!

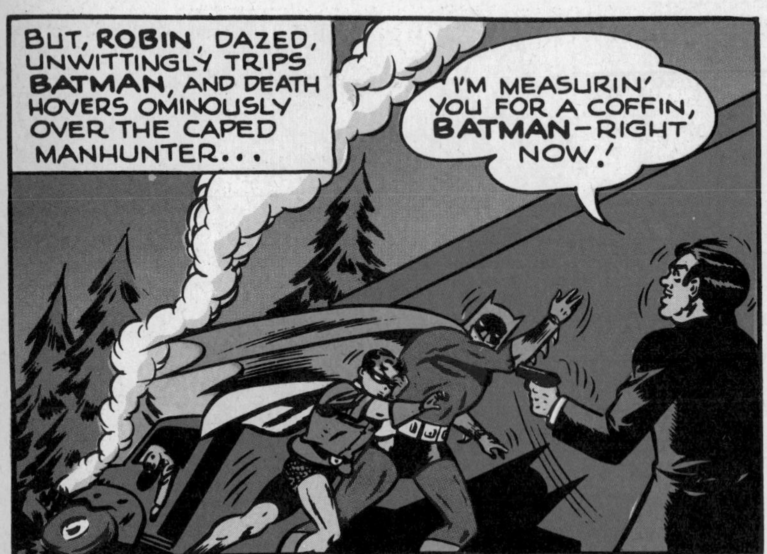
BUT, ROBIN, DAZED, UNWITTINGLY TRIPS BATMAN, AND DEATH HOVERS OMINOUSLY OVER THE CAPED MANHUNTER...
I'M MEASURIN' YOU FOR A COFFIN, BATMAN—RIGHT NOW!

ABRUPTLY, A BULLET FROM NOWHERE CLIPS THE MURDEROUS THUG...

BLAM!
UH...

WE HEARD THE CRASH! I DIDN'T WANT TO KILL THAT TRIGGERMAN, BUT IT WAS HIM OR YOU!
THE RADIO PATROL!
P.D.

SAY, THIS IS "FEETS" BORGAM! HE'S WANTED FOR A MURDER IN THE NEXT STATE! ALL STATE TROOPERS WERE TO WATCH FOR HIM IN CARS CROSSING THE STATE LINE!

HMM.. CONTAINER OF MILK... SANDWICHES... CIGARETTES... ALL THE COMFORTS OF HOME IN THAT SECRET COMPARTMENT!
THAT PROVES THE DRIVER KNEW HE WAS CARRYING "FEETS"!

A NEW RACKET, EH? SMUGGLING HOT CROOKS ACROSS THE LINE INTO OTHER STATES!
IT'S OBVIOUS THE DRIVER WASN'T ALONE IN THIS SET-UP! I WONDER IF THE OWNER OF THE LAND SEA-AIR TRANSPORT CO. IS TOP MAN?

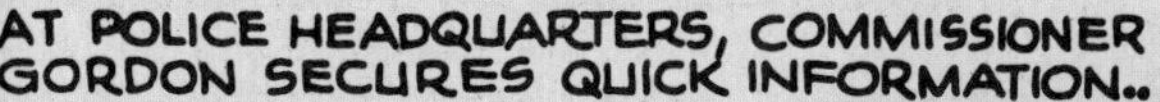

AT POLICE HEADQUARTERS, COMMISSIONER GORDON SECURES QUICK INFORMATION..

THE REPORT SAYS THE NEW L.S.A. OWNER BOUGHT OUT THE OLD OWNER, FIRED THE OLD TRUCKERS AND HIRED A NEW STAFF! THE OWNER'S NAME IS JOE CHILL! HERE'S A RADIO-PHOTO OF HIM...

THAT FACE... AFTER ALL THESE YEARS... IT'S HE! THE FACE OF THE MAN WHO KILLED MY PARENTS!

AND BATMAN'S THOUGHTS WHIRL HIM BACK TO A VIVID NIGHT MANY YEARS BEFORE...TO A NIGHT WHEN HE WAS WALKING WITH HIS PARENTS, THOMAS AND MARTHA WAYNE...

THIS IS A STICKUP! I'LL TAKE THAT NECKLACE YOU'RE WEARIN', LADY!

OH... NOT MY NECK-LACE...

YOU HOODLUM! DON'T YOU DARE PUT A HAND ON MY WIFE! UHHH...!

THOMAS!

MAYBE YOU'LL KEEP QUIET... NOW!

BLAM

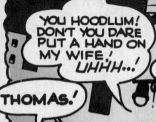

HAT SINGLE BULLET REALLY KILLED TWO EOPLE, FOR MARTHA WAYNE'S WEAK HEART TOPPED FROM THE SUDDEN SHOCK!
THEY'RE DEAD! YOU ILLED THEM... YOU KILLED MY MOTHER AND FATHER...
STOP LOOKIN' AT ME LIKE THAT!

SOMETHING ABOUT YOUNG BRUCE'S EYES MADE THE KILLER RETREAT... THEY WERE ACCUSING EYES THAT MEMORIZED HIS EVERY FEATURE... EYES THAT WOULD NEVER FORGET...

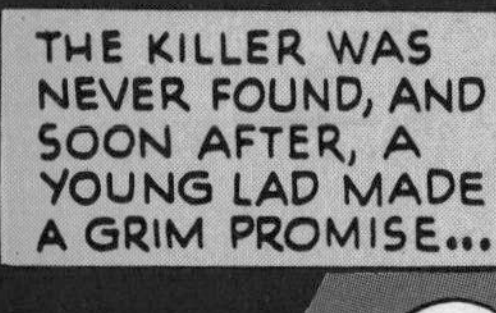
THE KILLER WAS NEVER FOUND, AND SOON AFTER, A YOUNG LAD MADE A GRIM PROMISE...
I SWEAR I'LL DEDICATE MY LIFE AND INHERITANCE TO BRINGING YOUR KILLER TO JUSTICE... AND TO FIGHTING ALL CRIMINALS! I SWEAR IT!

WAYNE
THOMAS MARTHA
THE YEARS PASSED AS BRUCE WAYNE PREPARED FOR HIS CHOSEN CAREER!
HE MASTERED SCIENTIFIC CRIMINAL INVESTIGATION!

HE TRAINED HIS BODY TO SUCH PHYSICAL AND ATHLETIC PERFECTION THAT HE COULD PERFORM ANY DAREDEVIL FEAT...

THEN, ONE DAY HE WAS READY FOR HIS NEW ROLE.
CRIMINALS ARE A SUPERSTITIOUS, COWARDLY LOT, SO I MUST WEAR A DISGUISE THAT WILL STRIKE TERROR INTO THEIR HEARTS! I MUST BE A CREATURE OF THE NIGHT, LIKE A... A...

AND, AS IF IN ANSWER, A WINGED CREATURE FLEW IN THROUGH THE OPEN WINDOW!
A BAT! THAT'S IT! IT'S LIKE AN OMEN! I SHALL BECOME A BAT!

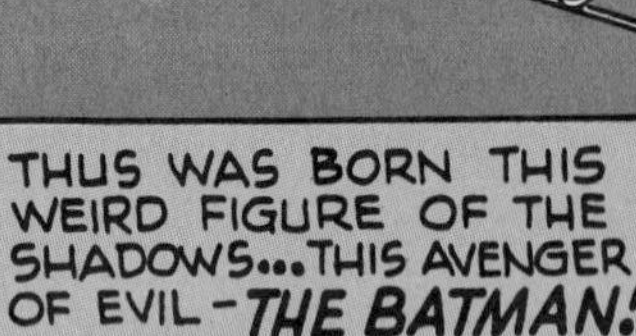
THUS WAS BORN THIS WEIRD FIGURE OF THE SHADOWS...THIS AVENGER OF EVIL–THE BATMAN!
SOME DAY, I'LL FIND THE KILLER OF MY PARENT ... SOME DAY...

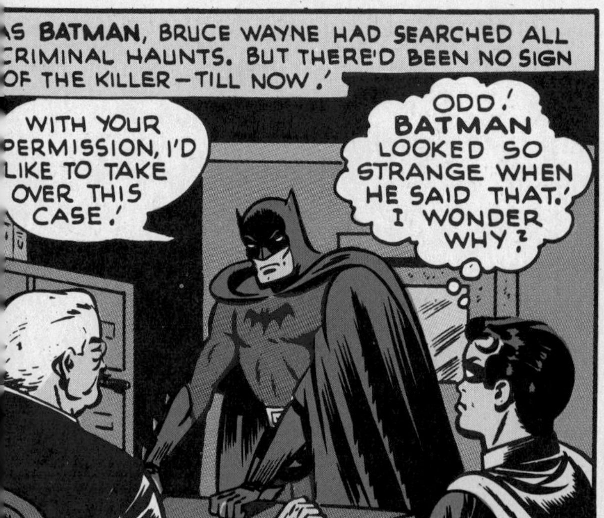
S BATMAN, BRUCE WAYNE HAD SEARCHED ALL RIMINAL HAUNTS. BUT THERE'D BEEN NO SIGN OF THE KILLER—TILL NOW.!
WITH YOUR PERMISSION, I'D LIKE TO TAKE OVER THIS CASE.!
ODD.! BATMAN LOOKED SO STRANGE WHEN HE SAID THAT.! I WONDER WHY?

AT HOME, AFTER BATMAN EXPLAINS TO HIS YOUNG PARTNER...
THE KILLER OF YOUR PARENTS, EH? WELL... LET'S GO GET HIM.!
SORRY, ROBIN, THIS IS ONE JOB I'M DOING ALONE! I DON'T HAVE TO EXPLAIN—YOU CAN UNDERSTAND WHY.!

THE NEXT DAY, A DISGUISED BATMAN CALLS AT THE L.S.A. TERMINAL...
LSA
LAND, SEA, AIR TRANSPORT COMPANY
YOU WANT A JOB AS A TRUCKER? THAT'S UP TO THE BOSS, BUD.!

O AT LONG LAST, BRUCE WAYNE OMES FACE TO FACE WITH THE AN HE HAD VOWED TO TRACK OWN.!
HE HASN'T HANGED! HE'S STILL RUEL... STILL A KILLER.!
ON YOUR WAY, PUNCHY! I ONLY HIRE GUYS I KNOW!

LATER...
HE'S CAGEY.! ONLY WANTS DRIVERS HE'S SURE HE CAN TRUST.! THAT KILLS MY CHANCES OF GETTING INSIDE HIS GANG.! WHAT NOW?

I'VE GOT IT! I'M GOING TO BRING BUSINESS TO JOE CHILL.!
SNAP!

THAT NIGHT, BATMAN RIDES WITH THE POLICE HARBOR PATROL...
SO THAT SHOWBOAT IS REALLY A GAMBLING SHIP, EH?
YES! RUN BY MONTY JULEP! HE HAS ALL HIS CREW COSTUMED LIKE OLDTIME MISSISSIPPI GAMBLERS! HIS SHOWBOAT PADDLES AROUND OUTSIDE THE LEGAL LIMIT SO WE CAN'T ARREST HIM!
POLICE 4

ONE HOUR LATER... ON THE GAMBLING SHIP, TWO SENTRIES IDLE AWAY THE TIME...
PETE, I THINK I'LL TRY SOME TARGET PRACTICE ON THAT SEA GULL!
YOU SAP! THE SHOTS WOULD PANIC THE CHUMPS AT JULEP'S TABLES! PUT YOUR GUN AWAY!

A GOOD THING, TOO... FOR THE "SEA GULL" IS IN REALITY A UNIQUE CAMOUFLAGE UNDER-WATER HELMET WORN BY BATMAN!

THEN, THE CHURNING STERNWHEEL CARRIES THE ACROBATMAN UNSEEN TO A TOP DECK!
TRICKY, BUT IT'S A SHORT-CUT TO THE WHEEL-ROOM!

JUST A LITTLE MUTINY, CAPTAIN!

SOON AFTER... A CYCLONIC FIGURE CHARGES INTO THE GAMBLING ROOM!
THROW IN YOUR CARDS, FOLKS! MONTY JULEP'S NOT DEALING ANOTHER HAND TONIGHT!
DON'T BE TOO SHORE, BATMAN! BOYS, COME A-RUNNIN'!

WHERE ARE YORE EYES? HIT HIM!
TELL HIM TO STAND STILL AND WE'LL DO IT.!

CASHING IN YOUR CHIPS, JULEP?
THEN I'LL GET HIM MYSELF... YII-II!

WITH ONE MIGHTY HEAVE, BATMAN WRENCHES UP THE ROULETTE WHEEL... AND IT BECOMES A DISCUS!
WATCH THE SPINNING WHEEL, FOLKS.

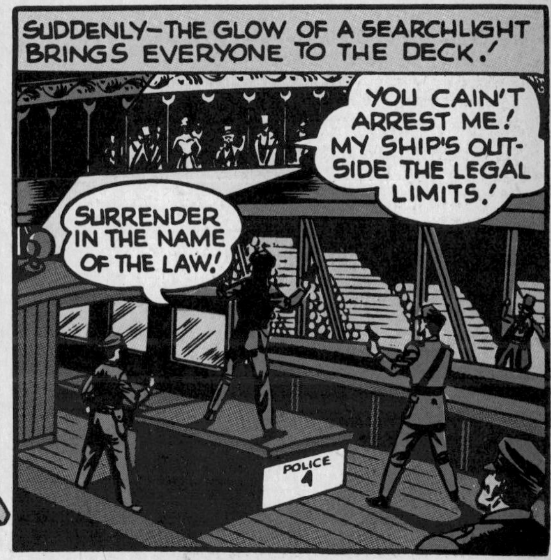
SUDDENLY—THE GLOW OF A SEARCHLIGHT BRINGS EVERYONE TO THE DECK!
YOU CAIN'T ARREST ME! MY SHIP'S OUTSIDE THE LEGAL LIMITS!
SURRENDER IN THE NAME OF THE LAW!
POLICE 4

NOT ANYMORE! I LASHED YOUR WHEEL AND STAGED THIS FIGHT SO YOU'D BE TOO BUSY TO NOTICE YOUR BOAT WAS TURNING INSIDE THE LIMIT!

POLICE POUR ON DECK, AND IN THE CONFUSION, MONTY JULEP RACES TO A SMALL MOTOR-BOAT HIDDEN FOR EMERGENCIES...
THEY AIN'T GOIN' TO ARREST ME! I'LL GET OUT O' THIS STATE MIGHTY FAST!

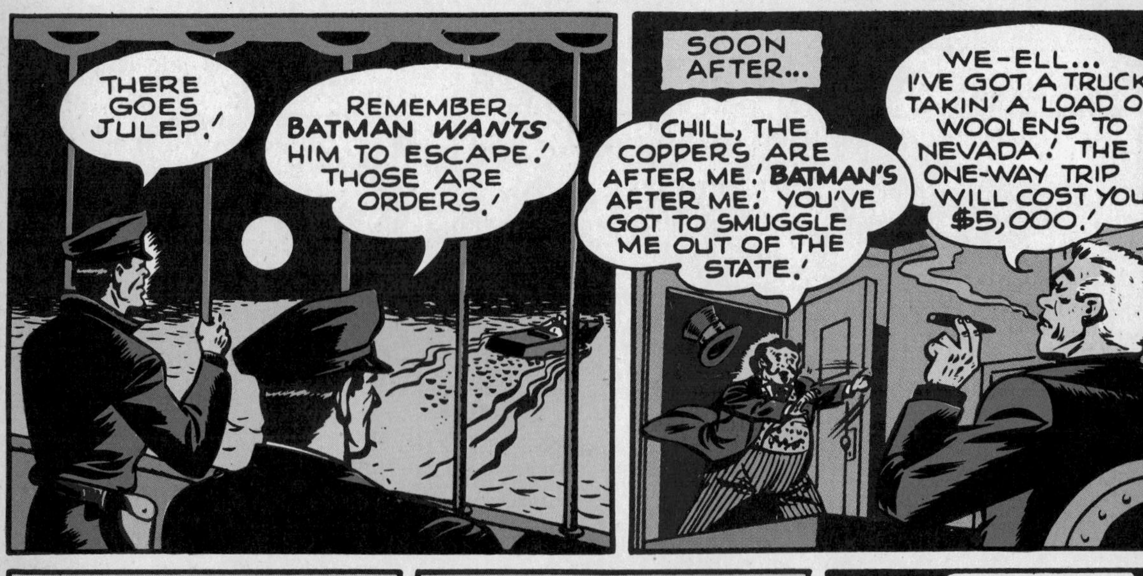
THERE GOES JULEP!
REMEMBER, BATMAN WANTS HIM TO ESCAPE! THOSE ARE ORDERS!
SOON AFTER...
CHILL, THE COPPERS ARE AFTER ME! BATMAN'S AFTER ME! YOU'VE GOT TO SMUGGLE ME OUT OF THE STATE!
WE-ELL... I'VE GOT A TRUCK TAKIN' A LOAD OF WOOLENS TO NEVADA! THE ONE-WAY TRIP WILL COST YOU $5,000!

ABRUPTLY, CHILL GETS UP AND SNAPS A SWITCH ON AN INSTRUMENT PANEL...
YOU'RE A-GOIN' TO LOOK AT TELEVISION... NOW?
NO! I'M JUST MAKIN' SURE YOU WEREN'T FOLLOWED! THIS IS REALLY A PERISCOPE THAT LOOKS OVER THE BACKYARD!

SUDDENLY, THE TELLTALE SCREEN REVEALS—
BATMAN! HE MUST'VE BEEN HIDDEN IN THE CABIN OF MY BOAT.
THIS IS A TRAP!

JULEP, YOU DIRTY DOUBLECROSSE I'M SENDING YOU O A ONE-WAY TRIP... AND I AIN'T CHARGIN' YOU A CENT!

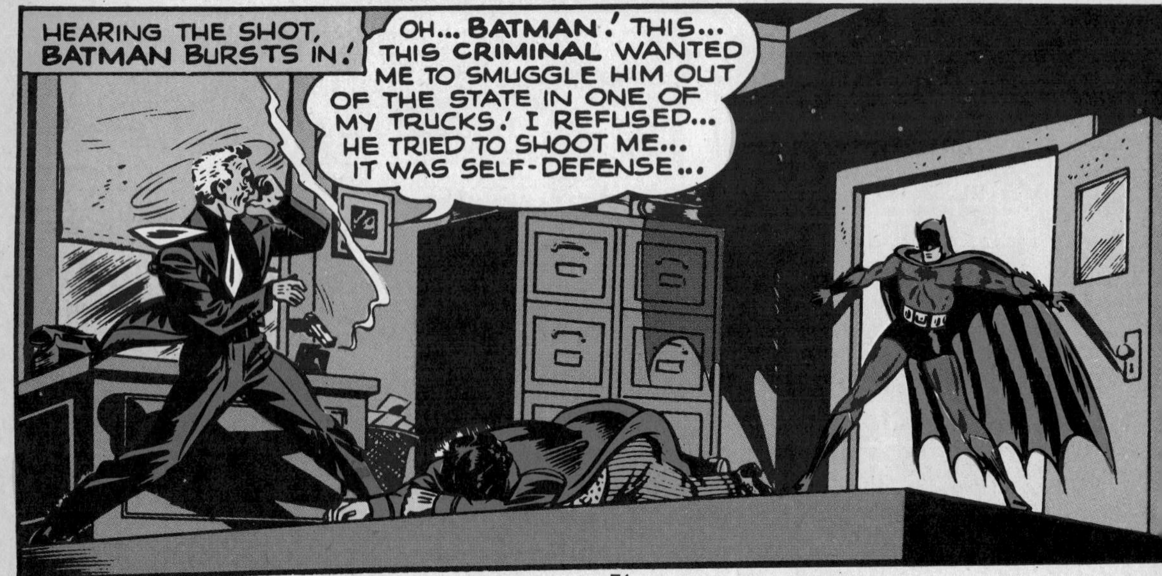
HEARING THE SHOT, BATMAN BURSTS IN!
OH... BATMAN! THIS... THIS CRIMINAL WANTED ME TO SMUGGLE HIM OUT OF THE STATE IN ONE OF MY TRUCKS! I REFUSED... HE TRIED TO SHOOT ME... IT WAS SELF-DEFENSE...

THAT NIGHT, A BROODING **BATMAN** WEIGHS HIS CASE AGAINST HIS ENEMY...

HM-MM! I'M CLOSING IN ON JOE CHILL— BUT HOW CAN I MAKE HIM CONFESS THAT HE KILLED MY FATHER?

THERE'S ONLY ONE WAY. IT'S A DESPERATE MOVE... BUT I **MUST** TAKE IT... EVEN IF IT MEANS **THE END OF BATMAN'S CAREER!**

PRESENTLY, **BATMAN** CALLS ON JOE CHILL!

CHILL, I WANT TO TELL YOU A STORY... WITHOUT AN ENDING! MAYBE YOU CAN SUPPLY IT! IT BEGAN SOME YEARS AGO IN GOTHAM CITY... WHEN THOMAS WAYNE, HIS WIFE, AND YOUNG SON, BRUCE, WERE STOPPED BY A BANDIT...

YOU SAID... W-WAYNE?

THE BANDIT KILLED THOMAS WAYNE... HIS WIFE DIED FROM THE SHOCK! FRIGHTENED, THE COWARDLY KILLER RAN AWAY ... BUT NOT BEFORE YOUNG BRUCE WAYNE MEMORIZED HIS FEATURES!

I BECAME BATMAN BECAUSE OF WHAT YOU DID AND I SWORE I'D ARREST YOU FOR IT SOME DAY! I CAN'T PROVE YOUR GUILT, BUT I'LL NEVER STOP HOUNDING YOU UNTIL I DO...

"WHATEVER YOU DO, I'LL BE WATCHING..."
Club Pelican

"WHEREVER YOU GO, I'LL BE WATCHING..."

I'LL ALWAYS BE WATCHING... AND SOMEDAY YOU'LL MAKE A MISTAKE... AND I'LL BE THERE... WAITING! REMEMBER THAT—AND THIS!

AND WHEN BATMAN LEAVES...
WHAT'LL I DO? BATMAN MEANS EVERYTHING HE SAID! HE PROVED IT BY REVEALING HIS IDENTITY! HE'LL GET ME... UNLESS I KILL HIM FIRST!

DESPERATE, CHILL RUNS TO THE REPAIR GARAGE OF HIS TERMINAL...
LISTEN, BOYS... I NEED HELP BAD! YEARS AGO, I KNOCKED OFF A GUY... AN' NOW HIS SON IS AFTER ME! THAT GUY'S SON IS THE BATMAN! HE JUST TOLD ME!
YOU... KNOCKED OFF BATMAN'S FATHER? YOU'R KIDDIN'!

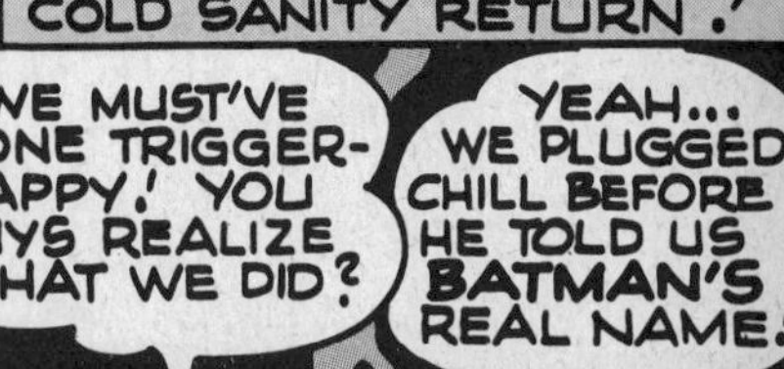

LOOK! HE'S STILL ALIVE! MAYBE HE'LL TALK!
CHILL! QUICK! WHO IS BATMAN?
HIS NAME-IS-IS-

WE GOTTA GET HIM BEFORE HE GETS US FOR THIS KILLING!
THIS IS WHAT I WANT—THE LEVER THAT SENDS THE CAR HOIST TURNING!
LSA
LAND, SEA, AIR, TRANSPORT COMPANY

THE HOIST SPINS... AND AT THAT INSTANT BATMAN SNATCHES UP A GREASE-GUN!
A GREASE SHAMPOO—NO EXTRA CHARGE!
AGGGH!
OOF!
THE ONLY WAY I CAN KEEP YOU AWAY FROM CHILL... IS TO KNOCK YOU OUT!

STILL WITH US, CHILL?
NOT... FOR LONG! FUNNY ...BECAUSE I STARTED YOU OFF AS BATMAN, THE BOYS... PLUGGED ME!

YEAH... I GUESS YOU GOT ME.... AFTER ALL! AHHHH...

AND SO, AT LAST, THE CASE IS CLOSED—THE CASE WITHOUT WHICH THERE WOULD NEVER HAVE BEEN A BATMAN!
Murder of Thomas Wayne
Closed
THE END

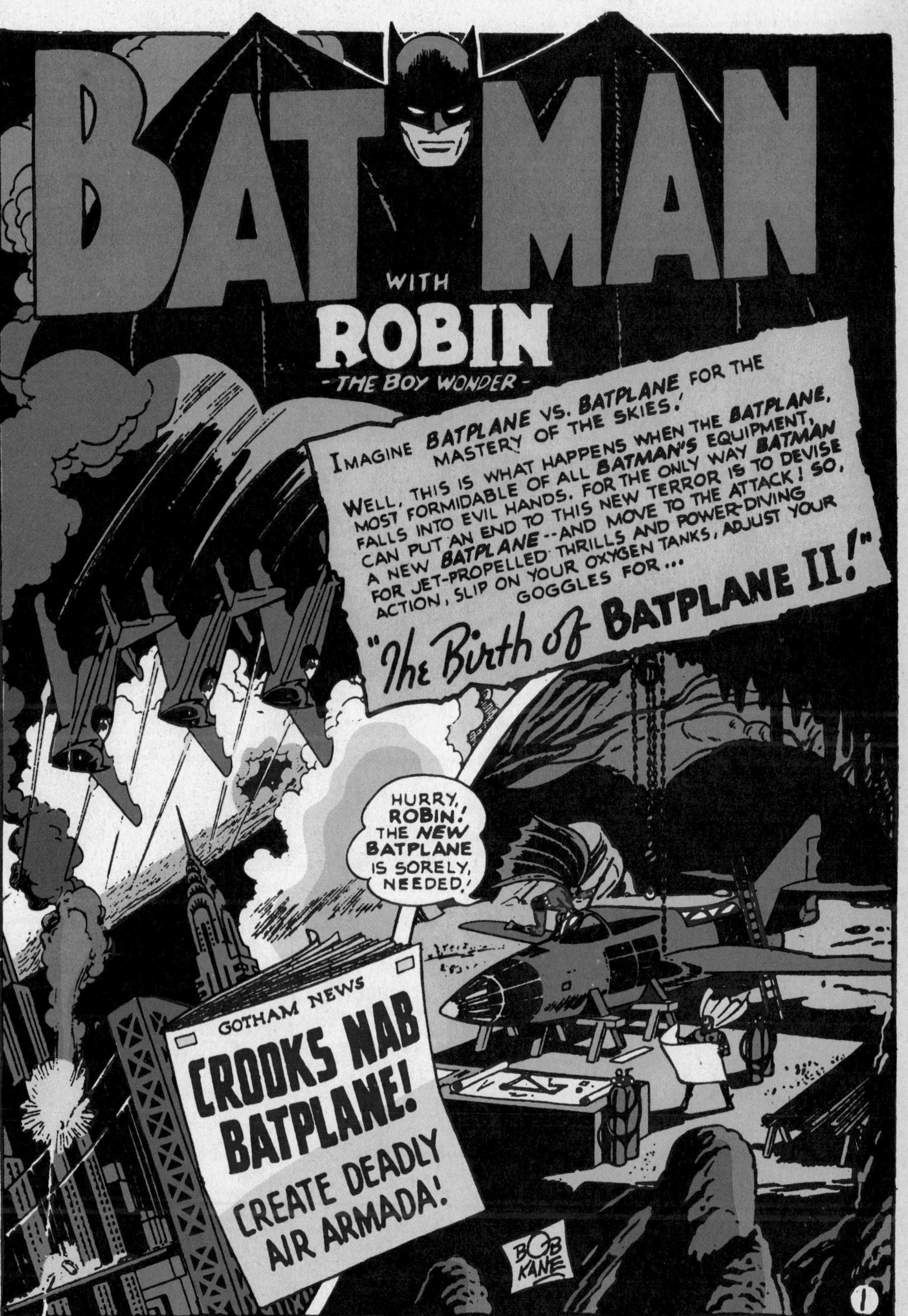

Art by Dick Sprang & Charles Paris/Coloring by Glenn Whitmore

ONE DAY, IN THE OFFICES OF GOTHAM AIRLINES...
I'M SORRY, HAGGERTY... THE DOCTORS HAVE TURNED DOWN YOUR REQUEST TO PILOT ONE OF OUR PLANES!
WHAT? WITH MY WAR RECORD—AND FLYING EXPERIENCE?

DESPERATELY, "FLYING TIGER" HAGGERTY PRODUCES PHOTOGRAPHIC TESTIMONY OF HIS SKILL...
SEE? THAT WAS ME PILOTING THAT MUSTANG, MR. LANE! I WAS CREDITED WITH SHOOTING DOWN 22 JAP PLANES!

WHY, I'VE HANDLED ALL TYPES OF AIRCRAFT! LOOK AT THIS CARGO SHIP I FLEW OVER THE TREACHEROUS ALPS!

I KNOW—BUT, YOU'VE GOTTEN OLDER—YOUR REFLEXES ARE SLOWER! AND YOU KNOW, SAFETY IS OUR MAIN CONCERN! BUT REMEMBER—COME SEE ME ANY TIME YOU'RE READY TO TAKE A DESK JOB...
DESK JOB! WHY, I'D NEVER BE ABLE TO STAND IT!

LATER, AS "FLYING TIGER" HAGGERTY MAKES ONE LAST-DITCH EFFORT TO STAY IN THE GAME HE LOVES...
BUT, COLONEL WEBB—YOU CAN'T TURN ME DOWN! FLYING'S MY WHOLE LIFE!
SORRY, HAGGERTY... REGULATIONS ARE REGULATIONS! I'D LOVE TO HAVE YOU--BUT I JUST CAN'T...

MEANWHILE, IN A WAITING ROOM NEAR COLONEL WEBB'S OFFICE...
I WONDER WHAT COLONEL WEBB WANTS OF US, BATMAN?
HE DIDN'T SAY! HE JUST TOLD COMMISSIONER GORDON IT WAS A MATTER OF EXTREME URGENCY AND SECRECY!

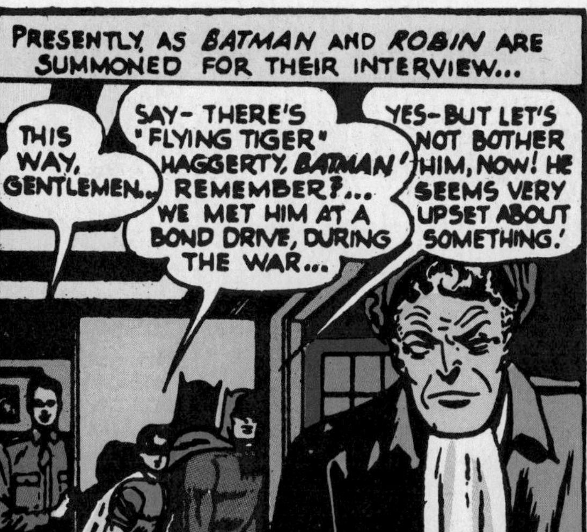
PRESENTLY, AS BATMAN AND ROBIN ARE SUMMONED FOR THEIR INTERVIEW...
THIS WAY, GENTLEMEN...
SAY- THERE'S "FLYING TIGER" HAGGERTY, BATMAN! REMEMBER?... WE MET HIM AT A BOND DRIVE, DURING THE WAR...
YES-BUT LET'S NOT BOTHER HIM, NOW! HE SEEMS VERY UPSET ABOUT SOMETHING!

AND WHEN THE DYNAMIC DUO IS ALONE WITH COLONEL WEBB...
SO YOU WANT US TO HELP YOU TEST AN IMPORTANT NEW WEAPON YOU'VE INVENTED, COLONEL!
YES, GENTLEMEN! IT'S NOT QUITE READY TO BE PRESENTED OFFICIALLY TO THE ARMY-- THAT'S WHY I PREFER NOT TO USE ARMY PLANES OR PERSONNEL IN THIS TEST...

WHAT I WOULD LIKE TO DO IS INSTALL THE WEAPON IN THE BATPLANE -AND USE MY PERSONAL PLANE AS THE TEST TARGET!
WHY, WE'LL BE GLAD TO ASSIST YOU, COLONEL!

NEXT DAY, AT AN ISOLATED AIRFIELD...
I CALL IT A "VACUUM BLANKET," BATMAN! WHEN TURNED ON DIRECTLY OVER ANOTHER PLANE, IT CREATES A VACUUM, WHICH CONKS OUT THAT PLANE'S ENGINE!

AND AS THEY TAKE TO THE AIR...
WHEN I GIVE THE SIGNAL, ROBIN, TURN ON THE "VACUUM BLANKET"!
RIGHT! AND IF IT WORKS, COLONEL WEBB SHOULD HAVE LITTLE TROUBLE GLIDING HIS PLANE TO A LANDING!

BUT AS ROBIN TURNS ON THE NEW WEAPON...
TURN IT OFF, ROBIN! SOMETHING'S GONE WRONG! THE BATPLANE'S CONTROLS HAVE FROZEN!
3

IT'S NO USE, ROBIN EVERYTHING'S JAMMED! WE'LL HAVE TO BAIL OUT!
AND HOW! IN A FEW MINUTES, WE'LL BE OVER THE OCEAN!

SECOND'S LATER...
WELL, THERE GOES THE BATPLANE! WE'VE LOST IT FOR GOOD, BATMAN!
YES—BUT WE CAN ALWAYS BUILD ANOTHER! LUCKY IT'S HEADED OUT TO SEA... WHEN IT RUNS OUT OF FUEL—AND CRASHES—NO ONE WILL BE HURT!

BUT LONG AFTER BATMAN AND ROBIN HAVE LANDED SAFELY, A PHENOMENON OF NATURE ALTERS THE BATPLANE'S COURSE...
...AS A FREAK CROSS-WIND SPINS IT AROUND AND HEADS IT BACK TO THE MAINLAND!

MEANWHILE, AT A SMALL AIRCRAFT FACTORY, NORTH OF GOTHAM CITY, RUN BY THE THREE BOLEY BROTHERS...
BULL, WE GOT A TIP THE COPS ARE ON TO US, FOR INCOME TAX EVASION!
AND WHEN THEY COME NOSIN' AROUND, THEY'RE SURE TO GET WISE THAT THIS FACTORY IS JUST A FRONT FOR OUR SMUGGLING RACKET!

AWRIGHT-AWRIGHT! SO WE'LL BLOW THIS JOINT BEFORE THEY COME. NOW, LEMME THINK... HOW'LL WE DO IT?
4

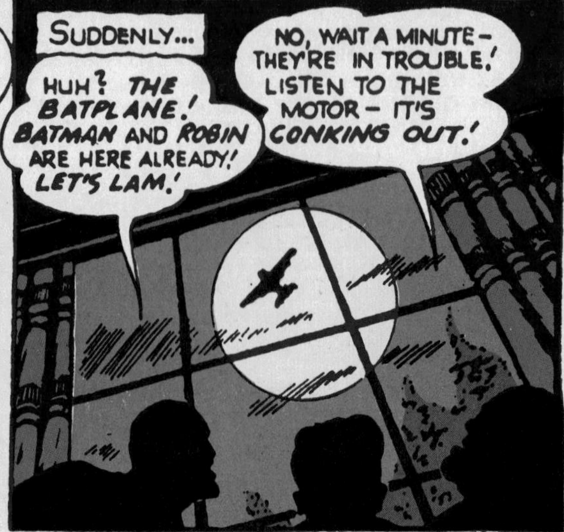
SUDDENLY...
HUH? THE BATPLANE! BATMAN AND ROBIN ARE HERE ALREADY! LET'S LAM!
NO, WAIT A MINUTE—THEY'RE IN TROUBLE! LISTEN TO THE MOTOR—IT'S CONKING OUT!

MOMENTS LATER...
LOOK! THE BATPLANE'S LANDED, LIGHT AS A FEATHER, IN THOSE PINE TREES! ARE THEY LUCKY!
MAYBE THEY'RE NOT SO LUCKY! HERE'S OUR CHANCE TO CATCH 'EM BY SURPRISE! SHOOT TO KILL!

BUT WHEN THE CROOKS CHARGE THE BATPLANE...
WHY-IT'S EMPTY! THEY AIN'T HERE! WHAT HAPPENED?
I DON'T KNOW, AND I DON'T CARE! WE JUST GOT OURSELVES A BATPLANE! WHAT AN IDEA THAT GIVES ME!

THINK OF THE JOBS WE CAN PULL WITH THE BATPLANE! ALL WE NEED IS A PILOT WHO CAN FIX THE MOTOR! THEN, WE'LL BUILD TWO MORE BATPLANES -ONE FOR EACH OF US! WHY, WE'LL RULE THE CRIME WORLD!

AT THAT MOMENT, IN THE BATCAVE, BATMAN AND ROBIN, IN THEIR EVERYDAY DISGUISES AS BRUCE WAYNE AND HIS YOUNG WARD, DICK GRAYSON, COMPLETE PLANS FOR A NEW BATPLANE...
COLONEL WEBB HAS CO-OPERATED IN KEEPING THE ACCIDENT OUT OF THE PAPERS, DICK!
HELICOPTER ASSEMBLY FOLDS INTO FUSELAGE
MAGNESIUM FIRED BATBEAM
THREE-WAY INTERCHANGING LANDING GEAR-WHEELS, PONTOONS, SKIS
"VACUUM BLANKET" ACTIVATOR
COMPLETE CRIME LAB WITHIN BATPLANE CABIN
SUPER RAM-JET POWER PLANT
HUMAN EJECTOR TUBES
TELEVISION, RADAR, RADIO ANTENNAE ALL CONTAINED IN THE WING STRUCTURES
GOOD, BRUCE! THERE'S NO SENSE IN LETTING CROOKS KNOW WE HAVEN'T GOT A BATPLANE! WILL THE BE SURPRISED WHEN THEY SEE THIS NEW ONE! BOY-IT'S A CORKER!

AND AS THE DAYS PASS...
A MINIATURE BUT COMPLETE CRIME LAB WILL FIT IN HERE! BEHIND IT WILL BE OUR STORAGE SPACE!
HMMM... THAT'S WHERE WE CAN KEEP PROVISIONS, EXTRA UNIFORMS, DUMMIES OF OURSELVES, SPARE EQUIPMENT-AND ALL THE OTHER THINGS THIS TERRIFIC PLANE WILL NEED!

MEANWHILE, AS THINGS GO BADLY FOR "FLYING TIGER" HAGGERTY...
THAT MUST BE THE FLYER THEY TOLD US ABOUT IN THAT FLEA-BAG OF A HOTEL...
YEAH! AN OLD ARMY PILOT WHO'D DO ANYTHING TO FLY AGAIN! AND DON'T FORGET HIS OLD FOLKS, DOWN IN MISSISSIPPI -- THAT'S OUR ACE IN THE HOLE!
5

WHEN THE CROOKS INVITE HAGGERTY FOR A RIDE..
YES, I COULD USE THE JOB! BUT ARE YOU SURE THIS FLYING DEAL YOU'RE OFFERING IS LEGITIMATE?
SURE, PAL! WE DID SOME REPAIRS ON THE BATPLANE FOR BATMAN AND ROBIN. NOW, ALL WE NEED IS A FERRY PILOT TO DELIVER THE PLANE!
SOON, AT THE BOLEY FACTORY...
ALL WE HAVE TO DO IS DELIVER IT TO THE MUNICIPAL AIRPORT... LET'S GO!
GOSH--THE BATPLANE! WHAT A SWEET JOB TO FLY!
HA-HA! HE'S FALLING FOR THE GAG!
WHILE AT GOTHAM CITY MUNICIPAL AIRPORT...
HERE COMES THAT DIAMOND SHIPMENT NOW, SIR...
RIGHT! WE'LL USE SECURITY PLAN "Y"! CLEAR THE FIELD-KEEP ALL INCOMING PLANES IN THE AIR-POSTPONE ALL TAKE-OFFS!
BUT AS THE TRANSPORT PLANE LANDS...
LOOK! THERE COME BATMAN AND ROBIN... PROBABLY TO LEND ADDITIONAL SECURITY! TELL THEM TO LAND AT ONCE!
SUDDENLY...
WHAT IS THIS!? WHERE'S BATMAN?
QUICK, SLATS-GRAB THE DIAMONDS!
ONE FALSE MOVE, HAGGERTY-AND I'LL DRILL YOU!
AND AS THE BRASH THIEVES MAKE THEIR GETAWAY...
OKAY, HAGGERTY-TAKE OFF! AND DON'T TRY TO BE A HERO! WE KNOW ALL ABOUT YOUR OLD FOLKS DOWN IN MISSISSIPPI...
YEAH-WE GOT FRIENDS DOWN THERE! YOU PLAY BALL OR YOU'LL NEVER SEE YOUR FAMILY AGAIN!
YOU RATS!

MINUTES LATER...
BUT HOW DID CROOKS EVER LAY HANDS ON THE BATPLANE, BATMAN?
PROBABLY BY SOME FREAK OF NATURE! THIS IS SERIOUS ROBIN! WE'VE GOT A REAL FIGHT ON OUR HANDS!

NO - I DIDN'T RECOGNIZE ANY OF THE CROOKS! BUT I COULDN'T MISTAKE THEIR PILOT - HE WAS "FLYING TIGER" HAGGERTY!
HAGGERTY! WE KNEW HE WAS DOWN AND OUT, BUT WE NEVER FIGURED HE'D TAKE UP WITH CRIMINALS! ROBIN, YOU KNOW WHAT THAT MEANS... WE MUST FINISH OUR NEW PLANE AHEAD OF SCHEDULE!

AND SO, THE BAT-CAVE SOON STARTS TO HUM WITH CONSTRUCTION ACTIVITY...
THE NEW BATPLANE CAN ALSO CONVERT INTO A HELICOPTER OR A SUBMARINE! SEE, DICK? THE WINGS AND RUDDER ASSEMBLY -FOLD INTO THE FUSELAGE!
WOW! A BATMARINE!

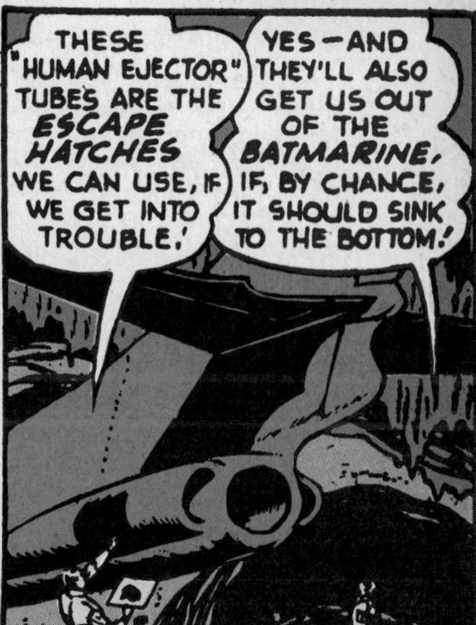
THESE "HUMAN EJECTOR" TUBES ARE THE ESCAPE HATCHES WE CAN USE, IF WE GET INTO TROUBLE!
YES - AND THEY'LL ALSO GET US OUT OF THE BATMARINE, IF, BY CHANCE, IT SHOULD SINK TO THE BOTTOM!

BUT ELSEWHERE, OTHER BATPLANES ARE ALSO TAKING SHAPE...
IN ANOTHER WEEK, THEY'LL BE FINISHED, BULL!
GOOD. I HEAR BATMAN IS BUILDING A NEW PLANE! BUT WAIT TILL WE MEET HIM. THREE BATPLANES AGAINST ONE!

BY THE WAY, HAGGERTY, I GOT A LETTER, HERE, FROM MY FRIEND IN MISSISSIPPI. HE'S KEEPIN' A SHARP EYE ON YOUR FOLKS-- WANNA READ IT?
DON'T RUB IT IN, BULL! I'M WORKING FOR YOU... ISN'T THAT ENOUGH?
7

DAYS LATER:..
THERE IT IS, DICK- THE NEW BATPLANE! COMPLETE WITH JET-PROPULSION, TELEVISION, RADAR, CRIME LAB...
..."VACUUM BLANKET," BATMARINE, EJECTORS, THE BAT-BEAM - GOSH, BRUCE - WE COULD GO ON AND ON!
ABRUPTLY...
FLASH! A BATPLANE, BELIEVED TO BE THE ONE IN POSSESSION OF CRIMINALS HAS BEEN SIGHTED IN THE AIR, NORTH OF GOTHAM CITY...
WHAT? WE DIDN'T FINISH A MOMENT TOO SOON!
DICK! IT'S TIME FOR BATMAN AND ROBIN TO TRY OUT THEIR NEW PLANE!
SOON, IN THE SKIES OVER GOTHAM CITY...
HERE COMES BATMAN, BULL! THIS COULD MEAN OUR FINISH!
HA-HA! NOT WITH DAVE AND SLATS HIDING IN THE CLOUDS ABOVE! REMEMBER- BATMAN DOESN'T USE GUNS -AND WE DO!
SUDDENLY, AS THE COLORFUL CRIME-BUSTERS APPROACH BULL'S PLANE...
LOOK! THREE BATPLANES! AND THEY'RE FIRING HEAVY CANNON!
TOO MUCH FIRE-POWER EVEN FOR THIS PLANE, ROBIN!
WITHIN SECONDS, SMOKE POURS FROM THE NEW BATPLANE, AND...
NICE AIM, BOYS! YOU SET 'EM AFIRE AND THEY'RE BAILING OUT! WHAT A TARGET THEY'LL MAKE, FLOATING DOWN TO EARTH!
SO WHAT! HA-HA! THE NEW BATPLANE DIDN'T LAST LONG, DID IT? AND BATMAN AND ROBIN ARE SHOT FULL OF HOLES!
IT'S MURDER, BULL! PLAIN COLD-BLOODED MURDER!

BUT AS THE NEW BATPLANE HITS THE WATER AND CHANGES INTO THE BATMARINE...
THOSE DUMMIES AND THE SMOKE BOMB WE RELEASED FOOLED THEM! I STILL HEAR THEM ON THE RADIO...THEY THINK WE'RE DEAD!
IT'S NO FUN TO RUN FROM A FIGHT, BUT IT'S OUR BEST STRATEGY! WE'LL DO BETTER TAKING THEM ONE AT A TIME!

THINKING US OUT OF THE WAY, THEY'LL PROBABLY FEEL THERE'S NO NEED TO COME OUT IN FORCE! THEY'LL STRIKE WITH ONE PLANE AT A TIME!
... AND THAT'S WHEN THEY'LL FALL INTO OUR TRAP!

NEXT DAY, AS THE LUXURY YACHT "TROY" CRUISES OFF-SHORE, WITH A GALA PARTY ABOARD...
LOOK--A BATPLANE! WHAT'S IT DOING?
HAVEN'T YOU READ THE PAPERS? A CROOK CONTROLS THAT PLANE NOW!

A MESSAGE FROM THAT PLANE, SIR! HE ORDERS US TO CHANGE COURSE--TO PUT IN AT BLACK HOOK COVE--OR HE'LL SINK US WITH BOMBS OR CANNON!
WHY--THE PIRATE! THERE'S A FORTUNE ABOARD THIS VESSEL! HE CAN'T GET AWAY WITH IT... RADIO FOR HELP!

BUT BEFORE A MESSAGE CAN BE SENT THROUGH..
HE'S TUNED TO OUR RADIO CHANNEL, SIR! HE SAYS IF HE HEARS ONE PEEP OF AN SOS, HE'LL SINK US ON THE SPOT!
GOOD GRIEF! HE MEANS BUSINESS, ALL RIGHT... AND I CAN'T RISK THE LIVES OF MY PASSENGERS! WE'LL HAVE TO OBEY!

MEANWHILE, AS BRUCE AND DICK MAINTAIN A CONSTANT VIGIL BEFORE A HUGE RADAR SCREEN IN THE BATCAVE...
THERE IT IS...THE OUTLINE OF A BATPLANE!
ACCORDING TO THE CO-ORDINATES, HE'S OUT AT SEA! COME ON-- TIME TO GET STARTED AS BATMAN AND ROBIN!
9

IMMEDIATELY, OUT AT SEA...
THERE HE IS, ROBIN! THIS LOOKS LIKE A GREAT OPPORTUNITY TO USE THE NOW-PERFECTED "VACUUM BLANKET"!
BOY— WILL HE BE SURPRISED!

AND, AS THE "VACUUM BLANKET" GOES TO WORK...
HE'LL HAVE TO BAIL OUT, ROBIN! RADIO THAT YACHT, DOWN THERE, TO PICK HIM UP AND HOLD HIM!
HUH? THE BATPLANE... WITH BATMAN AND ROBIN ALIVE! AND MY MOTOR... IT'S CONKING OUT! MY RADIO'S DEAD!

HE'D ORDERED THE CAPTAIN TO PUT IN AT BLACK HOOK COVE, BATMAN...
THEN HE MUST HAVE A HENCHMAN WAITING THERE TO HELP LOOT THE SHIP! LET'S TAKE A LOOK-SEE!

PRESENTLY, AT BLACK HOOK COVE...
THERE HE IS! WE'VE CAUGHT ANOTHER FISH!
I'VE GOT AN IDEA, ROBIN— TURN ON THE BATBEAM!

INSTANTLY, A POWERFUL FLASH OF LIGHT, AND...
UGH! A BAT! I CAN'T SEE!
WE'VE BLINDED HIM, ROBIN—AND STALLED HIS TAKE-OFF! NOW, QUICKLY... SHIFT TO HELICOPTER AND TURN ON THE "VACUUM BLANKET"! THEN, GET THE GRAPPLING HOOKS READY!
10

AS ROBIN CARRIES OUT HIS INSTRUCTIONS...
IT WORKED, ROBIN! WE'VE HOOKED HIM FORE AND AFT! NOW, WE'LL TOTE HIM TO POLICE HEADQUARTERS!
I GET IT... CARRY HIM JUST HIGH ENOUGH SO THAT HE CAN'T LEAP OUT WITHOUT A CHUTE—AND TOO LOW TO LEAP OUT WITH A CHUTE!
STILL CAN'T SEE... WH-WHAT'S HAPPENING?

THAT NIGHT, ON THE ROOF OF POLICE HEADQUARTERS
A T-MAN IDENTIFIED THE TWO MEN YOU CAPTURED AS SLATS AND DAVE BOLEY! THEY'VE GOT A BROTHER, BULL, AT AN AIRCRAFT FACTORY NORTH OF HERE...
THAT'S OUR MAN... AND HAGGERTY'S UNDOUBTEDLY WITH HIM! THANKS, COMMISSIONER--LET'S GO, ROBIN!

MEANWHILE, AT THE BOLEY FACTORY...
THEY GOT MY BROTHERS--BUT THEY AIN'T GETTIN' ME! C'MON, HAGGERTY-YOU'RE FLYIN' ME TO MEXICO!

ABRUPTLY...
YOU FORGOT SOMETHING, BULL! WITH YOUR BROTHERS IN JAIL, WHO'S GOING TO TIP OFF YOUR FRIENDS IN MISSISSIPPI, NOW THAT I'M NOT PLAYING BALL ANYMORE?

SECONDS LATER...
WHAT A PLEASURE IT'LL BE TO TURN YOU OVER TO BATMAN, YOU RAT!
BOLEY A

BUT IN THE SKIES OVER GOTHAM CITY, AS THE TWO BATPLANES MEET...
WE'VE GOT THEM BOTH, ROBIN--BOLEY AND HAGGERTY! LET'S JUST RUN THEM RAGGED, UNTIL WE CAN FORCE THEM DOWN ON AN OPEN FIELD!
BATMAN! BATMAN! DON'T--I'M A FRIEND... A FRIEND!

I CAN'T SET THIS PLANE DOWN HERE--AND I CAN'T BAIL OUT WITH BULL TIED UP BESIDE ME... THAT WOULD BE MURDER!
BOY-WATCH BATMAN FLY RINGS AROUND THOSE CROOKS! AND REMEMBER--BATMAN USES NO LETHAL WEAPONS!
11

HAGGERTY SEEMS TO BE *WAVING* AT US!
MOST LIKELY SHOUTING HIS DEFIANCE! I CAN'T UNDER STAND WHAT GOT INTO THE MAN--BUT I'M GOING TO SHOW HIM SOME FLYING EVEN *HE* NEVER SAW BEFORE!

SUDDENLY, BEFORE THE STUNNED EYES OF THE ONLOOKING CROUD...
LOOK! THE CROOKS' PLANE IS IN A TAILSPIN! THEY'LL BE KILLED!
BATMAN'S WON! BUT I THOUGHT HE *NEVER* USED LETHAL WEAPONS! HE CERTAINLY DID UP THERE!

THEY'RE OUT OF CONTROL-SPINNING INTO A CRASH!
I DON'T UNDERSTAND! I KNOW I BUZZED THEM PRETTY CLOSELY, BUT I DON'T THINK I *SHEARED OFF* ANY OF THAT PLANE!

THEN, A MIRACULOUS STROKE OF LUCK...
WOW! THE CROOKS LANDED RIGHT IN THAT TRUCKFUL OF *SOFT RAGS!* IT BROKE THEIR FALL! THEY WEREN'T HURT AT ALL!
GOTHAM PAPER CO.

LATER...
WE'RE SURE GLAD YOU'RE OKAY, HAGGERTY! BOLEY JUST CONFESSED! IT LOOKS LIKE WE HAD YOU PEGGED ALL WRONG!
BUT THERE'S ONE THING I DON'T UNDERSTAND... HOW COME YOU *CRACKED UP?* DID WE *DISABLE* YOUR PLANE?
12

OH, NO... I SIMPLY *BLACKED OUT!* THE DOCS WERE RIGHT, *BATMAN... MY FLYING DAYS ARE OVER!* I JUST HAD TO LEARN IT THE *HARD* WAY!
YOUR FLYING DAYS MAY BE OVER, HAGGERTY-BUT THERE ARE STILL PLENTY OF JOBS IN AVIATION FOR YOU! *ROBIN* AND I ARE GOING TO SEE THAT YOU *GET* ONE!
THE END

ROBIN
-THE BOY WONDER-

BOB KANE

HA-HA! THIS IS THE END OF THAT FAMOUS *ESCAPE ARTIST, ROBIN!*

C'MON, *ROBIN!* LET'S SEE YOU GET AWAY *THIS TIME!*

JUST HOW SMART DO YOU THINK YOU ARE? CLEVER ENOUGH, SAY, TO MATCH WITS WITH *ROBIN?* COULD **YOU** HANDLE YOURSELF IN A TIGHT SPOT WITH ALL THE RESOURCEFULNESS OF THE **BOY WONDER?** WELL--HERE'S YOUR CHANCE TO FIND OUT! SO--SHARPEN UP THOSE BRAINS--PAY KEEN ATTENTION--AS **ROBIN** LEADS YOU ON THE THRILL-LOADED...

OPERATION "ESCAPE"!

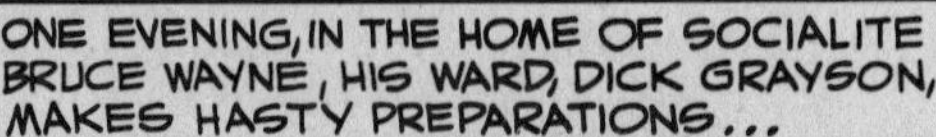

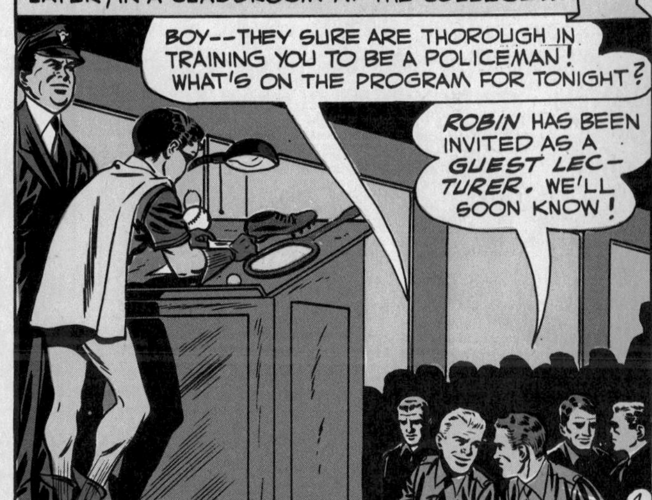

Art by Jim Mooney/Coloring by Shelley Eiber

LOOK! HE'S BROUGHT ALONG A *TENNIS RACKET*, A *GOLF BALL*, A *BASEBALL* AND A *BASE-BALL SHOE*! WHAT IN THE WORLD FOR??
YOU'VE GOT ME! IT'S CER-TAINLY AN ODD COLLECTION FOR A *CRIME LECTURE*!

THEN...
RESOURCEFULNESS AND INITIATIVE, TWO PRIME ASSETS FOR ANY WOULD-BE POLICEMAN, ARE THE SUBJECTS **ROBIN** WILL DISCUSS TONIGHT. PAY ATTENTION--FOR YOU'LL BE GIVEN A QUIZ DURING THE LECTURE!

PICTURES ARE ALWAYS BETTER THAN WORDS, SO I'M GOING TO SHOW YOU A MOVIE! THIS IS AN ACTUAL CASE HISTORY, AUTHENTICALLY RECONSTRUCTED ON COLOR FILM BY *BATMAN* AND MYSELF, FOR EDUCATIONAL PURPOSES!

AND, AS THE MOVIE FLASHES ON...
THE CASE STARTED WITH A ROBBERY AT THE DEMBER LIGHTER FACTORY. *BATMAN* WAS OUT OF TOWN, SO I RUSHED THERE ALONE...
DEMBER
D
LIGHTER CO.

"*REACHED BEFORE THEY COULD MAKE GOOD THEIR ROBBERY, THE CROOKS SOUGHT ES-CAPE ON THE ROOF OF THE FACTORY... BUT I WAS RIGHT AT THEIR HEELS...*"
CLICK!
A TRICKY ADVER-TISING DISPLAY... A LIGHTER THAT ACTUALLY CLICKS ON AND OFF! BUT I MUSN'T LET IT DISTRACT ME FROM THE JOB AT HAND!
DEMBER
D

"*AS YOU SEE, IT DEVELOPED INTO QUITE A BATTLE! TWICE, THAT LIGHTER ALMOST BURNED ME ALIVE!*"
CLICK!
WOW...THAT WAS TOO CLOSE FOR COMFORT! I'D BETTER POLISH OFF THESE FELLOWS IN A HURRY!
2

"BUT THEN, I SUDDENLY RECOG-NIZED ONE OF MY ADVERSARIES... AND MY PLANS CHANGED ABRUPTLY."
WHY... THESE ARE CHAMP TRASK'S BOYS--AND THAT MUST BE THEIR GETAWAY CAR DOWN THERE! WE'VE BEEN HUNTING TRASK FOR MONTHS--MAYBE THEY CAN LEAD ME TO HIM!

"I FEIGNED AN ACCIDENT AND SLIPPED OFF THE LIGHTER, GIVING THEM THE CHANCE TO GET AWAY--WHICH THEY TOOK!"
THEY FELL FOR IT! NOW TO TRAIL THEM IN THE BATMOBILE!

I CAN SEE THEM PLAIN AS DAY, BUT THEY'LL NEVER SPOT ME! SCORE ANOTHER SUCCESS FOR BATMAN'S SPECIAL INFRA-RED GOGGLES!

"WHEN THEY TURNED INTO AN OLD PRIVATE DRIVE-WAY, I KNEW WE WERE NEARLY THERE. I PARKED THE BATMOBILE, WENT THE REST OF THE WAY ON FOOT..."
SO THIS IS TRASK'S HIDEOUT! NOW FOR A SURPRISE PARTY ALL MY OWN!

"I BARGED RIGHT IN, CAUGHT THEM FLAT-FOOTED AS I HAD EXPECTED... BUT THEN--A BAD BREAK!"
LOOK! HE SLIPPED ON THAT WET SPOT--GRAB HIM!
CHAMP

"IN THE NEXT MOMENT, I WAS A PRISONER--PRISONER OF A CROOK WHO FANCIED HIMSELF AN ATHLETE AND WHO PRIDED HIMSELF ON HIS CONDITION.."
C'MON, CHAMP! LET'S UNMASK HIM NOW, AND KNOCK HIM OFF. HE'S BEEN PLENTY OF TROUBLE!
NO! I GOT AN HOUR TO PAY OFF LEFTY KAISER THE TEN GRAND I OWE HIM! YOU WERE SUPPOSED TO HEIST IT AT THE FACTORY--BUT YOU DIDN'T! ROBIN'LL KEEP! WE GOTTA GET THAT DOUGH FIRST!

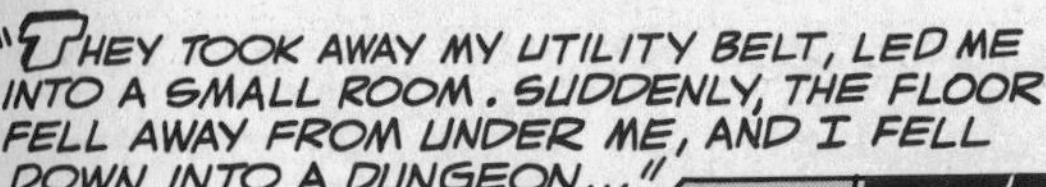

"THEY TOOK AWAY MY UTILITY BELT, LED ME INTO A SMALL ROOM. SUDDENLY, THE FLOOR FELL AWAY FROM UNDER ME, AND I FELL DOWN INTO A DUNGEON..."

CHAMP--WHAT'S IN THAT BAG DOWN THERE? KIN HE USE IT TO ESCAPE ??
NAH! JUST SOME OLD SPORTS EQUIPMENT! DON'T WORRY--WHEN I LET THIS TRAP DOOR SLAM UP, THERE'S NO WAY FOR ROBIN TO GET OUT!

"THE TRAP DOOR SLAMMED...AND THERE I WAS. IT WOULD'VE BEEN SENSELESS TO TRY TO SCALE THE WALLS--THEY WERE SLICK AS MARBLE..."
IF I COULD ONLY CLIMB A WALL AND GRAB THAT LOOP--THAT WOULD PULL THE TRAP-DOOR DOWN! BUT I CAN'T CLIMB HERE!

"IN DESPERATION, I TURNED TO THE BAG OF EQUIPMENT ON THE FLOOR..."

JUST AN OLD GOLF BALL, AN OLD BASEBALL, THE UNSTRUNG FRAME OF AN OLD TENNIS RACKET--AND ONE BASEBALL SHOE! SOME COLLECTION!

THAT WAS MY PROBLEM--HOW TO GET OUT OF THAT DUNGEON! AND NOW THAT'S YOUR PROBLEM, TOO! ALL RIGHT... TURN OFF THE PROJECTOR, PLEASE!

A GOLF BALL, A BASEBALL, A TENNIS RACKET FRAME AND A BASEBALL SHOE! THAT'S ALL YOU'VE GOT TO GET OUT OF THAT DUNGEON! HOW DO YOU DO IT!
SINCE SPEED WOULD BE OF THE ESSENCE, YOU'VE GOT EXACTLY TEN MINUTES TO TURN IN YOUR ANSWERS.

ALL RIGHT--
YOU CAN PLAY, TOO!

YOU'VE SEEN ALL THE CLUES--
YOU KNOW THE RULES!

ALLOW YOURSELF TEN MINUTES--
THEN TURN THE PAGE FOR THE EXCITING ANSWER!

4

TEN MINUTES HAVING PASSED, ROBIN IS READY TO RESUME HIS LECTURE ...
ALL RIGHT! WATCH CLOSELY AND YOU'LL SEE HOW IT WAS DONE!

"THE FIRST THING I DID WAS TO BREAK THE TOP HALF OF THE TENNIS RACKET FRAME!"
HMMM! A LITTLE ROUGH, PERHAPS, BUT IT WILL DO!

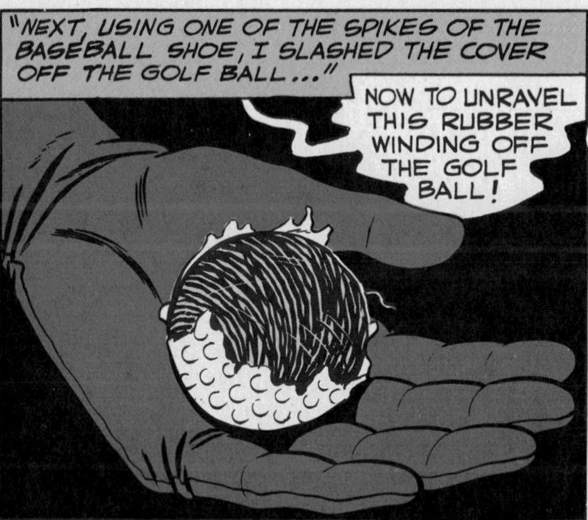
"NEXT, USING ONE OF THE SPIKES OF THE BASEBALL SHOE, I SLASHED THE COVER OFF THE GOLF BALL..."
NOW TO UNRAVEL THIS RUBBER WINDING OFF THE GOLF BALL!

"I UNWOUND ALL THE RUBBER, THEN BRAIDED IT INTO A SHORT BUT STRONG RUBBER CORD, WHICH I ATTACHED TO MY TENNIS RACKET FRAME..."

NOT A BAD SLING-SHOT, IF I SAY SO MYSELF!

"NOW I NEEDED AMMUNITION. THAT'S WHEN I REACHED FOR THE BASEBALL SHOE..."
ONE OF THESE SPIKES, REMOVED FROM THE SHOE, OUGHT TO BE JUST WHAT I NEED!

"NEXT, I TORE THE COVER OFF THE BASEBALL AND CAREFULLY UNWOUND THE TIGHT YARN UNDERNEATH. I TIED ONE END OF A LONG PIECE OF YARN TO THE SPIKE--AND NOW I WAS READY!"

ROBIN'S SLINGSHOT.
TENNIS RACKET FRAME
RUBBER CORD
SPIKE
YARN
5

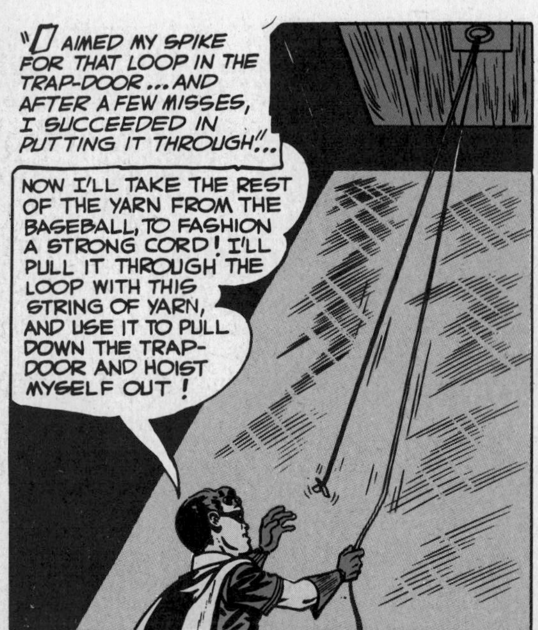
"I AIMED MY SPIKE FOR THAT LOOP IN THE TRAP-DOOR ... AND AFTER A FEW MISSES, I SUCCEEDED IN PUTTING IT THROUGH!"..
NOW I'LL TAKE THE REST OF THE YARN FROM THE BASEBALL, TO FASHION A STRONG CORD! I'LL PULL IT THROUGH THE LOOP WITH THIS STRING OF YARN, AND USE IT TO PULL DOWN THE TRAP-DOOR AND HOIST MYSELF OUT!

ONCE I GET TO THAT TRAP-DOOR, I CAN SWING MY-SELF UP THE REST OF THE WAY!

THAT'S IT! WHEN CHAMP AND HIS MEN RE-TURNED, I WAS READY FOR THEM WITH ANOTHER SURPRISE ATTACK ... AND THIS TIME, I DIDN'T MISS! TODAY, THEY'RE ALL IN JAIL, SERVING LONG TERMS!

LATER...
WELL, JOE... DID YOU HAVE THE ANSWER? I DIDN'T!
HECK, NO! NO WONDER THERE'S ONLY ONE ROBIN, THE BOY WONDER!
THE END!
6

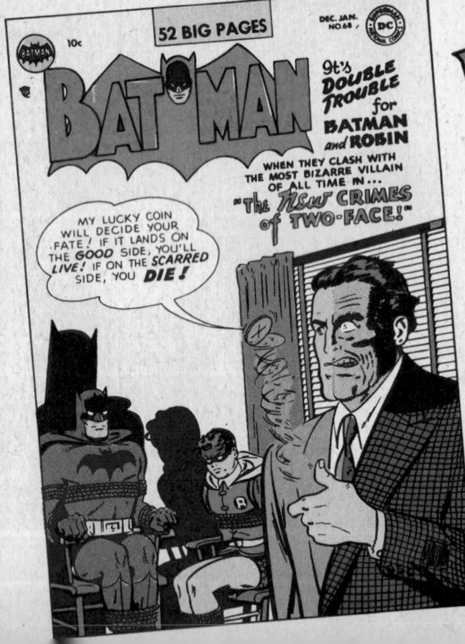
52 BIG PAGES
DEC. JAN. NO. 68
DC
10¢
BATMAN
It's DOUBLE TROUBLE for BATMAN and ROBIN
WHEN THEY CLASH WITH THE MOST BIZARRE VILLAIN OF ALL TIME IN...
"The New CRIMES of TWO-FACE!"
MY LUCKY COIN WILL DECIDE YOUR FATE! IF IT LANDS ON THE GOOD SIDE, YOU'LL LIVE! IF ON THE SCARRED SIDE, YOU DIE!

For The VERY BEST
SUPERMAN
DC
NATIONAL COMICS
in
COMICS READING

No. 120
FEB.
Ten Cents
Detective COMICS
BATMAN and ROBIN give The Penguin the bird in "Fowl Play"

Art by Dick Sprang & Charles Paris/Coloring by Helen Vesik

A PLANE MAKES A ROUTINE LANDING AT A SMALL GOTHAM CITY AIRPORT ---
--- AND ITS PILOT GETS A FEARFUL WELCOME!
WHAT-- A BLACK PANTHER-- HELP!
BUT BEHIND THE PANTHER APPEARS AN EVEN MORE SINISTER FORM!
CATWOMAN! SAVE ME FROM THAT PANTHER!
I WILL-- BUT ONLY IF YOU GIVE ME THAT CASE OF DIAMONDS YOU WERE HIRED TO DELIVER TO THE GOTHAM JEWELERS COMPANY!

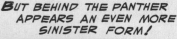

AND SECONDS LATER, A POWERFUL CRAFT ROARS AWAY INTO THE NIGHT!
AND NOW TO FLY TO MY SECRET HIDEOUT, WHERE NOT EVEN BATMAN CAN FIND US!
CATWOMAN STOLE THE DIAMOND SHIPMENT--- CALL THE POLICE!

SOON, AS THE ALARM GOES OUT, AN EERIE SIGNAL PIERCES THE NIGHT-SKY!
--- ESCAPED IN FAST PLANE!
LISTEN TO THAT POLICE FLASH-- IT'S CATWOMAN AGAIN!
AND THERE'S THE BAT-SIGNAL! WE'RE WANTED AS BATMAN AND ROBIN!
A SWIFT CHANGE, AND PLAYBOY BRUCE WAYNE AND HIS WARD, DICK GRAYSON, BECOME BATMAN AND ROBIN, THE BOY WONDER!
WE'LL GET THE BATPLANE OUT AND GO STRAIGHT TO THAT AIRFIELD!
SHE'LL BE GONE-- SHE STRIKES AS FAST AS THE CATS SHE LOVES!

AT THE AIRFIELD, BATMAN AND ROBIN HEAR AN INCREDIBLE STORY!
YOU SAY SHE USES A HUGE BLACK PANTHER IN HER ROBBERY? HOW COULD EVEN CATWOMAN CONTROL SUCH A BEAST?
IT'S UNCANNY! HMM --- IF WE HAD SOME CLUE TO WHERE SHE WENT, THE BATPLANE MIGHT STILL OVERTAKE HER!
2

THE TRAINED EYES OF THE WORLD'S GREATEST SLEUTHS DISCOVER WHAT OTHERS MIGHT HAVE MISSED!

THIS IS WHERE HER PLANE TOOK OFF-- YOU CAN SEE ITS WHEEL-MARKS!
THE DRIED MUD THAT FELL OUT OF HER TIRE-TREADS--- IT'S VOLCANIC CLAY OF A TYPE FOUND ONLY ON CERTAIN TROPICAL ISLANDS! COME ON, ROBIN!

PRESENTLY, THE MIGHTY BAT-PLANE'S JETS ROAR LOUDLY AS IT SCREAMS UP SKYWARD ON A TENUOUS TRAIL!
CATWOMAN HAS A START, BUT MAYBE WE CAN OVER-TAKE HER BEFORE SHE REACHES THOSE ISLANDS, ROBIN!
HMM... I KNOW SHE'S ALWAYS LIKED CATS, BUT I NEVER DREAMED SHE'D USE KILLER-CATS LIKE THAT PANTHER!

AS DAWN FLARES, THE BATPLANE HAS STREAKED FAR SOUTHWARD IN ITS GRIM PURSUIT!
THAT'S HER PLANE-- HEADING TOWARD A LARGE ISLAND!
HANG ON-- I'M GOING TO FORCE HER DOWN!

SO BATMAN TRAILED ME! WELL, HE'LL LEARN THAT THOSE WHO BOTHER CATS CAN GET SCRATCHED!
CLAW RETRACTOR

FROM THE CATWOMAN'S PLANE, GREAT RETRACTABLE STEEL CLAWS MECHANICALLY REACH FORTH!
NOW TO SUDDENLY THROTTLE DOWN AND LET THE BATPLANE ZOOM PAST CLOSE BENEATH ME, AND---
CW

--THEY'LL LEARN I STILL HAVE CLAWS!
SHE'S RIPPED OUR WINGS TO FORCE US DOWN! I'LL HAVE TO LAND AT ONCE!
3

WE'LL LAND HERE AND REPAIR OUR WINGS LATER, BUT FIRST, WE'LL GET AFTER THE CATWOMAN!
BATMAN, I SAW WHAT LOOKS LIKE A MINE HERE!
PRESENTLY, THE CAPED CRIME-FIGHTERS ENTER THE HEART OF THE TROPICAL JUNGLE ISLE!
WE'LL FIND OUT WHAT THOSE MINERS KNOW OF CATWOMAN. SHE MUST HAVE A LAIR HERE SOMEWHERE!
LOOK! NOT ONLY PANTHER TRACKS, BUT LION, LEOPARD AND TIGER TRACKS, TOO! THEY MUST HAVE BEEN MADE BY HER PETS -- BUT HOW CAN SHE HANDLE SUCH FIERCE BEASTS?
WELCOME, BATMAN AND ROBIN! I'M JOHN JARROW AND THIS IS MY SMALL DIAMOND-MINE --- AND I'M SURE GLAD TO SEE YOU TWO!
THEN YOU KNOW THAT CATWOMAN'S HERE?
WITH HER TERRIBLE FELINES, SHE'S USED THIS ISLE AS A CRIME-BASE AND WE'RE TOO AFRAID OF HER BEASTS TO STOP HER!
WE'RE AFRAID SHE'S AFTER THE DIAMONDS WE MINE! IF YOU COULD ONLY SET A TRAP TO PROTECT US AGAINST HER JUNGLE CATS...
WE CAN!
PRESENTLY...
IF ANY OF HER BEASTS COME HERE, THIS NOOSE-TRAP WILL CATCH THEM!
YES, CUTTING THIS TRIGGER-ROPE THAT HOLDS THE TREE DOWN WOULD TRAP ANYTHING---
WHRRHIP!
--EVEN BATMAN AND ROBIN!
HA, HA-- NICE OF THEM TO SET A TRAP FOR THEMSELVES! NOW WE'VE GOT THEM!
4

BATMAN THESE MEN ARE CROOKS-- PROBABLY WORKING WITH CATWOMAN. WE STEPPED RIGHT INTO IT!
HERE'S OUR CHANCE TO GET RID OF OUR BIGGEST ENEMY! ALL TOGETHER-- WE'LL FIRE IN A VOLLEY!
STOP!
BUT WHY STOP US, CATWOMAN? THEY'RE YOUR ENEMIES, TOO!
I'VE A BETTER IDEA! CUT THEM DOWN!
SO THEY ARE IN LEAGUE WITH CATWOMAN!
WHY NOT KNOCK THEM OFF AT ONCE?
I WANT THE PLEASURE OF HUNTING THEM DOWN, AS THEY HUNTED ME! TAKE AWAY THEIR UTILITY BELTS AND COSTUMES AND GIVE THEM JUNGLE CLOTHING SO THEY'LL HAVE NO TRICKS LEFT!
SOON, ANIMAL SKINS TRANSFORM THE DETECTIVE DUO INTO PRIMITIVE MEN OF THE JUNGLE!
I'LL GIVE YOU BOTH TEN MINUTES' START BEFORE I BEGIN TRAILING YOU WITH MY CATS! AND TAKING OFF YOUR MASKS WILL BE THE CLIMAX OF MY CHASE!
WHY, YOU FEMALE FELINE...
DON'T WASTE TIME, ROBIN-- LET'S GET GOING!
MY LITTLE PETS WILL ENJOY THIS HUNT!
A SWELL IDEA, CATWOMAN! I WISH I COULD SEE IT WHEN THOSE BEASTS OF YOURS TRACK THEM DOWN!
PRESENTLY, BATMAN AND ROBIN TRY TO LOSE THEMSELVES IN THE GREEN MAZE OF THE JUNGLE...
I STILL DON'T UNDERSTAND--IF THOSE CROOKS REALLY HAVE A DIAMOND MINE, WHY WOULD THEY BE IN WITH CATWOMAN?
THEY'RE AFRAID OF HER FELINES AND SHE DOMINATES THEM THAT WAY-- BUT QUICK, ROBIN, FOLLOW ME!
5

ARR-R-R-RGH!
FOLLOWING THIS STREAM MAY THROW THEM OFF OUR TRAIL!
BATMAN, THEY'RE ALREADY COMING UP ON US!

HURRY, ROBIN-- BREAK OFF ONE OF THESE HOLLOW REEDS!
I GET IT-- WE HIDE UNDER THE WATER, AND USE THE REEDS FOR BREATHING TUBES!

AND SECONDS LATER, AN UNEARTHLY HUNT SWEEPS BY!
GO ON, MY PETS -- THERE'S NOTHING HERE FOR YOU!

WHEN THE SOUNDS OF THE HUNT HAVE DIED AWAY...

WHEW-- THAT'S A RELIEF! I WAS AFRAID SHE'D SEE US IN THAT SHALLOW WATER, BUT SHE DIDN'T!

DIDN'T SHE, ROBIN? I WONDER! ANYWAY, WE'VE GOT WORK TO DO--- COME ON!

THEN, AS NIGHT BLANKETS THE JUNGLE, TWO EERIE FIGURES FOLLOW ON THE TRACK OF THE GREAT CATS!

WE CAN SOLVE THE MYSTERY OF THE DIAMOND MINE LATER -- AND TAKE CARE OF THOSE CROOKS! BUT RIGHT NOW I WANT TO FIND CATWOMAN'S SECRET LAIR-- AND THESE TRACKS SHOULD LEAD US THERE!

I STILL DON'T GET IT! WILD LIONS, TIGERS, AND LEOPARDS-- HOW DOES SHE CONTROL THEM, ANYWAY?

SUDDENLY, A RISING TROPIC MOON REVEALS A STRANGE AND AWESOME SIGHT!

WHY-- WHY, IT LOOKS LIKE AN OLD RUINED TEMPLE-- AND THE TRAIL ENDS THERE!

PROBABLY BUILT LONG AGO BY AN ANCIENT PEOPLE WHO WORSHIPPED CATS-- A FITTING LAIR FOR THE CATWOMAN!

6

AS SILENT AS TWO SHADOWS IN THE NIGHT, BATMAN AND ROBIN STEAL INTO THE SINISTER CAT-TEMPLE!
LIONS--- TIGERS--- LEOPARDS, THEY COULDN'T BE ALL NATIVE TO THIS ISLAND!
THEY'RE ANIMALS RAISED IN CAPTIVITY, ROBIN--- WILD LIONS NEVER HAVE BUSHY MANES LIKE THOSE IN ZOOS! THAT EXPLAINS WHY SHE'S ABLE TO HANDLE THEM! COME ON--- I WANT TO LOOK FOR SOMETHING!
PRESENTLY, SCOUTING AROUND THE AWESOME RUIN, BATMAN FINDS WHAT HE EXPECTED!
THESE ARE CIRCUS ANIMALS--- BROUGHT HERE BY CATWOMAN! AND THAT GIVES ME AN IDEA! LISTEN, ROBIN---
I'LL BE READY-- BUT BE CAREFUL, BATMAN! IF IT DOESN'T WORK---
I'M RELYING ON THE FACT THEY WERE CIRCUS ANIMALS, TO MAKE IT WORK!
A MOMENT LATER, A DRAMATIC FIGURE STRIDES INTO THE CATWOMAN'S NEW CATACOMB!
A CIRCUS TRAINER ALWAYS DISMISSES HIS ANIMALS WITH A VOLLEY OF FAST WHIP-CRACKS AND IT OUGHT TO WORK ON THESE BEASTS!
CRACK!
BATMAN. ARE YOU MAD, TO COME HERE---
AT THE CRACK OF THE LASH, THE STARTLED FELINES REVERT TO OLD TRAINING...
THEY MADE FOR THEIR CAGES AS BATMAN FIGURED---AND I CAN SHUT THEM IN!
CRACK
BUT A MORE DANGEROUS HUMAN FELINE REMAINS TO BE DEALT WITH!
YES, BATMAN! I BROUGHT TAME CIRCUS CATS HERE! YOU WERE CLEVER TO GUESS IT AND TRICK THEM, BUT NOT CLEVER ENOUGH!
JARROW AND HIS "MINERS" ARE YOUR CONFEDERATES, AND I THINK I KNOW WHAT YOU'VE BEEN UP TO!
7

UNKNOWN TO BATMAN, THE VERY CRIMINAL OF WHOM HE SPEAKS IS CLOSE AT HAND!
CATWOMAN FAILED TO GET HIM -- AND HE'S GOT HER! IF I SHOOT ONE OF THE DUO, THE OTHER MIGHT GET ME --- I'LL USE SOMETHING THAT WILL GET THEM BOTH!
RUTHLESS IN STRATEGY, THE EVIL JARROW UNLEASHES A THING OF TERROR...
THIS GORILLA MAY DESTROY CATWOMAN, TOO, BUT I DON'T CARE AS LONG AS IT GETS BATMAN AND ROBIN!
THEN, A CRY OF WARNING FROM BATMAN, BUT TOO LATE!
ROBIN, LOOK OUT!
YOU CAN'T SAVE ROBIN-- THAT GORILLA IS A KILLER!
ALL ANIMALS FEAR FIRE-- MY ONLY CHANCE---
ROBIN'S UNCONSCIOUS, BUT IT'S DROPPED HIM-- NOW IT'S AFTER ME--
WHIRLING THE BURNING BRAND IN CIRCLES, BATMAN DRIVES BACK THE RAGING MONSTER!
IT'S RECOILING INTO ITS CAGE-- NOW TO SLAM THE DOOR QUICK!
8

BUT AS THE CAGE DOOR CLICKS SHUT UPON THE MIGHTY APE...
NICE WORK, BATMAN-- BUT I'LL TAKE OVER NOW!

A GOOD THING I CAME TO MAKE SURE YOU'D GOT BATMAN! I'M TAKING HIM DOWN TO THE MINE AND WE'LL MAKE CERTAIN HE'S DONE FOR THIS TIME!
I MUST RELEASE MY PETS AGAIN!

LEAVE THOSE CRITTERS HERE-- WE DON'T LIKE THEM! GOOD THING THE GORILLA GOT THE BRAT!
HE DOESN'T KNOW ROBIN'S ONLY STUNNED! I WON'T SAY ANYTHING-- ROBIN IS NEAR THE FIRE AND THE BEASTS WON'T BOTHER HIM!

ONE SURE WAY TO GET RID OF HIM SO HE'LL NEVER BE FOUND--- TOSS HIM IN THE RIVER, TIED HAND AND FOOT!
WE'LL DO IT!

PUT HIS COSTUME BACK ON HIM SO IT WILL NEVER BE FOUND EITHER! I TOOK EVERYTHING OUT OF THE UTILITY BELT!
THAT'S A CLEVER IDEA, CATWOMAN! DO IT, BOYS! WE MUST DESTROY ALL THE EVIDENCE THAT COULD PROVE WE MURDERED HIM!

PRESENTLY, BOUND HAND AND FOOT, BATMAN IS TOSSED TO HIS DOOM!
HAW, HAW, THAT BIG FALL WON'T LEAVE ANY-THING OF HIM!
9

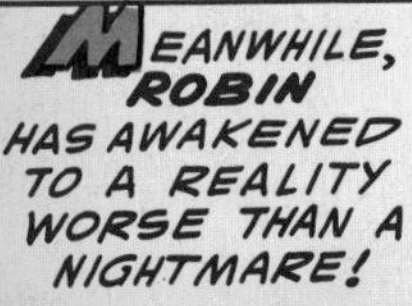

MEANWHILE, ROBIN HAS AWAKENED TO A REALITY WORSE THAN A NIGHTMARE!

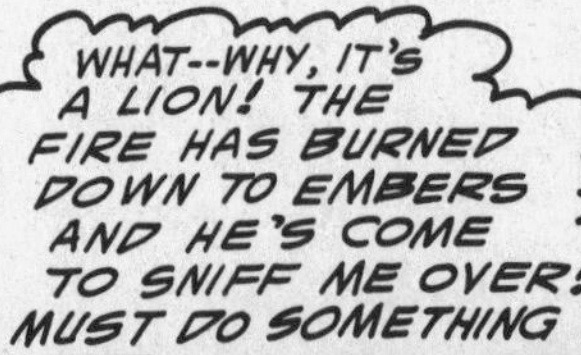

WHAT--WHY, IT'S A LION! THE FIRE HAS BURNED DOWN TO EMBERS AND HE'S COME TO SNIFF ME OVER! MUST DO SOMETHING TO GET RID OF HIM!

LACKING EVEN HIS UTILITY BELT THE BOY WONDER MOVES HIS HAND SLOWLY AND SOFTLY!

BY SLOWLY PRESSING THIS PLANT DOWN SO ITS GREEN TOP-LEAVES ARE IN THE HOT FIRE-EMBERS--

SNORT!
--AS I'D HOPED. HE DIDN'T LIKE THE SMOKE, AND IS LEAVING! WHAT A RELIEF!

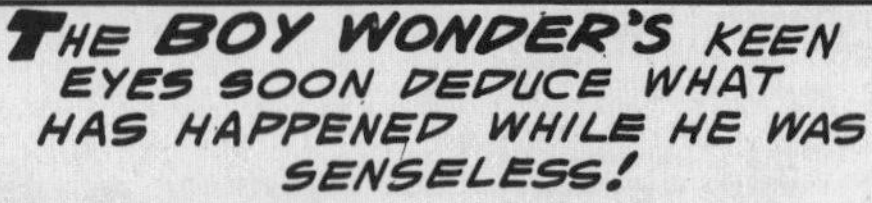

THE BOY WONDER'S KEEN EYES SOON DEDUCE WHAT HAS HAPPENED WHILE HE WAS SENSELESS!

JARROW'S AND CATWOMAN'S FOOTPRINTS OVER BATMAN'S HEADING TOWARD THAT MINE! THAT MEANS THEY FORCED HIM AHEAD OF THEM! I'VE GOT TO GO TO HIS AID---

I CAN USE THIS SMOKE-GAG ON A BIG SCALE AND DRIVE THE BEASTS TOWARD THE MINE! IF THEY STAMPEDE INTO ITS STREET, IT'LL CREATE SUCH A CONFUSION, I CAN SLIP IN AND FIND BATMAN!

MEANWHILE, HURLED INTO THE RAGING TORRENT WITH HANDS AND FEET BOUND, BATMAN HAS NOT SURRENDERED TO DESPAIR!

CATWOMAN SAID SHE TOOK EVERY-THING OUT OF MY UTILITY-BELT, BUT SHE SLIPPED UP! I CAN FEEL MY SILKEN CORD AND MY EMERGENCY KNIFE-BLADE STILL IN IT! GOT TO GET THE KNIFE OUT FAST AND CUT MY WRISTS FREE!

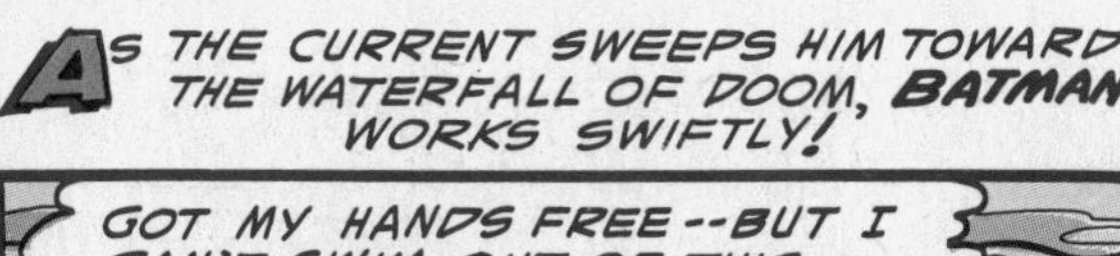
AS THE CURRENT SWEEPS HIM TOWARD THE WATERFALL OF DOOM, BATMAN WORKS SWIFTLY!

GOT MY HANDS FREE--BUT I CAN'T SWIM OUT OF THIS TERRIFIC CURRENT IN TIME TO ESCAPE THE FALLS! ONLY ONE CHANCE--THE SILKEN ROPE IN MY UTILITY BELT!

IF I CAN GET A NOOSE OF MY ROPE OVER A PROJECTING ROCK IN THE BOTTOM -- GOT IT! AND JUST IN TIME, FOR I'M RIGHT AT THE FALLS!

SECONDS LATER, CRIMINALS SEE THEIR GREATEST ENEMY APPARENTLY PLUNGE TO HIS DOOM!
THERE HE GOES, AND THAT FINISHES HIM! NO HUMAN BEING COULD SURVIVE THAT PLUNGE!
BATMAN GONE? IT--IT SEEMS IMPOSSIBLE!

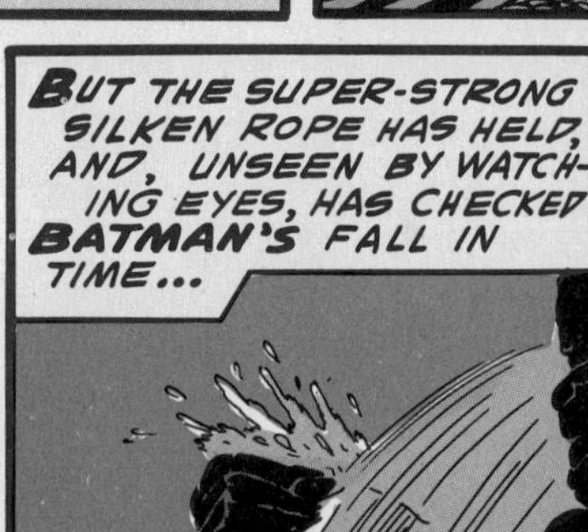
BUT THE SUPER-STRONG SILKEN ROPE HAS HELD, AND, UNSEEN BY WATCHING EYES, HAS CHECKED BATMAN'S FALL IN TIME...

THE ROPE HELD! NOW IF I SWING IN AND CUT LOOSE AT THE RIGHT MOMENT, I CAN LIGHT ON THOSE ROCKS AND GET UP TO SQUARE ACCOUNTS WITH THOSE THUGS!

BATMAN... GONE. AND I THOUGHT HE'D SAVE HIMSELF -- HE ALWAYS HAS IN THE PAST---
AND HE DID THIS TIME! I'LL JUST TIE YOU UP SAFELY WHILE I BREAK UP YOUR ACCOMPLICES' RACKET FOR GOOD!

WHAT WAS LEFT OF MY ROPE CAME IN HANDY! NOW FOR THESE "DIAMOND MINERS"!
11

SOON, IN ONE OF THE "MINE" BUILDINGS, BATMAN CONFIRMS HIS SUSPICIONS!
I THOUGHT SO! THEY GET STOLEN DIAMONDS FROM ALL OVER AND RE-CUT THEM--THEN PRETEND THEY MINED AND CUT THE GEMS THEMSELVES!
YOUR NUMBER'S UP, BATMAN! OUTSIDE!

YOU'RE HARD TO KILL, BUT THIS TIME WE'LL MAKE SURE WITH BULLETS!
JARROW, LOOK OUT--CATWOMAN'S BEASTS ARE STAMPEDING THIS WAY!

AND AS THE PANICKY CROOKS RECOIL FROM A JUNGLE STAMPEDE...
LOOKS LIKE I SENT MY "FRIENDS" HERE JUST IN TIME!
AND YOU'RE WELCOME! WE'LL JUST CAGE THESE HUMAN SPECIMENS NOW!

BUT MEANWHILE, A GREAT CAT HAS GONE LOYALLY TO ITS MISTRESS...

MY FAITHFUL PET-- YOUR SHARP CLAWS ARE HELPFUL NOW, THOUGH YOU DON'T KNOW IT!

12

AND WHEN THE DYNAMIC DUO FINISHES SECURING THE CROOKS, THEY GET AN AMAZING SURPRISE!

CATWOMAN! SHE'S GETTING AWAY, TO HER HIDDEN PLANE!

AND WE CAN'T FOLLOW TILL THE BATPLANE IS REPAIRED! I GUESS SHE ESCAPES US FOR NOW, THOUGH WE'VE BROKEN UP HER CRIME-SCHEME!

FUNNY, THAT SHE ACCIDENTALLY LEFT THAT KNIFE-BLADE AND SILKEN CORD IN YOUR UTILITY BELT.. OR WAS IT AN ACCIDENT? SHE'S ALWAYS BEEN SOFT ON YOU!

THAT WAS NO ACCIDENT, ROBIN. MURDER ISN'T IN THE CATWOMAN'S HEART. SENTIMENT IS HER WEAKNESS--AND THAT'S WHY WE'LL CATCH HER THE NEXT TIME!

THE END.

Art by Sheldon Moldoff / Coloring by Michele Wolfman

ONE DAY, AS BRUCE WAYNE AND HIS YOUNG WARD, DICK GRAYSON, CLEAN OUT THEIR ATTIC...
BRUCE! LOOK! I MUST HAVE TOUCHED A HIDDEN SPRING IN YOUR FATHER'S OLD DESK!
A SECRET DRAWER! AND THERE'S SOMETHING INSIDE IT!
TO HIS SURPRISE, BRUCE WITHDRAWS A FANTASTIC GARMENT...
IT'S... A KIND OF BATMAN COSTUME!
DICK, I THINK I'VE SEEN THIS COSTUME BEFORE-- ON MY FATHER--LONG, LONG AGO!
THEN THAT MEANS YOUR FATHER WAS A "BATMAN" BEFORE YOU!
BUT THAT'S IMPOSSIBLE! I WAS THE FIRST "BATMAN"! I ADOPTED THE FIRST BATMAN COSTUME YEARS AFTER I SAW MY PARENTS KILLED BY A ROBBER!
BRUCE'S THOUGHTS WHIRL BACK TO WHEN HE WAS A BOY AND MADE A PROMISE TO THE MEMORY OF HIS PARENTS...
I VOW THAT I'LL DEDICATE MY LIFE TO BRING YOUR KILLER TO JUSTICE... AND TO FIGHT ALL CRIME!
AS YEARS PASSED, BRUCE MASTERED SCIENTIFIC CRIMINAL INVESTIGATION... TRAINED HIS BODY TO ATHLETIC PERFECTION...
ONE NIGHT, HE WAS AT LAST READY FOR HIS CHOSEN CAREER, BUT HE NEEDED A DISGUISE THAT WOULD STRIKE TERROR INTO CRIMINAL HEARTS...
A BAT-- IT'S FLOWN IN THE WINDOW! IT'S LIKE AN OMEN! I SHALL BECOME A BAT-- A BATMAN!
YEARS PASSED, AND BATMAN NEVER GAVE UP HIS SEARCH FOR THE KILLER! THEN ONE DAY, WHILE INVESTIGATING A CRIMINAL NAMED JOEY CHILL...
IT'S THE MAN WHO KILLED MY PARENTS! HE'S OLDER NOW-- BUT I COULD NEVER FORGET THAT FACE!
2

BUT, IRONICALLY, JOEY CHILL WAS SHOT DOWN BY OTHER MOBSTERS WHO HAD A GRUDGE AGAINST HIM...

BANG!

HE'S DEAD! HIS OWN CRIMES FINALLY CAUGHT UP WITH HIM!

THIS THEN, WAS THE ORIGIN OF **BATMAN**! THEN HOW COULD HIS FATHER HAVE BEEN A **BATMAN** BEFORE HIM?

LOOK! HERE'S SOMETHING ELSE IN THE DRAWER! A CAN OF MOVIE FILM AND A DIARY!
LET'S LOOK AT THE FILM FIRST! I'LL SET UP THE PROJECTOR!

SOON, THE TWO VIEW AN EPISODE FROM THE PAST...

LADIES AND GENTLEMEN, AS YOU ALL KNOW, THE THEME OF THIS YEAR'S MASQUERADE BALL IS "**FLYING CREATURES**"!

AND OUR FIRST PRIZE FOR THE BEST "FLYING CREATURE" COSTUME GOES TO DR. THOMAS WAYNE FOR HIS **BAT-MAN** COSTUME!
MY FATHER!

SUDDENLY...
WE FIGURED THERE'D BE A DOC IN THIS CROWD! COME ON, DOC-- WE NEED YOU! MAKE IT SNAPPY!

YOU CAN'T THREATEN ME!
ATTABOY, DAD!
3

BETTER COME ALONG, DOC--OR SOMEBODY SURE IS GONNA GET HURT!
I--I HAVE NO CHOICE--NOW!

HERE THE MOVIE ABRUPTLY ENDS!
AT LEAST THE MOVIE TOLD US WHY YOUR FATHER WORE A BAT-MAN COSTUME!
LISTEN TO WHAT HIS DIARY SAYS...

"TONIGHT, MARTHA AND I ARE GOING TO THE ANNUAL MASQUERADE BALL! OUR LITTLE BOY SEEMS FASCINATED BY MY COSTUME..."
GEE, DADDY, I WISH I COULD WEAR A SUIT LIKE THAT!
I'LL SAVE IT FOR YOU, BRUCE--TO WEAR WHEN YOU GROW UP!

DICK, WHEN THAT BAT FLEW INTO MY ROOM, IT MUST HAVE PRODDED MY SUBCONSCIOUS MEMORY OF MY FATHER'S COSTUME! NOW I REALIZE I ADOPTED A BATMAN COSTUME BECAUSE I REMEMBERED MY FATHER WEARING ONE!

READING ON, BRUCE LEARNS WHAT HAPPENED AFTER THE HOODLUMS TOOK HIS FATHER FROM THE BALL...

"THE GUNMEN TOOK ME TO AN OLD WAREHOUSE WHERE THEIR BOSS WAS IN HIDING..."
YOU'RE LEW MOXON, THE BANK ROBBER THE POLICE ARE AFTER!
YEAH--ONE OF THEM WINGED ME! I WANT YOU TO REMOVE THE SLUG!

"I KNEW THAT ONCE I REMOVED THE BULLET, MOXON WOULD NEVER LET ME LIVE TO REVEAL HIS WHEREABOUTS TO THE POLICE..."
I'VE GOT TO DO SOMETHING--BUT WHAT?
4

"I SUDDENLY HOOKED ONE FOOT AROUND MOXON'S CHAIR AND..."
WHAT...?!

"THAT LEFT ONLY THE HOODLUMS TO DEAL WITH!"
I'LL LET THE POLICE TAKE OVER FROM HERE!

WOW! EVEN THOUGH HE DIDN'T HAVE ANY TRAINING IN FIGHTING CROOKS, YOUR FATHER PULLED A TYPICAL **BATMAN** STUNT!
MY FATHER WAS QUITE A GUY!

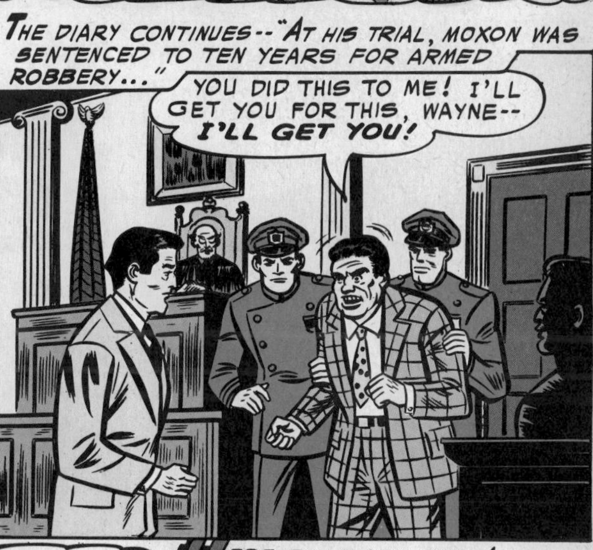

THE DIARY CONTINUES--"AT HIS TRIAL, MOXON WAS SENTENCED TO TEN YEARS FOR ARMED ROBBERY..."
YOU DID THIS TO ME! I'LL GET YOU FOR THIS, WAYNE-- **I'LL GET YOU!**

"TEN YEARS ROLLED BY! I'D INVESTED MY SAVINGS WISELY AND BECAME WEALTHY! I'D ALMOST FORGOTTEN MOXON UNTIL TODAY..."

MOXON-- FREE!

YEAH--I SERVED MY TEN YEARS IN JAIL-- WHERE **YOU** PUT ME! I SWORE I'D GET YOU, AND I WILL!

BUT I'M TOO SMART TO DO IT MYSELF! THE POLICE WOULD ARREST ME ON SUSPICION FAST! I'LL GET SOMEONE ELSE TO DO IT FOR ME!

HERE THE DIARY ENDS!

THIS MEANS JOEY CHILL ONLY **PRETENDED** TO BE A HOLDUP MAN-- ACTUALLY HE WAS MOXON'S **HIRED KILLER!** MOXON MUST HAVE ORDERED CHILL **NOT** TO KILL ME, TOO-- SO I'D BE ALIVE TO TESTIFY THAT MY PARENTS WERE KILLED BY A ROBBER!

GOSH, BRUCE-- MOXON USED **YOU** AS HIS **ALIBI!**

HE USED ME AS A COVERUP FOR HIS DELIBERATE MURDER OF MY PARENTS! PUT ON YOUR COSTUME, DICK-- **WE'VE JUST REOPENED THE WAYNE MURDER CASE!**

LATER, IN THE OFFICE OF POLICE COMMISSIONER GORDON...

COMMISSIONER, I'D LIKE TO KNOW THE WHEREABOUTS OF LEW MOXON!

I'LL HAVE THIS TELE-PHOTOED TO EVERY POLICE DEPARTMENT IN THE COUNTRY!

AND WHEN THE INFORMATION COMES...

MOXON IS NOW IN THE **BILLBOARD BLIMP** BUSINESS OUT WEST-- IN COASTAL CITY!

SOON AFTER, THE SLEEK **BATPLANE** RACES THROUGH THE SKIES...
WHY DID YOU HAVE ME BRING ALONG YOUR FATHER'S COSTUME, **BATMAN?**
IT GIVES ME THE FEELING THAT MY FATHER IS WITH ME ON THIS CASE!
HOURS LATER, AT THEIR DESTINATION, TWO FIGURES MOVE LIKE SHADOWS TOWARDS A BLIMP HANGAR...
MOXON SKY-HI ADVERTISING CO.

BUT, IN THE DARKNESS, **ROBIN'S** FOOT KICKS A MISPLACED GASOLINE CAN...
CLANK
BATMAN AND ROBIN! GET 'EM!
6

AS ROBIN DARTS FORWARD, A SWINGING SANDBAG TREACHEROUSLY FELLS HIM!
UH-H!
WE GOT THE BRAT! BATMAN WILL BE EASIER TO TAKE NOW!
BOP!
UNDER THE IMPACT OF FOUR THUGS, BATMAN IS BROUGHT DOWN...
...BUT NOT FOR LONG!
THIS'LL TAKE THE FIGHT OUT OF ALL OF YOU!.
LATER... LEW MOXON, I'M CHARGING YOU WITH THE MURDER OF DR. THOMAS WAYNE!
IS THAT WHAT YOU'RE AFTER ME FOR?
INCREDIBLY, A SMILE OF RELIEF PASSES OVER THE ACCUSED'S FACE...
I NEVER HEARD OF ANY DR. WAYNE! I'M EVEN WILLING TO TAKE THE LIE DETECTOR TEST TO PROVE IT!
ALL RIGHT, WE'LL SOON SEE IF YOU ARE LYING!
7

SOON...
DIDN'T YOU HIRE JOEY CHILL TO MURDER DR. WAYNE?
NO! I NEVER EVEN HEARD OF JOEY CHILL!

YOU KNOW YOU HATED DR. WAYNE, THAT YOU SWORE YOU'D GET HIM!
I DON'T KNOW ANY DR. WAYNE-- AND I DON'T KNOW WHAT YOU'RE TALKIN' ABOUT!

BATMAN CONTINUES TO HAMMER QUESTIONS AT THE PRISONER, AND WHEN THE INTERROGATION IS OVER...
SEE FOR YOURSELF, BATMAN-- THE NEEDLE DIDN'T JUMP ONCE. NOBODY CAN BEAT THE MACHINE-- SO HE MUST BE TELLING THE TRUTH!

HELPLESSLY, BATMAN SEES MOXON RELEASED ON BAIL FOR ASSAULT AND BATTERY...
HOW COULD MOXON BE TELLING THE TRUTH WHEN WE KNOW HE WAS INVOLVED IN YOUR FATHER'S MURDER? THAT'S SOMETHING NOBODY CAN FORGET!
FORGET? HMM-MM! I THINK I'LL PLACE A LONG DISTANCE PHONE CALL TO POLICE COMMISSIONER GORDON!

LATER...
YOU SAY MOXON WAS IN AN AUTOMOBILE ACCIDENT RIGHT AFTER DR. WAYNE WAS MURDERED?
YES! HE HAD A HEAD INJURY! ONE DAY HE WANDERED AWAY FROM THE HOSPITAL AND NOBODY EVER SAW HIM AFTER THAT!
ROBIN, THAT HEAD INJURY GAVE MOXON AMNESIA, LOSS OF MEMORY! HE DOESN'T REMEMBER MY FATHER OR ANYTHING THAT HAPPENED BEFORE THE AUTO ACCIDENT!
GOLLY! WHAT'LL WE DO NOW?
KEEP AFTER MOXON! HE MUST BE INVOLVED IN SOMETHING SHADY--OTHERWISE HIS MEN WOULDN'T HAVE JUMPED US! TONIGHT WE'RE GOING TO TRAIL HIS BLIMP!
8

THAT NIGHT, A FLOATING BILLBOARD FLASHES ITS SKY-HIGH ELECTRIC SIGN...
NOTHING SUSPICIOUS HAPPENING SO FAR, BATMAN!
SUDDENLY, THE ELECTRIC LIGHTS WINK OUT, LEAVING THE DARK BLIMP ALMOST UNSEEN AGAINST THE NIGHT SKY...
LOOK! A MAN IS BEING LOWERED TO THAT PENTHOUSE! SO THAT'S MOXON'S ANGLE-- USING HIS BLIMP TO PULL SKY-HIGH BURGLARY JOBS!
AFTER SETTING THE VERSATILE BATPLANE ON ROBOT STABILIZER CONTROLS...
ROBIN, YOU GO AFTER THE MAN ON THE ROOF-- I'LL TAKE THE GONDOLA!
LIKE A HAWK, ROBIN PLUMMETS DOWN ON HIS QUARRY!
LOOKS LIKE I'VE GOT THE DROP ON YOU!
MEANWHILE, THE ACROBATMAN TRAPEZES THROUGH SPACE...
...AND SWIFTLY SCALING THE BLIMP'S ROPE LADDER, BURSTS INTO ITS GONDOLA!
BATMAN!
THIS BLIMP'S NEXT STOP WILL BE POLICE HEADQUARTERS!
LATER, AFTER THE PRISONERS ARE JAILED...
NOW LET'S PICK UP MOXON! BUT FIRST YOU'D BETTER CHANGE TO YOUR SPARE BATMAN COSTUME-- THAT LAST SCRAP REALLY SHREDDED THIS ONE!
OH, OH! I FORGOT TO PACK A SPARE IN THE BATPLANE!
9

SAY--HOW ABOUT WEARING **YOUR FATHER'S COSTUME?**
YES--IT WOULD BE APPROPRIATE! IT'D BE ALMOST AS IF DAD WERE ARRESTING MOXON!

LATER, ALONE IN HIS OFFICE, MOXON LOOKS UP TO SEE A GRIM FIGURE FRAMED IN THE DOORWAY!
WHO--?!

THAT COSTUME--I'VE SEEN IT BEFORE--LONG AGO! I'M BEGINNING TO REMEMBER--A DOCTOR--DOC WAYNE--HE WORE THAT COSTUME!

GREAT SCOTT! I DIDN'T REALIZE THE SHOCK OF SEEING THIS COSTUME WOULD JAR MOXON'S MEMORY!
GO AWAY! YOU'RE DEAD! I HAD JOEY CHILL KILL YOU! LEAVE ME ALONE!

FEAR-RIDDEN, MOXON WRENCHES OPEN A SIDE-DOOR AND RUSHES OUT INTO THE NIGHT...

HE'S COME BACK TO HAUNT ME! I'VE GOT TO GET AWAY--**GET AWAY!...**

MOXON! LOOK OUT! THAT TRUCK!

A SCREECH OF BRAKES--A CRY--AND MOXON'S CAREER OF VIOLENCE ENDS IN VIOLENCE...
I WANTED TO TAKE HIM ALIVE... TO STAND TRIAL FOR HIS CRIMES... BUT HIS OWN GUILT CONVICTED HIM!
10

SOON AFTER, A COSTUME OCCUPIES AN HONORED SPACE IN THE **BAT-CAVE'S TROPHY ROOM!**

FROM THE WAYNE MURDER CASE
CASE FINALLY SOLVED BY THIS COSTUME ONCE WORN BY THE FIRST BAT-MAN

THE END.

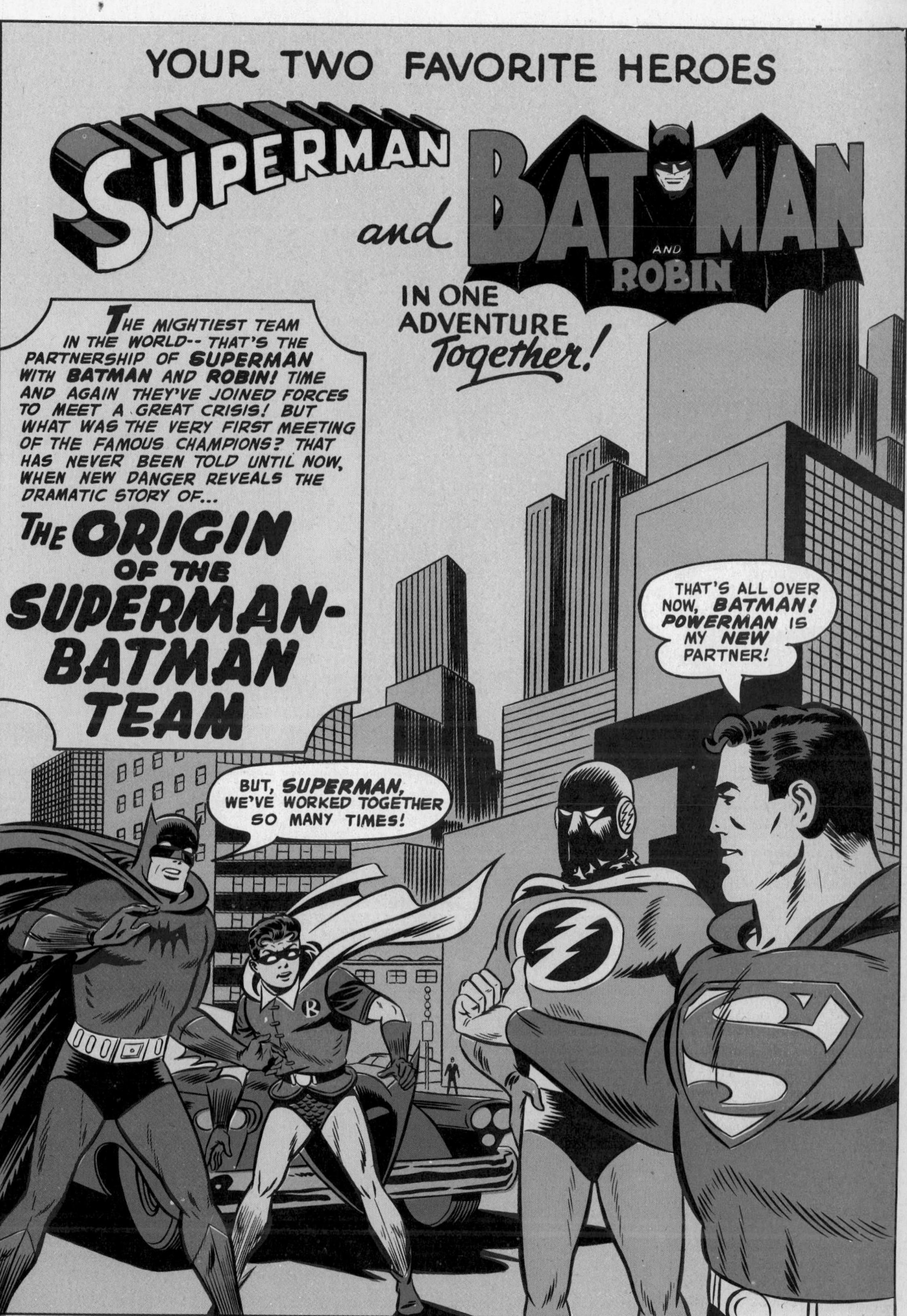

Art by Dick Sprang & Stan Kaye/Coloring by Daniel Vozzo

ONE NIGHT, IN THE GOTHAM CITY MANSION OF SOCIALITE BRUCE WAYNE AND HIS WARD, DICK GRAYSON...
AND HERE'S A BULLETIN FROM METROPOLIS! LUTHOR, THE SCIENTIFIC GENIUS OF CRIME, HAS ESCAPED FROM PRISON!
OH, OH-- THAT MEANS TROUBLE AHEAD!
LUTHOR ALWAYS BOASTED THAT SOME DAY HE'D HAVE HIS REVENGE ON BOTH SUPERMAN AND METROPOLIS!
LET'S NOT WASTE TIME, DICK-- WE'RE GOING TO METROPOLIS!
AND IN THE BAT-CAVE UNDER THE MANSION, THE TWO SWIFTLY CHANGE TO-- BATMAN AND ROBIN, THE BOY WONDER...
SUPERMAN MAY NEED OUR HELP IF LUTHOR USES KRYPTONITE FOR HIS VENGEANCE!
YES---KRYPTONITE WEAKENS SUPERMAN, BUT IT DOESN'T AFFECT ORDINARY PEOPLE LIKE US!
A SWIFT RIDE BY BATMOBILE BRINGS THEM WITHIN A FEW HOURS TO THE OUTSKIRTS OF METROPOLIS...
SUPERMAN WILL SEE OUR IMPROVISED BAT-SIGNAL AND COME HERE-- THEN WE'LL PLAN HOW TO DEAL WITH LUTHOR!
THERE HE COMES NOW-- BUT SOMEONE'S WITH HIM!
HELLO, SUPERMAN! WE FIGURED YOU MIGHT NEED HELP IF LUTHOR USED KRYPTONITE!
THANKS, BATMAN-- BUT MY NEW PARTNER, POWERMAN, WILL HELP ME, IF NECESSARY--
-- WHICH RELIEVES YOU! AND---ER--- POWERMAN DOESN'T WANT ANY MORE PEOPLE ON OUR TEAM!
SUPERMAN AND I CAN HANDLE THIS JOB BY OURSELVES!
2

WE CAN'T WASTE ANY MORE TIME HERE! WE MUST FIND LUTHOR!
YOU'RE RIGHT, POWERMAN! SORRY, BATMAN--!

WHOEVER POWERMAN IS, HE HASN'T SUPER-POWERS-- SUPERMAN IS CARRYING HIM!
AFTER ALL OUR CASES TOGETHER, HOW COULD SUPERMAN REJECT US LIKE THAT?

IT HURTS TO HAVE AN OLD FRIEND CAST YOU OFF!
IT JUST ISN'T LIKE SUPERMAN! MAYBE THIS POWERMAN MADE HIM DO IT-- HE MAY HAVE SOME HOLD ON SUPERMAN!

THAT MIGHT BE IT! POWERMAN DID SPEAK TO SUPERMAN DOMINEERINGLY! WE'LL GO ON TO METROPOLIS AND SECRETLY WATCH THEM, TO FIND OUT!

LATER, AS THE MAN OF STEEL AND HIS MYSTERIOUS NEW PARTNER SEARCH THE CITY...
AS LONG AS WE STAY BEHIND LEAD, LIKE THIS ORNAMENTAL CORNICE, SUPERMAN CAN'T SPOT US!
HE'S USING HIS X-RAY VISION FROM ABOVE WHILE POWERMAN SEARCHES ON FOOT!
PRODUCTS

IT WASN'T LIKE THIS THE FIRST TIME WE MET SUPERMAN, WHEN HE WAS MENACED BY KRYPTONITE, TOO!
YES, I REMEMBER!
3

"WE'D READ OF HIS FEATS WITH ADMIRATION, BUT HAD NEVER MET HIM---"
WOW, THAT SUPERMAN CAN DO ANYTHING! HE'S TERRIFIC!
I AGREE-- BUT WE'D BETTER GET ALONG WITH OUR SEARCH!
GOTHAM DAILY NEWS
SUPERMAN AVERTS METEOR DANGER
"WE'D BEEN LOOKING FOR THE LEADERS OF A SMUGGLING RING, AND THAT NIGHT OUR HUNT CAME TO AN END..."
HERE'S YOUR SHARE, BOYS!
SMUGGLING IN THAT KRYPTONITE WAS THE BEST-PAYING JOB YET!
GOTHAM IMPORT CO.
YOU'RE OUT OF BUSINESS--
CRUCK
--BUT YOU'LL LEARN A NEW TRADE IN JAIL!
"OUR PRISONERS WOULDN'T ANSWER QUESTIONS"...
THEY MENTIONED KRYPTONITE! IT'S THE ONE ELEMENT THAT WEAKENS SUPERMAN!
IT MUST BE FOR SOMEONE TO USE IT AGAINST HIM! WE'RE GOING TO METROPOLIS TO WARN HIM! LET'S GET THE BATPLANE...
GEE, BATMAN, WE'RE GOING TO MEET SUPERMAN HIMSELF!
"WHEN WE REACHED METROPOLIS..."
BATMAN, LOOK-- A HELICOPTER SNATCHING UP AN ARMORED CAR!
4

THEY'RE GETTING AWAY, BATMAN!
WE DAREN'T RISK FORCING IT TO CRASH IN THE STREETS-- WE'LL HAVE TO FOLLOW!

"SUDDENLY, ACROSS THE SKY STREAKED AN INCREDIBLE FIGURE!"
BATMAN LOOK-- IT'S HIM-- SUPERMAN!

"FOR THE FIRST TIME, WE SAW SUPERMAN IN ACTION!"
THERE HE COMES-- GET THE GUN READY!
YOU KNOW THAT GUNS DON'T STOP ME!

BUT THIS GUN WILL! IT SHOOTS LIQUID KRYPTONITE!

"TO OUR ASTONISHMENT, WE SAW SUPERMAN FALL HELPLESSLY!"
BATMAN, WHAT'LL WE DO?
WE'VE GOT TO PREVENT HIM FROM FALLING INTO THE CROWDED STREETS--

"I SENT THE BAT-PLANE INTO A SCREAMING POWER-DIVE..."
5

GOT HIM!
AND JUST IN TIME-- HE'S INVULNERABLE, BUT IF HE FELL INTO THE CROWD BELOW, HE'D INJURE MANY PEOPLE!
THOSE THIEVES ESCAPED WHILE WE DIVED TO CATCH SUPERMAN!
BATMAN, I CAN'T ROUSE HIM! PUT ON THE AUTOMATIC PILOT, AND HELP ME!
HE'S SPATTERED WITH THAT KRYPTONITE SOLUTION! WE'VE GOT TO GET IT OFF HIM FAST, AND I THINK I KNOW HOW!
"WE RIGGED A ROPE SLING AND THEN, ZOOMING TOWARD A NEARBY WATERFALL..."
THIS SHOULD WASH EVERY PARTICLE OF KRYPTONITE OFF HIM!
HE'S STIRRING, BATMAN!
"PRESENTLY..."
BATMAN! I'VE HEARD OF ALL YOUR GREAT FEATS! YOU CAME IN THE NICK OF TIME!
BUT WE WERE TOO LATE TO WARN YOU OF THE KRYPTONITE DANGER!
WE'RE IMMUNE TO KRYPTONITE, SO WE CAN HELP YOU AGAINST THOSE CROOKS, IF YOU WISH!
IF I WISH? IT WOULD BE AN HONOR TO WORK WITH BATMAN AND ROBIN!
6

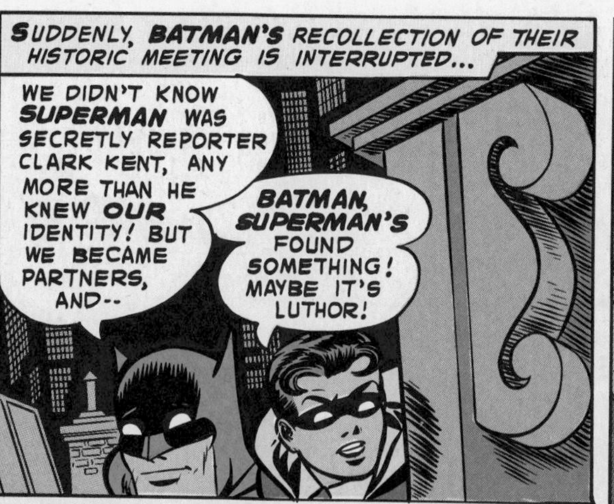
SUDDENLY, BATMAN'S RECOLLECTION OF THEIR HISTORIC MEETING IS INTERRUPTED...
WE DIDN'T KNOW SUPERMAN WAS SECRETLY REPORTER CLARK KENT, ANY MORE THAN HE KNEW OUR IDENTITY! BUT WE BECAME PARTNERS, AND--
BATMAN, SUPERMAN'S FOUND SOMETHING! MAYBE IT'S LUTHOR!

THERE'S GAS LEAKING FROM A LOOSE MAIN UNDER THE BUILDING! IT'LL EXPLODE AT THE FIRST SPARK--

THERE'S NO ONE IN THE BUILDING. I'LL LIFT IT AND LET THE GAS DISSIPATE! POWERMAN CAN TIGHTEN THE LOOSE PIPE!

POWERMAN IS MAKING THE REPAIR! HE MAY NOT HAVE SUPERPOWERS, BUT HE'S STRONG!
MAYBE HE'S A PROFESSIONAL STRONG-MAN···BUT WHY WOULD SUPERMAN CHOOSE HIM?

IT'S SAFE NOW! WE'VE GOT TO GO ON LOOKING FOR LUTHOR!
I'M RIGHT WITH YOU!

I STILL DON'T UNDERSTAND WHY SUPERMAN WOULDN'T LET US HELP HIM SEARCH FOR LUTHOR, TOO.
IT WAS POWERMAN WHO OBJECTED TO US! IF WE FIND OUT WHO HE IS, WE MAY LEARN THE REASON!
7

WE DIDN'T HAVE TO WATCH FROM A DISTANCE IN OUR FIRST ADVENTURE WITH SUPERMAN! WE WENT AFTER THOSE KRYPTONITE-USING CROOKS TOGETHER---
"---AND WHAT A THRILL IT WAS TO GO INTO ACTION WITH SUPERMAN!"
WE'VE SEARCHED METROPOLIS AND HAVEN'T FOUND ANY HANGAR WHERE THAT HELICOPTER IS HIDDEN!
LET'S LAND-- MY X-RAY VISION DETECTS SOMETHING!
"YES, HIS AMAZING SIGHT HAD PENETRATED AN ASTOUNDING CAMOUFLAGE!"
YOU MEAN-- THAT OLD WINDMILL IS THE HELICOPTER?
CUNNING, ISN'T IT? LET'S GO INSIDE--NO ONE'S IN THERE, SO THE FARMHOUSE MUST BE THEIR BASE!
FIGURING YOU WERE KNOCKED OUT BY KRYPTONITE, THEY WERE SURE NO ONE ELSE COULD SEE THROUGH THE DISGUISE!
I CAN SEE THEM IN THAT FARMHOUSE, WITH THEIR LOOT AND THAT KRYPTONITE-GUN!
THAT KRYPTONITE WILL ENDANGER YOU! LET US GO IN AFTER THEM!
NO, YOU TWO WATCH THE OTHER SIDE OF THE HOUSE SO THEY DON'T SLIP AWAY! I'LL WAIT HERE AND CATCH THEM BY SURPRISE WHEN THEY TRY TO USE THE 'COPTER AGAIN!
"BUT WHEN WE CREPT AROUND BEHIND THE HOUSE, SUPERMAN'S REASON FOR RESTRAINING US BECAME APPARENT..."
THEY'VE GOT A MACHINE-GUN, AS WELL AS THE KRYPTONITE-GUN! SUPERMAN WAS AFRAID WE'D BE HURT!
THAT'S WHY HE SENT US HERE! HE DOESN'T WANT TO ENDANGER US!
8

WE CAN'T LET SUPERMAN FACE THAT KRYPTONITE GUN TO PROTECT US!
I'VE AN IDEA-- LET'S SLIP BACK TO THE BAT-PLANE!

"AND INSIDE THE PLANE..."
MY DISGUISE WILL BE FINISHED IN A MINUTE!
AND SO WILL THE MAKESHIFT COSTUME--LUCKY FOR US WE USE COLORED PARACHUTES FOR IDENTIFICATION!

"MINUTES LATER, MY DISGUISE WAS COMPLETE..."
YOU'RE A DEAD RINGER FOR SUPERMAN NOW, BATMAN!
I ONLY HOPE MY PLAN WORKS!

BUT AGAIN, BATMAN'S MEMORIES OF THEIR FIRST GREAT CASE WITH SUPERMAN ARE INTERRUPTED...
BATMAN, WE'VE LOST THEIR TRAIL! I DON'T SEE SUPERMAN AND POWERMAN ANYWHERE AHEAD!
WE'RE HERE, ROBIN!

YOU COULDN'T KEEP THE BATMOBILE SHIELDED. I GLIMPSED YOU FOLLOWING ME!
AND NOW WE'VE REACHED THE AREA WHERE LUTHOR MUST BE HIDING, WE DON'T WANT YOU AROUND!

LET US GO WITH YOU, SUPERMAN! IF LUTHOR USES KRYPTONITE, YOU'LL NEED OUR HELP!
I'M ALL THE HELP SUPERMAN NEEDS!
9

I AGREE WITH POWERMAN-- YOU MUST LEAVE!
YOU'RE REJECTING YOUR FRIENDS FOR THIS POWERMAN, WHOEVER HE IS!
IT'S ALL RIGHT, ROBIN-- WE'LL GO!

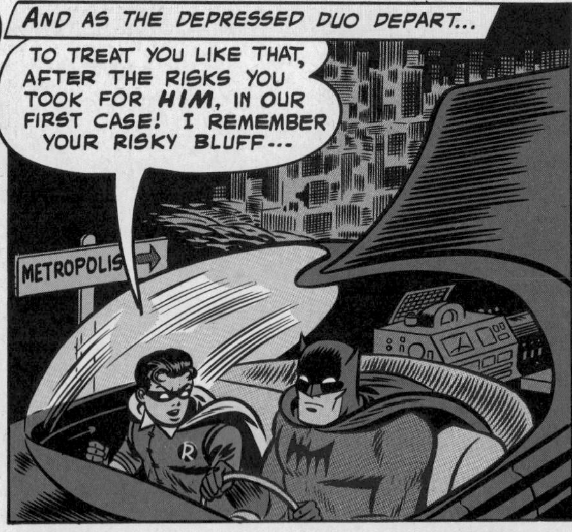
AND AS THE DEPRESSED DUO DEPART...
TO TREAT YOU LIKE THAT, AFTER THE RISKS YOU TOOK FOR HIM, IN OUR FIRST CASE! I REMEMBER YOUR RISKY BLUFF---
METROPOLIS

"---GOING RIGHT INTO THE CROOKS' HIDEOUT, DISGUISED AS SUPERMAN..."
IT'S SUPERMAN!
THIS KRYPTONITE-GUN WILL STOP HIM AGAIN!

"AGAIN, THEY USED THE KRYPTONITE WEAPON, BUT THIS TIME..."
IT DOESN'T AFFECT HIM THIS TIME!
NOT A BIT-- I CAN PROTECT MYSELF AGAINST IT NOW!

"BUT, ALL AT ONCE..."
LOOK, THE SPRAY WASHED MAKE-UP OFF HIS FACE! HE'S NOT SUPERMAN!
SO THAT'S WHY KRYPTONITE DIDN'T STOP HIM-- BUT THE MACHINE-GUN WILL!

"THAT'S WHEN I WENT INTO ACTION!"
SUPERMAN! NOW'S YOUR CHANCE--
GUN THEM DOWN! GET THAT KRYPTONITE-GUN BACK TO USE ON THE REAL SUPERMAN!
10

BATMAN! I'D NEVER HAVE LET YOU TAKE THE RISK IF I'D KNOWN!
THE BLUFF WORKED, THOUGH! WE'VE ROUNDED THEM UP!
"LATER, WHEN WE PARTED..."
I'LL NEVER FORGET HOW WE WORKED TOGETHER, BATMAN-- BUT I NEVER WANT YOU TO RISK YOUR LIFE FOR ME AGAIN!
MAYBE YOU CAN PAY BACK THE FAVOR SOME DAY, SUPERMAN!
AND NOW THAT'S HOW HE REPAYS YOU-- CASTING YOU OFF FOR THIS POWERMAN!
ROBIN, YOU JUST REMINDED ME OF SOMETHING THAT SUGGESTS WHY SUPERMAN HAS BEEN ACTING THIS WAY!
SUPERMAN WOULD ONLY REJECT US BECAUSE, AS IN OUR FIRST CASE, HE WOULDN'T ENDANGER US TO HELP HIM! I'VE GOT AN IDEA-- I WANT TO SEE HOW LUTHOR ESCAPED FROM JAIL!
METROPOLIS PRISON
AND, SHORTLY AFTER, IN THE METROPOLIS PRISON...
SUPERMAN ASKED ME NOT TO TELL ANYONE, BUT, OF COURSE, THAT WOULDN'T INCLUDE YOU, BATMAN! LUTHOR SECRETLY MADE A DESTRUCTIVE RAY DEVICE, AND CUT RIGHT OUT THROUGH THE WALL!
I SEE BITS OF SILICON WERE LEFT, SO HIS RAY DIDN'T AFFECT THAT ELEMENT!
BECAUSE LUTHOR'S RAY COULD DESTROY US, SUPERMAN WOULDN'T LET US HELP! BUT I KNOW HOW WE STILL CAN!
I DON'T GET IT! IF HE WOULDN'T ENDANGER US, WHY WOULD HE IMPERIL POWERMAN?
11

SHORTLY, AS SUPERMAN AND HIS NEW ALLY CLOSE IN ON LUTHOR'S HIDEOUT...
THAT'S LUTHOR'S RAY, WHICH HE'LL USE TO TAKE REVENGE ON METROPOLIS! BUT IT CAN'T HURT ME! I'M GOING IN!
BUT LUTHOR WILL USE KRYPTONITE ON YOU, SUPERMAN-- SO WE'RE GOING IN INSTEAD!
METROPOLIS WAREHOUSE COMPANY
BATMAN! THAT RAY WILL DESTROY YOU---
I LEARNED THAT IT DOESN'T AFFECT SILICON, SO I IMPROVISED SOME SILICON SHIELDS! COME ON, ROBIN!
AND BEFORE SUPERMAN CAN STOP THEM...
THEIR SHIELDS DEFLECT THE RAY, BUT OUR KRYPTONITE WILL STOP SUPERMAN!
YOU WON'T GET A CHANCE TO USE IT, LUTHOR!
I'VE GOT THE KRYPTONITE, SUPERMAN!
COVER IT, SO I CAN GET HIM!
SOON...
IT'S LIKE OUR FIRST CASE TOGETHER, BATMAN!
BUT YOUR FRIEND POWERMAN DIDN'T DO ANYTHING--
HE'S A ROBOT, WITH A TAPE-PLAYER SPEECH DEVICE, THAT I OPERATED BY REMOTE CONTROL. RATHER THAN ENDANGER YOU TWO, I PLANNED TO USE HIM IF I RAN INTO KRYPTONITE!
WE MIGHT HAVE KNOWN YOU'D NEVER REPLACE US WITH A REAL NEW PARTNER!
12
THE END

Art by Sheldon Moldoff & Charles Paris/Coloring by Carl Gafford

"WHERE IS BATMAN?" ROBIN WONDERS! AND THE FAMED CRIME-FIGHTER SOON WONDERS, TOO-- FOR HIS WHEREABOUTS IS A MYSTERY TO HIMSELF!
ALL BATMAN KNOWS IS THAT HE IS BEING SWEPT ALONG BY SWIRLING LIGHTS THROUGH VAST REACHES OF SPACE...

THEN SAND CRUNCHES UNDER HIS FEET--AND AN UNFAMILIAR LANDSCAPE ENCIRLES HIM!
TWIN MOONS! I'M ON AN ALIEN PLANET!

THOSE SWIRLING LIGHTS-- WERE THEY AN ALIEN ENERGY THAT TRANS-MITTED ME HERE? I--I CAN'T REMEMBER! MAYBE ALIENS DELIBERATELY ERASED MY MEMORY! BUT WHY? WHAT IS IT THEY DON'T WANT ME TO REMEMBER?

MY UTILITY-BELT IS GONE-- WITH MY BAT-ROPE AND BATARANGS! I'VE BEEN MADE DEFENSELESS -- THRUST ON AN ALIEN WORLD -- AND I DON'T KNOW WHY!

THEN BATMAN IS TOUCHED BY A TINY FEAR -- THE INSTINCTIVE FEAR OF ANY MAN WHO IS ISOLATED AND WEAPONLESS -- AND CONFRONTED BY THE UNKNOWN!
IT'S NOT KNOWING THAT'S SO DISQUIETING! AND SOMEHOW I SENSE TERRIBLE DANGER -- WAITING! I--I'VE NEVER FELT SO ALONE IN ALL MY LIFE...

SO, BATMAN TRUDGES ON THROUGH THE ALIEN LAND, UNTIL...
THE RUINS OF A DESERTED CITY! IT'S SO ANCIENT THE PLANTS HAVE TAKEN OVER!

WITHOUT WARNING, SOMETHING SHOOTS OUT AT HIM...
GREAT SCOTT! THAT PLANT'S TENDRIL HAS ELONGATED AND WRAPPED ITSELF AROUND ME! GOT TO YANK MYSELF LOOSE!

BUT BEFORE BATMAN CAN MOVE...
UH--CAN'T FREE MY ARM! I'M HELPLESS!

THEN AS THE TERRIBLE PLANT RELENTLESSLY TIGHTENS ITS GRIP...
IF ONLY ROBIN WERE HERE TO HELP ME! ROBIN! WHERE ARE YOU, ROBIN? ROBIN!

SUDDENLY, A FAMILIAR, STURDY FIGURE RACES FORWARD...
I'LL GET YOU FREE!
ROBIN!
3

ALL RIGHT NOW?
CRACK
YES-- THE TENDRILS HAVE RELAXED THEIR GRIP!

ROBIN--HOW DID YOU GET HERE?
NO TIME TO TALK NOW! MORE PLANTS ARE COMING! THEY CAN WALK! LET'S GET AWAY FROM HERE--FAST!

LATER...
THE SUN! DAWN'S APPROACHING!
WHY DO I FEEL SO UNEASY? WHY DO I FEEL THAT THERE ARE EYES WATCHING-- EYES WITH HUMAN INTELLIGENCE?

LOOK! A GIANT STATUE!
IT MUST BE AN IDOL THAT THE ALIENS WORSHIP!

THEN, AMAZINGLY, THE STONE FIGURE SUDDENLY REARS ERECT!
IT'S ALIVE-- AND COMING AFTER US! RUN, ROBIN-- RUN!
4

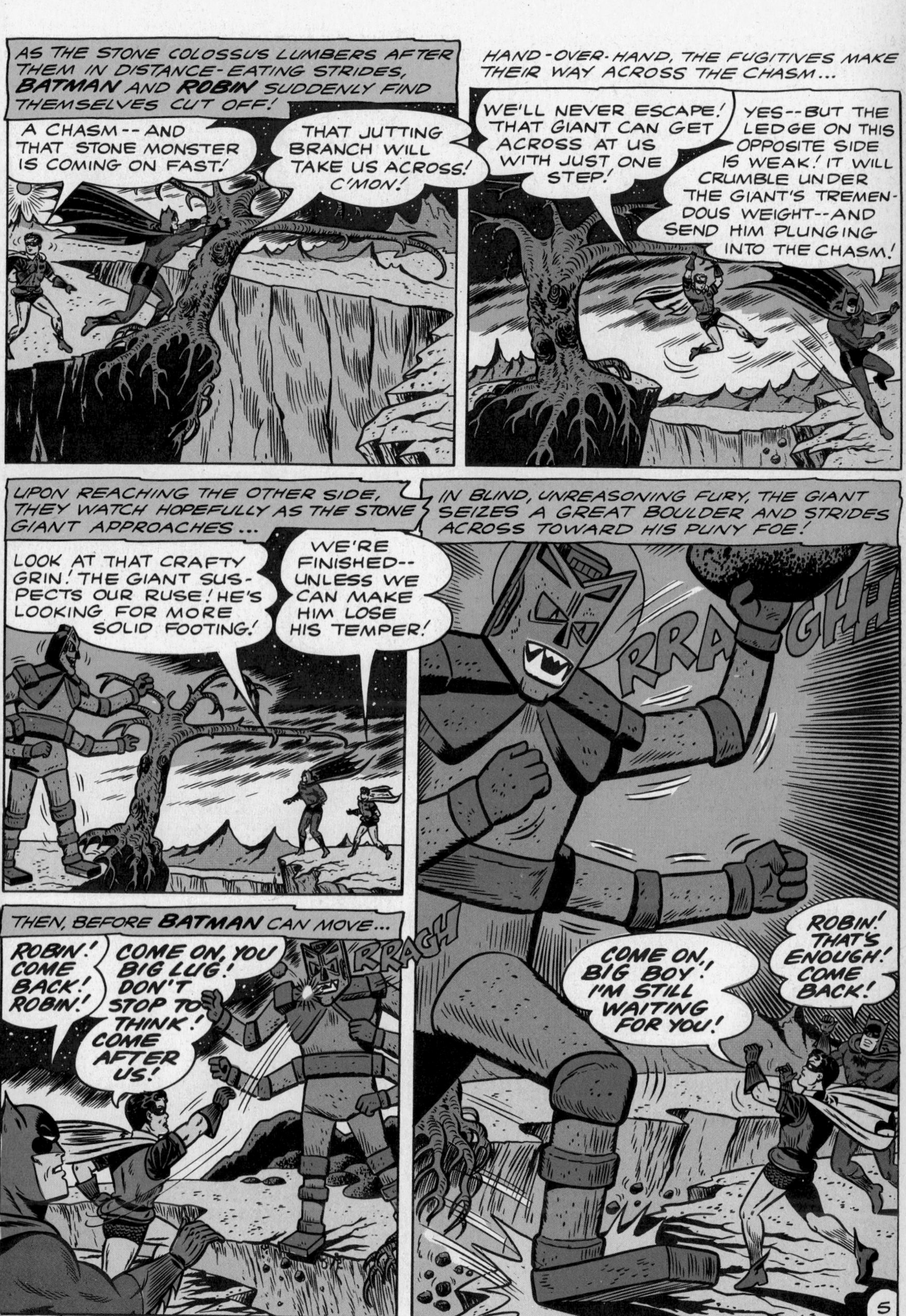
AS THE STONE COLOSSUS LUMBERS AFTER THEM IN DISTANCE-EATING STRIDES, BATMAN AND ROBIN SUDDENLY FIND THEMSELVES CUT OFF!
A CHASM--AND THAT STONE MONSTER IS COMING ON FAST!
THAT JUTTING BRANCH WILL TAKE US ACROSS! C'MON!
HAND-OVER-HAND, THE FUGITIVES MAKE THEIR WAY ACROSS THE CHASM...
WE'LL NEVER ESCAPE! THAT GIANT CAN GET ACROSS AT US WITH JUST ONE STEP!
YES--BUT THE LEDGE ON THIS OPPOSITE SIDE IS WEAK! IT WILL CRUMBLE UNDER THE GIANT'S TREMENDOUS WEIGHT--AND SEND HIM PLUNGING INTO THE CHASM!
UPON REACHING THE OTHER SIDE, THEY WATCH HOPEFULLY AS THE STONE GIANT APPROACHES...
LOOK AT THAT CRAFTY GRIN! THE GIANT SUSPECTS OUR RUSE! HE'S LOOKING FOR MORE SOLID FOOTING!
WE'RE FINISHED--UNLESS WE CAN MAKE HIM LOSE HIS TEMPER!
THEN, BEFORE BATMAN CAN MOVE...
ROBIN! COME BACK! ROBIN!
COME ON, YOU BIG LUG! DON'T STOP TO THINK! COME AFTER US!
RRAGH
IN BLIND, UNREASONING FURY, THE GIANT SEIZES A GREAT BOULDER AND STRIDES ACROSS TOWARD HIS PUNY FOE!
RRAGHH
COME ON, BIG BOY! I'M STILL WAITING FOR YOU!
ROBIN! THAT'S ENOUGH! COME BACK!
5

AS THE WEAK LEDGE CRUMBLES UNDER THE GIANT'S COLOSSAL WEIGHT...
ROBIN! WATCH OUT!-- THAT BOULDER!
UHHH!

ROBIN!

EVEN AS HE FEELS FOR A PULSE BEAT, BATMAN KNOWS IT IS NO USE!
HE--HE'S DEAD! ROBIN'S DEAD!

THE DAWN SUN RISES, LOOKING DOWN AT A MAN STUNNED BY THE SHOCK OF TERRIBLE CATASTROPHE!
ROBIN SACRIFICED HIMSELF FOR ME! HE DIED SO I COULD LIVE! OH, ROBIN... ROBIN...

LATER, ON THIS HOSTILE, ALIEN WORLD -- A MOUND OF STONES BECOME ROBIN'S CRYPT -- ROBIN'S FINAL RESTING PLACE!
6

MUCH LATER, WEAKENED BY THIRST-- CRUSHED BY TRAGEDY--A LONE FIGURE STAGGERS OVER BURNING DESERT SANDS..
EYES--I CAN FEEL EYES WATCHING ME--EYES WITH HUMAN INTELLIGENCE-- WATCHING--ALWAYS WATCHING...
I KNOW YOU'RE OUT THERE! WHY DON'T YOU SHOW YOURSELVES? WHY ARE YOU WATCHING ME?
THEN A GREAT BULK HUNCHES UP FROM THE SANDS ..
A BEAST--AN ALIEN BEAST! I'M TOO WEAK TO RUN OR FIGHT IT...
LET IT COME! I DON'T WANT TO LIVE! IT'S MY FAULT ROBIN DIED! I DON'T WANT TO LIVE...
LET IT COME! I DON'T WANT TO LIVE! IT'S MY FAULT ROBIN DIED! I DON'T WANT TO LIVE...
HE'S HAD ENOUGH! GET HIM OUT OF THERE!
7

SWIFTLY, A HATCH OPENS--FIGURES HURRY TO BATMAN'S SIDE...
WHAT...? ROBIN--ALIVE! I--I...
EASY, BATMAN--EVERYTHING'S UNDER CONTROL! YOU'RE IN THE TEST CHAMBER--REMEMBER?
THE TEST--I REMEMBER NOW! I DIDN'T WANT YOU TO WORRY--I LEFT A LETTER WITH GORDON FOR YOU--TO BE GIVEN TO YOU AFTER TWO DAYS...
YES--I GOT THE NOTE--AND I'VE BEEN COMING HERE EVERY DAY SINCE THEN, TO LOOK IN ON YOU!
WELL, DOC--HOW DID I DO?
YOU DID FINE! YOU MADE A SIMULATED "FLIGHT" INTO SPACE IN THIS CHAMBER THAT DUPLICATES CONDITIONS AN ASTRONAUT MIGHT UNDERGO IF HE FOUND HIMSELF ALONE ON SUCH A SPACE FLIGHT!
BATMAN, BY VOLUNTEERING FOR THIS TEST, YOU'VE MADE A GREAT CONTRIBUTION TO SPACE MEDICINE!
YES, INDEED! THE DATA COLLECTED ON THESE SENSITIVE RECORDING INSTRUMENTS WILL ENABLE US TO GAUGE EFFECTS ON AN ASTRONAUT'S NERVOUS SYSTEM!
YOUR REACTIONS WILL HELP US DETERMINE HOW LONG, AND WHAT KINDS OF STRAINS AN ASTRONAUT CAN ENDURE IN LONELINESS, BEFORE HIS MIND STARTS IMAGINING THINGS...
IMAGINING THINGS... I HAD AN HALLUCINATION...
WE GUESSED THAT WHEN WE HEARD YOU YELLING! YOU CAN TELL ME ABOUT IT TOMORROW--BUT RIGHT NOW YOU NEED SLEEP!
8

THE FOLLOWING DAY, AFTER MANY TESTS, BATMAN DICTATES HIS HALLUCINATION INTO A TAPE RECORDER...
THOSE EYES I SENSED WATCHING ME-- NOW I REALIZE THEY WERE YOUR EYES WATCHING THROUGH THE OBSERVATION WINDOW! STRANGE, HOW AFRAID I WAS OF BEING ALONE...
NOT SO STRANGE!...

ONE OF MAN'S MOST PRIMITIVE FEARS IS LONELINESS! WHEN A MAN IS ISOLATED TOO LONG, THE MIND PLAYS STRANGE TRICKS... IN YOUR CASE, YOU IMAGINED THAT YOU WERE INDIRECTLY GUILTY OF ROBIN'S DEATH... YOUR CONSTANT CONCERN ABOUT THE BOY'S SAFETY CAME TO THE SURFACE IN YOUR HALLUCINATIONS!

LATER, AS BATMAN LEAVES FOR HOME...
DOCTOR, YOU LOOK WORRIED...
I AM! BATMAN'S A HARDY SPECIMEN, WITH AN ABOVE-AVERAGE MIND-- BUT EVEN A BATMAN CAN SUCCUMB TO STRESS AND SHOCK! I JUST HOPE THERE WON'T BE ANY AFTER-EFFECTS...
9
CONTINUED IN CHAPTER 2

CHAPTER 2 ROBIN DIES AT DAWN

HOMEWARD BOUND, ROBIN BRIEFS BATMAN ON THE ANT-MAN CASE, WHEN...
ACME LOAN CO.
ROBIN, DO YOU SEE WHAT I SEE? GORILLAS ESCAPING WITH MONEY FROM THAT LOAN COMPANY!

THEY'RE ONLY MEN WEARING GORILLA COSTUMES, BATMAN! ACCORDING TO POLICE REPORTS, THE GORILLA GANG HAS BEEN OPERATING IN VARIOUS CITIES! NOW THEY'VE COME TO GOTHAM CITY--SO LET'S GIVE THEM A FITTING "WELCOME"!

SWIFTLY, SILENTLY, BATMAN AND ROBIN DART UP THE FIRE-ESCAPE--AND CHARGE INTO THE GORILLA GANG!

NOW LET'S MAKE MONKEYS OUT OF THESE APES!

BATMAN AND ROBIN! QUICK--WE'LL HAVE TO ESCAPE TO THE NEXT BUILDING, OVER THE DANGLING GIRDER!

ACME LOAN

10

AS ROBIN RACES AHEAD TOWARD THE FLEEING BANDITS, BATMAN SUDDENLY STARES AT THE TALL CONSTRUCTION CRANE...

...AND IT SEEMS TO ALTER...

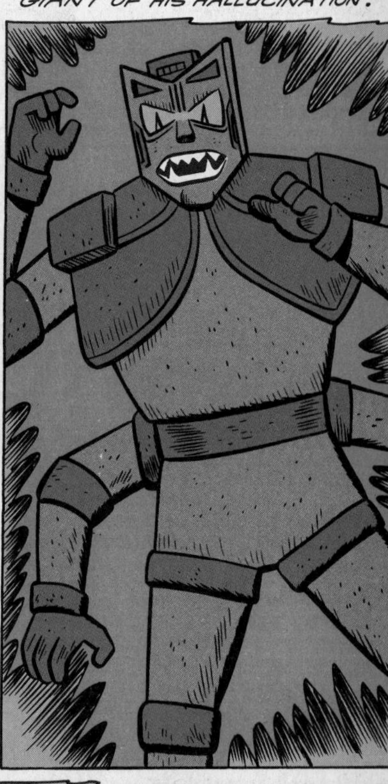
...TO BECOME THE STONE GIANT OF HIS HALLUCINATION!

ONCE AGAIN BATMAN SEEMS TO SEE ROBIN IN PERIL, AND ACTS INSTINCTIVELY!
NO, ROBIN-- NO!

BUT, TO ROBIN'S EYES, THE SCENE IS A VERY DIFFERENT ONE!
BATMAN! YOU'RE TAKING US OVER THE EDGE OF THE ROOF!

ROBIN'S SUDDEN SHOUT JOLTS BATMAN'S LAPSE OF MEMORY--AND HE INSTANTLY FLINGS OUT A HAND THAT CLINGS WITH AN IRON GRIP!
IT'S OKAY, ROBIN-- WE'RE SAFE NOW!
WOW!
11

LATER, AFTER BATMAN TELLS OF HIS MOMENTARY HALLUCINATION...
SORRY, ROBIN--I GUESS I'M STILL A LITTLE SHAKY FROM THE TEST! I--I'LL BE BACK TO NORMAL BY TOMORROW!
I SURE HOPE SO--FOR BATMAN'S SAKE

LATER, AT THE WAYNE MANSION, BRUCE'S RETURN IS EAGERLY AWAITED BY TWO LOYAL FRIENDS!
ALFRED! ACE! AH, IT'S GOOD TO BE BACK HOME AGAIN!
WE ALL MISSED YOU, SIR!

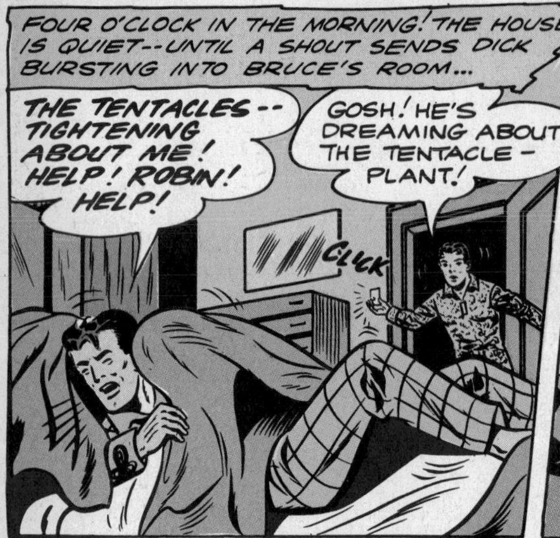
FOUR O'CLOCK IN THE MORNING! THE HOUSE IS QUIET--UNTIL A SHOUT SENDS DICK BURSTING INTO BRUCE'S ROOM...
THE TENTACLES--TIGHTENING ABOUT ME! HELP! ROBIN! HELP!
GOSH! HE'S DREAMING ABOUT THE TENTACLE-PLANT!
CLICK

AS THE SUDDEN ILLUMINATION AWAKENS BRUCE...
UH...? I'M HOME! OH, I HAD A NIGHTMARE! IT WAS AWFUL--AWFUL...
BRUCE, I'LL HAVE ACE SLEEP IN HERE TONIGHT--SO YOU WON'T FEEL SO ALONE...

Y-YES... MAYBE THAT WOULD BE BETTER...

THE FOLLOWING NIGHT, AS DICK DESCENDS TO THE BAT-CAVE...
YOU'RE NOT REALLY GOING ON PATROL?
I CERTAINLY AM! I FEEL FINE TODAY! BESIDES, WITH THE GORILLA GANG IN TOWN, THE POLICE MAY NEED OUR HELP! GET DRESSED, DICK!
12

LATER--EVER ON THE ALERT, THE **DYNAMIC DUO** INSTANTLY DASHES TO THE SOURCE OF A CLANGING BURGLAR ALARM!
A LUCKY BREAK FOR US! IT'S THE **GORILLA GANG** AGAIN!
THEY'VE CRACKED THE TRUCKING COMPANY'S VAULT! QUICK--CIRCLE AROUND THEM, **ROBIN**! WE'LL HIT THEM FROM TWO DIRECTIONS!
CLANG
GOTHAM TRUCKING CO.
UNEXPECTEDLY, THE **GORILLA GANG** PILES INTO A GETAWAY CAR HIDDEN IN THE DARKNESS...ITS MOTOR ROARS...AND HEADLIGHTS FLASH ON...
UH--THAT DAZZLING LIGHT!
RUN HIM DOWN!

HALF-BLINDED BY THE SUDDEN GLARE, **BATMAN** STANDS TRANSFIXED--LIKE A MOTH HYPNOTIZED BY FLAME...

...AND IN HIS MIND'S EYE, THE CAR SUBTLY CHANGES SHAPE...

...UNTIL HE IS ONCE AGAIN RELIVING HIS HALLUCINATION!

LET IT COME! I DON'T WANT TO LIVE! IT'S MY FAULT **ROBIN** DIED! I DON'T WANT TO LIVE...

REALIZING WHAT HAS HAPPENED, THE **BOY WONDER** LEAPS AT THE BANDIT CAR AND...
HE'S YANKED THE WHEEL! GOTTA SHOVE HIM OFF!

WHEW! IT JUST MISSED **BATMAN**!
ACME CAMPHOR FLAKES
SCREEE--EECH
CRACK
13

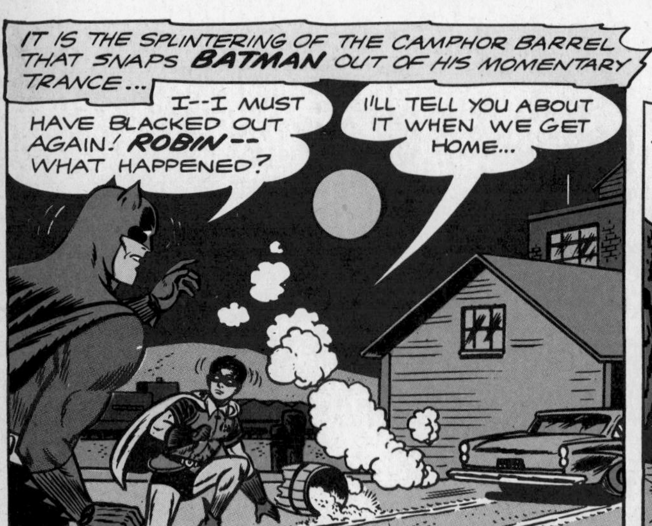

IT IS THE SPLINTERING OF THE CAMPHOR BARREL THAT SNAPS BATMAN OUT OF HIS MOMENTARY TRANCE...
I--I MUST HAVE BLACKED OUT AGAIN! ROBIN-- WHAT HAPPENED?
I'LL TELL YOU ABOUT IT WHEN WE GET HOME...

LATER, BATMAN AT LAST REALIZES THERE IS SOMETHING VERY, VERY WRONG WITH HIM...
LET'S FACE REALITY! WHILE I HAVE THESE MENTAL BLACKOUTS, I ENDANGER YOUR LIFE! I CAN'T EVER LET THAT HAPPEN AGAIN! THERE'S ONLY ONE THING I CAN DO...

...I MUST PUT AWAY MY BATMAN COSTUME AND RETIRE FROM CRIME-FIGHTING!
OH, BATMAN! SOB

THE FOLLOWING NIGHT--ONLY ONE MEMBER OF THE FAMED TEAM DONS CRIME-FIGHTING GARB...
I'VE AN APPOINTMENT WITH PROFESSOR CARSON--ABOUT THE TESTIMONY WE'LL GIVE AT THE ANT-MAN'S TRIAL! I--I'LL BE BACK AS SOON AS I CAN!
I-IF YOU RUN INTO CRIMINAL ACTIVITY, BE EVEN MORE CAREFUL THAN YOU WOULD BE IF I WERE ALONG!

BUT ONE THING ROBIN KEEPS FROM BATMAN IS A SECRET APPOINTMENT WITH THE ARMY DOCTOR...

I WAS AFRAID OF THIS! BATMAN WILL NEED TREATMENT! THEN, EVENTUALLY, HE WILL BE HIMSELF AGAIN-- BUT IT WILL TAKE TIME...

HOURS PASS, AND KEEPING HIS VIGIL IN THE BAT-CAVE, BRUCE IS GETTING WORRIED, WHEN...

BBZZZZZ

THE EMERGENCY BAT-SIGNAL FROM COMMISSIONER GORDON! I'D BETTER CONTACT HIM AT ONCE ON THE BATMOBILE'S TWO-WAY RADIO!

14

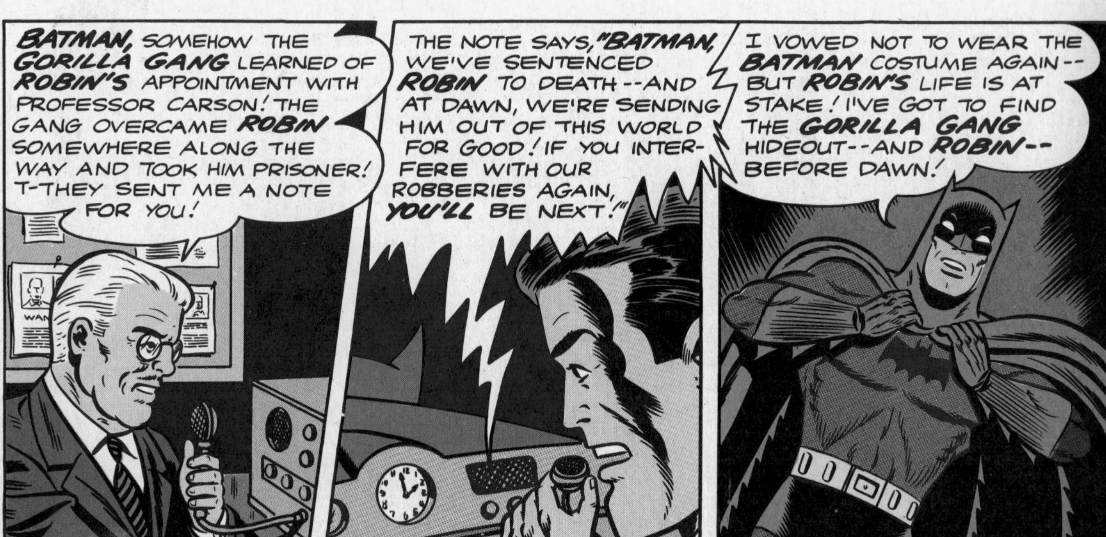

"LAST NIGHT"! THOSE WORDS SUDDENLY HELP BATMAN RECALL SOMETHING THAT OCCURRED THE PREVIOUS NIGHT!

THE GETAWAY CAR TIRES PASSED THROUGH SPILLED CAMPHOR FLAKES! CAMPHOR SCENT IS VERY STRONG--TAKES QUITE A WHILE TO FADE AWAY COMPLETELY! THAT CAMPHOR SCENT WOULD BE TOO FAINT FOR ME TO TRAIL--BUT NOT FOR A DOG'S KEEN SENSE OF SMELL!

SHORTLY, WITH ACE IN HIS BAT-HOUND IDENTITY, THE MOVE AGAINST THE GORILLA GANG STARTS THIS NIGHT--WHERE LAST NIGHT'S ENDED!

OKAY, BAT-HOUND--THE CAMPHOR SMELL ON THE GETAWAY CAR TIRES SHOULD LEAD YOU RIGHT TO THE GANG'S HIDEOUT!

SNIFF! SNIFF!

15

SOON--DAWN! SHAFTS OF SUNLIGHT PROBE EVERYWHERE--ESPECIALLY THROUGH A SLIDING ROOFTOP...
SUNRISE--AND ROBIN'S GONNA RISE UNTIL HE'S OUTA THIS WORLD! HA, HA! ONE WHACK OF THIS SHARP AX AND...
HOLD IT, PETE! I HEARD SOMETHING--SOUNDS LIKE FOOTSTEPS! LUKE, TAKE A LOOK OUTSIDE AND SEE IF ANYBODY'S SNOOPING AROUND!
CHECK!
MINUTES PASS AS THE CRIMINALS WAIT FOR THE RETURN OF THEIR COMPANION...
WELL? ANYBODY OUTSIDE?
YES...
...ME!
BATMAN! HE KAYOED LUKE--AND GOT INTO LUKE'S SUIT TO CATCH US OFF-GUARD! I'LL FIX HIM!
THEN, A SHAGGY SHAPE HURTLES FORWARD LIKE A MISSILE...
THE AX--IT'S CUT THE MOORING ROPES!
FREED, THE BALLOON STARTS TO RISE, THE ROPES TRAILING LIKE TENTACLES AROUND BATMAN'S SHOULDERS!..
"LIKE TENTACLES"! WILL THOSE ROPES CAUSE BATMAN TO BLACK OUT AGAIN? WILL HE IMAGINE HE IS IN THE GRIP OF THE TENTACLE-PLANT?
16

SO IT SEEMS AS BATMAN SWEEPS THE ROPES ASIDE, LUNGES DESPERATELY FOR THE FALLEN AXE, AND HURLS IT UPWARD...
IS BATMAN WILDLY BATTLING THE "TENTACLES" OF HIS IMAGINARY WORLD?

THE ANSWER COMES IN THE NEXT INSTANT...
MY AIM WAS PERFECT! AS THE GAS ESCAPES, THE BALLOON WILL COLLAPSE--AND GENTLY FLOAT DOWN TO THE FLOOR!
HISSSSSS

LATER, WHEN POLICE ARE SUMMONED TO JAIL THE GORILLA GANG...

GOSH! YOU WERE LIKE YOUR OLD SELF! YOU DIDN'T BLACK OUT THIS TIME!

NO! YOU SEE, ROBIN, IN MY HALLUCINATION, I ONLY IMAGINED YOU DIED AT DAWN! BUT THIS WAS A REAL DAWN--AND YOU FACED A REAL DEATH! WELL, THE REALITY OF THE SITUATION WAS SO TERRIBLE, IT SHOCKED ME RIGHT BACK TO NORMAL!

17

DAWN--ONCE AN OMEN OF ROBIN'S DEATH--IT IS NOW A FITTING SIGN THAT BATMAN'S CRIME-FIGHTING CAREER HAS RETURNED TO LIFE!

The End

Story by Gardner Fox/Art by Carmine Infantino & Joe Giella/Coloring by Helen Vesik

THROUGH THE SURGE AND HEAVE OF A STORM-BATTERED SEA, A CABIN CRUISER LIFTS AND DIPS HELP-LESSLY IN THE TROUGH AND SWELL OF MAD-DENED WATERS...

THE YELLOW SCRATCH OF LIGHTNING AGAINST A BLACKENED SKY HIGHLIGHTS THE RENDING CRASH AND SPLINTERING OF A WOODEN PROW ON JAGGED, KNIFE-LIKE ROCKS...
HAVE TO ABANDON SHIP! WHAT A MISERABLE WIND-UP TO A DAY OF DEEP-SEA FISHING!
CRAACK!

LIGHTNING SPOTLIGHTS THE FIGURE OF BRUCE (BATMAN) WAYNE AS HE SPLITS THE WAVES IN A CLEAN DIVE FROM THE DECK OF THE TOSSING, DYING VESSEL BEING POUNDED TO PIECES AGAINST THE RUTHLESS ROCKS...
SPOTTED AN ISLAND CLOSE BY! GOT TO MAKE A SWIM FOR IT!

A WET, BEDRAGGLED FIGURE STAGGERS ASHORE A LITTLE LATER AS THE FULL FURY OF THE STORM SMASHES OVERHEAD IN A DIAPASON OF DEADLY DESTRUC-TION!...
PANT! WONDER IF THERE'S ANY SHELTER FURTHER INLAND? ANYTHING'D BE BETTER THAN THIS!

THEN IN A LULL BETWEEN THE OMINOUS CRESCENDO OF CRASHING THUNDER, BRUCE WAYNE HEARS A CRY, A WAIL OF DESPAIR, OF UTTER HOPE-LESSNESS...
HELP!...HELP! PLEASE--SOMEBODY... HELP ME!
GOOD GOSH! SOUNDS LIKE SOMEONE'S WORSE OFF THAN I AM!

HE LURCHES FORWARD BLINDLY THROUGH THE AWESOME DOWN-POUR--AND COMES TO A DEAD STOP WHEN HE SEES...
A BOY--CAUGHT IN A QUICK-SAND BED! KEEP CALM, YOUNGSTER--DON'T THRASH ABOUT SO MUCH! YOU'RE ONLY MAKING YOURSELF SINK DEEPER...

HIS POWERFUL HANDS BREAK OFF A BRANCH AND THRUST IT OUT OVER THE GRIPPING QUAG-MIRE! HIS VOICE SOOTHES AND COMFORTS...
JUST RELAX...AND YOU WON'T STIR UP THE SANDS THAT DRAW YOU DOWNWARD! ATTABOY! NOW--GRAB HOLD OF THIS BRANCH AND I'LL HAVE YOU OUT IN A JIFFY!
2

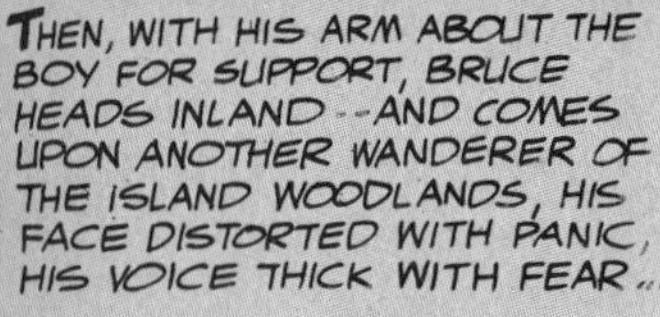
THEN, WITH HIS ARM ABOUT THE BOY FOR SUPPORT, BRUCE HEADS INLAND--AND COMES UPON ANOTHER WANDERER OF THE ISLAND WOODLANDS, HIS FACE DISTORTED WITH PANIC, HIS VOICE THICK WITH FEAR...

MARK! MARK--IS THAT YOU? I WAS SO WORRIED! WHAT HAPPENED TO YOU?
HE FELL INTO A QUICKSAND BOG--BUT HE SHOULD BE OKAY BY MORNING!

AND IN THE MORNING A GRATEFUL ROLAND DESMOND GRIPS BRUCE WAYNE BY THE HAND AS CLEAR SKIES REVEAL A CHANGE IN WEATHER...
THANKS AGAIN FOR SAVING MY BROTHER MARK'S LIFE! IF THERE'S ANYTHING I CAN DO--
THE OVERNIGHT SHELTER YOU PROVIDED SQUARED THINGS AS FAR AS I'M CONCERNED! NOW IF YOU'LL JUST TAKE ME BACK TO THE MAINLAND...

THE DAYS SLIP INTO WEEKS AND THE WEEKS INTO MONTHS. THEN ONE EVENING AS BATMAN AND ROBIN MAKE THEIR PATROL OF THE BUSINESS DISTRICT OF GOTHAM CITY...
TAKE A GANDER AT THAT! A BIG HOLE IN THAT WALL--AND POLICE PROWL CARS GATHERED TO INVESTIGATE IT!
ODD THAT WE DIDN'T HEAR ANY EXPLOSION ON OUR ROUNDS!

THERE WAS NO EXPLOSION, BATMAN! A SINGLE MAN MADE THAT OPENING--WITH SHEER BRUTE STRENGTH!
WHAT?!

"YES, HE SLAMMED INTO THAT WALL LIKE A FULLBACK RAMMING THE LINE--CLEAVING A PATH THROUGH BRICK AND CONCRETE AS IF MADE OF TISSUE PAPER!..."
CRASSH!

"INSIDE THE BANK HE STUFFED A DOUBLE KNAPSACK FULL OF MONEY! WE SAW HIM COMING OUT--AND WHEN HE IGNORED OUR WARNING TO STOP..."
OUR BULLETS FLATTEN OUT WHEN THEY HIT HIS BODY--AND BOUNCE OFF!
THINGS LIKE THIS ARE ONLY SUPPOSED TO HAPPEN IN HORROR MOVIES!
POW!
POW!
3

"AS IF TO SHOW HIS DEFIANCE OF US, HE LIFTED MY PARKED SQUAD CAR HIGH INTO THE AIR WITH ONE HAND..."
GNAAGH!
"THEN, SETTING THE CAR DOWN, HE RACED OFF INTO THE NIGHT..."
MAN, WHAT A NIGHT-MARE EVENING THIS HAS TURNED OUT TO BE!

A STUNNED **ROBIN** GIVES VOICE TO THE THOUGHTS THAT SWIRL ABOUT IN EVERYONE'S MIND...

WOWEE! HOW DOES ANYONE FIGHT A **BLOCKBUSTER** LIKE THAT!

BLOCKBUSTER!! SAY, THAT'S A TERRIFIC HEADLINE NAME FOR HIM! THE "**BLOCK-BUSTER BANDIT**"! YEAH!

SOON AFTERWARD IN THE **BATCAVE**, THE **MASKED MANHUNTER** AND THE **BOY WONDER** BUCKLE DOWN TO SEVERAL HOURS' WORK...

IF THAT **BLOCK-BUSTER** IS GOING TO HAUNT OUR NIGHTLY PATROLS--WE'D BETTER BE READY TO DEAL WITH HIM!

WITH SOME **VERY** SPECIAL WEAPONS AND EQUIPMENT TO HANDLE HIS VERY **SPECIAL** CASE!

4

ONE NIGHT--TWO NIGHTS--A THIRD NIGHT SLIPS BY WITH-OUT INCIDENT! THEN ON THE SHORT-WAVE RADIO OF THE **BATMOBILE** COMES THE ALARM THEY HAVE BEEN WAITING FOR...

ATTENTION, ALL UNITS! AN OFFICER ON THE BEAT HAS REPORTED SEEING THE **BLOCKBUSTER BANDIT** CRASHING INTO THE **TOLLIVER ART GALLERY**!
WE'RE ONLY A COUPLE OF BLOCKS FROM THERE, **ROBIN**!

MOMENTS AFTERWARD, TWO GRIM FIGURES VAULT FROM THE **BATMOBILE**--LADEN WITH THEIR **BLOCKBUSTER-BANDIT-CONTROL-GEAR**...

MY ORDERS WERE NOT TO INTERFERE WITH THE **BLOCK-BUSTER**--JUST GIVE THE ALARM!
HOLD THE POLICE RE-INFORCEMENTS OUT HERE WHEN THEY ARRIVE--WHILE WE TAKE A CRACK AT HIM WITH OUR SPECIAL WEAPONS!

TOWERING LIKE A COLOSSUS IN THE ART GALLERY, THE BLOCKBUSTER BANDIT TURNS A SAVAGE FACE TOWARD THE ON-RUSHING CRIME-FIGHTERS...
GYAAGH!
WOW! COMPARED TO THIS BABY, FRANKENSTEIN'S MONSTER WAS A LITTLE LORD FAUNTLEROY!

AS DEFTLY AS A WELL-OILED MACHINE, THE DARING DUO MOVES INTO ACTION! A LEAPING BATMAN RAMS A FIST INTO A JUTTING JAW...
HAD TO THROW A PUNCH AT HIM FIRST--JUST TO SATISFY MYSELF THAT IT WOULDN'T WORK! IT DIDN'T--!
SOK!

AND AS THE CREATURE REACHES OUT TO GRASP AND CRUNCH HIM, ROBIN DARTS BENEATH THOSE ARMS TO SNAP TIGHT THE SPECIAL STEEL MANACLES PREPARED FOR THIS MOMENT..
GOT HIM!

A GLARE OF INSENSATE RAGE CROSSES THE FEATURES OF THE TITANIC TERROR AS HIS MUSCLES BULGE AND BUNCH! STEEL STRAINS--CRACKS--FLIES WIDE APART...
GYAAAGH!
SHADES OF SUPERMAN! THOSE LINKS ARE MADE OF THE STRONGEST STEEL POSSIBLE! WE'LL HAVE TO GO THROUGH WITH OUR FOLLOW-UP PLAN!
CRAAK!

NOW THE TEEN-AGE THUNDERBOLT HURLS A GAS PELLET--EVEN AS THE COWLED CRUSADER WHIRLS A STEEL-CABLED BOLA...
GYAAGH!
SEEMS LIKE BLOCKBUSTER HAS ONLY A ONE-WORD VOCABULARY!
BATMAN AND I ARE PROTECTED FROM THIS TEAR-GAS--BUT BLOCKBUSTER ISN'T!
5

ONCE AGAIN THE BELLOW OF THE MADDENED GIANT SOUNDS IN THE GALLERY AS STEEL CABLES SNAP AND FLY...

GYAAAGH!

NOT A TEAR IN HIS EYE! DOESN'T ANYTHING BOTHER THIS FREEP*?

*Editor's Note; SLANG FOR A COMBINATION FREAK AND CREEP!

A MASSIVE HAND DARTS OUT--AND CLOSES IN A GRIP OF UNIMAGINABLE POWER ...
HE'S GOT ROBIN! IF THIS BRUTE HAS A WEAK SPOT, I'D BETTER FIND IT FAST!
THUD!

FISTS THAT HAVE NEVER MET THEIR EQUAL BASH AND THUD UP AND DOWN THAT ROCK-LIKE BODY! BATMAN FIGHTS AS HE HAS NEVER FOUGHT BEFORE--TO FREE HIS YOUNG COMPANION FROM THAT AWESOME GRIP...
LIKE BANGING ONE'S HEAD AGAINST THE PROVERBIAL WALL...
POW!

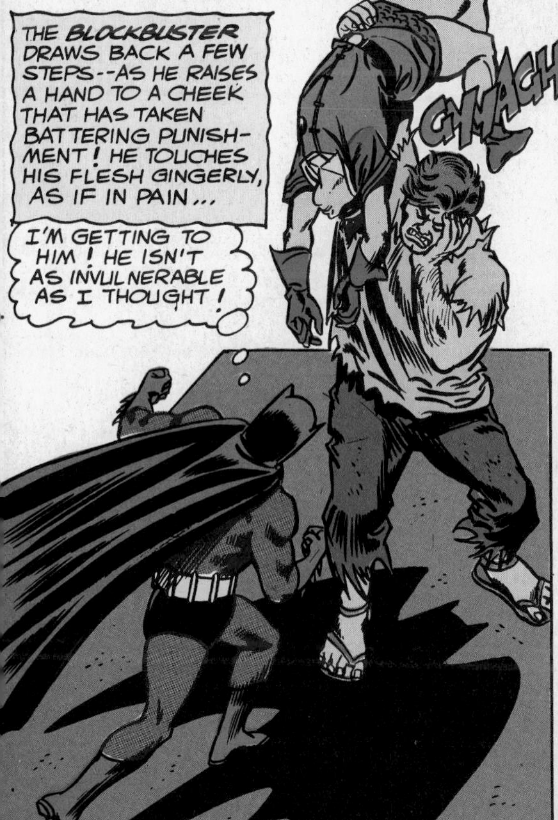

THE BLOCKBUSTER DRAWS BACK A FEW STEPS--AS HE RAISES A HAND TO A CHEEK THAT HAS TAKEN BATTERING PUNISHMENT! HE TOUCHES HIS FLESH GINGERLY, AS IF IN PAIN...
I'M GETTING TO HIM! HE ISN'T AS INVULNERABLE AS I THOUGHT!
GYAAAGH!

AGAIN THE COWLED CRUSADER HITS--AND YET AGAIN--WITH BLOWS THAT WOULD FELL AN OX! AND STUNG TO A WILD, ANIMALISTIC FURY--THE BLOCKBUSTER BANDIT ROARS WITH ANGER...
GYAAAGH
THUNNK!
THUNNK!

OUTSIDE THE GALLERY WAITS A FORCE OF EAGER, WELL-TRAINED POLICEMEN...
DON'T INTERFERE! GIVE BATMAN AND ROBIN A CHANCE TO "GET THEIR MAN"!
WHAT A BATTLE THEY MUST BE PUTTING UP!
BLAPPP!
VOOOMP!

AND THEN-- WITH A CRASH OF MASONRY AS HE KICKS THROUGH BRICK AND MORTAR-- COMES THE CRIME COLOSSUS...
CRASH!
MAN ALIVE! HE GOT 'EM BOTH!

HIGH ABOVE HIS HEAD ARE LIFTED THE MASKED MANHUNTER AND TEEN-AGE THUNDERBOLT-- INERT WEIGHTS IN THE MIGHTY HANDS OF THE BLOCKBUSTER BANDIT...
GYAAAGH!

THEN THEY ARE FLUNG LIKE CANNON-BALLS AT THE STUNNED POLICE-- BOWLING THEM OVER LIKE TENPINS...
WHAM
7

THE BLOCKBUSTER RACES OFF--SMASHING HIS WAY THROUGH ANOTHER BUILD-ING WALL--THEN BLASTING DOWN INTO A CELLAR...
CRAK!

HE MAKES HIS WAY INTO A SEWER-WAY, SPLASHING ALONG AT EVERY STEP...

UNTIL HE COMES TO AN ABAN-DONED SUBWAY TRACK, WHERE HE SCAMPERS OFF INTO THE DISTANCE...

BEHIND HIM HE LEAVES A SERIES OF GAPING HOLES, CRUNCHED-THROUGH BUILDING WALLS, THAT POINT A PATH TO THE NO-WHERE INTO WHICH THE CRIME COLOSSUS HAS DISAPPEARED...
THE TRAIL HAS PETERED OUT! HE'S GONE!
BUT HE'LL BE BACK--AND NEXT TIME WE'LL REALLY BE READY FOR HIM! LET'S GO SEE COMMISSIONER GORDON, ROBIN!
8

DETECTIVE COMICS
12¢
JUNE NO. 376
BATMAN-- WHAT'S WRONG? YOU LOOK LIKE YOU JUST SAW A GHOST!

BATMAN
12¢
AUG. NO. 183
HOT-LINE CALL, BATMAN! LET'S GET GOING!
NOT TONIGHT, KID! I'M STAYING IN THE BATCAVE TO WATCH MYSELF ON TELEVISION!
THE ADVENTURES OF BATMAN
HOLY EMERGENCY! WHAT'S THE REAL REASON BATMAN'S GOOFING OFF? THE TELLTALE CLUE IS ON THIS COVER!
POP CORN

DURING THE NEXT SEVERAL HOURS, THE DISGRUNTLED DUO CONFERS WITH THE GOTHAM CITY POLICE COMMISSIONER...
THEN IT'S AGREED! NEXT TIME HE APPEARS--WE LET HIM STEAL WHAT HE WANTS!
WHILE WE'LL BE ABOVE THE CITY IN THE BAT-COPTER--TO FOLLOW AND SEE WHERE HE GOES!

FOR THE NEXT TWO NIGHTS THE DARK, GRIM SHAPE OF THE BATCOPTER HOVERS LIKE A GREAT BIRD OF PREY ABOVE THE CITY ROOFTOPS...
WE'LL FIGHT HIM ON HIS HOME GROUND--AND HOLD HIM UNTIL THE POLICE ARRIVE WITH ELECTRIFIED NETS!

THEN ON A CLOUDY NIGHT, WHEN DARKNESS CLOAKS THE CITY--THE BEHEMOTH OF BANDITRY CRASHES INTO A CITY MUSEUM..
THERE HE GOES! NOW KEEP YOUR EYES PEELED FOR HIM WHEN HE COMES OUT!
RIGHTO, BATMAN! MY PUPILS ARE ALREADY PANTING!

ALL GOTHAM CITY HAS BEEN ALERTED TO THE TERRIBLE DANGER! LET THE BLOCKBUSTER BANDIT COME AND GO WITHOUT INTERFERENCE...
GYAAGH!

MINUTES LATER, HOLLOW FOOT-FALLS SPEED ALONG THE DESERTED CITY STREETS--WHILE OVERHEAD THAT DREAD FORM IS SHADOWED BY THE GOTHAM GANGBUSTERS...
HE'S HEADING TOWARD THE WHARVES!

INTO THE SEA HE PLUNGES, SWIMMING WITH POWERFUL STROKES AS THE ALMOST SILENT ROTORS OF THE BATCOPTER FOLLOW OVER-HEAD...

SAY, HE'S HEADING TOWARD THE ISLAND WHERE I RESCUED THAT BOY, MARK DESMOND! I WONDER IF THERE CAN BE ANY CONNECTION?

9

THEN ABOVE THE ISLAND--CRIES ARE WRUNG FROM STARTLED THROATS AS THE WHIRLYBIRD DIPS AND BEGINS TO FALL !...

THE COPTER'S OUT OF CONTROL ! WE'VE RUN INTO SOME SORT OF HIGH-FREQUENCY INTERFERENCE THAT'S JAMMED THE MOTOR!

OUR RADIO'S GONE DEAD! WE CAN'T CONTACT THE POLICE! BATMAN-- WE'RE ON OUR OWN!

FROM A FOOTPATH BELOW THE WRECKED BATCOPTER THE BLOCKBUSTER BANDIT RECOGNIZES HIS FIGHTING FOES! A MAD SHRIEK TEARS FROM HIS THROAT...

GYAAGH!

SOUNDS LIKE HE HASN'T INCREASED HIS VOCABULARY ANY! BOY, WHAT I WOULDN'T GIVE TO MAKE HIM CRY "UNCLE"!

DODGING AROUND TREES--CHANGING DIRECTION ABRUPTLY--THEY COME IN SIGHT OF ...
A HOUSE!
THE ONE I'VE BEEN LOOKING FOR--WHERE ROLAND DESMOND LIVES WITH HIS BROTHER MARK!

ON FEET THAT FLY LIKE THOSE OF OLYMPIC SPRINTERS, THE CRIME-FIGHTING COUPLE DASHES INTO THE CELLAR-WAY OF THE HOUSE,..
OKAY! NOW I CAN GET SET TO STOP THE BLOCKBUSTER!
LET ME KNOW WHEN YOU'RE SET--AND I'LL CALL GO!
SLAMM!

THE MADDENED MIGHT OF THE CRIME COLOSSUS IS NOT TO BE DENIED! HE LUNGES FOR-WARD--AND THE HEAVY OAK DOOR SPLINTERS BEFORE HIM..
NOW, BATMAN?
NOT YET, ROBIN!
CRUNCH

JELLING IN THE ALERT, DEDUCTIVE BRAIN OF BATMAN IS THE ONE POSSIBLE HOPE OF VICTORY IN THIS UNEQUAL STRUGGLE...
ROBIN--I THINK THE BLOCKBUSTER IS THE SAME FELLOW I SAVED FROM THE QUICKSAND BED--MARK DESMOND! THERE'S JUST ENOUGH FACIAL STRUCTURE LEFT SO THAT THEY LOOK ALIKE! IF THAT'S SO--I CAN STOP HIM!
BUT YOU TOLD ME MARK WAS A SCRAWNY KID! THIS ONE'S A--A BLOCK-BUSTER!

DESPERATELY THE BOY WONDER FLINGS HIMSELF UPON THE MASKED MANHUNTER! HIS VOICE PLEADS AS HIS HANDS RESTRAIN...
NO, NO, BATMAN! YOU CAN'T FIGHT THE BLOCK-BUSTER! HE'S TOO TOUGH AN OPPONENT!
TOO TOUGH FOR BATMAN--BUT NOT FOR BRUCE WAYNE!

AS BATMAN THROWS OFF HIS UNIFORM TO STAND IN SLACKS AND SHIRT--THE BEHEMOTH BANDIT PAUSES! ACROSS HIS FACE FLITS A STRANGE EXPRESSION! IS HE REMEMBERING THAT NIGHT MONTHS AGO, WHEN THIS VERY MAN SAVED HIS LIFE--AS MARK DESMOND?...
NO SIGN OF RECOGNITION YET! ROBIN, GO FIND THE OTHER MAN-- HIS BROTHER ROLAND! IF MY HUNCH IS RIGHT, HE'S THE BRAINS BEHIND THIS CHARACTER! THE SAME ONE WHO BROUGHT DOWN OUR 'COPTER AND CUT OFF OUR RADIO!
GYAAGH!

THEN THAT EXPRESSION FADES AS A MAMMOTH FIST BASHES OUT! ONLY THE INSTANT REFLEXES OF BRUCE (BATMAN) WAYNE SAVE HIM...
GYAAGH!
POW!

MOMENTS LATER, BRUCE IS RUNNING FOR HIS LIFE ALONG AN ISLAND TRAIL! BEHIND HIM COMES THE THUDDING FOOTBEATS OF THE BLOCKBUSTER..
GOT TO--GET TO THAT QUICKSAND...

A SPLASH OF SANDY WATERS! A THUMP OF HEAVY FEET! AND NOW IT IS BRUCE WAYNE HIMSELF WHO WILDLY THRASHES IN THE STEADY TUG OF THE DEADLY BOG...
I MUST DUPLICATE EVERY MOVE MARK MADE WHEN HE WAS IN THE QUICKSAND--TO HELP HIM REMEMBER OUR FIRST MEETING--THAT HE OWES HIS LIFE TO ME--AND WILL SPARE MINE!

THE COLOSSUS SWAYS! HIS EYES GLAZE OVER! HIS DAZED BRAIN STRUGGLES FOR THOUGHT, FOR MEMORY...
GYAH? GYAAGH?! GYAACH!!

SUDDENLY HIS HANDS HOLD OUT THE VERY SAME BRANCH WHICH BRUCE WAYNE USED TO RESCUE HIM!...
HE REMEMBERED! HE KNOWS--BRUCE WAYNE IS HIS FRIEND!

AND YET--I'M IN A QUANDARY! I CAN'T BECOME BATMAN AGAIN--OR BLOCKBUSTER WILL ATTACK ME! BUT IF I REMAIN AS BRUCE WAYNE--HIS BROTHER ROLAND WILL TUMBLE ON TO THE SECRET OF MY DOUBLE IDENTITY!
12

AT THIS MOMENT, ROBIN IS ON THE ATTACK! HE, TOO, REALIZES THE DILEMMA CONFRONTING BRUCE WAYNE--AS HIS FIST THUNDERS AGAINST THE JAW OF ROLAND DESMOND...
ZOK!
I MUST KAYO HIM--FAST!

THEN, AS BRUCE APPEARS IN THE DOORWAY, THE TEEN-AGE THUNDERBOLT IS STARTLED BY HIS COMMAND...
TAKE ROLAND TO HIS BOAT! AND HURRY! THE THREE OF US ARE GETTING OUT OF HERE!
B-BUT WHAT ABOUT THE BLOCKBUSTER? I GUESS HE'S YOUR "FRIEND" NOW--BUT WE CAME HERE TO CAPTURE HIM!

WHILE ROBIN LUGS ROLAND TO THE BOAT, BRUCE RETURNS TO THE CELLAR WHERE...
WHEN ROBIN GIVES IT SOME THOUGHT, HE'LL REALIZE THAT BLOCKBUSTER MUST STAY ON THE ISLAND UNTIL WE CAN RETURN, AND THAT ROLAND MUSTN'T SEE ME--AS BATMAN!

WHILE BLOCKBUSTER WANDERS AROUND THE ISLAND, BATMAN SNEAKS OFF TO THE WAITING BOAT...
YEAH, YOU CAUGHT ME! AND YOU'RE RIGHT ABOUT MARK! HE'S THE BLOCKBUSTER--BUT HE ONLY OBEYS ME! AND HE'LL GET YOU YET--BECAUSE I'LL NEVER TELL HIM NOT TO!
MARK WAS ALWAYS THE GENIUS OF THE FAMILY, BUT HE WAS A SCRAWNY KID! SO HE WORKED OUT A SERUM THAT WOULD AFFECT CERTAIN ENDOCRINE GLANDS TO MAKE HIM GROW BIG AND STRONG! BUT HE WAS OVER-ANXIOUS--HE NEVER BOTHERED TO TEST HIS DISCOVERY FIRST!
WHAT NATURE GAVE WITH ONE HAND, IT TOOK AWAY WITH THE OTHER! AN OVER-ACTIVE ANTERIOR LOBE OF THE PITUITARY GLAND MADE HIM SHOOT UP LIKE A GIANT--WITH TREMENDOUS STRENGTH! BUT SIMULTANEOUSLY, A FAULTY ENDOCRINE GLAND RETARDED HIS MENTAL DEVELOPMENT...
13

IN THE BATCAVE, AFTER ROLAND DESMOND HAS BEEN TURNED OVER TO THE AUTHORITIES...
I'LL BET I KNOW WHERE WE'RE GOING NOW--BACK TO THE ISLAND TO ROUND UP THE BLOCKBUSTER!
THAT WASN'T HARD TO FIGURE OUT! THE TRICK IS HOW TO DO IT!

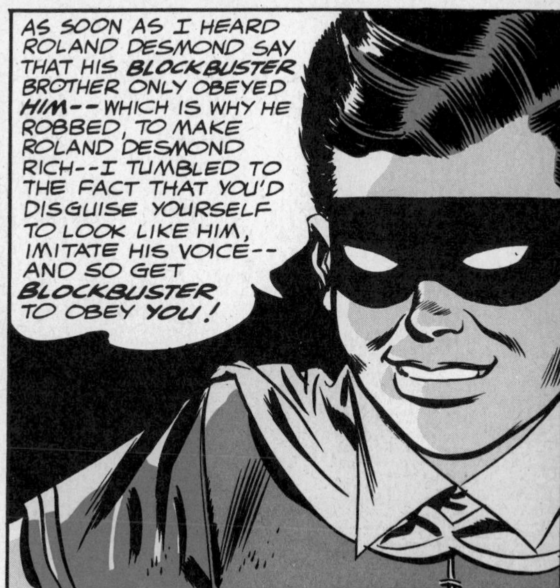
AS SOON AS I HEARD ROLAND DESMOND SAY THAT HIS BLOCKBUSTER BROTHER ONLY OBEYED HIM--WHICH IS WHY HE ROBBED, TO MAKE ROLAND DESMOND RICH--I TUMBLED TO THE FACT THAT YOU'D DISGUISE YOURSELF TO LOOK LIKE HIM, IMITATE HIS VOICE--AND SO GET BLOCKBUSTER TO OBEY YOU!

AND SO BRUCE WAYNE--DISGUISED AS ROLAND DES-MOND--RETURNS ONCE MORE TO BLOCKBUSTER ISLAND...
HIS FOOTPRINTS--LEADING INTO THE SEA! SOME ANIMAL INSTINCT MUST HAVE WARNED HIM IT WOULD BE DANGEROUS TO STAY HERE!
WHEREVER HE'S GONE, THE BLOCKBUSTER HAS CUT HIMSELF OFF FROM THE WORLD--DOOMED HIMSELF TO LIVE APART FROM HIS FELLOW HUMAN BEINGS! IN THIS MANNER, IRONICALLY ENOUGH, HE IS SERVING A SENTENCE OF SOLITARY CONFINEMENT FOR HIS CRIMES!
A FORTH-COMING ISSUE OF DETECTIVE COMICS WILL REVEAL THE SURPRISING AND THRILLING WIND-UP TO THE CASE OF THE BLOCKBUSTER BANDIT!
The End
14

JULY NO. 353
STARRING
12¢
DETECTIVE COMICS
BATMAN
THE BOY WONDER
Out of the pages of the FLASH storms the WEATHER WIZARD...
...to nleash a listering TTACK gainst ATMAN AND OBIN!
CRAAACK

For The VERY BEST
SUPERMAN
DC
NATIONAL COMICS
in COMICS READING

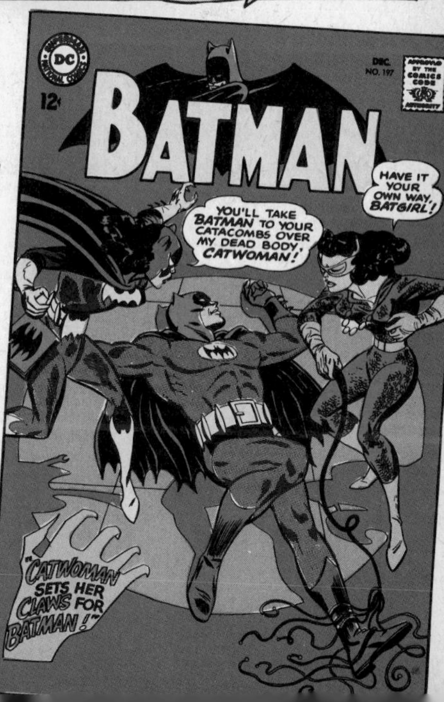
DEC. NO. 197
12¢
BATMAN
HAVE IT YOUR OWN WAY, BATGIRL!
YOU'LL TAKE BATMAN TO YOUR CATACOMBS OVER MY DEAD BODY, CATWOMAN!
"CATWOMAN SETS HER CLAWS FOR BATMAN!"

YOU ARE STANDING ON A WINDSWEPT CLIFF SOMEWHERE IN CENTRAL **SPAIN**, LOOKING THROUGH THE EYES OF A SOLITARY WATCHER... OBSERVING A SPECK OF AN AIR-CRAFT IN THE DISTANCE...

IT IS CLOSER, AND YOU HEAR ITS ENGINE SPUTTERING--YOU SEE THAT IT IS A FRENCH-MADE **NIEUPORT 17**--A MOTORIZED KITE THAT WAS USED IN THE WORLD'S FIRST AIR-COMBAT IN 1916...

SUDDENLY IT FLIPS OVER AND HURLS TOWARD THE ROCKS BELOW YOU...AND YOU KNOW, WITH CHILL CERTAINTY, THAT YOU ARE WITNESSING A **MURDER**--

THE GROUND SHUDDERS AS THE PLANE SPLINTERS AGAINST THE CLIFF'S SNOWY FACE...
LEAVE, NOW THE EYES OF THE DREAD--
BATMAN
AND FOLLOW THE CAPED AVENGER THROUGH A TANGLE OF CRIME AND INTO THE BLEAKEST CORNER OF A MAN'S SOUL...A MAN WHO MUST BECOME...
GHOST OF THE KILLER SKIES!

Coloring by Tatjana Wood

SWIFT AS HIS FLYING NAME-SAKE, THE BATMAN SWOOPS TO THE BROKEN CRAFT...

...AND HEEDLESS OF PERSONAL DANGER, PULLS FROM THE WRECK A BROKEN, LIFELESS THING THAT HAD BEEN A MAN--

INCREDIBLE--! I SAW THERE'D BEEN FOUL PLAY... BUT NOT THE KIND I THOUGHT!
THE PILOT'S BEEN... STRANGLED! HE MUST HAVE BEEN DEAD BEFORE THE CRASH...
STRANGLED IN MID-AIR... IN A SINGLE-SEATER PLANE...

UP THERE, MR. ANSON!
YOU THINK I DON'T KNOW, BOOB? SO WE CLIMB!
THE FILM CREW--! IT WON'T DO TO LET THEM SEE THE BATMAN HERE IN SPAIN... AT LEAST NOT JUST YET!

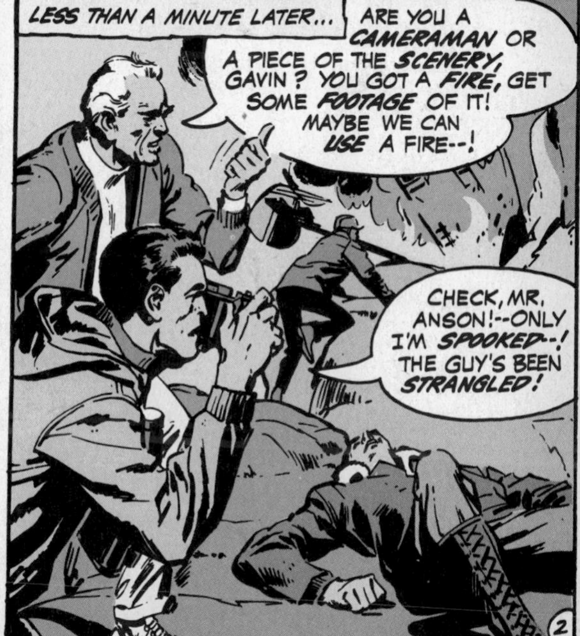
LESS THAN A MINUTE LATER...
ARE YOU A CAMERAMAN OR A PIECE OF THE SCENERY, GAVIN? YOU GOT A FIRE, GET SOME FOOTAGE OF IT! MAYBE WE CAN USE A FIRE--!
CHECK, MR. ANSON!--ONLY I'M SPOOKED--! THE GUY'S BEEN STRANGLED!
2

DID SOMEONE SAY *DEAD?*
LIKE A DOORNAIL, MR. WAYNE!
BRUCE, BABY, WHAT THIS PICTURE IS...IS *JINXED!* THAT PILOT WAS ONE OF THE *FEW* LEFT WHO CAN FLY THOSE *WORLD WAR I* CRATES!

NOTHIN' BUT *TROUBLE* SINCE WE STARTED--! WE COME TO *SPAIN* 'CAUSE WE CAN MAKE IT *CHEAP* HERE, AND WHAT HAPPENS?
PROPS ARE MISSING... FILM-STOCK CATCHES FIRE... SOUND TRACKS GET ACCIDENTALLY ERASED...AND NOW *THIS!*
I'M READY TO *GIVE UP!*
PERHAPS WE SHOULD RETURN TO THE SET AND CALL A *MEETING!*

SHORTLY, ON THE MAIN SET OF THE MOVIE-IN-PROGRESS, TENTATIVELY TITLED "*THE HAMMER OF HELL*"...

YOU WANT *REASONS* WHY WE SHOULD PACK OUR BAGS AND SCOOT, I'LL GIVE 'EM, BRUCE!

NOT ONLY HAVE WE HAD SETBACKS WHICH *ALREADY* PUT US A LOT OVER OUR BUDGET, BUT I HEAR *ANOTHER* OUTFIT IS MAKIN' A GERMAN WAR PIC! IT'LL *KILL* OUR MARKET!

...BUT THE OTHER COMPANY DOESN'T HAVE A DIRECTOR LIKE *YOU*, ANSON-- A THREE-TIME ACADEMY AWARD WINNER...

AND...THEY AREN'T TELLING THE STORY OF *BARON HANS VON HAMMER*... THE MOST ENIGMATIC FLYER WHO EVER LIVED!

3

I BELIEVE IN "THE HAMMER OF HELL"-- AND THE THINGS IT CAN SAY TO AUDIENCES ABOUT THE NATURE--AND FOLLY-- OF WAR!
THAT'S WHY I PUT MONEY INTO IT...AND WHY I'LL CONTINUE TO FINANCE IT!
PARDON ME, PLEASE!
COME ON IN, FRANZ!

I HAVE HEARD ABOUT... ACCIDENT, NO? MY FELLOW PILOT KILLED?
MORE THAN KILLED... STRANGLED!

BRUCIE, MEET HEINRICH FRANZ --OUR TECHNICAL EXPERT! HEINRICH, THIS IS BRUCE WAYNE--ONE OF THE BANK-ROLLERS OF THIS MESS WE'RE WORKING ON!
YOU'VE DONE A FINE JOB KEEPING OUR ANTIQUES IN THE AIR, HERR FRANZ!

I AM SORRY FOR TROUBLES, MEIN HERR! PERHAPS WE ARE NOT FATED TO COMPLETE ZIS FILM, EH?
VON HAMMER VAS A GREAT BELIEVER IN FATE... THE DESTINY OF THE KILLER SKIES, HE CALLED IT!
PERHAPS... VON HAMMER'S GHOST IS OUR ENEMY, EH?

UMMM, WELL... I HAVE SOME BUSINESS TO ATTEND TO!
MAYBE THE BATMAN CAN FIND THE ANSWER TO THAT...ON THE MOVIE SET!
4

AND SO, IN BRUCE WAYNE'S HOTEL ROOM...
I THOUGHT THERE WAS SOMETHING FAMILIAR ABOUT FRANZ... THE RESEMBLANCE IS UNCANNY!

HE LOOKS ALMOST EXACTLY LIKE THE MAN IN THIS OLD PHOTO... THE REAL BARON HANS VON HAMMER!
AS ALICE SAID, "CURIOUSER AND CURIOUSER..."

NIGHT, THICK AS A VELVET CLOAK, ENSHROUDS THE CARDBOARD AND CANVAS CASTLE, AND THE MAKE-SHIFT AIRFIELD WHICH LIES NEARBY...
HURRY... LIGHT THE FUSES AND RUN--
SI, SEÑOR HAMMER!
THEN YOU WILL GIVE US THE PESOS YOU PROMISED, SEÑOR?

SOMETHING MOVES IN THE DARKNESS!
USE YOUR FLASH, IDIOT!
MY ASKING YOU TO SURRENDER-- IN ENGLISH OR SPANISH-- WOULD DOUBTLESSLY FALL ON DEAF EARS-- SO...
5

AIEEE! EL HOMBRE MURCIELAGO!*
* TRANS: LITERALLY, THE BATMAN!

MARTINEZ... THE FUSE! DESTROY THE PLANES!
SI, SEÑOR HAMMER!
AND I SHALL PLACE MY BLADE IN THIS... THIS MONSTER!

UGGNH
HE MOVES SWIFTLY AS THE SHARK--!

NO... MORE SWIFTLY THAN A SHARK, THIS RELENTLESSLY TRAINED BODY, POWERED BY UNQUENCHABLE WILL... STRIKES--

...AND STRIKES AGAIN, WITH DEVASTATING PRECISION...

FOR THIS IS THE BATMAN... ONE WHO KNOWS A SPECIAL SORT OF GREATNESS!
6

AT LEAST TWO OF MY PLAYMATES WERE HIT HARD ENOUGH TO STAY COOLED--
--BUT THAT THIRD ONE MIGHT STILL BE UP TO ANOTHER ROUND--
--COULDN'T GIVE BOTH HIM AND THE EXPLOSIVE ATTENTION THEY NEEDED!
AS I THOUGHT... HE'S TRYING FOR A QUICK EXIT!

HE RUNS LIKE A REJECT FROM AN OLD FOLKS HOME--
UN MOMENTO, HOMBRECITO!

DEAR FRIEND, IF YOU VALUE YOUR FINE TEETH, YOU WILL SPEAK OF THE MAN WHO HIRED YOU TO DO EVIL THINGS! HIS NAME, OR--*
THIS I KNOW NOT, MAN OF THE BATS! ALWAYS, HE IS MASKED IN GOGGLES AND SCARF--EVEN AS YOU ARE MASKED!*
* TRANSLATED FROM THE SPANISH!

HE PAYS US MANY PESOS TO RUIN THE WORK OF THE AMERICAN FILM-MAKERS--
--BUT I SWEAR ON THE GRAVE OF MY MOTHER, I HAVE NOT HIS TRUE IDENTITY!
DID HE REQUIRE YOU TO TAMPER WITH THE AIRPLANE?
THIS WE DID NOT DO...

I CHOOSE TO BELIEVE YOU--FOR THE MOMENT! GO... SEEK A POLICEMAN AND SURRENDER YOURSELF AND YOUR COMPANIONS!
SHOULD YOU ATTEMPT TO FLEE, I WILL HUNT YOU THOUGH YOU HIDE AT THE END OF THE EARTH!

MOTIVE... OPPORTUNITY... AND ONE VERY BAD SLIP OF THE TONGUE--
IT'S GOT TO BE HIM MASQUERADING AS "VON HAMMER"!-
7
SO, THE BATMAN IS CERTAIN HE HAS SOLVED THE MYSTERY! ARE YOU AS CERTAIN...

I HAVE NO WAY OF KNOWING EXACTLY WHERE HE FLED--BUT IT IS PROBABLE HE RETURNED HERE... TO THE COMPANY'S LIVING AREA--
YES--; THERE'S A LIGHT IN HIS TRAILER--

AS I HOPED... HE'S STOPPED TO COLLECT HIS BLOOD MONEY--

FINISH COUNTING... I'M CURIOUS TO LEARN EXACTLY HOW MUCH THE RIVAL MOVIE OUTFIT PAID YOU TO SABOTAGE "THE HAMMER OF HELL"--
THE BATMAN?

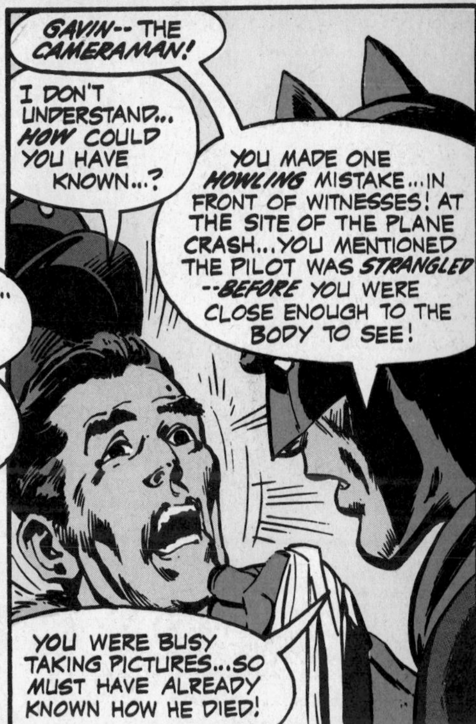
GAVIN-- THE CAMERAMAN!
I DON'T UNDERSTAND... HOW COULD YOU HAVE KNOWN...?
YOU MADE ONE HOWLING MISTAKE... IN FRONT OF WITNESSES! AT THE SITE OF THE PLANE CRASH... YOU MENTIONED THE PILOT WAS STRANGLED --BEFORE YOU WERE CLOSE ENOUGH TO THE BODY TO SEE!
YOU WERE BUSY TAKING PICTURES... SO MUST HAVE ALREADY KNOWN HOW HE DIED!

BUT... I WASN'T ANYWHERE NEAR THAT PLANE...
NO... BUT ONE OF THOSE SPANISH GOONS YOU HIRED COULD'VE HIDDEN IN THE COCKPIT OF THE NIEUPORT 17, PUT A GUN ON THE PILOT, FORCED HIM TO TAKE OFF-- THEN STRANGLED HIM IN THE AIR AND BAILED OUT BEHIND THE MOUNTAIN! YOU ALSO HAD A THUG SABOTAGE THE PLANE AS INSURANCE! I NOTICED THAT ONE OF THE NIEUPORT'S FLAPS WAS STUCK IN THE HALF-DOWN POSITION...
8

THAT'S WHY THE CRAFT ROLLED JUST BEFORE THE CRASH...
I DIDN'T DO ANYTHING TO THE PLANE...I HAVE NO REASON TO LIE--NOW!

SHOTS--!
BLAM
BLAM

:UH: HURT... BAD...NOT GONNA MAKE IT...

ANSON... HE'S BEEN HIT IN THE CHEST--!

EASY, FELLA... CAN YOU SPEAK? TELL ME WHAT HAPPENED?

G-GHOST OF VON HAMMER... BLASTED ME... WENT AWAY... TOWARD AIRFIELD-- ...AAH!

DEAD... CUT DOWN BY SOMEBODY WITH A BIG CALIBER PISTOL! YET... IT COULDN'T HAVE BEEN GAVIN! HE WAS WITH ME!

TOUGH ON MY DIRECTOR BUDDY... BUT A LUCKY BREAK FOR ME! I CAN MAKE MY GETAWAY WHILE THE BATMAN'S TENDING TO ANSON!

THERE'S ONLY ONE POSSIBLE ANSWER...TWO MEN SABOTAGING THE FILM--!

AND THE SECOND HAS TO HAVE KNOWLEGE OF VINTAGE AIRCRAFT--

UNLESS I BUY THE GHOST THEORY-- WHICH I DON'T!

POW
GAVIN'S EVEN WORSE AT THE 100-YARD DASH THAN HIS EMPLOYEE...
HE'LL STAY PUT UNTIL I GET AROUND TO COLLECTING HIM--
9

SOMEBODY'S STARTING AN ENGINE... SOUNDS LIKE THE OLD FOKKER TRIPLANE--
ANSON SAID HIS KILLER WENT TOWARD THE STRIP.. GOT TO RUN LIKE I'VE NEVER RUN BEFORE!

THE FOKKER'S READY TO GO! BUT I DON'T SEE A PILOT--!
PLEASE, TURN AROUND SLOWLY SO I MAY LOOK AT YOU!

YOU ARE THE AMERICAN LAWMAN-- THE BATMAN!
YES...I DON'T BELIEVE WE'VE MET!
YOU MAY CALL ME THE GHOST OF HANS VON HAMMER--!

I'D RATHER NOT--! I'D RATHER CALL YOU BY YOUR NAME!
HEINRICH FRANZ AT YOUR SERVICE!
YOU'RE THE ONE WHO'S BEEN SABOTAGING THE MOVIE!

GUILTY AS CHARGED! THIS... FILTHY AMERICAN FILM IS AN INSULT TO THE MEMORY OF GERMANY'S FINEST HERO--
--VON HAMMER WAS AS A GOD! THE AMERICANS SHOW HIM AS A SOFT, SNIVELING WEAKLING...
...PUTTING INTO HIS MOUTH WORDS OF COMPASSION ...OF MERCY... OF RESPECT FOR THE ENEMY!

BAH! HE WAS RUTHLESS, WAS MY ANCESTOR-- MAGNIFICENTLY RUTHLESS!
NOT THE WAY I READ HIS STORY! I SEE THE BARON AS A MAN CAUGHT BETWEEN HIS FEELING OF DUTY AND HIS OWN BEST INSTINCTS... A TRAGIC, TORMENTED AND SOMEWHAT PITIFUL SOLDIER--
10

AS YOU WILL! I AM NOT GOING TO ARGUE HISTORY! RATHER, I AM GOING TO KILL!
SHOOT AN UNARMED ENEMY? IS THAT HOW VON HAMMER WOULD'VE ACTED? OR WOULD HE HAVE WELCOMED A FAIR FIGHT?

YES, YES... YOU ARE RIGHT! A CONTEST OF SKILL--THAT IS THE WAY OF VON HAMMER!
THE NIEUPORT IS FUELED AND READY--
I SHALL MEET YOU-- IN THE KILLER SKY!

ONCE, A LONG TIME AGO, AN OLD STUNT-PILOT SHOWED ME HOW TO FLY THESE CRATES...
I HOPE I REMEMBER ALL HE SAID! BECAUSE IF I DON'T--
THAT MANIAC WILL GO FREE... AND I'LL BE DEAD!

AS THE FIRST LIGHT OF THE DAY BREAKS OVER THE CLOUDS EAST OF THE FIELD, TWO FRAIL THINGS-- BARELY MORE THAN STICKS COVERED WITH CANVAS-- CLIMB SLOWLY AWAY FROM THE EARTH...

...THEY TURN IN SCREAMING ARCS AND BEGIN A DEATH-DUEL--!
11

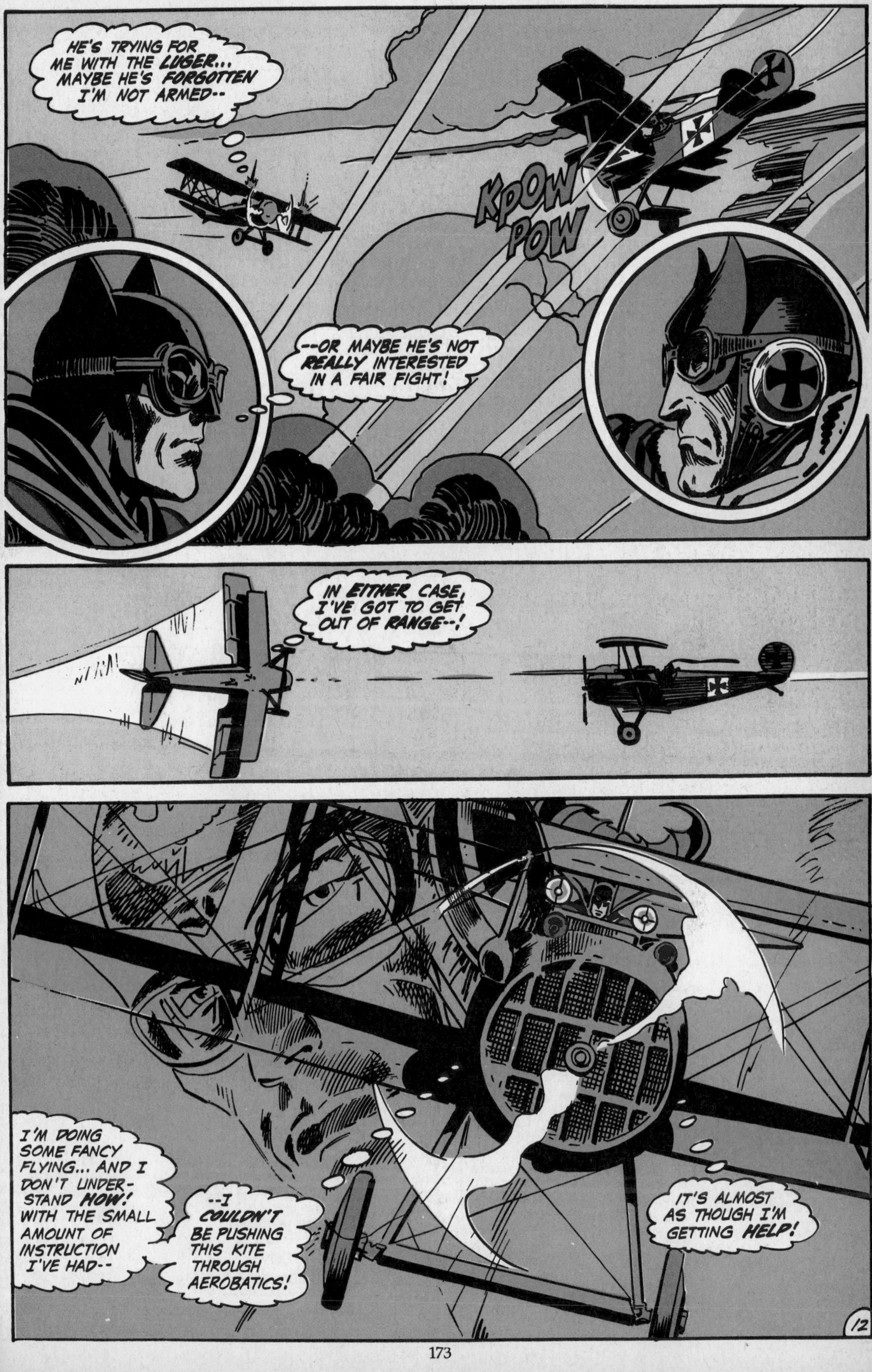

HE'S TRYING FOR ME WITH THE *LUGER*... MAYBE HE'S *FORGOTTEN* I'M NOT ARMED--

KPOW POW

--OR MAYBE HE'S NOT *REALLY* INTERESTED IN A FAIR FIGHT!

I'M DOING SOME FANCY FLYING... AND I DON'T UNDERSTAND *HOW*! WITH THE SMALL AMOUNT OF INSTRUCTION I'VE HAD--

--I *COULDN'T* BE PUSHING THIS KITE THROUGH AEROBATICS!

IT'S ALMOST AS THOUGH I'M GETTING *HELP*!

12

HE'S DIVING... STRAIGHT AT ME--! DOES HE PLAN TO CRASH--?

NO...HE'S USING HIS PROP TO CAUSE TURBULENCE... HOPING THAT I'LL BE BOUNCED AROUND UNTIL I MAKE A MISTAKE...
--A FATAL MISTAKE!

IF THE PLANE CAN TAKE IT--SO CAN I! FIRST JOB IS TO GET OUT OF HIS BACK-WASH...BY GOING UPSTAIRS--

...AND THEN I'LL TRY A STUNT OF MY OWN--HUH? THE ENGINE'S QUITTING...
ONE OF THE SLUGS MUST HAVE CUT THE FUEL-LINE...

I'M A SITTING DUCK... BUT HE CAN'T HAVE MORE THAN ONE BULLET LEFT--
GOT TO MAKE HIM WASTE IT...

--BY DOING THE TOTALLY... UNEXPECTED!
13

YOU ARE A COURAGEOUS FOE! IT IS ALMOST WITH RESPECT THAT I DESTROY YOU!

I SHALL SALUTE YOU AS YOU FALL-- AS THE GREAT BARON SALUTED VALIENT ENEMIES!

THUNK!

SURELY THIS IS NOT WORTHY OF THE BATMAN...EXPECTING ME TO BELIEVE I AM ATTACKED FROM BEHIND--
FRANZ... BEHIND YOU!
--WHILE WE RIDE THE WINDS HIGH ABOVE THE GROUND--!

NO... YOUR SCARF--!
G-EHHH!!
14

IT CAUGHT IN THE PROP.. YANKED HIM OUT OF THE COCKPIT--
YAAAARRRRGGHHH
I WONDER IF FRANZ WAS REALLY VON HAMMER'S DESCENDANT-- OR JUST ANOTHER VICTIM OF THE MOST TERRIBLE OF LOVES--
--THE LOVE OF WAR!
I GUESS I'LL NEVER KNOW...
End
A TRIBUTE TO THE GREAT
Joe Kubert & Robert Kanigher
FROM
DENNY O'NEIL (SCRIPTER) NEAL ADAMS DICK GIORDANO (ART) JULIUS SCHWARTZ (EDITOR)
15

IT IS HUSHED, HERE... THE ONLY SOUNDS ARE THE MUFFLED MURMURINGS OF SWAMP BEASTS AND THE GENTLE LAP OF WATER AGAINST GRASSY BANKS... AND THE ONLY SIGHTS THE GAUNT SHAPE OF AN ANCIENT VESSEL AND THE AWESOME FIGURE OF THE DREAD--
BATMAN
BUT BE NOT DECEIVED BY THE SERENITY! THERE IS DANGER IN THIS PEACEFUL PLACE, MYSTERY, AND THE SHADOW OF DEATH... FOR HERE LURKS...
"HALF AN EVIL"
STORY BY: DENNY O'NEIL
ART BY: NEAL ADAMS & DICK GIORDANO
EDITED BY: JULIE SCHWARTZ
1

Coloring by Gene D'Angelo

IT BEGINS AT THE ANNUAL GOTHAM CITY MERCHANTS' PARADE... A MERRY PROCESSION OF FLOATS THROUGH THE BUSINESS DISTRICT, CELEBRATING THE PRODUCTS AND SERVICES OF THE MIGHTY METROPOLIS...
JACK'S HOT DOGS
DOUBLY DELICOUS

NONE OF THE GRINNING SPECTATORS ARE AWARE THAT A CRIME IS BEING COMMITTED BEFORE THEIR EYES...
KEEP THAT SMILE IN PLACE, SISTER... AND THE MOUTH BUTTONED! THIS'LL ALL BE OVER IN A WINK...
...AND YOU JUST MIGHT LIVE THROUGH IT!
MUSTARD

THERE! IT'S CUT!
OKAY! LET'S SPLIT, BEFORE SOMEBODY TUMBLES TO WHAT'S HAPPENIN'!

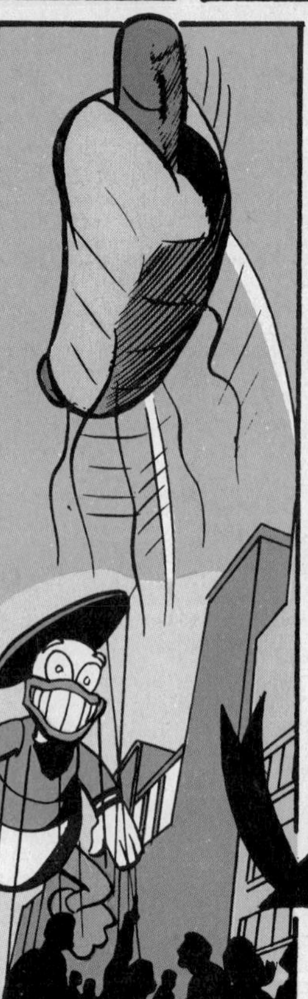

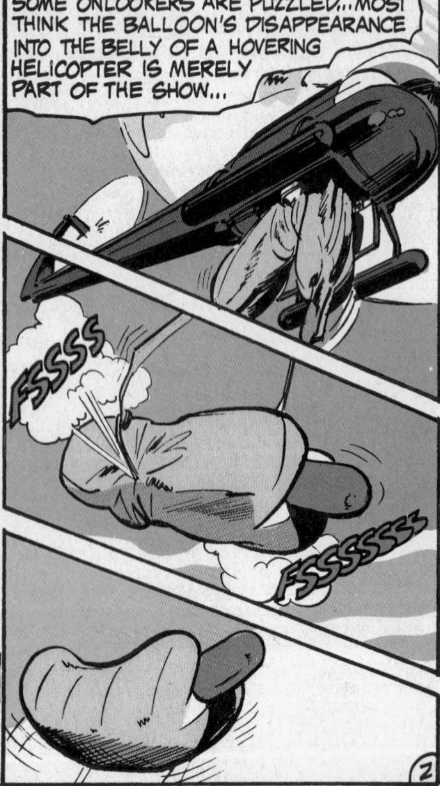
SOME ONLOOKERS ARE PUZZLED... MOST THINK THE BALLOON'S DISAPPEARANCE INTO THE BELLY OF A HOVERING HELICOPTER IS MERELY PART OF THE SHOW...
FSSSS
FSSSSSS
2

THE BATMAN?
DON'T GAB... BLAST HIM!
NOT LIKELY!
THE OTHER ONE--PITCHING A SMOKE-GRENADE! THEY'RE WELL-EQUIPPED FOR COMMON RIP-OFF ARTISTS!
SSSSSSSSS
UH!...
I'VE GOT TO COUNT THE GRENADE-TOSSER AS A DEAD LOSS... NO WAY OF FOLLOWING HIM THROUGH THE FUMES!
BUT THIS CHARMER ISN'T GOING ANYWHERE... EXCEPT INTO A ROOM OF FRESH AIR!
WAK
STAY BACK, BATMAN... OR SO HELP ME, I'LL SCRAMBLE YOUR BRAINS! I DON'T WANNA MIX WITH YOU--!
JUST...KEEP AWAY!
NO NEED TO GET UPSET!...
...YOU'RE NO DANGER--NONE AT ALL!
5

THE POLICE WILL ARRIVE SHORTLY! IF YOU'D CARE TO BE HEALTHY WHEN THEY TAKE YOU AWAY, YOU'LL ANSWER MY QUESTIONS!
S-SURE... ANYTHING!

WHOM ARE YOU WORKING FOR?
I DUNNO...I SWEAR I DON'T! HE'S A WEIRDO... FACE HIDDEN ALL 'A TIME...
...AN' HE KEEPS TOSSIN' SOME KINDA COIN!

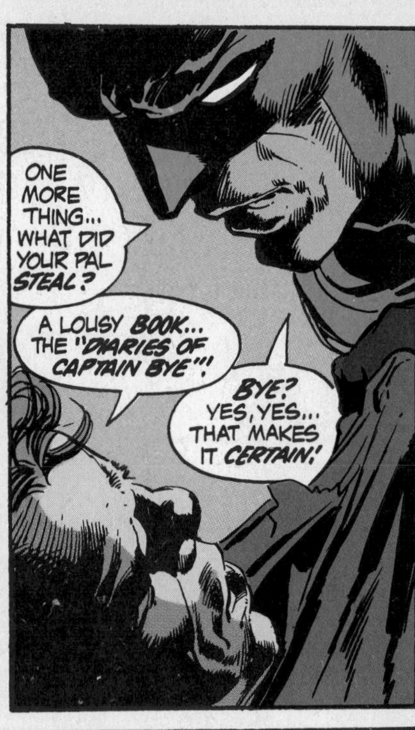
ONE MORE THING... WHAT DID YOUR PAL STEAL?
A LOUSY BOOK... THE "DIARIES OF CAPTAIN BYE"!
BYE? YES, YES... THAT MAKES IT CERTAIN!

YOUR BOSS IS ONE OF THE STRANGEST CRIMINAL GENIUSES WHO EVER LIVED! ONE OF THE MOST TRAGIC...AND ONE OF THE DEADLIEST!

AT THAT MOMENT, IN A SHACK NEAR THE GOTHAM CITY DOCKS...
YOU GOT IT?... THE DIARY?
YEAH... ONLY MY BUDDY WAS NABBED!

THAT'S VERY UNFORTUNATE... FOR HIM! IT'S NO CONCERN OF MINE, HOWEVER! THIS IS THE IMPORTANT THING...
...THIS WRITING! A CIPHER-EXPERT I MET IN PRISON TOLD ME THERE IS IN THESE PAGES THE CODED CLUE TO A FORTUNE!

AND I HAVE THE KEY TO THE CODE! BUT WILL I USE IT? WILL I ACTUALLY COMMIT THE CRIME?
THAT IS FOR THE COIN TO DECIDE!

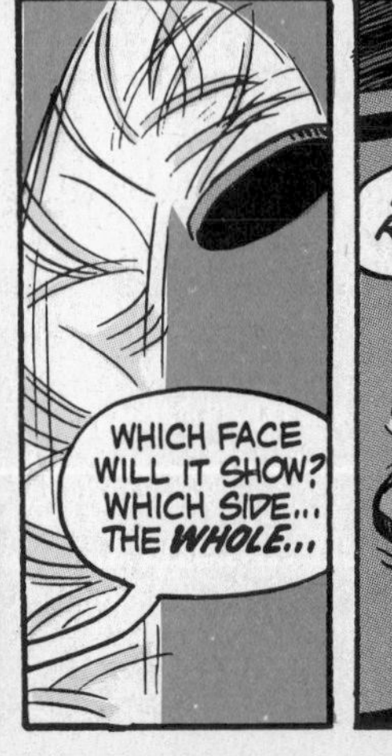
WHICH FACE WILL IT SHOW? WHICH SIDE... THE WHOLE...

...OR THE RUINED?
6

THE COIN HAS DECIDED! THE EVIL PART OF MY NATURE WINS... AND SO TWO-FACE MUST STRIKE!
AS THE BELLS OF GOTHAM CITY TOLL MIDNIGHT, WEALTHY SOCIALITE BRUCE WAYNE STANDS ON THE BALCONY OF HIS PENTHOUSE, CONFERRING WITH HIS BUTLER, ALFRED...
A KNOTTY PROBLEM, MASTER BRUCE?
WORSE, ALFRED! I SUSPECTED THAT OUR OLD ENEMY TWO-FACE WAS BEHIND THE BALLOON THEFT...
...HE COULDN'T RESIST THE SLOGAN ON THE FLOAT--"DOUBLY DELICIOUS!" OR THE NAME "JANUS".. THE TWO-FACED ROMAN GOD!
ARE YOU SURE, SIR? ISN'T TWO-FACE STILL IN JAIL?
HE ESCAPED.. SEVERAL MONTHS AGO! HOW COULD ANY JAIL HOPE TO HOLD A MAN SO CLEVER AND DEVIOUS AS HARVEY?
TSSSSS
"REMEMBER, ALFRED, HOW TWO-FACE CAME TO BE? HOW MANY YEARS AGO WAS IT WHEN THAT TWO-BIT GANSTER HURTLED A VIAL OF ACID INTO THE FACE OF GOTHAM'S MOST BRILLIANT DISTRICT ATTORNEY, HARVEY DENT..."
7

"...WHAT A MAD AND DIABOLICAL CHASE HE LED *ROBIN* AND *ME* WHEN HIS HALF-RUINED FACE TWISTED HIS MIND TOWARD CRIME..."

"IT WAS ONLY THANKS TO MODERN METHODS OF PLASTIC SURGERY THAT THE PERSONALITY OF HARVEY DENT WAS BROUGHT BACK FROM THE EDGE OF MADNESS..."

"ONCE AGAIN HE RE-ENTERED LAWFUL SOCIETY AND SPENT HIS ENERGIES ON THE SIDE OF JUSTICE...UNTIL ONE UNHOLY DAY HARVEY ATTEMPTED TO STOP A ROBBERY..."
ALL RIGHT, YOU TWO! STAND WHERE YOU ARE--!

"SO INTENT WAS HE ON CAPTURING THE THIEVES, HE FAILED TO SPOT THE SPUTTERING FUSE THEY HAD SET..."

BLAM

"IT WASN'T UNTIL HE STAGGERED HOME AND LOOKED INTO A MIRROR THAT THE FULL EXTENT OF HIS TRAGEDY TOOK HOLD OF HIS MIND ONCE AGAIN..."
THE PLASTIC SURGERY! IT'S *ALL* BEEN UNDONE! IT CAN NEVER BE REPAIRED THIS TIME! I'M DOOMED TO REMAIN *TWO-FACE... FOREVER...*
TWO-FACE... FOREVER!

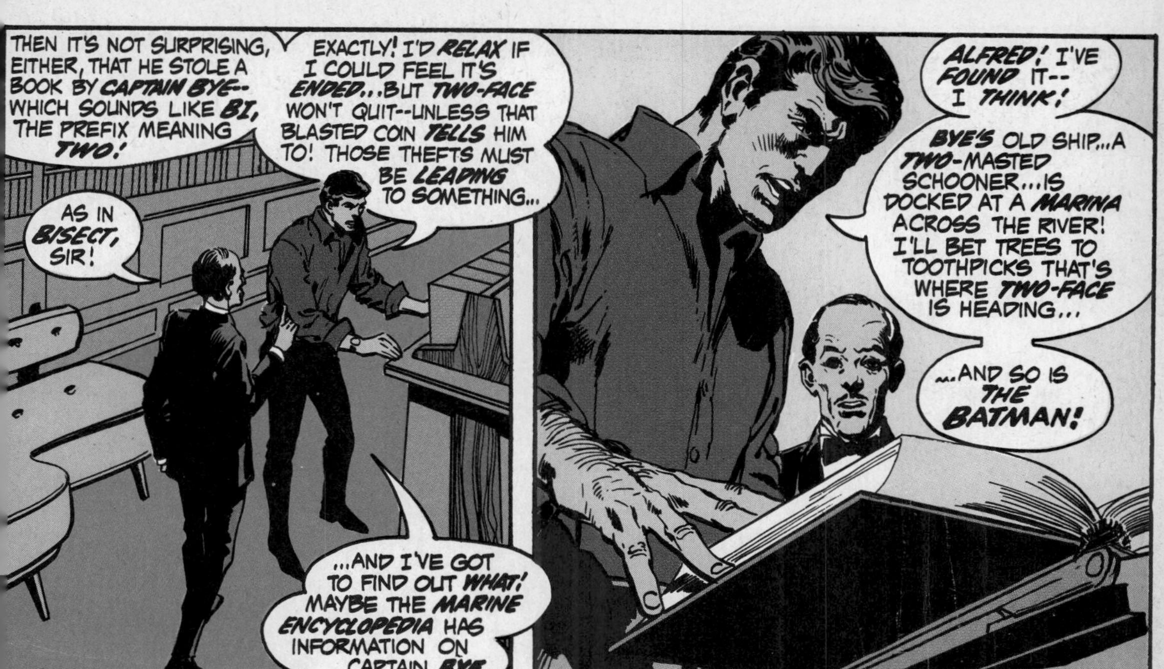

THEN IT'S NOT SURPRISING, EITHER, THAT HE STOLE A BOOK BY CAPTAIN BYE-- WHICH SOUNDS LIKE BI, THE PREFIX MEANING TWO!
EXACTLY! I'D RELAX IF I COULD FEEL IT'S ENDED... BUT TWO-FACE WON'T QUIT--UNLESS THAT BLASTED COIN TELLS HIM TO! THOSE THEFTS MUST BE LEADING TO SOMETHING...
AS IN BISECT, SIR!
...AND I'VE GOT TO FIND OUT WHAT! MAYBE THE MARINE ENCYCLOPEDIA HAS INFORMATION ON CAPTAIN BYE...
ALFRED! I'VE FOUND IT-- I THINK!
BYE'S OLD SHIP...A TWO-MASTED SCHOONER...IS DOCKED AT A MARINA ACROSS THE RIVER! I'LL BET TREES TO TOOTHPICKS THAT'S WHERE TWO-FACE IS HEADING...
...AND SO IS THE BATMAN!

A SLEEK ROADSTER CUTS THROUGH THE DARKNESS, ACROSS A MAMMOTH BRIDGE...

...AND HURTLES ONTO A PIER FRONTING ONE OF GOTHAM'S TWIN RIVERS!

MY GUESS WAS GOOD! THE OLD SCHOONER'S BEEN CUT LOOSE... IT'S DRIFTING INTO THE CURRENT!

...AND THOSE THUGS MUST BE TWO-FACE'S NEW PLAYMATES!

9

THAT CAR AIN'T ONE OF OURS!
PROB'LY THE HEAT! GIVE IT TO 'EM!

HE CAN'T SEE... HE'S FIRING AT WHERE HE FIGURES I AM! THE AUTOMATIC PILOT-TYPE CONTROLS IN THAT MODEL BAT-MOBILE ARE PRECISION PERFECT!

I'VE BEEN IN THIS SITUATION TOO OFTEN TO DO THE OBVIOUS!
AYIEEEE

BRAKATAK
NUMBER TWO'S GETTING INTO THE ACT! THIS CALLS FOR A SUBTERRANEAN ATTACK!
CHOK

10

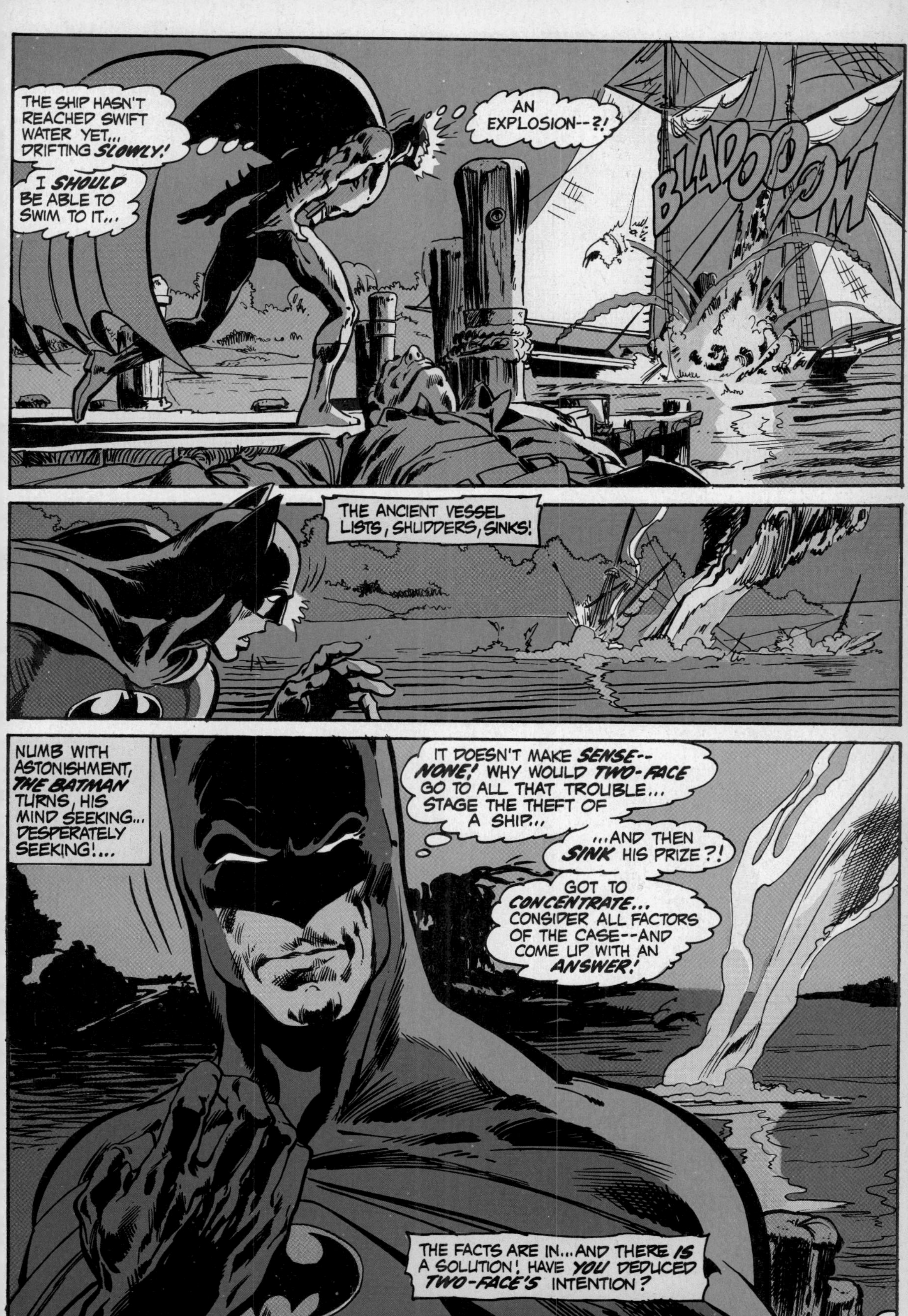
THE SHIP HASN'T REACHED SWIFT WATER YET... DRIFTING SLOWLY!
I SHOULD BE ABLE TO SWIM TO IT...
AN EXPLOSION--?!
BLADOOOOM
THE ANCIENT VESSEL LISTS, SHUDDERS, SINKS!
NUMB WITH ASTONISHMENT, THE BATMAN TURNS, HIS MIND SEEKING... DESPERATELY SEEKING!...
IT DOESN'T MAKE SENSE-- NONE! WHY WOULD TWO-FACE GO TO ALL THAT TROUBLE... STAGE THE THEFT OF A SHIP...
...AND THEN SINK HIS PRIZE?!
GOT TO CONCENTRATE... CONSIDER ALL FACTORS OF THE CASE--AND COME UP WITH AN ANSWER!
THE FACTS ARE IN... AND THERE IS A SOLUTION! HAVE YOU DEDUCED TWO-FACE'S INTENTION?
11

MEET NOW, BILLY THE TRAMP... HAVING AN EARLY MORNING NAP IN A BACKWATER BAY SOUTH OF GOTHAM. HE'S HAD A HARD NIGHT, BILLY HAS--

BUT NOT NEARLY AS HARD AS HIS MORNING WILL BE! FOR THE TOP-MAST OF A SHIP POKES ABOVE THE BAY NEAR HIS HEAD...

...AND...

NEARBY, THE BATMAN LURKS...
RIGHT ON TIME! THE TIDE-CHARTS SHOWED THAT IF A FLOATING OBJECT WERE SUNK NEAR THE PIER WHERE I COOLED TWO-FACE'S HENCHMEN...
...BUT NOT ENTIRELY SUNK--IT WOULD DRIFT HERE!

TWO-FACE HASN'T ARRIVED YET! I'LL BE WAITING FOR HIM WHEN HE DOES!
AND ON HIS WAY TO JAIL, I'LL EXPLAIN THAT I DEDUCED WHY HE NEEDED A BIG BALLOON--
--TO PUT IN THE HOLD OF THIS TUB, RIGGED TO INFLATE AFTER A PROPER INTERVAL!
--TO RAISE IT IN A QUIET COVE WHERE HE CAN WORK UNDISTURBED!
12

EH? WHO THE DEUCE IS THAT IN THE RIGGING? LOOKS LIKE A HOBO! HOW IN THE NAME OF ALL THAT'S HOLY DID HE GET THERE?

KAK
I'LL HAUL HIM DOWN...
I DON'T WANT ANY DISTRACTIONS WHEN THE FIREWORKS BEGIN... UNNNGH!

QUICKLY, THE WET-SUITED CRIMINAL PRODUCES A LENGTH OF WIRE-ROPE, AND BEGINS LASHING THE CAPED CRUSADER TO A MAST...

I WAS SURE THE BATMAN WOULD TAKE A HAND! SO I HID IN THE SHIP'S HOLD, BREATHING WITH AN OXYGEN MASK...

GROGGY... BUT... NOT OUT... GOT TO EXPAND MY MUSCLES ...PREVENT HIM TYING LINE TIGHTLY--

DON'T PRETEND YOU'RE NOT AWAKE, OLD FOE! I WANT YOU TO SEE-- HOW YOU'LL DIE! UGLY, YOU'LL DIE... UGLY AS THE ACCIDENT THAT MADE ME A FREAK!

I PUT A HOT EMBER TO THE BALLOON WHICH HELD THIS SCOW AFLOAT ONCE--AND FOR THE SECOND TIME...
PAWOO

...AND WHILE THE GAS ESCAPES, I SMASH AWAY THIS MOLDING...
13

BEHOLD, A FORTUNE IN GOLD COMES SPILLING,,, GOLD DOUBLOONS, JUST AS CAPTAIN BYE'S DIARY PROMISED!

HAVING FILLED HIS SACK, TWO-FACE WHIRLS TO A LIFEBOAT, AND,,,
WITHIN MOMENTS, THIS SCOW WILL HAVE SUNK...TAKING A BATMAN WITH IT!
NOT ONLY ME! LOOK-- UP IN THE RIGGING!

ARE YOU GOING TO LET HIM DROWN-- AN INNOCENT, OLD MAN?
HIS MISFORTUNE, BATMAN...AND NO CONCERN OF MINE!

YOU'VE ALWAYS PRIDED YOURSELF ON BEING AS GOOD AS YOU ARE EVIL! WAS YOUR PRIDE A MERE POSE?
QUIET, BATMAN! MY DECISION IS FINAL!

ONCE MORE CAPTAIN BYE'S SCHOONER SETTLES, WATER CREEPING RAPIDLY UP ITS HULL--! TWO-FACE TRIES TO IGNORE IT...

...BUT CAN'T! RELUCTANTLY, HE REMOVES THE DOUBLE-HEADED COIN FROM HIS POUCH, FLIPS IT... AND...
14

BATMAN-- YOU'RE FREE?!
I MIGHT HAVE KNOWN--
IT WASN'T DIFFICULT! I EXPANDED MY MUSCLES WHILE YOU WERE ROPING ME! BY CONTRACTING THEM, I GOT ENOUGH SLACK TO SLIP OUT OF THE KNOTS!
DO YOU WANT TO SURREN-DER?

NEVER! THE COIN DICTATED I SAVE THE OLD MAN... YOU REMAIN MY ENEMY!

AND THUS IT ENDS...PERHAPS!

Coloring by Tatjana Wood

DAWN... AND A DESERT IN NEW MEXICO IS SHAKEN BY...
... A MASSIVE UNDERGROUND NUCLEAR TEST-
BLAST!
A.E.C. STA-72A.7
SHORTLY, FAR TO THE WEST... STILL SHUDDERING FROM THE FIRST SHOCK-WAVES...
... MIGHTY HOOVER DAM IS STRUCK AGAIN... BY SWARMS OF PANIC-BLINDED BATS!
?!
THEY DIDN'T EVEN "SEE" IT!--AS IF THEIR "SONAR-GUIDANCE SYSTEMS" WERE... KNOCKED OUT!
LATE THAT NIGHT...
... A SILENT LOOMING HORROR STRIKES AT VEGAS!
CASA
DRIVE-IN
EVEN LATER, AS BIG SPENDERS OF THE "STRIP'S" ROUND-THE-CLOCK GAMBLING CASINOS CALL IT A NIGHT...
DON'T LOOK LIKE SLEEP, THELMA-- NOT THE WAY HE'S SPRAWLED!
COLLAR RIPPED OPEN-- AND... LOOK!
WELL, I NEVER...! SOME FOLKS DON'T CARE WHERE THEY SLEEP IT OFF...
AGH!
THOSE UGLY MARKS IN HIS NECK-- THAT DEAD-WHITE SKIN!
J-JUST LIKE-- LIKE...
DON'T DARE SAY IT, SAM!
THAT SORT OF STUFF ONLY HAPPENS IN -- "DRACULA" MOVIES!
2

WITHIN THE HOUR, ALL OF VEGAS IS ABUZZ...
YOU SURE, QUINT?
NO OTHER POSSIBILITY?
NONE, CHET! I DON'T BELIEVE IN THESE "THINGS," EITHER, BUT...
...ESPECIALLY THE USUALLY DEAD-SILENT POLICE-MORGUE!
...WITH EYEWITNESS REPORTS FLOODING IN OF A KING-SIZE "VAMPIRE-BAT" FLYING OFF-- HOW ELSE DO YOU EXPLAIN IT?

WILD THEORIES QUICKLY FILL THE AIR-WAVES...
...THE LATEST GUESSES NOW LINK UP THREE SEEMINGLY "ISOLATED" EVENTS!
ONE: THE NUCLEAR BLAST!
TWO: IT'S FAR-FLUNG SHOCK-WAVES WHICH SPLIT OPEN AN UNDISCOVERED NETWORK OF CAVES...

WHILE IN GOTHAM, HOME OF ANOTHER "CREATURE OF THE NIGHT"... ...THE BATMAN...
VAMPIRES? IN NEVADA--SO FAR NORTH OF THEIR NATURAL HABITAT?
ALFRED-- I WONDER IF KIRK LANGSTROM HAS HEARD OF THIS YET...?
...RELEASING SWARMS OF PANICKED VAMPIRE-BATS TO SMASH INTO HOOVER DAM!
AND THREE: HERE IN VEGAS...

SHOULD BE RIGHT DOWN HIS ALLEY, SIR...
...AS CURATOR OF NOCTURNAL MAMMALS AT GOTHAM NATURAL HISTORY MUSEUM!
...THE SMART MONEY HAS IT THAT THE "VEGAS RAIDER" IS A NUCLEAR-CREATED...
...MONSTER-MUTANT VAMPIRE-BAT!

THE "SMART MONEY" HAS BEEN SEEING TOO MANY "HORROR MOVIES"!
A "MUTANT" BAT-- HUH!
MIGHT I SUGGEST, MASTER BRUCE-- THAT LANGSTROM HIMSELF WAS ONCE A "MUTANT" BAT?
IN SPECIFIC-- A MAN-BAT!

TRUE-- BUT HE BROUGHT THAT ON HIMSELF...AND HIS WIFE... BY RECKLESS EXPERIMENTS!
...TO SHED SCIENTIFIC LIGHT ON THESE THEORIES...
...WE TAKE YOU TO THE CAVE-SITE WHERE VISITING BAT-SPECIALIST, PROFESSOR KIRK LANGSTROM...
LANGSTROM-- DOWN THERE?
3

YOU WERE NEAR HERE AT THE TIME, PROFESSOR--ON AN EXPLORATORY FIELD-TRIP...
WHAT IS YOUR OPINION OF THESE "MUTANT" THEORIES?
SHEER NONSENSE!
FACT: THE NUCLEAR SHOCK-WAVES DID UNCOVER THESE POSSIBLY "PREHISTORIC" CAVES...
LVC

... REVEALING A SURVIVING SPECIES OF BAT--THE "DIPHYLLA VAMPYRUS"--NEVER SEEN THIS FAR NORTH!
A TROPIC-ZONE VAMPIRE PREYING MAINLY ON ANIMALS, AND RARELY--ON MEN!

THEN, IN YOUR CONSIDERED VIEW, SIR--THE "CREATURE" OVER VEGAS WAS...
...A FIGMENT OF MASS-HYSTERIA!
A MIND-TRIP... DIG?
YOU MEAN...?
...YOUR "MUTANT" WAS A TINY STRAGGLER FROM THIS CAVE--CRAZED BY HUNGER--WHO HAPPENED UPON A LONE MAN!

THANK YOU, PROFESSOR--AND YOUR LOVELY WIFE, FRANCINE!
HE'S COVERING, ALFRED--I'D SWEAR IT!

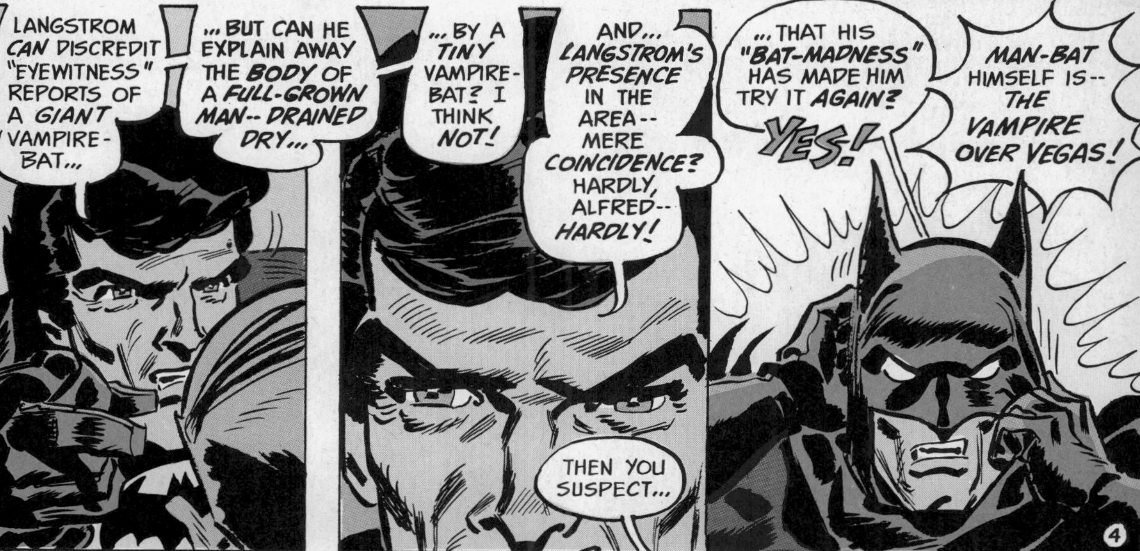
LANGSTROM CAN DISCREDIT "EYEWITNESS" REPORTS OF A GIANT VAMPIRE-BAT...
...BUT CAN HE EXPLAIN AWAY THE BODY OF A FULL-GROWN MAN--DRAINED DRY...
...BY A TINY VAMPIRE-BAT? I THINK NOT!
AND... LANGSTROM'S PRESENCE IN THE AREA--MERE COINCIDENCE? HARDLY, ALFRED--HARDLY!
THEN YOU SUSPECT...
...THAT HIS "BAT-MADNESS" HAS MADE HIM TRY IT AGAIN?
YES!
MAN-BAT HIMSELF IS--THE VAMPIRE OVER VEGAS!
4

THE FOLLOWING NIGHT, HIGH ABOVE THE VEGAS "STRIP"...

WHO ELSE CAN IT BE? YET... I MUST BE SURE BEFORE I "NAB" LANGSTROM!

AND IF IT IS HIM... IS HE FULLY RESPONSIBLE FOR HIS ACTIONS?

HAD A DEVIL OF A TIME PERSUADING THE POLICE HERE NOT TO SHOOT ON SIGHT... GIVING ME FIRST CRACK AT THE "VAMPIRE"!

ACES

JUST BELOW HIS ROOFTOP STAKEOUT... IN THE "ACES-HI" SKYTOP CABARET...

GEE, JUST A DAY BEFORE THEIR MARRIAGE-- AND THAT "THING" HAS TO KILL HER BOY FRIEND!

YOU OKAY, DEBBIE...?

I-I'LL MAKE IT, TAMMY-- LEAST TILL DANCE-BREAK!

POOR DEBBIE -- A REAL TROUPER! HER HEART BREAKING-- BUT YOU'D NEVER KNOW IT!

BUT THEN I HIT THE ROOF FOR FRESH AIR! I'M STIFLING IN HERE...

LATER...
SURE YOU DON'T WANT COMPANY, DEBBIE? I MEAN, YOU THINK IT'S WISE...
WHAT'S "WISE" NOW, TAMMY...? I CAN'T BE HURT ANYMORE THAN I'VE BEEN!
THANKS, HONEY-- BUT I'D RATHER BE ALONE!

ALONE... JUST ME AND THE BATMAN!
THE LEAST I CAN DO TO AVENGE JIM'S DEATH...
...IS AGREEING TO ACT AS BAIT!
5

BRAVE KID! SHE DIDN'T HAVE TO BUY MY SCHEME...
...BUT I HAD TO HAVE A LIVE TARGET TO LURE MAN-BAT WITHIN STRIKING DISTANCE!
HERE HE COMES NOW!
I'M COUNTING ON THIS NEON-GLARE TO BLIND HIM TO MY PRESENCE...
...FORCE HIM TO FOCUS ON DEBBIE!
SKEEEK..!
EEEEEE!
GOTTA EVEN THE ODDS...!
...BRING HIM DOWN!
THE EQUALIZER... A BATARANG FOR THE MAN-BAT!
KRANNGG
6

GET BELOW, DEBBIE! THAT THING IS STILL DANGEROUS...
--MORE THAN THE BATMAN REALIZES! AND ONCE ALONE...
LANGSTROM! WHAT MAD CRAVINGS MADE YOU GO THIS FAR?
MAN-BAT WAS EVIL ENOUGH! BUT NOW... A VAMPIRE-BAT?

AAGHH

SKREEGK
DON'T FIGURE...! MY BATARANG HEAD-SHOT SHOULD'VE PUT HIM OUT FOR HOURS!

WHAT NEW POWERS DOES THIS FIEND HAVE...?

IT'S BREAK... NOW OR NEVER!
SKRAK!
7

RISING TO ATTACK... FROM THE AIR?!

JUST HOPE MY WEIGHT CAN COUNTERACT HIS WINGS!

PULLING HIM BACK DOWN-BUT...
...WHAT'S HE DOING NOW?

USING THE LADDER AS LEVERAGE...
...TO SHAKE ME LOOSE!

SLIPPING...
GRIP SLIPPING...
8

CRASHING DOWNWARD, THE BATMAN CLUTCHES DESPERATELY AT COLD-LIGHT NEON-TUBES...
...SNAPPING THEM OFF LIKE — FRAGILE ICICLES!...

BUT A RAVENING MAN-BAT INTENT ONLY ON SATISFYING HIS VAMPIRE-TASTES...
...FOLLOWS HIS PREY DOWN IN A CRASH-DIVE!...

...GIVING THE MASKED MAN-HUNTER ONE LAST GRAB AT LIFE...!
ONLY HOPE... HIS BATWINGS BREAK OUR FALL!

KARASH!
9

STARK HORROR...
...IN THE GAMBLING CASINO!...
...AS FLAILING BATWINGS CUSHION THE MASSIVE IMPACT!
WHOMP!

MASS-PANIC SCATTERS THE PATRONS... BLOCKING THE BATMAN!
GOTTA GRAB HIM-- 'FORE HE...

BUT A FAST-REACTING "BOUNCER" HAS THE SAME IDEA!...
I'LL GIT 'IM, BATMAN...!

MAN-BAT IS FASTER THAN BOTH!
?!

CRIPES! DIDN'T MEAN TO...
KNOW YOU DIDN'T...!
LANGSTROM! CAN'T LOSE HIM NOW! MUSTN'T...
10

INSTANTS LATER...
HAD EVERY CONTINGENCY COVERED... EVEN MAN-BAT'S ESCAPE!
... WITH A BORROWED POLICE-COPTER TO MATCH HIS WINGS!
POLICE

LANGSTROM'S GOT A BIG LEAD, BUT I'VE GOT TO RUN HIM TO EARTH... BEFORE HE RAVAGES THE COUNTRYSIDE!
HE'S BLOOD-HUNGRY NOW... FRUSTRATED... AT HIS MOST DANGEROUS!

MANY FEVERED MILES LATER...
HE'S STYMIED ME -- CAN'T FOLLOW HIM INTO THAT NARROW CRACK WITH THIS!

RISING ABOVE THE COLORADO RIVER GORGE TO FIND A LANDING SPOT...
LANGSTROM'S BASE CAMP!
PITCHED RIGHT BY THE FISSURE LEADING DOWN TO THE VAMPIRE-BAT CAVES... WHERE MAN-BAT MUST BE HIDING NOW!

THEN, SPURRED BY A SUDDEN HORRIFYING THOUGHT...
WHAT'S THIS?...
COULD HE BE FAR GONE ENOUGH NOW TO MAKE A TRY FOR HIS OWN WIFE, FRANCIE? MUST WAKE HER BEFORE...

... CLINGING TO MY GLOVE...
... A BANDAID!?
NOW WHERE DID THAT COME FROM ...?
11

MMM... ONLY ONE PLACE I COULD'VE PICKED THIS UP!
--DURING MY BATTLE WITH MAN-BAT! BUT... WAS IT HIM?
WAIT!
I RECALL WHEN I FIRST SAW THIS... DURING THAT TV INTERVIEW WITH THE LANGSTROMS!*
* REMEMBER, READER? Ed.

GOOD G--! IF I REMEMBER RIGHTLY...
...KIRK LANGSTROM CAN'T POSSIBLY BE THE VAMPIRE OF VEGAS!

THIS PROVES IT!
B-BATMAN...?! WHAT'RE YOU DOING HERE...?

TRYING TO SAVE YOUR WIFE'S LIFE!
FRANCIE? WHY, SHE'S PERFECTLY SAFE...
...HERE IN BED...
?!

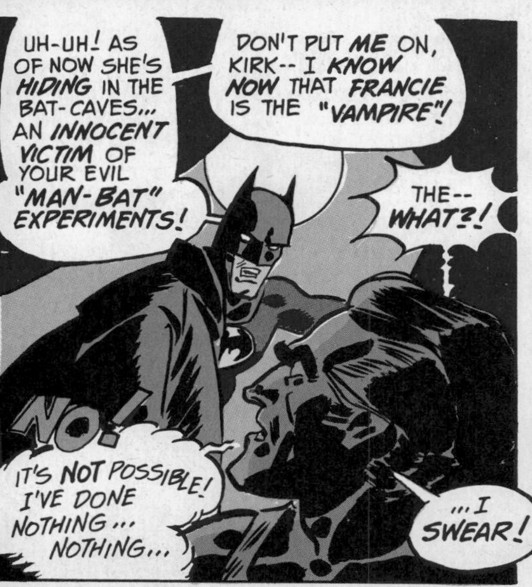
UH-UH! AS OF NOW SHE'S HIDING IN THE BAT-CAVES... AN INNOCENT VICTIM OF YOUR EVIL "MAN-BAT" EXPERIMENTS!
DON'T PUT ME ON, KIRK-- I KNOW NOW THAT FRANCIE IS THE "VAMPIRE"!
THE-- WHAT?!
NO!
IT'S NOT POSSIBLE! I'VE DONE NOTHING... NOTHING...
...I SWEAR!

THEN EXPLAIN THIS BANDAID TORN OFF YOUR WIFE'S WRISTS-- WHEN SHE TRIED TO KILL ME OVER VEGAS TONIGHT!
OH, LORD-- FRAN WAS WEARING A BANDAID!
EVER SINCE THAT SCRATCH SHE GOT-- HANDLING OUR FIRST DEAD SPECIMENS OF THE "HOOVER-DAM" BATS!
UGH!
THOSE UGLY VAMPIRE FANGS--COULD THEY HAVE...?
12

WHAT COUNTS NOW IS FINDING FRANCIE-- SOMEWHERE IN THESE UNEXPLORED CAVES!
I'LL BRING "SPELUNKING"* GEAR, BATMAN-- WE'LL NEED IT!
*CAVE-EXPLORATION GEAR.

WHILE SEEKING AN EXIT DEEP INSIDE THE DARK CAVERNS... A BEWILDERED HUMAN "VAMPIRE" FINDS HERSELF COMPLETELY LOST!...
SKREEK
EEEK
EEK
SKREEEK

FINALLY... EXHAUSTED... THE FORLORN "CREATURE" COLLAPSES INTO A DEEP SLEEP!...

...UNAWARE THAT OUTSIDE DAWN IS BREAKING...

...SIGNALLING AN END TO THE EVIL SPELL THE FULL MOON HAS OVER HER!...

...OBLIVIOUS EVEN TO THE FRANTIC, ECHOING CALLS OF TIRELESS RESCUERS...
FRAN
FRANCIEEEEE
FRANCIEEEE
...WHICH LAST TILL SUNDOWN...
UH-H, BATMAN-- WILL WE EVER FIND HER? WILL I EVER SEE FRAN AGAIN...?
NOT UNLESS WE KEEP GOING, KIRK! I'VE MARKED OUR WAY TO THIS FORK...
...BUT HERE WE SPLIT! NO OTHER CHOICE...
13

WHILE IN THE TIMELESS DARKNESS... A DAZED, VERY HUMAN GIRL NOW... AWAKENS TO A TERRIFYING SITUATION!
WH-WHERE AM I...?
S-SO COLD... D-DAMP...
...LIKE AN ICY TOMB!

OH-H, KIRK-- KIRK! HELP MEEEE... PLEASE?
HELP
PLEASE
KIRK
KIRK
KIRK
FRAN?
KIRK

HERE!
...UP HERE-- KIRK, DEAREST!
DARLING... WHERE ARE YOU?
HANG ON, LOVE! I'LL GET YOU DOWN-- FAST AS I CAN!

WHILE OUTSIDE...

NEAR EXHAUSTION, A DEVOTED HUSBAND FIGHTS HIS WAY UPWARD... UNTIL...
ALMOST THERE, FRAN...
GASP
...A LITTLE MORE...
PANT
...AND WE'RE TOGETHER AGAIN!

SKREEEEK
NO!
ARGHH
14

ONCE MORE UN-HUMAN... STARVED FROM HER LONG "FAST"!...
...NO LONGER AWARE IT'S HER OWN HUSBAND'S THROAT SHE HUNGERS FOR...
...THE MOONSTRUCK VAMPIRE...
STRIKES!
SKREEEK
YAHHH!!

SUDDENLY, FROM THE BLACKNESS BELOW... A SEARCHING GRAPNEL SNAKES UPWARD... AND...!

FOLLOWED BY...

CAME AS FAST AS I COULD, KIRK...
...AFTER HEARING YOUR ECHOING SHOUTS!
15

YAGHHHH
SHE'S AFTER MY THROAT NOW...!
GOTTA BE STOPPED ANY WAY I CAN...

Y-YOU'RE SO RIGHT, BATMAN...
SOB
...FRAN'S NO LONGER RESPONSIBLE FOR WHAT SHE DOES... CAN NEVER BE NOW!
MUST BE STOPPED-- FOREVER!

NO, KIRK-- NO!
WE DO IT--MY WAY!

SWIFTLY TWIRLING THE TRAILING BATROPE INTO RESTRAINING LOOPS...
GOT HER-- ALIVE!
NOW FRAN'S VAMPIRE NIGHTMARE IS ABOUT OVER-- IF WE CAN FIND ENOUGH OF HER BLOOD-TYPE IN A VEGAS HOSPITAL!

AND... AS THEY SPEED BACK TOWARD THE "STRIP"...
A FULL TRANSFUSION, BATMAN?
THEN TAKE MINE-- WE'RE THE SAME TYPE!
NONE OF YOURS, KIRK! MY GUESS IS...
...THAT YOUR "BAT-SERUM" ORIGINALLY CONTAMINATED HER BLOOD-- LEAVING HER VULNERABLE TO THE MERE SCRATCH OF A TINY VAMPIRE-BAT!
POLICE
NO--IF YOU LOVE HER, LANGSTROM-- YOU'LL REALIZE THAT ONLY A TRANSFUSION OF FRESH, PURE BLOOD CAN SAVE HER NOW!
I HOPE... AND PRAY!
THE END
16

"The BATMAN NOBODY KNOWS!"

Story by Frank Robbins Art by Dick Giordano Edited by Julius Schwartz

DEEP IN THE WOODS FAR FROM *GOTHAM*, THREE GHETTO-HARDENED KIDS -- GUESTS OF MILLIONAIRE *BRUCE WAYNE* -- GET THEIR FIRST BREATH OF SMOG-FREE AIR, THEIR FIRST SIGHT OF THE GREAT OUTDOORS...

...AND THEIR FIRST EARFUL OF THE *UNKNOWN!*...

HOOOOT! HOOO-OOOT!

W-WHAT WAS *THAT?*

A *OWL*, YA DUMMY! AIN'T IT, *MR. WAYNE?*

RIGHT, *RONNIE!*

HUH! A LUCKY GUESS!

TH' ONLY BIRDS *RONNIE* EVER SEEN WAS *JAIL*-BIRDS AN' *SNOW*-BIRDS!

S-1473

YEAH? WELL, I KNOW LOTSA THINGS *YOU* DON'T, *ZIGGY!*
YE-AH? LIKE ANY JERK KNOWS *THAT* IS A PLAIN OL' *BAT!*

SHOWS HOW MUCH YOU TWO WISE GUYS KNOW!
THAT WAS *THE BATMAN!* HISSELF... IN *PERSON!*

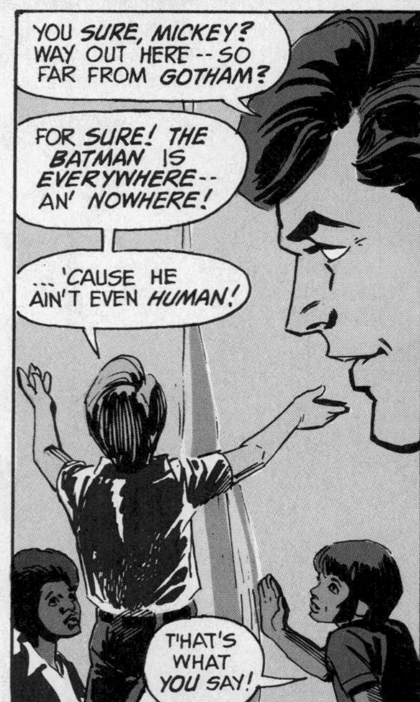

YOU *SURE, MICKEY?* WAY OUT HERE -- SO FAR FROM *GOTHAM?*
FOR *SURE! THE BATMAN* IS *EVERYWHERE* -- AN' *NOWHERE!*
... 'CAUSE HE AIN'T EVEN *HUMAN!*
T'HAT'S WHAT *YOU* SAY!

Coloring by Anthony Tollin

I'LL *PROVE* IT TO YUH ABOUT *THE BATMAN!* INNA FIRST PLACE-- IF YUH EVER SAW HIM...

"...HE'S SO BIG-- HE COVERS *ALL* O' *GOTHAM!* LIKE A KING-SIZE BLANKET!..."

HE'S GOT *X-RAY EYES!* SEES THRU WALLS AN' STUFF! *NOTHIN'* ESCAPES HIM!

"MAN, *BATS* SLIPS RIGHT THRU WALLS-- LIKE THEY WASN'T EVEN THERE!"

HEY! THOUGHT YOU SAID HE WAS AS BIG AS THE WHOLE CITY?
LIKE... HOW COME HE SHRINKS DOWN SMALL ENOUGH TO GET INSIDE A BUILDING?

"EVEN BULLETS ZIP THRU HIM LIKE NOTHIN'!"

'CAUSE, LIKE I SAID-- HE AIN'T HUMAN!

"BUT-- HEH!-- WHEN THE BATMAN CONNECTS, IT'S WITH A FIST OF IRON!"
"SENDS THOSE CREEPS STRAIGHT INTO JAIL-- NON-STOP!"
2

OH, MAN, MICKEY-- WHAT YOU DON'T KNOW 'BOUT THE BATMAN WOULD FILL A BOOK!
YE-AH? LIKE WHAT DO YOU DIG-- THAT I DON'T?

THAT OL' BATWINGS IS A REAL LIVE DUDE!
NOTHIN' SPOOKY 'BOUT HIM--
'CEPT HOW HE COMES ON!

"HE'S LOADED WITH TRICK-GADGETS! GOT SHINY PLASTIC WINGS RUN BY MOTORS--JET-PROPELLED BY TINY ROCKETS!"

"AN' HE JUST SNIFFS OUT TROUBLE--LIKE A HOUNDDOG--USIN' ONE O' THEM ELECTRONIC SNIFFIN' GIZMOS..."

SO YOU SEE THE BATMAN AS A SUPER-MOD CRIME-FIGHTER, RONNIE?
NOT SUPER, MR. WAYNE! HE'S ONE DOWN-TO-EARTH HIP-DUDE!

"...A ONE-MAN ARMY! THE BATMAN IS MUHAMMED ALI--JIM BROWN--SHAFT--AN' SUPER-FLY ALL ROLLED INTO ONE!"
3

LIKE WOW, RONNIE-- YOU MAKE THE BATMAN SOUND LIKE A "BROTHER"!
WHAT ELSE COULD A COOL CAT LIKE HIM BE, ZIGGY?

NOT ACCORDING TO TH' WAY I HEAR IT-- RIGHT FROM THE HORSE'S MOUTH!
IN FACT, FROM WILLIE THE HORSE HIMSELF!

Y'MEAN THE CON WHAT ONCE GOT SENT UP BY THE BATMAN?
YE-AH! HANGS 'ROUND MY BLOCK, FEEDS US KIDS THE INSIDE INFO--TO KEEP US "STRAIGHT," HE SAYS!
HMM, MAYBE NOW WE'LL GET A TRUE PICTURE OF "ME"!
WILLIE THE HORSE SHOULD KNOW... I COLLARED HIM!

"LIKE WILLIE TELLS IT... HE WAS CASIN' THE ROOFS ONE NIGHT, LOOKIN' FOR AN 'EASY-ENTRY'! THAT'S WHAT BURGLARS CALL A HEIST WHERE YUH DON'T GOTTA BREAK IN..."

"...WHEN SUDDENLY--FROM OUTA NOWHERE--COMES THIS GIANT SHADOW!"

"TEN FEET TALL HE WAS! WITH BIG BAT-EARS--WHAT COULD HEAR A PIN DROP MILES AWAY!"
"THAT'S HOW HE SPOTTED WILLIE-- EVEN THOUGH WILLIE WAS WEARIN' HUSH-SNEAKERS!"
4

BUT THE "HORSE" WASN'T GONNA GET NABBED SO EASY-- NOT WITHOUT A FIGHT! ...

"... HE HITS THAT GIANT BATGUY WITH A RUNNIN' SHOULDER-BLOCK-- RIGHT OFF THE ROOF!"

"WHICH MAKES NO NEVER-MIND TO THE BATMAN! 'CAUSE HE BOUNCES RIGHT BACK UP FROM A CLOTHESLINE BELOW..."

OH... NO! WILLIE SURE PILED IT ON THICK TO MAKE HIMSELF LOOK GOOD!
FIRST, ME "TEN FEET" TALL WITH "BAT'S EARS"... AND NOW MY HANDY BATROPE TURNS INTO A BOUNCING CLOTHESLINE!

SO WHA' HAPPEN THEN, ZIGGY?
"...COMIN' UP LIKE A BAT OUTA HELL, HE UPPERCUTS WILLIE-- IN MID-AIR, YET!"
"POOR GUY DIDN'T KNOW WHAT HIT HIM -- TILL HE'S STANDING IN FRONT OF THE JUDGE! LIKE WILLIE SAYS NOW-- NEVER MESS AROUND WITH THE BATMAN!"
5

AND THAT'S WHAT THE REAL "BATMAN" IS LIKE!
WHOO-HOO! LIKE MAN, ZIGGY-- HOW STRAIGHT CAN Y' GET? BELIEVIN' A CON-MAN LIKE "THE HORSE"...
WELL, I DUNNO, RONNIE...
LET'S ASK MR. WAYNE WHAT HE THINKS! HE'S KINDA GROWN-UP...

MR. WAYNE-- WHERE'D HE GO?
LET ME TELL YOU WHAT I THINK, FELLAS...

... THE BATMAN LOOKS LIKE THIS!

AW, C'MON-- MR. WAYNE! YOU'RE TOO BIG FOR THAT KINDA KID-STUFF!
NO WAY, MAN--NO HOW! EVERY COSTUME-CAT THINKS HE CAN BE THE "MAN"-- THE REAL "BLACK BATMAN"!
YUH WANTA PLAY, MR. WAYNE YAWN! YOU'RE ON YOUR OWN! I'M GONNA TURN IN...
6

SHORTLY...
HMM, WHATEVER ELSE IT PROVES-- THE BATMAN'S FRIGHTENING IMAGE SCARES THE GUILTY...
... NOT THE INNOCENT!
THE END

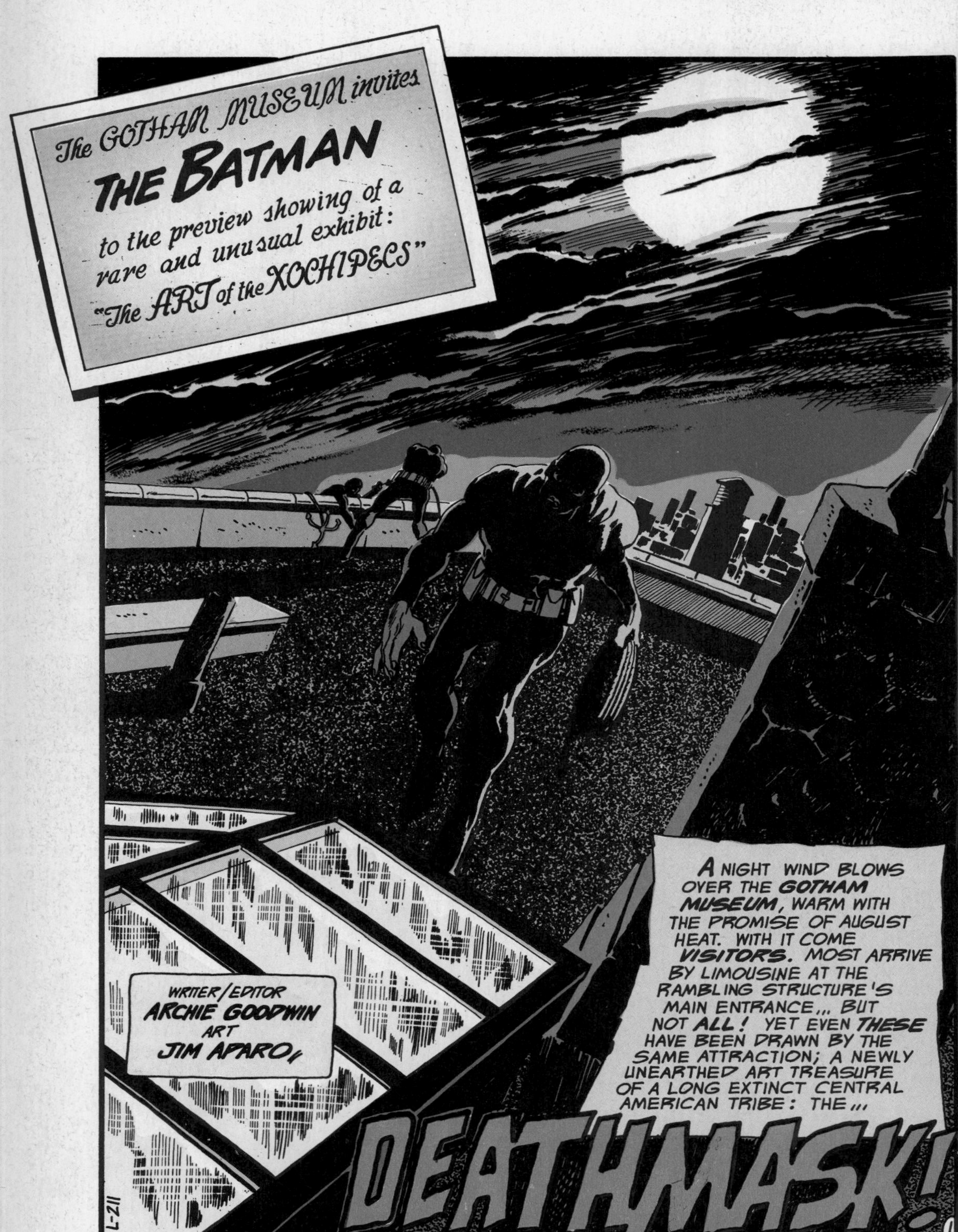
The GOTHAM MUSEUM invites
THE BATMAN
to the preview showing of a
rare and unusual exhibit:
"The ART of the XOCHIPECS"
A NIGHT WIND BLOWS OVER THE GOTHAM MUSEUM, WARM WITH THE PROMISE OF AUGUST HEAT. WITH IT COME VISITORS. MOST ARRIVE BY LIMOUSINE AT THE RAMBLING STRUCTURE'S MAIN ENTRANCE... BUT NOT ALL! YET EVEN THESE HAVE BEEN DRAWN BY THE SAME ATTRACTION; A NEWLY UNEARTHED ART TREASURE OF A LONG EXTINCT CENTRAL AMERICAN TRIBE: THE...
WRITER/EDITOR ARCHIE GOODWIN
ART JIM APARO
DEATHMASK!
L-211
1

Coloring by Petra Scotese

2

LADIES AND GENTLEMEN, I'VE JUST LEARNED OF AN ATTEMPT TO STEAL THE KEY ITEM OF TONIGHT'S EXHIBIT...!

AN ATTEMPT-- COMMISSIONER GORDON HERE ASSURES ME-- WHICH WAS FOILED BY NONE OTHER THAN...
THE BATMAN!

SO LET'S TOAST THE MASKED MANHUNTER!
AND ONCE OUR DIRECTOR, MARCUS WINGATE, FINISHES SOME LAST TOUCHES ON THE EXHIBIT, WE'LL ALL SEE --

JUDD THAXTON, EXECUTIVE ASSISTANT TO THE MUSEUM DIRECTOR, ALLOWS A DRAMATIC BEAT TO PASS. THEN, GESTURING HIGH ABOVE THE CROWD...

--THE MASK OF THE XOCHIPECS' GOD OF DEATH... MATUCHIMA!

ISN'T THERE SOME SORT OF CURSE..?

IS THE ORIGINAL AS GRUESOME AS THIS REPLICA...?

ISN'T THERE ALWAYS? VENGEANCE FOR REMOVING IT FROM ITS RIGHTFUL PLACE ...LATE SHOW STUFF!

BUT NOT ALL SPECULATION IS ABOUT THE MASK OF MATUCHIMA...

EXCUSE ME... HAVE YOU SEEN BRUCE WAYNE, COMMISSIONER? HE PROMISED TO MEET ME HERE!

WHAT? BRUCE WAS SUPPOSED TO MEET ME...!

3

I'M SORRY, LADIES, I--
ACTUALLY, I THOUGHT MEETING BOTH OF YOU WOULD BE A FINE COMPROMISE!
BUT WITH THE COMMISSIONER'S POLICE CARS SURROUNDING THE PLACE... ONE VERY NEARLY COULDN'T GET IN AT ALL!
I DIDN'T REALIZE SO MANY OF YOUR MEN WERE ART LOVERS, GORDON...
BRUCE--!
COULDN'T JUST A FEW GET BACK TO FIGHTING CRIME? WITH ALL THE TAXES I PAY...
...I HATE SEEING IT LEFT ENTIRELY TO SOME CAPED AND COWLED FREELANCE VIGILANTE!
BRUCE WAYNE'S PRACTICALLY BECOME A NEW PERSON THESE PAST FEW MONTHS... NOT ONE I PARTICULARLY CARE FOR!
HAVING BOLSTERED MY EFFETE SNOB IMAGE FOR THE EVENING, MAYBE I CAN RELAX AND ENJOY THE--
UH-UH! WHAT'S THIS...?
SPIRES, WILL YOU STOP? YOU'RE CAUSING A SCENE!
YOU BET I AM, THAXTON! WHAT RIGHT DOES THAT FOOL WINGATE HAVE TAMPERING WITH MY EXHIBIT?!
ISN'T IT ENOUGH THAT HE WAITED TILL I WAS RISKING MY LIFE IN THE CENTRAL AMERICAN JUNGLE...
...THEN COAXED THE BOARD OF TRUSTEES INTO MAKING HIM MUSEUM DIRECTOR INSTEAD OF ME?!
YOU?! MY FUND-RAISING KEEPS THIS PLACE GOING! WINGATE WAS PROMOTED ON THE STRENGTH OF IT!
IF ANYONE'S DESERVING OF HIS JOB... I AM!
JUDD THAXTON AND CHIEF ARCHAEOLOGIST AUSTIN SPIRES ANGRILY PART, FADING INTO THE MILLING CROWD. A SHORT TIME LATER...
THAT'S FROM THE XOCHIPEC EXHIBIT HALL!
YAAAAHHHHHH
4

WHAT'S GOING ON HERE? WHAT--
L-LORD..! IT'S MATUCHIMA... COME TO LIFE!
WHATEVER IT IS, IT'S DONE SOMETHING TO MR. WINGATE! LOOK BEHIND THAT ALTAR THING--!
USE YOUR GUNS, MEN! USE--

BLAM
GET 'IM!

BRUCE! THAT WAS A SHOT! WHAT SHOULD WE--
BRUCE--! WHERE--??
HE'S HANDSOME, HE'S RICH... SO HE'S NOT BRAVE! TWO OUT OF THREE ISN'T BAD THESE DAYS!

THE OLD BRUCE WAYNE-- GUTSY, INVOLVED-- COULDN'T DIS-APPEAR WHEN TROUBLE POPPED UP WITHOUT CAUSING SUSPICION...
...BUT FOR THE NEW ONE... IT'S TOTALLY IN CHARACTER!
NOW TO THE CAR AND A QUICK CHANGE TO--

--THE BATMAN!
KARASH
5

AND A KILLING BLOW IS TURNED INTO A GLANCING ONE... STILL, THE ROOM WHIRLS, ITS FLOOR BECOMES QUICKSAND COUNTERING ALL EFFORTS TO STAND. YET THE BATMAN TRIES.

EASY, MAN! GIVE YOURSELF TIME TO RECOVER!

MY MEN ARE OUTSIDE... THEY'LL GET HIM SOON ENOUGH!

MOMENTS PASS. A THROBBING HEAD BEGINS TO CLEAR... AND AN EXAMINATION IS MADE.

SO THIS IS THE VICTIM... A FOURTH THIEF! PROBABLY WAS SCOUTING THE ROOF WHEN I SURPRISED HIS FRIENDS... THEN TRIED IT ALONE!

AND WAS BEATEN TO DEATH BY OUR ...DEMON! BUT--

COMMISSIONER! THAT THING GOT AWAY... INTO THE PARK! AN' WHEN WE WENT AFTER IT, WE FOUND...

6

...MARCUS WINGATE, THE MUSEUM'S DIRECTOR!
MUST HAVE BEEN DRAGGED HERE EARLIER BY THAT CREATURE! PERHAPS EVEN KILLED HERE...
THIS MAN WASN'T MURDERED, COMMISSIONER... HE DIED OF A HEART SEIZURE!
THE STRAIN... OR FRIGHT... OF THE ENCOUNTER COULD HAVE DONE IT!

WHAT ABOUT THIS SCRATCH...? LOOKS RECENT!
BUT SUPERFICIAL... PROBABLY FROM ONE OF THE BUSHES, BATMAN!

THAT CERTAINLY WAS NO ONE NORMAL I FOUGHT... BUT A SPIRIT? BOTH HIS MASK AND ROBE WERE ON DISPLAY ... ANYONE MIGHT HAVE DONNED THEM...
GORDON, WHERE WERE AUSTIN SPIRES AND JUDD THAXTON DURING ALL THIS?
MISSING! MANY PEOPLE FLED THE MUSEUM!
THAXTON LIVES UPTOWN, SPIRES ACROSS THE PARK! SHOULD WE--

I'LL CHECK SPIRES, YOU TAKE THAXTON, COMMISSIONER! BOTH WANTED WINGATE'S JOB...
SOME QUESTIONS ARE IN ORDER!
THE BATMAN BECOMES ONE WITH THE NIGHT, VANISHING INTO ITS ENFOLDING DARKNESS...

...TO EMERGE SOMETIME LATER!
SOMETHING I READ IN THE ADVANCE PUBLICITY ABOUT THE MASK KEEPS NAGGING AT ME... WELL, IT'LL COME...
...MEANTIME, THERE'S SPIRES' PENTHOUSE! OF THE TWO SUSPECTS, HE SEEMED MOST BITTER, MOST DESPERATE...
7

AND AT THE MOMENT... MOST IN NEED OF HELP!
MATUCHIMA!!
THAT CLEARS SPIRES, ACCORDING TO MY SUSPICIONS ...

... AND LEAVES THAXTON!
SPIRES! GET OUT OF HERE...! GET TO POLICE PROTECTION!

BUT MY SUSPICIONS DON'T EXPLAIN HOW THAXTON-- OR ANYONE ELSE--
CAN DO WHAT THIS BRUTE KEEPS DOING!

AND AS THOUGH IN RESPONSE TO THOSE THOUGHTS...

FALL RELAXED... ROLL AS YOU HIT... UP FAST! SECOND NATURE FOR THE BATMAN... BUT SEEMINGLY THE SOLE NATURE OF HIS DEATH-MASKED FOE...

...IS TO ATTACK MERCILESSLY...

...TO KILL BRUTALLY!

8

YET MANY HAVE TRIED TO KILL THE BATMAN; SOME AS MERCILESS, SOME AS BRUTAL...
...ALL HAVE FAILED.
BUT BY THE TIME AUSTIN SPIRES' APARTMENT IS REGAINED...
MATUCHIMA'S GONE! NOTHING LEFT BUT THE WRECKAGE...
...LOOKS LIKE SPIRES HAS BEEN BRINGING WORK HOME... THESE ARE XOCHIPEC PLAQUES! AND THIS NOTEBOOK...
HE'S BEEN TRANSLATING THE PLAQUES... LOT OF MATERIAL ON XOCHIPEC CULTURE... APPARENTLY LIKE OTHER INDIAN TRIBES...
THEY EXPERIMENTED WITH NARCOTICS AND--HOLD IT! HERE'S A SECTION ON THE DEATH GOD'S MASK!
"IT WAS BELIEVED TO BE A GIFT FROM MATUCHIMA... IN HIS LIKENESS, GRANTING THE USER HIS DEATH-DEALING POWERS! WARRIORS WHO WORE IT IN BATTLE ALWAYS LED THE TRIBE TO TRIUMPH...
"...AND USUALLY PERISHED SOON AFTER! A SAYING CAME INTO BEING-- 'WHO WEARS THE DEATHMASK CONQUERS ALL... ALL BUT THE FINAL CONQUEROR!'"
THAT'S WHAT I READ EARLIER! AND THAT--COUPLED WITH THE OTHER INFORMATION ABOUT THE DRUGS--
IS THE ANSWER TO THIS ENTIRE TERRIBLE BUSINESS!
9

A SHORT WHILE LATER, A POLICE CAR SCREECHES TO A HALT IN FRONT OF THE **GOTHAM MUSEUM**. AND...

BATMAN! YOU'RE JUST IN **TIME!**

THERE'S NO TRACE OF THAXTON AT HIS **HOME**... BUT WE'VE JUST BEEN CALLED **ABOUT** A **NEW DISTURBANCE** HERE!

I'M NOT **SURPRISED**, COMMISSIONER... WAS THE CALL FROM **AUSTIN SPIRES?**

YES! PHONED FROM HIS **OFFICE** HERE, ABSOLUTELY **FRANTIC** AND--

BUT **HOW** DID YOU--

BATMAN! GOOD LORD! THERE'S SPIRES **NOW**...

AND **MATUCHIMA** IS MOVING IN FOR THE **KILL!**

GOOD LORD! IT WAS THAXTON!
SHOT AND SHOT... HE WOULDN'T FALL..!
DIDN'T GIVE ME ANY CHOICE... YOU SAW...

I SAW YOUR PLAN NEARLY BACKFIRE! JUDD THAXTON HAD A MUCH STRONGER HEART THAN WINGATE, DIDN'T HE, SPIRES?
BATMAN, WHAT... ?

SPIRES FOUND MORE THAN RELICS IN THE JUNGLE... HE FOUND THE SECRET NARCOTIC XOCHIPEC PRIESTS USED TO MAKE THE MASK WORK..!

TO MAKE IT TURN THE WEARER INTO A BERSERKER... WITH MADMAN'S STRENGTH! SIMILAR TO THE MOROS IN THE PHILIPPINES WAR...
ONLY THE MASK-WEARER'S HEART BURSTS IN TIME FROM THE STRAIN!

THERE MUST BE A TINY SPUR INSIDE THE MASK THAT, ANNOINTED WITH THE NARCOTIC... SCRATCHES THE VICTIM'S NECK WHEN HE PUTS IT ON!
ALL RIGHT! YOU FOUND MY NOTES... YOU GUESSED! THAXTON AND WINGATE STOOD BETWEEN ME AND THE DIRECTOR'S JOB! MONUMENTAL EGOS LIKE THEIRS COULDN'T RESIST TRYING THE MASK OF A GOD, DEFYING A PRIMITIVE CURSE... !

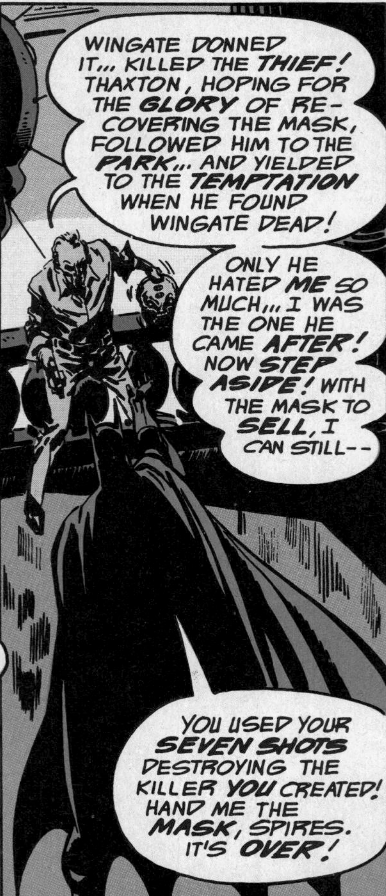
WINGATE DONNED IT... KILLED THE THIEF! THAXTON, HOPING FOR THE GLORY OF RE-COVERING THE MASK, FOLLOWED HIM TO THE PARK... AND YIELDED TO THE TEMPTATION WHEN HE FOUND WINGATE DEAD!
ONLY HE HATED ME SO MUCH... I WAS THE ONE HE CAME AFTER! NOW STEP ASIDE! WITH THE MASK TO SELL, I CAN STILL--
YOU USED YOUR SEVEN SHOTS DESTROYING THE KILLER YOU CREATED! HAND ME THE MASK, SPIRES. IT'S OVER!

NOT WHILE THERE'S THIS WAY OUT!
NO, SPIRES! EVEN IF YOU CAN HANG ON--
11

--THE SUPPORT WIRES CAN'T TAKE YOUR WEIGHT!
PWEENG
PWEENG
PWEENG

NOOOOOOOOOOOO

SO THIS IS THE WAY IT ENDS... EVEN THE MASK OF MATUCHIMA WAS DESTROYED! I SUPPOSE THE MUSEUM WILL REALIZE A GOOD DEAL FROM THE JEWELS, BUT--
I KEEP THINKING OF THE XOCHIPEC SAYING, COMMISSIONER --"WHO WEARS THE DEATHMASK CONQUERS ALL..."

SOMEHOW THAT TEMPTED REASONABLY INTELLIGENT MEN LIKE WINGATE AND THAXTON... EVEN KNOWING THE REST OF THE SAYING!
THERE'S STILL PLENTY OF TEMPTATION IN THE WORLD, GORDON...
I'M JUST AS HAPPY KNOWING THE DEATH-MASK WON'T BE CONTRIBUTING ITS PART!
THE END
12

BUT NEXT ISSUE, BATMAN... A MONSTER WALKS WAYNE MANOR!

PROLOGUE:

EARLIER, A **FLASH STORM** HAD SHATTERED THIS SPRING EVENING IN **GOTHAM!** BUT NOW, A CLEAR SKY AND A FULL MOON HELPS US FOCUS ON ONE OF THE CITY'S NEW FASHIONABLE HIGH-RISES — IN THE **PENTHOUSE** OF WHICH WE FIND AERONAUTICAL ENGINEER **MASON TERRELL** RECEIVING A LATE AND UNEXPECTED VISITOR...

BING BONG
YES — COMING!
WELL —! I'M IMPRESSED! WHEN THE DOORMAN SAID WHO WAS COMING UP, I WASN'T SURE JUST WHAT TO EXPECT!
THANK HEAVEN I REACHED YOU, MASON!
IT'S HARD TO KNOW WHERE TO BEGIN, BUT —
50A

HOW 'BOUT A NIGHTCAP?
I WAS FIXING MYSELF ONE WHEN YOU RANG! THERE'S ICE IN THE BUCKET —
HELP YOURSELF WHILE I LET IN A LITTLE OF THIS VIEW THAT I'M PAYING SIX BILLS A MONTH FOR — AHH! THAT'S BETTER!

OH, MY GOD!
BEN DANCER!! IT CAN'T BE!

L-325

1

WHEN YOU PATROL THE CITY DARKNESS, WHEN YOU STALK THOSE WHO WOULD PREY UPON OTHERS.. YOU ARE ALERT—PREPARED—FOR THE SOUNDS OF VIOLENCE—GUNFIRE! BUT GUNFIRE FROM THE TWIN VICKERS MACHINE GUNS OF A SPAD XIII—?! FROM A GHOSTLY WHITE-BLEACHED RELIC OF A WAR ENDED OVER A HALF-CENTURY AGO ?! CAN ANYONE BE PREPARED FOR THIS NIGHT WHEN...

AND AT DIZZYING HEIGHTS ABOVE THE DESERTED CITY STREETS...
THEN, WITH BONE-WRENCHING SWIFTNESS AND FORCE, THE GHOSTLY SPAD.. LOOPS!
HE WAS READY FOR ME!
I CAN'T...
HANG...
...ON!
LOOP BROUGHT US BACK.. OVER WATER TOWER!
GOT TO BRING MY FREEFALL UNDER CONTROL... AND
HIT
FEET
FIRST
NOW!
KRAK
3

AND ATOP THE BUILDING ...

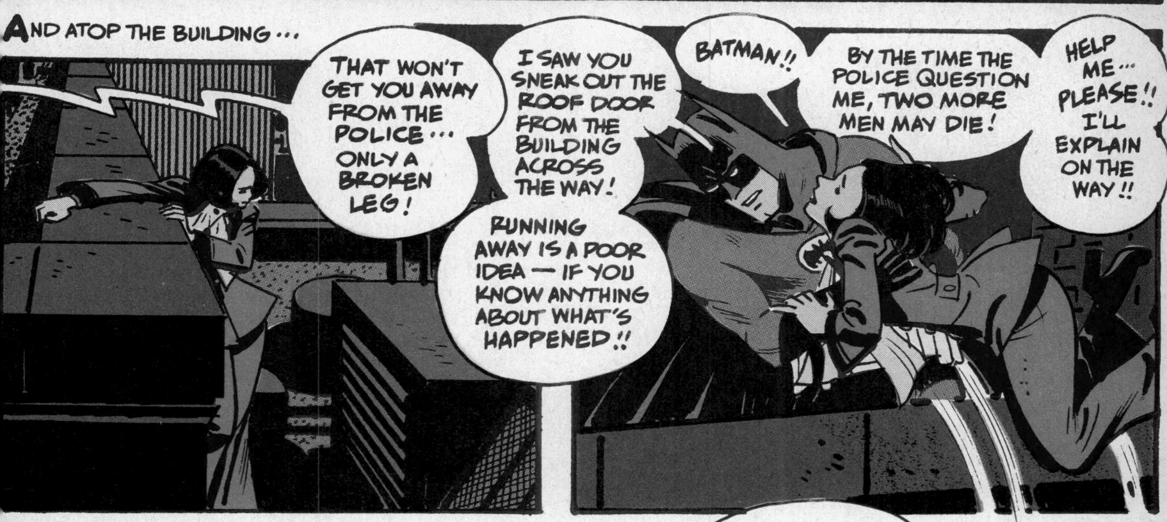

LATER — THE TWO RACE NORTHWARD IN THE CAR OF ...

... EVE DANCER?

WAS YOUR FATHER THE KOREAN WAR ACE WHO DIED IN A CRASH A FEW YEARS AGO?

YES! — IT WAS SUICIDE!!

.. AND NOW THE THREE MEN WHO DROVE HIM TO IT ARE BEING KILLED —

— UNLESS WE CAN REACH THE RICHTHOFEN AERODROME IN TIME!!

4

MY FATHER MADE HEADLINES FLYING JETS, BATMAN.. BUT HIS REAL LOVE WAS RESTORING AND FLYING OLD WWI BI-PLANES!
"AFTER RETIRING, HE GATHERED UP A GROUP OF AMATEUR PILOTS WHO SHARED HIS INTEREST...
...DOUG GARTH...
...MASON TERRELL...
...AND RICK HALSTROM!"

"POOLING THEIR MONEY, THEY GRADUALLY ACQUIRED AND REBUILT THE OLD PLANES THEY WANTED... AND DADDY TAUGHT THEM HOW TO FLY AND MAINTAIN THEM..."

"..UNTIL THEY HAD SORT OF A SQUADRON, FLYING EVERY WEEKEND — FOR THE SHEER JOY OF IT! OR SO DAD THOUGHT!"

THEN...
HI, BEN!
DOUG'S JUST INHERITED A FARM, NORTH OF GOTHAM! IT'S ALL PASTURED LAND, AND PERFECT FOR AN AIR STRIP FOR US TO PUT ON AIR SHOWS!
WHICH WOULD GIVE US A CHANCE TO MAKE OUR OL' KITES PAY THEIR OWN WAY AS WE FLY 'EM—!
IT'S A BIT OF A GAMBLE... BUT YOU KNOW ME, BEN..I LIKE GAMBLING!

MASON, DOUG, AND I HAVE DISCUSSED CALLING THE PLACE "RED BARON FIELD" OR "RICHTHOFEN AERODROME"...
SOMETHING CORNY WITH APPEAL, BEN! GET OLD WWI COSTUMES.. EXAGGERATED STUFF.. AN' DO DOGFIGHTS .. COMIC SEND-UPS OF THE "OLD DAYS"! CROWDS WILL EAT IT UP!
A CIRCUS!

TURN THIS OL' SPAD.. A THING I'VE LOVED, AND SWEATED OVER.. INTO A CHEAP CARNIVAL JOKE?! I WON'T DO IT— EVER!!
WE'RE ALL EQUAL PARTNERS, BEN — IF IT COMES TO A VOTE, YOU WON'T HAVE ANY CHOICE!

"DOUG GARTH WAS BOTH RIGHT..AND WRONG! WHEN A LONG, BITTER LAWSUIT WENT AGAINST HIM, DADDY DECIDED TO MAKE ONE MORE FLIGHT..."

"...HIS LAST!"

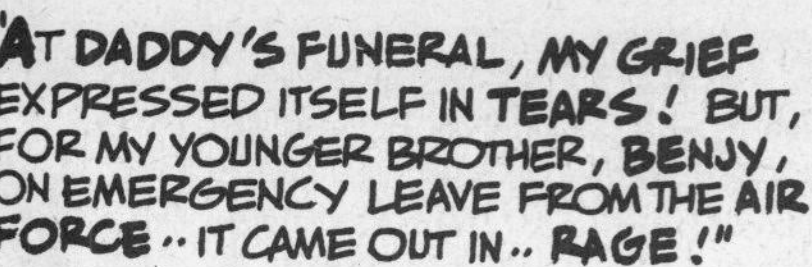
"AT DADDY'S FUNERAL, MY GRIEF EXPRESSED ITSELF IN TEARS! BUT, FOR MY YOUNGER BROTHER, BENJY, ON EMERGENCY LEAVE FROM THE AIR FORCE .. IT CAME OUT IN .. RAGE!"

TERRELL, GARTH, AND HALSTROM DROVE DAD TO THIS END, EVE ...
.. AND I'M GOING TO MAKE THEM PAY .. AND PAY .. FOR IT !!

"BENJY RESIGNED HIS AIR FORCE COMMISSION, AND VANISHED! THEN, MONTHS LATER .. A CALL SUMMONED ME TO A SMALL, SELDOM-USED AIRFIELD ..."
BENJY! .. THIS SPAD ...
.. YOU'VE MADE IT OVER TO LOOK EXACTLY LIKE -
- THE OLD MAN'S!
- WHEN I GET THESE GUNS INTO WORKING ORDER, I'LL SETTLE WITH THOSE 'RICHTHOFEN AERODROME' CLOWNS!

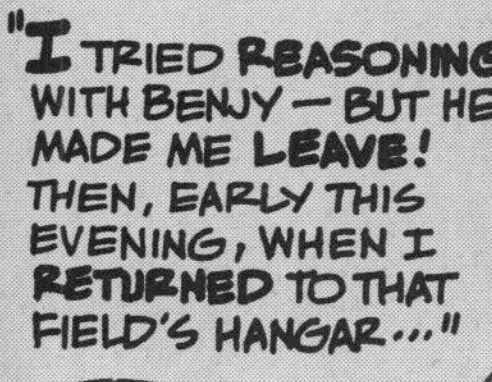
"I TRIED REASONING WITH BENJY — BUT HE MADE ME LEAVE! THEN, EARLY THIS EVENING, WHEN I RETURNED TO THAT FIELD'S HANGAR ..."
EMPTY! N-NO!
IF ONLY THERE'S TIME ENOUGH TO WARN THE OTHERS!
MUST KEEP THE POLICE OUT OF THIS — FOR BENJY'S SAKE!

.. BUT THERE WERE PROBLEMS! ... I COULDN'T REACH GARTH OR HALSTROM DUE TO TONIGHT'S STORM KNOCKING OUT PHONE LINES UP HERE —
— WHEN I FINALLY GOT TO TERRELL, IT WAS JUST THEN THAT BENJY ATTACKED!!
IS THAT THE TURN-OFF UP AHEAD, EVE?

YES!
THERE'S DOUG GARTH'S FARM!
— BUT HE'S SUPPOSED TO BE WORKING AT THE AERODROME —
— WHICH SHOULD BE JUST BEYOND THIS NEXT —!
FIRE!!
OH, DEAR LORD!
6

AS THE BATMAN REACHES THE WINDOW.. DANGER!

FOR AN INSTANT, HE HESITATES WHERE HE LIES...

THEN, AS THE BUILDING WALLS CRUMBLE...

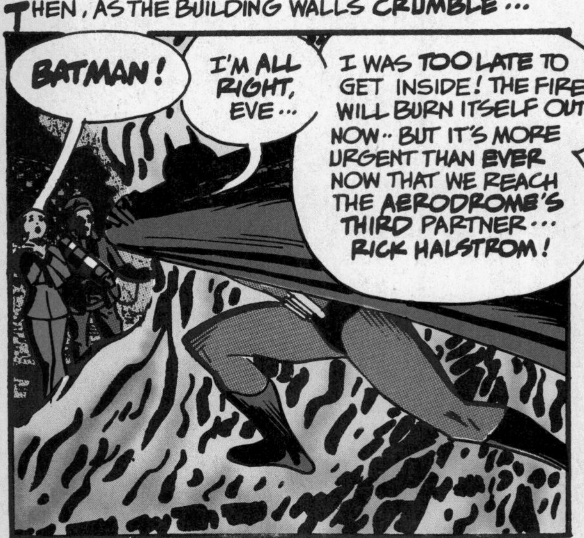

SOON, WITH EVE AT THE CONTROLS, THE HANOVERANER CL-II TAKES OFF INTO THE NIGHT SKY! IN ITS OBSERVER'S SEAT ... THE BATMAN!!
I'VE HAD SOME EXPERIENCE IN THESE ANTIQUES* ... BUT EVE HAS OBVIOUSLY HAD MORE!
THAT, AND MY BEING FREE TO ACT, COULD MAKE THE DIFFERENCE GOING UP AGAINST THAT KILLER SPAD!
* DETECTIVE COMICS #404: "GHOST OF THE KILLER SKIES"

AND AS THE GERMAN TWO-SEATER NEARS ITS DESTINATION ...
BATMAN! THAT CAR.. IT'S BEEN STRAFED!
BENJY MUST'VE CAUGHT HALSTROM COMING HOME! WE'RE TOO LATE ... AGAIN!
NO!
LISTEN AHEAD..
MACHINE GUN FIRE!

VICKERS MACHINE GUN FIRE — AND A MAN ... RUNNING FOR HIS LIFE!

BUT BEFORE THE BLAZING TRACERS CAN FIND THEIR TARGET ...
GOOD WORK, EVE!
OUR WHEEL GLANCED HIS WING!
JARRED HIM ENOUGH SO HALSTROM COULD REACH COVER! NOW-
WUMP

NOW I'M PULLING ALONGSIDE HIM! ONCE BENJY SEES IT'S ME, HE'LL SURELY COME TO HIS SENSES!
THIS MADNESS MUSTN'T GO ON ANY FURTHER!!
WAIT! NO! THAT'S..
8

THE BATMAN'S SHOUT IS CARRIED AWAY BY THE SCREAMING SLIPSTREAM, AS EVE DEFTLY BRINGS THE HANOVERANER WING-TO-WING WITH THE GHOSTLY SPAD...
A PISTOL!
BENJY! NO!!
I'M YOUR SISTER!!

BUT VICKERS AND MAGNUM WEAPONS ARE NOT THE ONLY AIRBORNE WEAPONS THIS NIGHT!...

ANOTHER IS THE BATARANG!...
TCHOK!
SWIFTLY, A CAPED FORM MOVES ACROSS THE WING OF THE HANOVERANER...

THEN— THE SPAD ROLLS!
HE'S TRYING TO SHAKE ME LOOSE.. LIKE BEFORE!
..BUT - BY LETTING GO AS THE ROLL PEAKS...
... I FALL TOWARD THE COCKPIT!!
KRAK!
9

NOW TWO PAIRS OF HANDS BATTLE FOR THE STICK!

GIVE IT UP, MAN!
CAN'T YOU SEE--
THAT YOU CAN OUTMATCH ME —?!?

MAYBE ANOTHER TIME, HERO! —BUT NOT—

—WHEN I'VE GOT A SAFETY BELT.. AND—
—YOU DON'T!

NO SAFETY BELT.. BUT A GUARDIAN ANGEL, YES! —FOR EVE'S PULLED UP HER PLANE— RIGHT UNDER THE SPAD!... AND JUST IN TIME!

AND AN ADVENTURE THAT BEGAN WITH A WATER TOWER... ENDS WITH ANOTHER!
KABOOOMMS!
BENJY! ..OH, GOD! BENJY!!
I TRIED TO WARN HIM THAT TOWER WAS AHEAD!
—BUT HE WOULDN'T LISTEN!
EVE! TAKE COMFORT—
THAT PILOT WASN'T YOUR BROTHER!
10

AFTER LANDING THE HANOVERANER NEARBY, AND JOINING A SHAKEN RICK HALSTROM, EVE AND THE BATMAN UNMASK THE GHOST SPAD'S PILOT...

DOUG GARTH!
BUT HOW?! THE FIRE.. IN HIS OFFICE—
—WAS STARTED WHEN HE STRAFED AND BOMBED THE AERODROME HIMSELF!!

I HAD TO HIT THE GROUND OUTSIDE HIS OFFICE'S BACK WINDOW, EVE.. AND I SAW FOOTPRINTS .. PARTIALLY WASHED AWAY BY THAT EARLIER RAINSTORM...
...THAT MEANT SOMEONE SNEAKED OUT THAT WAY DURING THE STORM.. WELL BEFORE THE STRAFING!

...SO GARTH KILLED TERRELL, ATTACKED THE FIELD, AND THEN WENT FOR MR. HALSTROM!... BUT WHY?!
—AND HOW COULD HE HOPE TO EXPLAIN HIS TURNING UP—ALIVE—LATER?
BY FAKING AN INJURY, THEN SAY HE GOT IT LEAPING OUT THE WINDOW DURING THE FIELD ATTACK.. AND HAD WANDERED OFF.. DAZED! SINCE ALL SUSPICION WAS ALREADY ON YOUR BROTHER —WHO WOULD QUESTION IT?!

AS FOR THE WHY.. TERRELL AND I LEARNT THAT DOUG WAS USING AERODROME PROFITS TO COVER HIS GAMBLING DEBTS! THEN WE MADE THE MISTAKE OF ALLOWING HIM TIME TO MAKE IT UP!

SO HE BOMBED HIS OWN OFFICE TO DESTROY THE INCRIMINATING RECORDS! BUT, IF GARTH DID ALL THAT, THEN WHAT'S HAPPENED TO BENJY?! AND WHERE IS HE, BATMAN?!

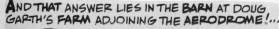

AND THAT ANSWER LIES IN THE BARN AT DOUG GARTH'S FARM ADJOINING THE AERODROME!...

BENJY!! HOW DID YOU GUESS, BATMAN?
GARTH HAD TO HAVE THE SPAD NEARBY, AND THIS BARN WAS HIS ONLY HIDING PLACE! HE'D WANT TO HOLD YOUR BROTHER, TOO... SO THAT, WITH HIS PARTNERS FINISHED, HE COULD WRECK THE SPAD, LEAVING THE POLICE A DEAD 'KILLER' TO FIND IN THE COCKPIT... BENJY!!

I-I WAS A FOOL, EVE! THINKING I COULD AVENGE DAD BY CHALLENGING THOSE GUYS INTO REAL DOGFIGHTS! GARTH PRETENDED TO BE WILLING WHEN I APPROACHED HIM... UNTIL HE COULD GRAB ME AND THE SPAD, AND...

...ACCIDENTALLY DID YOU THE BIG FAVOR OF YOUR LIFE, BENJY—KEEPING YOU FROM BECOMING A KILLER INSTEAD OF HIM!—THINK ABOUT IT... AND HOW BIG A FAVOR THAT IS!

END

BATMAN
TWENTY-ONE YEARS AGO, THIS NEIGHBORHOOD WAS THE DWELLING PLACE OF THE RICH AND SOON-TO-BE RICH... A PLACE OF GOURMET RESTAURANTS AND FASHIONABLE THEATERS... OF ELEGANT WOMEN AND SUAVE MEN...
BUT THE DRY ROT OF TIME SET IN, AND THE LAUGHTER STOPPED AND THE LIGHTS DIMMED, AND THOSE ELEGANT WOMEN AND SUAVE MEN SOUGHT THEIR PLEASURES ELSEWHERE... AND NOW, ONLY THE FORLORN AND THE DESPERATE WALK THESE STREETS...
FOR ONE NIGHT, TWO BRUTAL SLAYINGS OCCURRED SIGNALING THE BEGINNING OF THE END... THE AREA KNOWN AS PARK ROW ACQUIRED A NEW NAME -- CRIME ALLEY... AND --
S-2177
"THERE IS NO HOPE IN CRIME ALLEY!"
Story by DENNY O'NEIL
Art by DICK GIORDANO
Edited by JULIUS SCHWARTZ

Coloring by Julia Lacquement

IT BEGAN THREE HOURS AGO, FAR FROM CRIME ALLEY--AT THE LAVISH UPTOWN PENT-HOUSE OF MILLIONAIRE BRUCE WAYNE...
OFF IN PURSUIT OF THE JEWEL SMUGGLERS, MASTER BRUCE?
NOT TONIGHT, ALFRED!
SMUGGLERS BAFFLE POLICE!
BUT SURELY THE BATMAN IS INTERESTED!
ACCORDING TO THE PAPER, THE POLICE ARE BAFFLED, THE FBI IS STYMIED, THE TREASURY DEPARTMENT IS PERPLEXED...
I DON'T CARE... NOT TONIGHT!
JUST TEND TO YOUR DUTIES AND STAY OUT OF MY BUSINESS!
I'LL BE BACK AT DAWN!
I DO NOT UNDERSTAND! ALTHOUGH I PRIDE MYSELF ON BEING THE BATMAN'S CLOSEST CONFIDANT --NEXT TO MASTER ROBIN--
--HE HAS NEVER EXPLAINED WHERE HE GOES ON THIS DATE EVERY YEAR... OR WHY!
STRANGE... HE ALWAYS SEEMS NERVOUS... AGITATED... APPREHENSIVE-- AS IF SOMETHING FOUL WERE AFOOT...
ELSEWHERE...
WHILE I RIP OFF THE HUBCAPS... SNATCH THE RADIO!
2

GOT IT, HARRY--
--AND YOU CAN PUT IT BACK!

TH-THE BATMAN?
D-DON'T HURT ME, MAN! I'M BEGGIN' YA!
I WON'T! THE RADIO-- BACK!

WHILE YOUR PAL IS UNDOING THE HARM HE'S DONE, YOU'LL TALK!
S-SURE... ANYTHING!
WHERE'S LESLIE THOMPKINS?

THOMPKINS?
WHATTAYA WANT WITH THAT OLD CREEP?

DON'T YOU INSULT LESLIE THOMPKINS-- EVER-- UNDERSTAND?
Y-YEAH!

ONCE MORE... WHERE IS LESLIE?
I...I THINK I SEEN THE OLD... THOMPKINS NEAR THE WAREHOUSE!
3

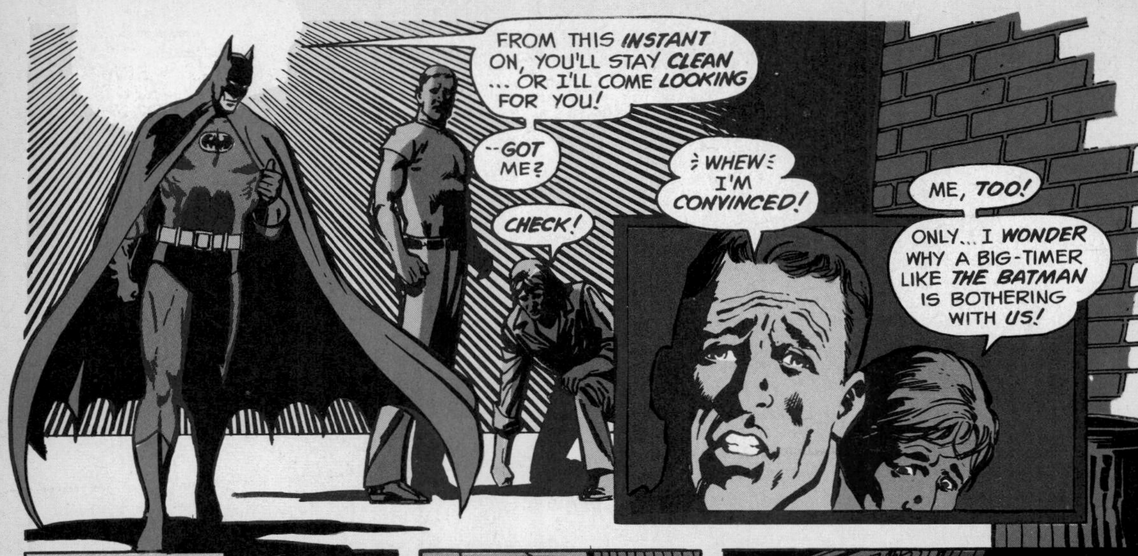
FROM THIS INSTANT ON, YOU'LL STAY CLEAN ... OR I'LL COME LOOKING FOR YOU!
--GOT ME?
WHEW I'M CONVINCED!
CHECK!
ME, TOO!
ONLY... I WONDER WHY A BIG-TIMER LIKE THE BATMAN IS BOTHERING WITH US!

MINUTES LATER...
PLEASE, SONNY... YOU AIN'T GONNA TAKE MY LAST DOLLAR? I NEED IT TO EAT!
THINGS ARE TOUGH ALL OVER, GRAMPS! --GIMME!

H-HELP!
GO AHEAD-- YELL YOUR FOOL HEAD OFF! IN CRIME ALLEY, NOBODY PAYS ATTENTION!

YOU CAN'T OUTRUN ME, NEITHER!
AN' 'CAUSE YOU TRIED, I'M GONNA WASTE YOU A LITTLE!

HUH--?
4

YOUR CHOICE, PUNK! DROP THE KNIFE...
...OR HAVE IT CRAMMED DOWN YOUR THROAT-- SIDEWAYS!
NO!
SUDDENLY... FEAR! THE PANIC OF THE COWARDLY DRIVES THE MUGGER FORWARD BLINDLY--
STUPID! REAL DUMB--
--BETTER THUGS THAN YOU HAVE HAD A GO AT STICKING ME--
--AND THEY FAILED--
--ALWAYS!
K-CHOK!
UNNGH
WAIT A FEW SECONDS, SIR, AND I'LL ACCOMPANY YOU HOME--
SOON AS I GIFT-WRAP THIS SPECIMEN FOR THE POLICE!
TH-THANK YOU, BATMAN!
5

MAY I ASK YOU A *QUESTION?*
SHOOT--

YOU CHASE *INTERNATIONAL CRIMINALS*... THEY SAY YOU'RE THE WORLD'S *GREATEST DETECTIVE!*
SO HOW COME YOU'RE PREVENTING A COMMON *MUGGING?*
CRIME IS *CRIME*...

... AND TO YOU, THE LOSS OF A *DOLLAR* IS MORE IMPORTANT THAN THE LOSS OF *THOUSANDS* TO A *BANKER!*

NOW, *MY* TURN TO DO THE ASKING--
--HAVE YOU SEEN *LESLIE THOMPKINS?*
WHY... YES! LESLIE WAS RUNNING A *STREET FAIR* OVER TO *SULLIVAN STREET* EARLIER TODAY!

STAY *WELL*, SIR!
WHATEVER COULD *HE* WANT WITH *LESLIE?*
6

THEN...
HEY, BATS! HOW YA DOIN', PAL?
YA SURE GAVE ME A HAND LAST YEAR ... WHEN THOSE KIDS WERE HASSLIN' ME!
YEAR AGO 'ZACTLY, RIGHT?
RIGHT! HAVE YOU SEEN LESLIE THOMPKINS?
ROW STREET FAIR
50¢
LEMME SEE... LES WAS HEADIN' FOR THE FAMILY HOUSE!
MEANWHILE...
READY, GOOCH?
YEAH... PLENTY READY!
PUT THE HEAT AWAY, WILL YA? A GUN AIN'T NECESSARY FOR--
X-RATED
...THERE SHE IS!
OUR PIGEON... RIPE FOR PLUCKIN'!
7

WAIT UP, LADY!
WHAT IS IT, BOYS?

LET LOOSE OF YOUR PURSE!
I'D LIKE TO... I REALIZE YOU'RE PROBABLY BROKE!
A LOT OF PEOPLE ARE THESE DAYS--

--BUT I'VE GOT THE RECEIPTS FROM THE STREET FAIR...
...AND THE MONEY IS EARMARKED FOR THE CHILDREN OF THE NEIGHBOR-HOOD... TO GIVE THEM A CHANCE YOU BOYS NEVER HAD!

I HAVE A MODEST BANK ACCOUNT! I'LL WRITE YOU A CHECK--
I DUNNO IF YOU'RE CRAZY-- OR JUST DUMB...

...AN' I DON'T CARE! GRAB THE PURSE, ALFIE!
SONNY... YOU PICKED ON THE WRONG PERSON-- AS YOU'RE ABOUT TO REGRET!

8

ANYONE WHO PASSES LESLIE THOMPKINS HAS TO ANSWER TO HER FRIEND--
--THE BATMAN!
UNNGH--
IN PERSON... AND ANXIOUS FOR YOU TO DO SOMETHING CLEVER...
...LIKE PLAYING TOUGH!
K-KEEP AWAY--
...OR I'LL S-SNUFF YOU!
YOU DARE--
--PULL A GUN ON ME--
--PULL A GUN ON ME HERE--
--DO YOU?
DO YOU?
9

TREMBLING WITH FURY, THE BATMAN CRASHES HIS FIST INTO GOOCH AGAIN AND AGAIN...
...AND HIS MIND REELS... SPINS LIKE A DERVISH INTO THE PAST...
...TO 21 YEARS AGO THIS VERY NIGHT, WHERE HE AND HIS PARENTS WERE STANDING ON THIS EXACT SPOT, CHATTING ABOUT THE MOVIE THEY'D JUST SEEN...
WHEN A GUN-MAN EMERGED FROM THE SHADOWS...
...AND AS THE BOY WATCHED IN HORROR, TWO SHOTS WERE FIRED...
...AND HIS FACE CONTORTED IN A SILENT SCREAM AS HIS MOTHER AND FATHER CRUMPLED TO THE COLD PAVEMENT...
LATER, THERE WERE POLICE-MEN AND REPORTERS... BUT NO-BODY NOTICED THE BOY WRACKED WITH ENDLESS SOBS...
...NOBODY EXCEPT A WOMAN, WHO KNELT BY HIM AND SAID...
"I'M LESLIE THOMPKINS. COME WITH ME. I'LL... I'LL DO WHAT I CAN."
AND IN ALL THE WORLD, THERE WAS NOTHING... NOTHING EXCEPT THE WARMTH OF HER ARMS AND THE COMFORT OF HER SOOTHING WORDS...
10

STOP... STOP!
YOU'VE HIT HIM ENOUGH!
SORRY... I LOST MY HEAD!
I'LL LET THE AUTHORITIES SWEEP UP THE SCUM!
YES! YOU SHOULD CALM YOURSELF! IT'S NOT HEALTHY TO LOSE YOUR TEMPER!
I'VE BEEN EXPECTING YOU, BATMAN -- YOU ALWAYS COME TO VISIT ON THIS DAY!
I CONFESS I'VE NEVER UNDERSTOOD THE REASON!
CALL IT A MEMORIAL... A REMINDER OF WHO I AM!...OF MY BEGINNING... AND MY PROBABLE END!
AND YOU, MISS THOMPKINS! WHAT IS YOUR REASON FOR CONTINUING TO LIVE IN CRIME ALLEY?
OH... I ONCE SAW A HIDEOUS THING--A CHILD WHOSE PARENTS WERE MURDERED IN FRONT OF HIS EYES!
I'VE NEVER FORGOTTEN THE LAD! I'VE DEVOTED MY LIFE TO DOING WHAT I CAN TO PREVENT SUCH TRAGEDY!
FORGIVE ME... BUT I LIVE FOR THE TIME WHEN YOU AND YOUR KIND WILL BE UNNECESSARY!
I'VE HEARD THERE'S NO HOPE IN CRIME ALLEY, MISS THOMPKINS-- THAT'S WRONG!
11

YOU... AND THOSE LIKE YOU... YOU'RE THE HOPE OF CRIME ALLEY--
MAYBE THE ONLY HOPE OUR TORMENTED CIVILIZATION HAS LEFT!

GOOD-BYE, MISS THOMPKINS! TAKE CARE!

AT LAST, THE LONG NIGHT IS OVER... AND THE RISING SUN BRIGHTENS CRIME ALLEY AND THE HAUNTS OF THE RICH ALIKE...

...INCLUDING THE WAYNE PENTHOUSE...
BREAKFAST, MASTER BRUCE! I'VE PREPARED YOUR FAVORITES-- EGGS BENEDICT AND...
12

HE'S ASLEEP AND...
HOW STRANGE!
HE'S SMILING!
END

DEATH STRIKES at midnight and three
by Dennis O'Neil & W.M. Rogers

At eight o'clock the special prosecutor died. He had just stepped from the humid warmth of the lobby of the Gotham Towers Hotel into the late February chill of West Forty-Eighth Street and was hurrying toward the limousine at the curb, hunched in his camel's-hair overcoat, talking to the man who was accompanying him.

"I think we've finally got the Lewes mob on the ropes, Bruce," the prosecutor said.

"I hope so, Bernie," Bruce Wayne replied. "At least, I'll take your word for it. Crime is a little out of my line."

The prosecutor smiled condescendingly. "To put it mildly."

"Buy you dinner?" Wayne asked.

"Sorry, I've got an important meeting tonight and a bit of homework—"

The prosecutor stopped, wheezed. His left shoulder sagged and he murmured, "Oh, damn."

Coloring by Bill Wray

His knees buckled and he collapsed quickly and awkwardly, as though all his joints had been severed at once. His head bounced on the sidewalk before Wayne could catch him.

Kneeling, Wayne shouted to the waiting chauffeur, "Get a doctor!" To the prosecutor, he said, "Take it easy, Bernie. Help's on the way."

The prosecutor's chest heaved and his eyes darted rapidly, frantically, as though he were desperately searching for something that was impossible to see. His bloodless lips barely moved as he said, "Meet blind man . . . midnight and three . . . safe till then . . . ."

"**Where**, Bernie?," Wayne asked urgently. "Where are you going to meet him?"

The eyes stopped darting and the headlights of a passing taxi shone in them.

Wayne stood and for a moment gazed at the corpse of his friend. "I'll get him for you, Bernie," he whispered.

"Doctor's coming, Mister Wayne," the chauffeur shouted from the limousine, clutching a small microphone.

"Pardon me," Wayne said, shivering violently. "I've got to get inside. I'm . . . I'm terribly upset."

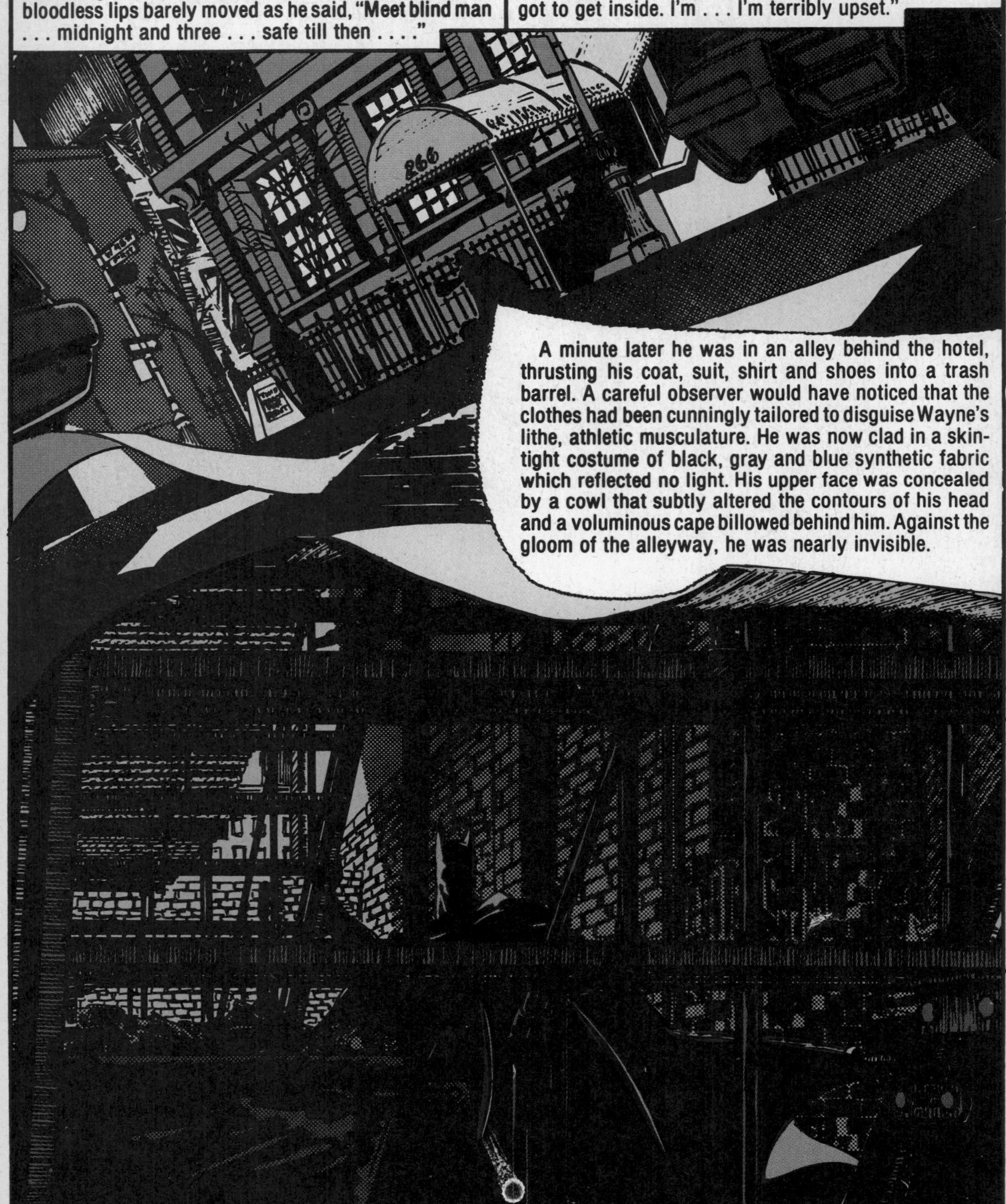

A minute later he was in an alley behind the hotel, thrusting his coat, suit, shirt and shoes into a trash barrel. A careful observer would have noticed that the clothes had been cunningly tailored to disguise Wayne's lithe, athletic musculature. He was now clad in a skintight costume of black, gray and blue synthetic fabric which reflected no light. His upper face was concealed by a cowl that subtly altered the contours of his head and a voluminous cape billowed behind him. Against the gloom of the alleyway, he was nearly invisible.

He moved to a service entrance, removed a sliver of metal from a compartment in his belt and applied it to the lock. The door swung open and he slipped through into a long, low area full of gleaming kitchen equipment. In a corner, next to a high, stainless steel vat, a fat man in a white apron sat sipping from a bottle of cooking sherry and scanning a racing form.

"You!"

The man looked up and gasped, "**The Batman!**"

The sherry bottle shattered on the tile floor.

"Look," the man stammered. "Sure, I maybe cheated a little on the income tax, but with three ex-wives, I got expenses you can't **believe**—"

Ignoring the confession, The Batman said, "There was somebody new working the charity backgammon tournament in the main ballroom today—a cook, a waiter, perhaps a busboy."

"Yeah, that's right. A waiter. Beefy guy, built like a rassler, real surly."

"Where is he now?"

"The waiters are goin' off shift. I guess he'd be in the locker room."

At the exit, The Batman said, "You'll pay the tax money you owe."

"Yeah, I was gonna do it anyhow, tomorra morning, you bet."

The Batman was leaning against a wall, arms folded, when the burly waiter emerged from the locker room.

"Shall we talk?" The Batman asked.

The waiter bolted for a flight of stairs at the end of the narrow corridor.

Instead of chasing him, the caped figure glided to a window, raised it and climbed onto a fire escape. Within seconds, he was standing on the roof, 40 stories above the avenue, silhouetted in the glow of the night-lit city.

The waiter emerged onto the roof, panting and wiping his brow on his sleeve, and immediately felt The Batman's hand on his shoulder.

"Ready for our talk?"

The waiter jumped back, fumbling in the pocket of his pea jacket.

"I'll begin," The Batman said. "A while ago, you contrived to serve Bernard Sorrel a snack loaded with poison, probably tubocurarine chioride in a neutralizing solution to delay the action."

Still fumbling, the waiter demanded, "How'd you know I was coming up here?"

"Call it instinct. I've watched a lot of cowards run."

"Coward, huh?" The waiter finally produced a blackjack, 20 ounces of leather-covered lead on a spring handle. "I'm gonna pound you, baby, pound you to hamburger."

The Batman shrugged. "Take your best shot."

The blackjack swung in an arc. Halfway to The Batman's skull, it halted as The Batman caught the waiter's forearm in hooked fingers and squeezed. With an abrupt, startled howl, the waiter dropped his weapon and sank to his knees as The Batman calmly forced the arm downward.

"Milo Lewes hired you to murder Bernard Sorrel. Don't bother to deny it. What proof I haven't got will be easy to get."

"O-**kay!**"

"The question is, **why?**"

"The blind man was gonna snitch to Sorrel."

"When?"

"Sometime late tonight."

"Where?"

"I dunno. Lewes only paid me to hit Sorrel. The rest of the stuff I got from keeping my ears open."

The Batman relaxed his grip and allowed the murderer to rise.

"You'll surrender yourself to the police," The Batman said.

"You crazy?"

Sighing, The Batman thumbed a nerve in the waiter's neck and eased the suddenly unconscious murderer to the tar paper.

Twelve miles away, a telephone rang in the hush of an oak-paneled bedroom. Alfred Pennyworth put his dust cloth on the desk top and lifted the receiver.

"Wayne residence. Alfred Pennyworth, butler, speaking."

"Alfred, is Dick around?"

"No, Master Bruce. He planned to leave for Hudson University directly after viewing a film of Mister Buster Keaton's at a theater devoted to revivals of cinema classics. 'A dynamite flick,' was his description. I confess I am baffled by youthful vernacu—"

"Right. I could've used his help, but we'll manage without it. See what the computer has on somebody nicknamed 'the blind man'—part of Milo Lewes' mob."

"A moment sir,"

Alfred touched a stud at the base of a lamp: a portion of the desk slid back to reveal the keys of a computer terminal and a row of stately volumes parted to bare a large display screen. Alfred tapped keys and the screen flashed information.

"Give, Alfred," The Batman said impatiently.

" 'Anthony Toombs, a.k.a. Tony the Tomb, a.k.a. Blindman Tony, a.k.a. the Blind Man,' " Alfred read.

"That's him," The Batman said.

" 'Born Rockford, Illinois, 19 July, 1927. Mother: Bertha Toombs. Father unknown. Awarded scholarship to State College at Billington—"

"Skip the background. Get to his association with Lewes."

" 'Entered the employ of Milo Lewes approximately 5 November, 1967, as accountant. No overt criminal activity noted. Struck by .25-cal. bullet, 24 December, 1968. Extensive damage to optical nerve resulted in total blindness."

"Anything on who shot him?"

"Nothing, Master Bruce."

"Outstanding personal characteristics? Talents?"

Alfred pushed keys, paused, and read: "Subject has total recall."

"Makes sense," The Batman said. "He probably has enough stored in his head to blow Lewes' operation apart, and for some reason, that's just what he wants to do. I wonder why?"

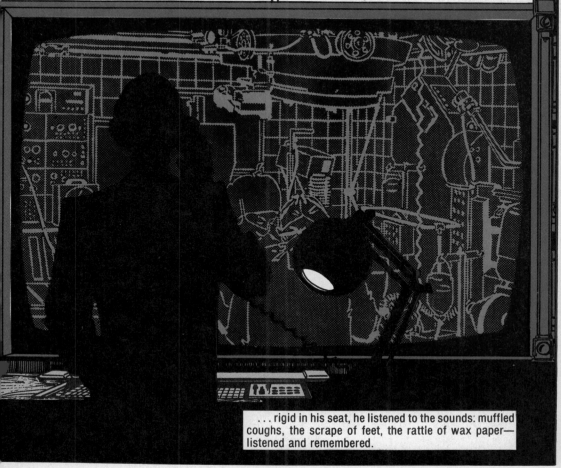

. . . rigid in his seat, he listened to the sounds: muffled coughs, the scrape of feet, the rattle of wax paper—listened and remembered.

He had been in the tiny alcove beneath the stairs, the private, hidden place where he liked to sit by himself, away from the crude humor of the others, constantly reminding him of his loss. He recognized the footfalls of Lewes, his boss; and Benny, Lewes' newly-hired bodyguard.

"You keep that blind guy around for laughs, huh?" Benny speaking, causing a sharp pang in the listener.

"No, no, Benjamin. Our Anthony is quite useful."—Milo Lewes.

The footfalls stopped. Snick of lighter. Odor of tobacco.

"How's zat?"

"He learns things, instantly and totally. With his memory available, I need not worry about records—names and numbers written on paper. And what is not recorded cannot be used as evidence against me."

"Neat." Benny was admiring. "Guess he has the memory 'cause he was born blind, huh?"

"Once more, you're mistaken, Benjamin. He was injured by a bullet."

Then Milo Lewes chuckled, and spoke the words that gave focus to ten years of rage and pain and hate. He said, "What our Anthony doesn't know is that I fired the bullet. I was a bit tipsy—this was Christmas Eve—and I was playing with a gift from a dear friend of mine, a .25-caliber Llama automatic. I didn't realize the little devil was loaded until it discharged and hit Anthony, who was sleeping in the next room. Pulled his shades permanently."

"He never guessed, huh?"

"He never will. One of Anthony's lovelier traits is trust. Game of pool, Benjamin?"

"Sure, Mister Lewes."

For an hour, he had sat and mentally reviewed the agonies and humiliations he had suffered for the past decade.
Then he had crept from his refuge to the telephone and asked the operator for the special prosecutor's number . . . .
". . . Commissioner Gordon to collect Sorrel's killer from the roof of the Towers," The Batman was telling Alfred. "He shouldn't have much trouble wringing a confession from him."
"Indeed. His spirit is broken, I presume?"
"Badly bent. I didn't have time to give him the full treatment. Lewes isn't the type to take chances. He won't be content with eliminating Bernie Sorrel. He'll have guns looking for the blind man, too. I've got to reach him first."
"Good luck, Master Bruce."

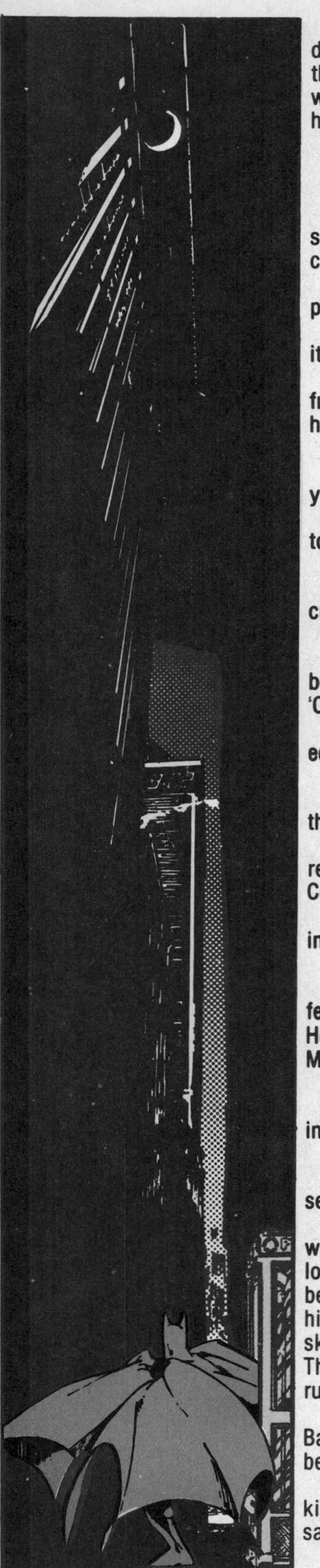

The Batman stepped from the booth and glanced upward at the digital clock atop the Arch Building. Nine-oh-two. At twelve-oh-three—midnight and three—the blind man would leave his haven, wherever it was, and become the prey of Lewes's hunters. The Batman had precisely three hours and one minute to find him.

Where would a blind man hide? Where could he be?

The Batman decided to ask Milo Lewes.

"Interesting news," Lewes said. And: "Eight ball in the side pocket."

He bent low over the felt-covered table and twitched his cue stick, sending the white ball into the black ball and the black ball into the corner pocket. Milo Lewes grinned and turned to his bodyguard.

"That's ninety dollars you owe me, Benjamin. Now, repeat for me, please—what did Boilerplate say?"

"That him and the Gimp spotted the blind man and in a couple hours it'll be cool to snuff 'im."

"Ah." Lewes chalked his stick and fastidiously flicked chalk dust from the velvet collar of his Japanese silk dressing gown. "And where has our Anthony been secreting himself?"

"Boilerplate didn't say."

"You didn't inquire? Benjamin, has anyone ever informed you that your intelligence is limited?"

Benny pouted. "My neighborhood, where I grew up, you didn't have to be smart, only tough."

"Or sneaky and mean?"

Lewes and Benny whirled as The Batman strode from behind heavy crimson drapes.

"Good evening, gentlemen."

Lewes brushed a lock of ginger-colored hair from his forehead and bowed slightly. "Ah, the gallant our smarmier tabloids refer to as the 'Caped Crusader.' You circumvented our alarm system?"

"Alarms? Those? No, **toys**, Milo. You should invest in some decent equipment."

"I shall."

"And pay for it with the income from the filth you put in the veins of the helpless."

"I prefer to think of my product as a respite from woe. Can I offer you refreshment? I have an excellent brandy sent me by a dear friend in the Cognac region of France."

"No, thanks. I'm afraid there might be something other than brandy in it—tubocurarine chloride, for instance."

"Poison you in my own home? No, dear me. That **would** be tacky."

"Let's cut the repartee, Milo. Your conversation gives me a slimy feeling in the pit of my stomach and besides, we're boring Benny there. He's itching to grab for the nine-millimeter Browning in the Berns-Martin spring holster under his jacket."

Benny gaped. "It hadda be a **guess**!"

"Close observation, Benny—plus a knowledge of the habits of the insect population."

Lewes snickered. "I do believe you've been insulted, Benjamin."

Benny had been practicing. Benny was fast. The sleek blue pistol seemed to appear in his fist from nowhere, rising, aiming.

By contrast, The Batman seemed to be moving in slow motion. He wafted into the air like a leaf being borne aloft on a gentle breeze, his long body pivoting on fingertips that barely touched the table. Yet before Benny could squeeze the trigger, The Batman's heels drove into his solar plexis. Benny rose on his toes, and his jaw sagged, and his skin darkened to an ashen hue, and he gulped like a beached guppy. As The Batman completed his leap, Benny was falling to the thick Persian rug.

"Splendid." Lewes was slapping his palms together. "Mikhail Baryshnikov has a peer. You missed your calling. You should have been a ballet dancer."

"You might as well talk, Milo. You're finished. The punk you hired to kill Sorrel will sing and you'll stand trial for murder. If you help me save the blind man, maybe the jury will take it into consideration."

"You **do** underestimate me, my agile detective. When the police

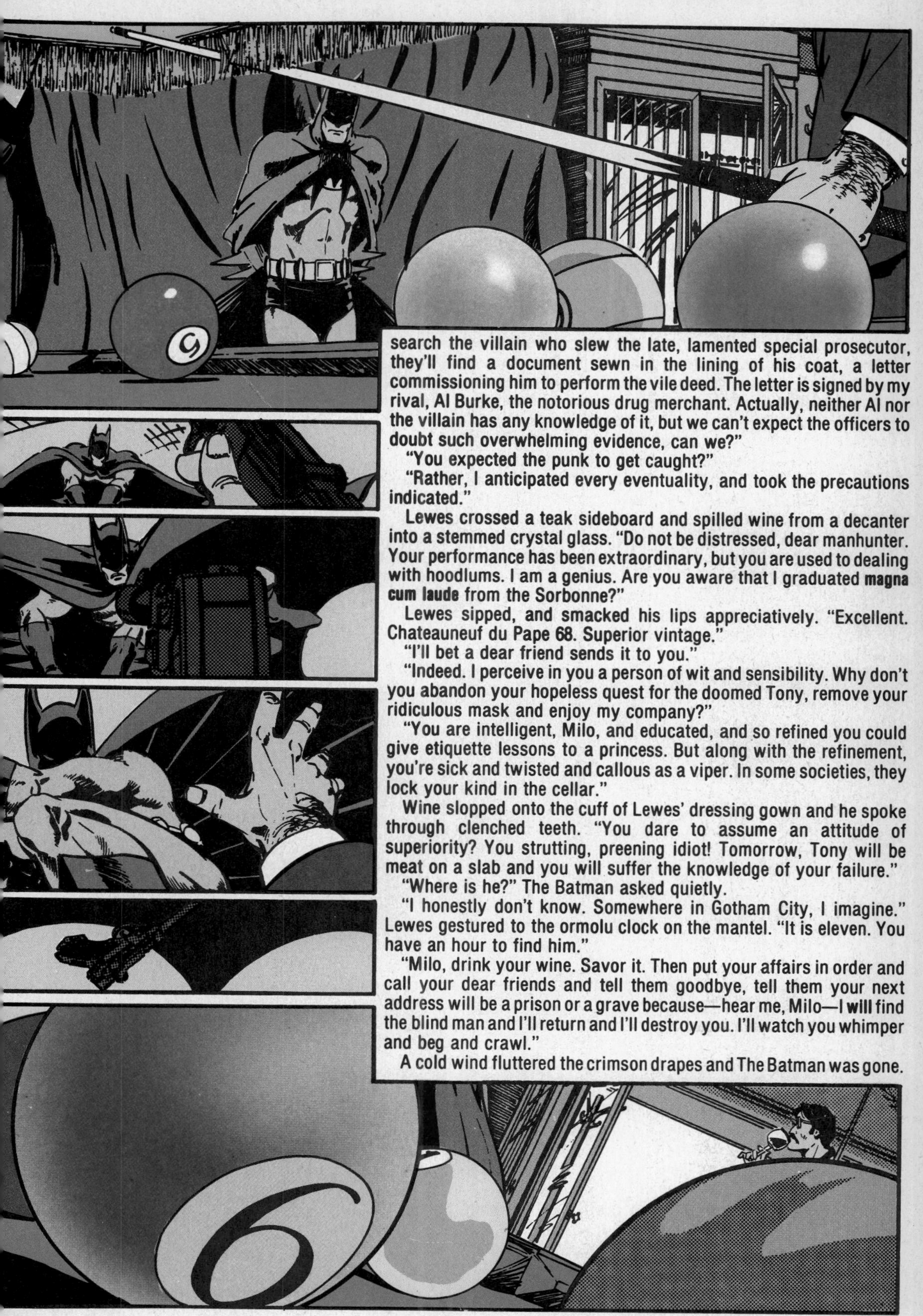

search the villain who slew the late, lamented special prosecutor, they'll find a document sewn in the lining of his coat, a letter commissioning him to perform the vile deed. The letter is signed by my rival, Al Burke, the notorious drug merchant. Actually, neither Al nor the villain has any knowledge of it, but we can't expect the officers to doubt such overwhelming evidence, can we?"

"You expected the punk to get caught?"

"Rather, I anticipated every eventuality, and took the precautions indicated."

Lewes crossed a teak sideboard and spilled wine from a decanter into a stemmed crystal glass. "Do not be distressed, dear manhunter. Your performance has been extraordinary, but you are used to dealing with hoodlums. I am a genius. Are you aware that I graduated **magna cum laude** from the Sorbonne?"

Lewes sipped, and smacked his lips appreciatively. "Excellent. Chateauneuf du Pape 68. Superior vintage."

"I'll bet a dear friend sends it to you."

"Indeed. I perceive in you a person of wit and sensibility. Why don't you abandon your hopeless quest for the doomed Tony, remove your ridiculous mask and enjoy my company?"

"You are intelligent, Milo, and educated, and so refined you could give etiquette lessons to a princess. But along with the refinement, you're sick and twisted and callous as a viper. In some societies, they lock your kind in the cellar."

Wine slopped onto the cuff of Lewes' dressing gown and he spoke through clenched teeth. "You dare to assume an attitude of superiority? You strutting, preening idiot! Tomorrow, Tony will be meat on a slab and you will suffer the knowledge of your failure."

"Where is he?" The Batman asked quietly.

"I honestly don't know. Somewhere in Gotham City, I imagine." Lewes gestured to the ormolu clock on the mantel. "It is eleven. You have an hour to find him."

"Milo, drink your wine. Savor it. Then put your affairs in order and call your dear friends and tell them goodbye, tell them your next address will be a prison or a grave because—hear me, Milo—I **will** find the blind man and I'll return and I'll destroy you. I'll watch you whimper and beg and crawl."

A cold wind fluttered the crimson drapes and The Batman was gone.

Somewhere in Gotham City . . . .
It is a monster sprawled along 25 miles of eastern seaboard, stirring and seething and ever-restless. Eight million human beings live on streets that, if laid end-to-end, would stretch all the way to Tokyo, crammed into thousands of neighborhoods from the fire-gutted tenements of Chancreville, where rats nestle in babies' bedclothes and grandmothers forage in garbage cans, to the penthouses of Manor Row, where the cost of a single meal served by liveried servants would support an immigrant family for a year. It is countless chambers and crannies and corners in bars, boats, houses, hotels, elevators, offices, theaters, shacks, tunnels, depots, shops, factories, restaurants, newsstands, hospitals, junkyards, cemeteries, buses, cars, trains, trams, bridges, docks, sewers, parks, jails, mortuaries—the shelters of living and dead, millionaires and bums, fiends and saints.
Napoleon's armies could search for a lifetime and leave places unseen.
An exceptionally energetic investigator could visit the likely ones in a month.

The Batman had less than sixty minutes.

Wrapped in his cape, oblivious to the mocking echoes of distant traffic and the pale fingers of mist arising from the river, he permitted his being to flow outward, to probe the fibers of the monster.

He knew that two gunmen had located the blind man, probably by accident.

Two rootless mercenaries, hungry for Saturday night pleasure, would seek the smoky haunts at the city's center. It was there, then, that they had glimpsed their quarry.

And a blind man would not be able to stray far from the city's ugly heart, not if he planned to meet someone at a prearranged time.

He would fear everyone and everything, insist the meeting be away from the spies who had infiltrated the palaces of the law, insist on neutral territory.

He would go where his enemies would not expect him to be.

He would cower in darkness, hoping to use it to his advantage.

A darkness that would vanish at midnight and three . . . .

Of course! The answer was obvious!

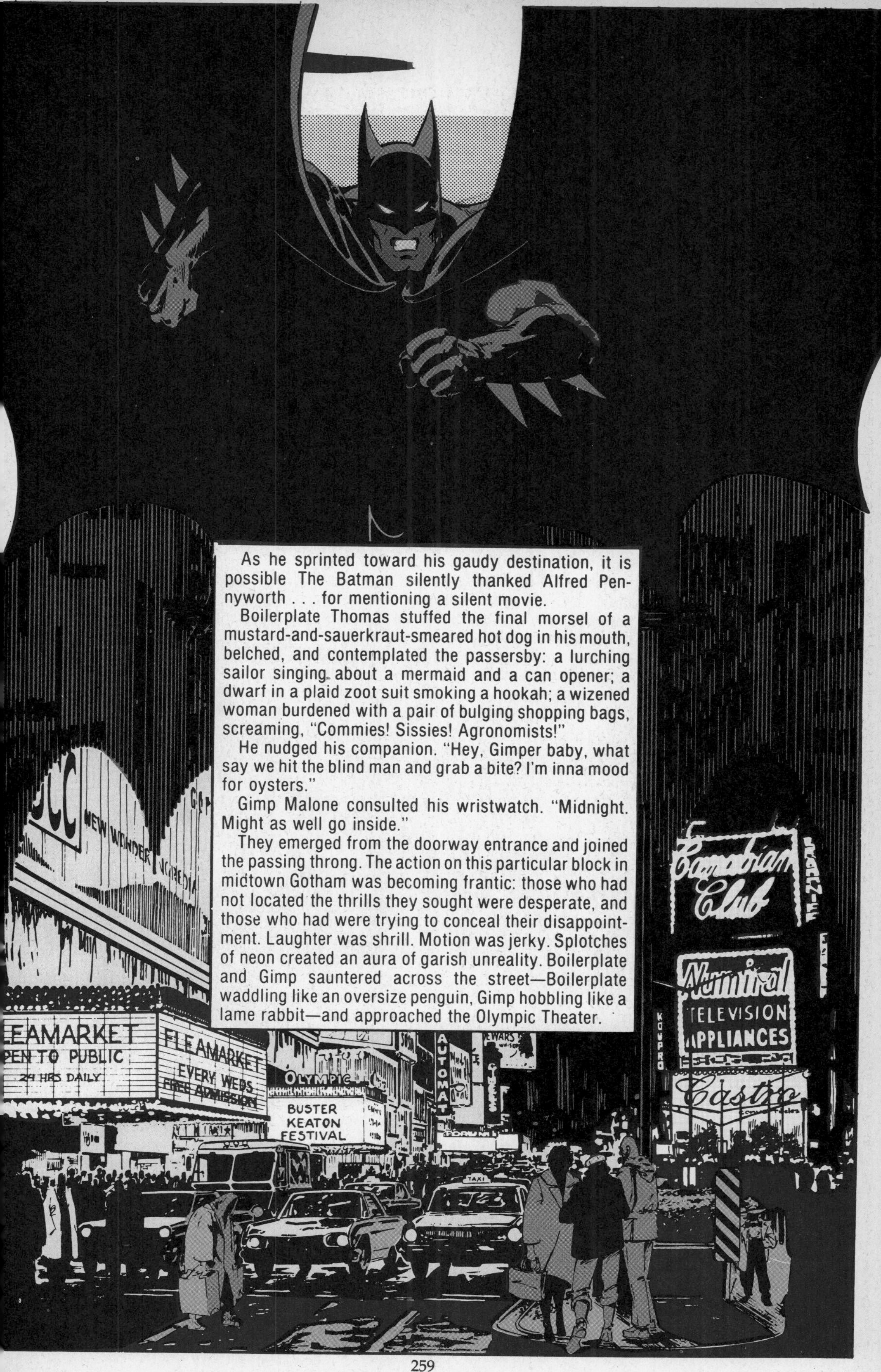

As he sprinted toward his gaudy destination, it is possible The Batman silently thanked Alfred Pennyworth . . . for mentioning a silent movie.

Boilerplate Thomas stuffed the final morsel of a mustard-and-sauerkraut-smeared hot dog in his mouth, belched, and contemplated the passersby: a lurching sailor singing about a mermaid and a can opener; a dwarf in a plaid zoot suit smoking a hookah; a wizened woman burdened with a pair of bulging shopping bags, screaming, "Commies! Sissies! Agronomists!"

He nudged his companion. "Hey, Gimper baby, what say we hit the blind man and grab a bite? I'm inna mood for oysters."

Gimp Malone consulted his wristwatch. "Midnight. Might as well go inside."

They emerged from the doorway entrance and joined the passing throng. The action on this particular block in midtown Gotham was becoming frantic: those who had not located the thrills they sought were desperate, and those who had were trying to conceal their disappointment. Laughter was shrill. Motion was jerky. Splotches of neon created an aura of garish unreality. Boilerplate and Gimp sauntered across the street—Boilerplate waddling like an oversize penguin, Gimp hobbling like a lame rabbit—and approached the Olympic Theater.

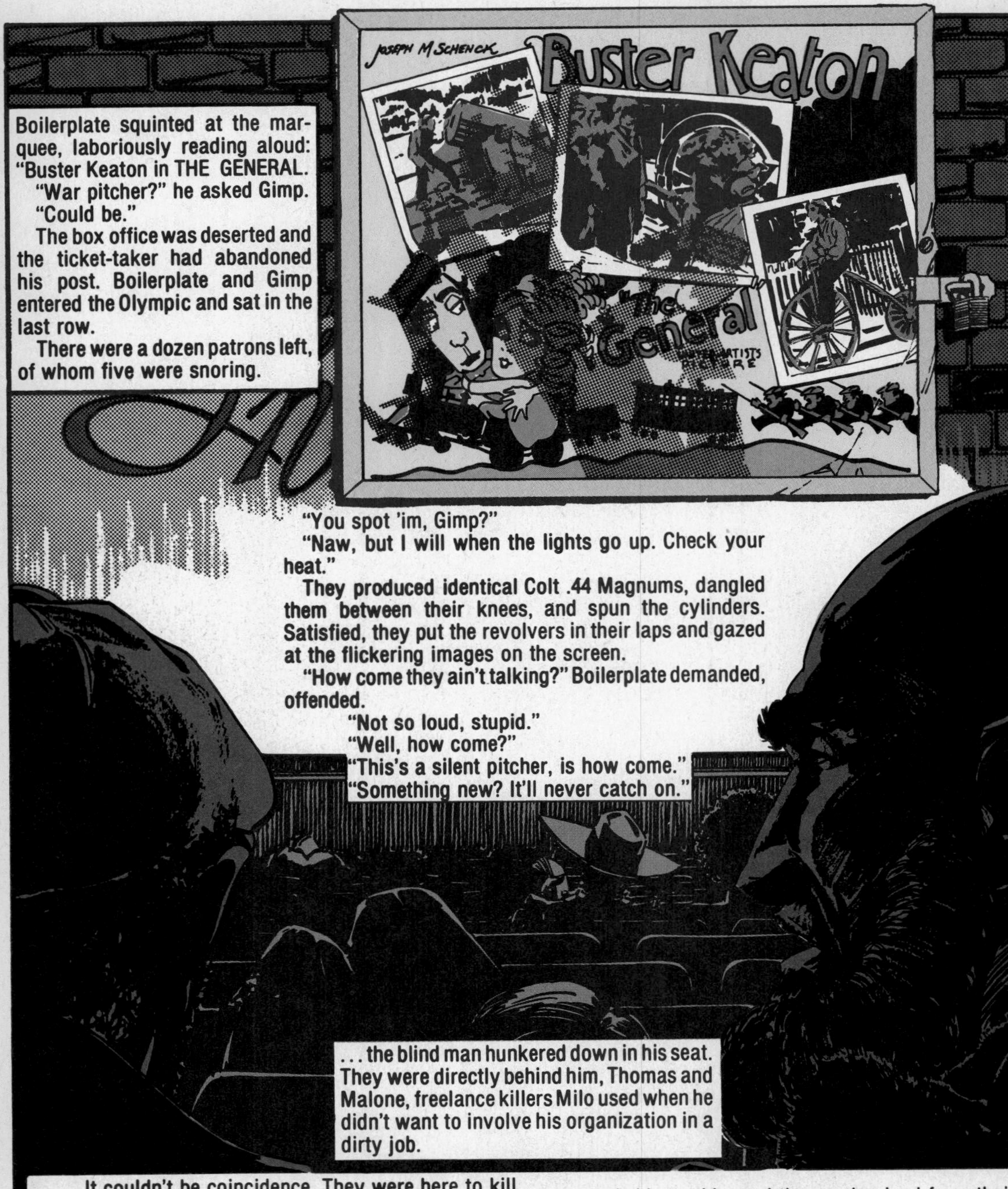

JOSEPH M SCHENCK
Buster Keaton
The General
Boilerplate squinted at the marquee, laboriously reading aloud: "Buster Keaton in THE GENERAL.
"War pitcher?" he asked Gimp.
"Could be."
The box office was deserted and the ticket-taker had abandoned his post. Boilerplate and Gimp entered the Olympic and sat in the last row.
There were a dozen patrons left, of whom five were snoring.
"You spot 'im, Gimp?"
"Naw, but I will when the lights go up. Check your heat."
They produced identical Colt .44 Magnums, dangled them between their knees, and spun the cylinders. Satisfied, they put the revolvers in their laps and gazed at the flickering images on the screen.
"How come they ain't talking?" Boilerplate demanded, offended.
"Not so loud, stupid."
"Well, how come?"
"This's a silent pitcher, is how come."
"Something new? It'll never catch on."
. . . the blind man hunkered down in his seat. They were directly behind him, Thomas and Malone, freelance killers Milo used when he didn't want to involve his organization in a dirty job.
It couldn't be coincidence. They were here to kill him. His throat dried, a nerve in his cheek twitched, his temples throbbed. Could he sneak by them? Reach the exit unobserved? No. The rap of his cane would alert them, or he'd stumble, and the searing lead from their guns would rip his flesh . . . . He tried to remember a prayer.

"Hiya Tony."

The blind man felt warm breath on his neck and smelled mustard and sauerkraut, and sweat stung the corners of his sightless eyes.

"We been waitin', Tony," Gimp Malone said. "Waitin' till there ain't no crowds and no cops."

"Show's over, Tony." This was Boilerplate Thomas. "You didn't notice."

"What you're gonna do, Tony, is you're gonna go where we lead you, real quiet and peaceful."

Helpless, the blind man allowed himself to be nudged forward. He lost all sense of direction, but he realized they were urging him to the front of the theater, to the vacant area at the rear of the screen.

"I got savings," he said. "I can pay."

"Swell," Thomas said. "You can buy yourself a nice funeral."

Later, Anthony Toombs would wonder if it was an hallucination, an illusion fomented by his immense fear and the startling, unexpected hope of salvation. Illusion or not, however, he would cherish those few moments of violence the rest of his days, would remain almost convinced that at twelve and three his personal darkness had been briefly lifted and he had seen:

The Batman, stark and implacable against the expanse of white, a grim figure congealing from the shadows.

"Looking for a target, gentlemen?" He asked pleasantly. "I volunteer."

Thomas and Malone jerked up their Colts and orange and blue flame gouted from the barrels. The screen shook and two holes puckered its gleaming surface, but The Batman remained untouched; as he had congealed, now he seemingly dissolved.

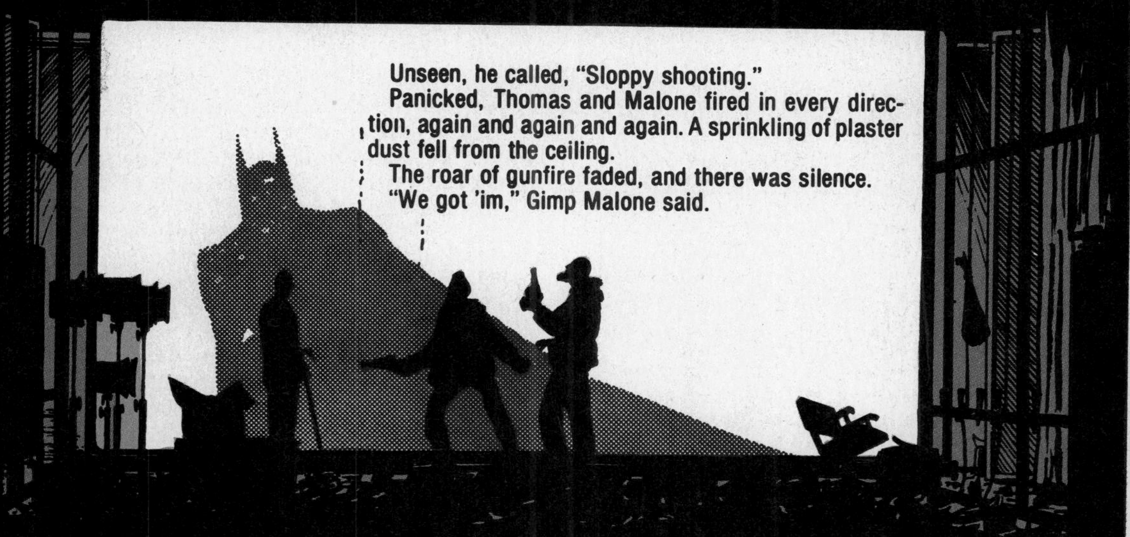

Unseen, he called, "Sloppy shooting."
Panicked, Thomas and Malone fired in every direction, again and again and again. A sprinkling of plaster dust fell from the ceiling.
The roar of gunfire faded, and there was silence.
"We got 'im," Gimp Malone said.

The blind man knew he was wrong. The blind man could **see** The Batman's fist pitch Malone into the aisle where he lay like refuse.

Then The Batman faced Boilerplate Thomas.

Thomas started to raise the Colt.

"You could conceivably succeed," The Batman said. "If you're quick, and if your gun isn't empty, you might be able to nail me before I stuff it in your ear."

And the blind man **saw** Thomas extend the weapon to The Batman, butt first.

The familiar darkness gathered in his sight, and he was comforted.

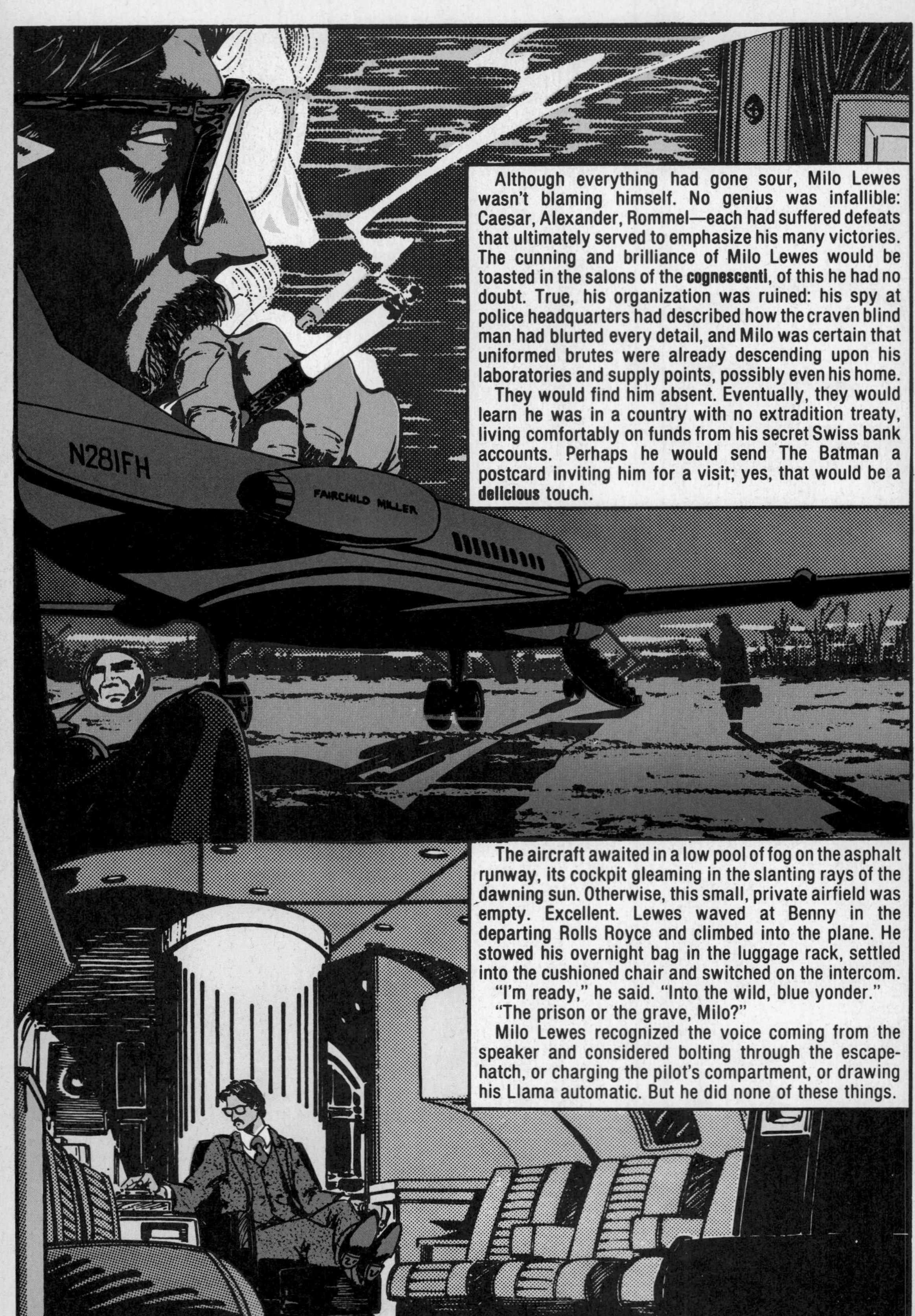
Although everything had gone sour, Milo Lewes wasn't blaming himself. No genius was infallible: Caesar, Alexander, Rommel—each had suffered defeats that ultimately served to emphasize his many victories. The cunning and brilliance of Milo Lewes would be toasted in the salons of the **cognescenti**, of this he had no doubt. True, his organization was ruined: his spy at police headquarters had described how the craven blind man had blurted every detail, and Milo was certain that uniformed brutes were already descending upon his laboratories and supply points, possibly even his home.
They would find him absent. Eventually, they would learn he was in a country with no extradition treaty, living comfortably on funds from his secret Swiss bank accounts. Perhaps he would send The Batman a postcard inviting him for a visit; yes, that would be a **delicious** touch.
N281FH
FAIRCHILD MILLER
The aircraft awaited in a low pool of fog on the asphalt runway, its cockpit gleaming in the slanting rays of the dawning sun. Otherwise, this small, private airfield was empty. Excellent. Lewes waved at Benny in the departing Rolls Royce and climbed into the plane. He stowed his overnight bag in the luggage rack, settled into the cushioned chair and switched on the intercom.
"I'm ready," he said. "Into the wild, blue yonder."
"The prison or the grave, Milo?"
Milo Lewes recognized the voice coming from the speaker and considered bolting through the escape-hatch, or charging the pilot's compartment, or drawing his Llama automatic. But he did none of these things.

Instead, he struggled to control an urge to whimper.
To beg.
To crawl.
End

AN ALMOST LEGENDARY FIGURE, THE COWLED SHADOW OF THE BATMAN PROWLS THROUGH THE NIGHT, PREYING UPON THE CRIMINAL PARASITE LIKE THE WINGED CREATURE WHOSE NAME HE HAS ADOPTED!
NOW, ACCOMPANIED BY THE EQUALLY-LEGENDARY LAUGH OF ROBIN, THE TEEN WONDER, HE STALKS THE MAMMOTH SHADOWS OF HIS HIDDEN BATCAVE, DRINKING IN ITS ECHOES!
SO THE PENGUIN GOES DOWN AGAIN, EH?*
HE WAS SO MAD, HE WAS FIT TO BE TIED! OL' PUDGY THOUGHT HE'D REALLY PUT IT OVER ON US THIS TIME!
--AND-- WHAT CAN I SAY? HE HAD ME SUCKERED!
BUT YOU CAN'T BEAT THE BATMAN!
AT LEAST, ROBIN-- NOT SO FAR! BUT WAIT FOR--
*CARRY OVER FROM LAST ISSUE.--JULIE
ORPHANED AS A CHILD WHEN HIS PARENTS WERE KILLED BEFORE HIS EYES, BRUCE WAYNE TRAINED HIMSELF TO WAGE RELENTLESS WAR AGAINST CRIME AS THE DREAD AVENGER OF THE NIGHT...
THE BATMAN
CREATED BY BOB KANE
THE DEADSHOT RICOCHET
STEVE ENGLEHART * STORY
MARSHALL ROGERS * PENCIL-ART
TERRY AUSTIN * INK-ART
BEN ODA * LETTERER
TRUST
1947
J

Coloring by Julianna Ferriter

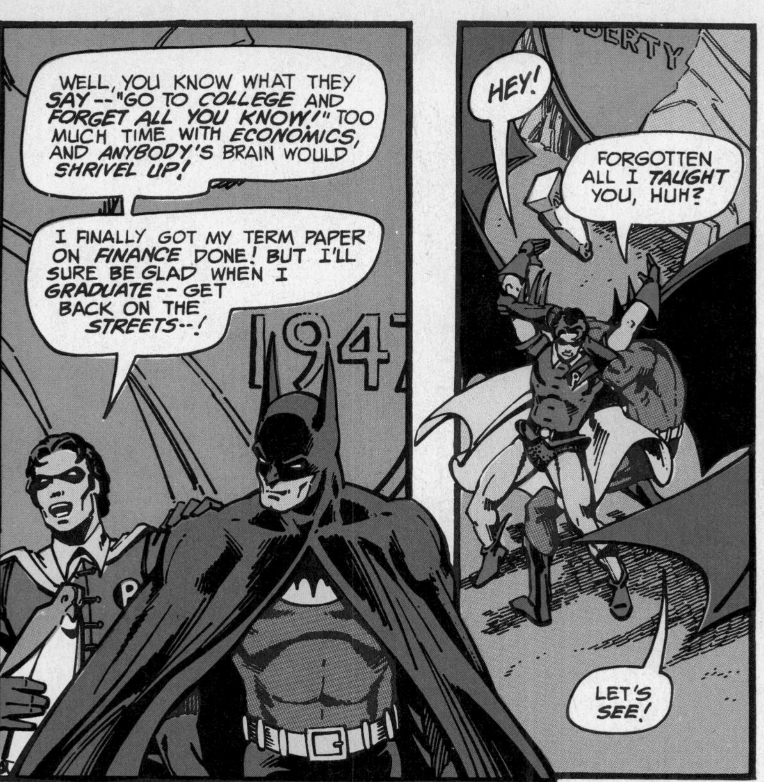

I CAN MATCH YOU ANY TIME I WANT TO, OLD-TIMER!

"OLD-TIMER"!?

HA!

CLIP

DOUBLED--

--AND REDOUBLED--"SMALL-FRY"!

2

IT'S NOT OFTEN THAT LAUGHTER ECHOES IN THE BATCAVE-- NOT TRUE, BREATHLESS LAUGHTER, SHARED BY TWO OLD FRIENDS!
YOU LOOK PRETTY FIT TO ME, KID!
JUST A LITTLE WET BEHIND THE EARS, STILL!
WHAT--?

NUTS! MY BELT-RADIO!
NOW WHAT--?
BZZZZ

ROBIN--WONDER GIRL CALLING!
COME TO GABRIEL'S HORN AT ONCE!
THIS IS THE MOST IMPORTANT MEETING SINCE THE TEEN TITANS STARTED!*
*AND WHY IT'S IMPORTANT WILL BE REVEALED IN THE FEBRUARY ISSUE OF TEEN TITANS, #53!--Julie

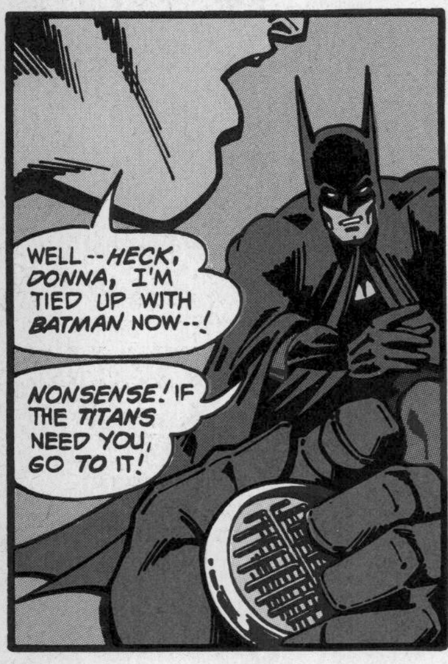
WELL--HECK, DONNA, I'M TIED UP WITH BATMAN NOW--!
NONSENSE! IF THE TITANS NEED YOU, GO TO IT!

BUT--I SAID I'D STICK WITH YOU TILL WE TOOK CARE OF BOSS THORNE--!
AND I APPRECIATE IT! BUT I CAN HANDLE HIM ALONE IF I HAVE TO!

OKAY! I WONDER WHAT THE BIG DEAL IS ON THIS MEETING, THOUGH?
ON MY WAY, WG!

YOU'RE SEEING A LOT OF WONDER GIRL AND THE HARLEQUIN THESE DAYS, I HEAR!
LIKE YOU SAID, BRUCE--I LEARNED A LOT FROM YOU--
--ABOUT BOTH GUNMEN AND GIRLS!

YOU JUST LOOK AFTER SILVER ST. CLOUD, AND LEAVE THE HEAVY STUFF TO THE EXPERTS!
ALL RIGHT! THAT DOES IT!
OUT!

CATCH YA LATER, BRUCE!
GOOD LUCK, DICK--AND THANKS!
IT WAS GOOD TO SEE YOU... PAL!
3

MEANWHILE

IN THE MAXIMUM-SECURITY SECTION OF GOTHAM PRISON...

30 a
INSIDE, COBBLEPOT-* WE'VE KEPT YOUR CELL WARM FOR YOU!
*OSWALD CHESTERFIELD COBBLEPOT, THAT IS--THE PENGUIN'S REAL NAME. --Julie

GREETINGS, PENGUIN! I SEE YOU'RE BACK AGAIN!

DON'T GET CUTE, LAWTON!
AT LEAST I COME AND GO, WHILE YOU JUST STAY AND STAY!

AS A MATTER OF FACT, MY FELONIOUS FRIEND, I'M ABOUT TO GO AGAIN-- WITH THIS INGENIOUS LITTLE DEVICE!
BUFFOONS! THEY CANNOT CAGE A CREATURE AS CLEVER AS I!
WHAT ARE YOU JABBERING ABOUT? THAT'S ONLY YOUR MONOCLE!

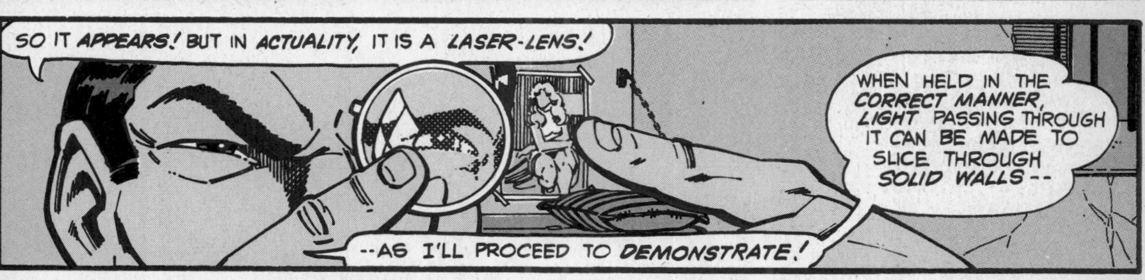
SO IT APPEARS! BUT IN ACTUALITY, IT IS A LASER-LENS!
WHEN HELD IN THE CORRECT MANNER, LIGHT PASSING THROUGH IT CAN BE MADE TO SLICE THROUGH SOLID WALLS--
--AS I'LL PROCEED TO DEMONSTRATE!

NO! IF IT'S THAT GOOD--I WANT IT!
AWRK

NOT A CHANCE, PENGY! YOU'RE RIGHT-- I'VE BEEN HELD HERE FOR YEARS--EVER SINCE THE BATMAN BEAT ME--
GIVE THAT BACK TO ME, YOU--
--WHILE THE SCARECROW, RIDDLER, CATWOMAN AND YOU PASSED THROUGH--
4

--BUT NOW--
--DEADSHOT IS FREE ONCE MORE!
WHAT TH--!

KRAK KRAK
WE WON'T BE SEEING THE PENGUIN AGAIN FOR A WHILE--
AWKK AWKK
CHK
CHK
--AND IT'S PROBABLY JUST AS WELL!

BUT WE'LL BE SEEING PLENTY MORE OF THIS MAN!
I MADE IT!
NOW, ONCE I ARM MYSELF, I'LL BE OFF ON A BAT-HUNT!

MEANWHILE, HOWEVER, WHY DON'T WE SPY ON BOSS RUPERT THORNE--?

SKRITCH SKRITCH

SKRITCH

GOOD EVENING, THORNE!
GOOD--
--LORD!
5

WELL! IF THIS IS SUPPOSED TO INTIMIDATE ME--
LET'S CUT THE PRETENDING, THORNE! THERE ARE NO VOTERS AROUND TO IMPRESS!
I CAME TO TALK ABOUT THIS "CEASE-AND-DESIST" ORDER YOU SLAPPED ON ME!

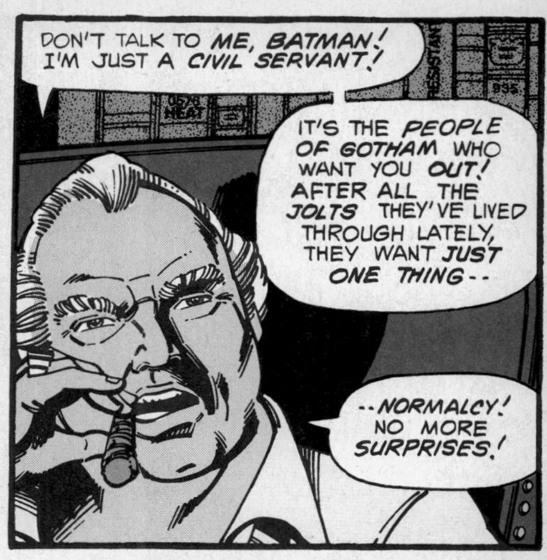

DON'T TALK TO ME, BATMAN! I'M JUST A CIVIL SERVANT!
IT'S THE PEOPLE OF GOTHAM WHO WANT YOU OUT! AFTER ALL THE JOLTS THEY'VE LIVED THROUGH LATELY, THEY WANT JUST ONE THING--
--NORMALCY! NO MORE SURPRISES!

A CAPED CREATURE OF THE NIGHT ONLY STIRS THINGS UP! THE ORDER STAYS!
YOU CAN'T STOP PRETENDING EVEN NOW, CAN YOU? YOU'RE ALWAYS ON STAGE!
DO YOU THINK I DON'T KNOW IT WAS YOU AND YOUR CROP OF ROTTEN APPLES WHO STAGE-MANAGED THIS? DO YOU THINK I DON'T KNOW WHAT THE PEOPLE REALLY THINK?

LET ME TELL YOU SOMETHING, THORNE! I GAVE YOU THIS ONE CHANCE TO SETTLE OUR BUSINESS PEACEFULLY, EVEN THOUGH I KNEW YOU PROBABLY WOULDN'T TAKE IT!

NOW, WE'LL SETTLE IT THE BATMAN'S WAY!

WHEW HE'S GONE!
BUT WHAT HE SAID-- HAVE TO BE READY--
CLICK
6

YOU'D BETTER BE READY FOR ME, TOO, THORNE!
WHA--HUGO STRANGE--!

B-BUT YOU'RE-- DEAD--!
AT YOUR HANDS, THORNE--OR AT LEAST BY YOUR ORDER--

NO!
I MEAN-- I DON'T BELIEVE THIS! YOU AIN'T NO SPOOK!
THERE AIN'T NO SPOOKS! BATMAN'S PULLING A CON-JOB!

THIS IS MY SECOND WARNING, THORNE!* YOUR MURDEROUS LIFE HAS RUN ITS COURSE!
WHEN YOU SEE ME A THIRD TIME, IT WILL BE--
* THE FIRST ONE CAME LAST ISSUE! -- Julie

--THE END.!
THIS IS A TRICK--!
IS IT?

THIS HAS GOTTA BE A TRICK! IT'S--
--GOTTA--
--GOTTA BE--!

OH, GEEZ!
7

NOON, THE NEXT DAY! AS A 24-HOUR TOWN, GOTHAM CITY SEES ITS RESIDENTS KEEP TO ALL SORTS OF SCHEDULES BESIDES THE TYPICAL 9-TO-5... BUT ONLY THE RICH AND THE FREE-LANCE KEEP THE HOURS BRUCE WAYNE KEEPS!
BRUCE! HI!
SILVER, MY DEAR, ONLY FOR YOU WOULD I GET UP AT THE CRACK OF DAWN!

YOU KNOW, IF I THOUGHT YOU MEANT ALL THAT MALARKY YOU SPOUT--!
I INVITED YOU TO SEE MY WORK, BRUCE, BECAUSE I LIKE MY WORK! DOING SOMETHING WELL IS IMPORTANT TO ME!
TO ME, TOO, SILVER!

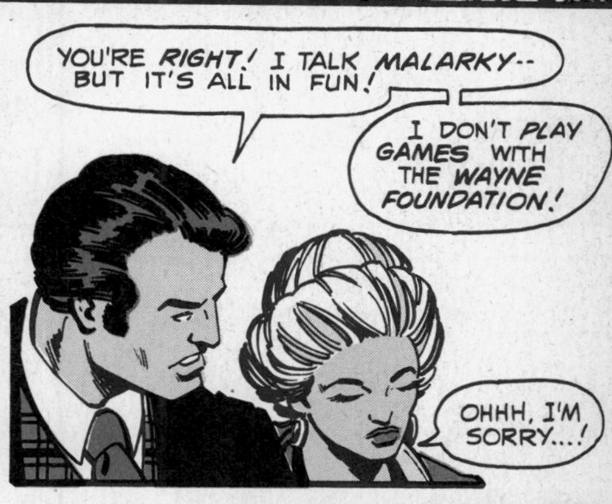

YOU'RE RIGHT! I TALK MALARKY-- BUT IT'S ALL IN FUN!
I DON'T PLAY GAMES WITH THE WAYNE FOUNDATION!
OHHH, I'M SORRY...!

A LOVER'S SPAT! OUR FIRST! THIS IS GETTING SERIOUS!
IT'S BEGINNING TO REALLY MATTER WHAT SHE THINKS OF ME!
AND YET--

--SHE DOESN'T REALLY KNOW ME--NOT INSIDE! THERE'S A PART OF ME SHE CAN'T EVER KNOW!
ALWAYS, THE SAME PROBLEM-- EVER SINCE THE FIRST GIRL I LOVED, JULIE MADISON!*
THEY LOVE BRUCE WAYNE--

*BACK IN DETECTIVE #31! YOU CAN FIND OUT WHAT BECAME OF HER IN WORLD'S FINEST #248! -- Julie

--BUT BRUCE WAYNE HAS BECOME A DAYTIME MASK FOR THE BATMAN!

THE PROBLEM IS-- WOULD I HAVE IT ANY OTHER WAY?

SO, SHOW ME YOUR WORK, SWEETHEART!
I'VE NEVER BEEN QUITE CLEAR ON WHAT IT IS ANYWAY!
IN THAT CASE--

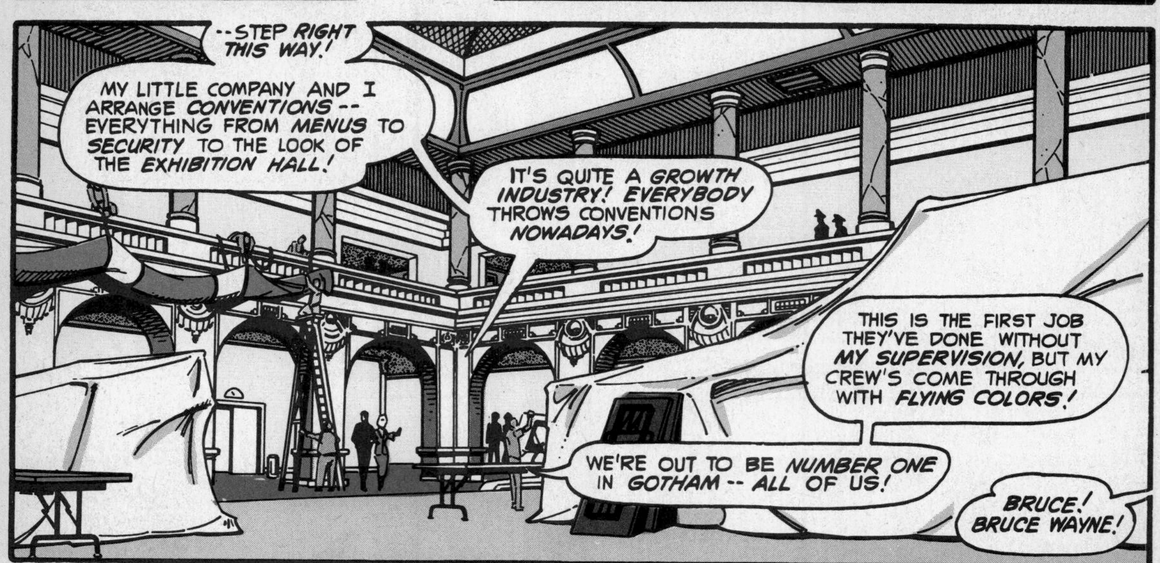
--STEP RIGHT THIS WAY!
MY LITTLE COMPANY AND I ARRANGE CONVENTIONS -- EVERYTHING FROM MENUS TO SECURITY TO THE LOOK OF THE EXHIBITION HALL!
IT'S QUITE A GROWTH INDUSTRY! EVERYBODY THROWS CONVENTIONS NOWADAYS!
THIS IS THE FIRST JOB THEY'VE DONE WITHOUT MY SUPERVISION, BUT MY CREW'S COME THROUGH WITH FLYING COLORS!
WE'RE OUT TO BE NUMBER ONE IN GOTHAM -- ALL OF US!
BRUCE! BRUCE WAYNE!

COMMISSIONER GORDON!
I RUN INTO YOU IN THE DARNEDEST PLACES, BRUCE!

CAN I HELP YOU, COMMISSIONER? I'M IN CHARGE HERE--!
MY BOYS WILL BE FINISHED SOON, MA'AM! A DANGEROUS CRIMINAL HAS ESCAPED, AND HIS LAST-KNOWN HIDEOUT WAS ON THIS BLOCK, SO WE'RE CANVASSING THE AREA!
OH? WHO WAS IT, COMMISSIONER?

FELLOW NAME OF FLOYD LAWTON-- A.K.A. DEADSHOT!
TANGLED WITH THE BATMAN ONCE, AND LOST!* HE WAS PRETTY BITTER ABOUT IT, FROM ALL REPORTS!
*IN BATMAN #59! --Julie
9

OH, YES... I REMEMBER HIM NOW! WASN'T HE A MASTER MARKSMAN?
THAT'S HIM! MASQUERADED AS A HERO-- WHILE PLANNING TO MURDER THE BATMAN!
WELL, I GUESS WE'RE FINISHED, MA'AM! THANK YOU FOR YOUR COOPERATION!

AND NOW, I'D LIKE TO REQUEST YOUR COOPERATION FOR LUNCH AT THE FOX GARDENS!
YOU'RE ON, BIG SPENDER! I'M FAMISHED!
BUT ONLY FOR LUNCH! THIS SHOW OPENS AT 7 TONIGHT!

A THREE-BLOCK WALK LATER...
FOX GARDENS

--CHENIN BLANC FOR THE LADY, AND PERRIER FOR ME!
VERY GOOD, MR. WAYNE!
BRUCE...CAN I ASK YOU A QUESTION?

SHOOT, SILVER!
WELL, YOU'RE A WELL-KNOWN MAN IN GOTHAM--AND ONE OF THE THINGS YOU USED TO BE KNOWN FOR WAS AN INTEREST IN CRIME!
YOU WERE A FRIEND OF COMMISSIONER GORDON'S, AND THE PAPERS EVEN SAID YOU HELPED CONTACT THE BATMAN SOMETIMES!
UH OH!

OBVIOUSLY, YOU'RE STILL A FRIEND OF THE COMMISSIONER'S--BUT WHAT ABOUT THE BATMAN?
YOU SEEM SO BORED WITH CRIME, AT LEAST SINCE I'VE KNOWN YOU!
SHE'S WATCHING ME SO INTENTLY!
THIS ISN'T JUST A CASUAL QUESTION!
DOES SHE SUSPECT?

THE DARK KNIGHT MEASURES HIS WORDS CAREFULLY...
WHEN I WAS YOUNGER, SILVER--HAD FEWER RESPONSIBILITIES TO WAYNE ENTERPRISES AND THE FOUNDATION--
--SURE, I LIKED TO FOLLOW THE CRIME REPORTS!
BUT THAT'S ALL PAST!
10

AND -- DID YOU KNOW THE BATMAN?
WELL, YES--
--WE MET ON A NUMBER OF OCCASIONS! BUT ALFRED KNEW HIM BETTER -- HE WAS SOMETHING OF AN AMATEUR DETECTIVE AND HELPED THE BATMAN ON A FEW CASES!

YOUR ORDER, SIR!

SHE DOES SUSPECT! I THOUGHT SHE DID, THE NIGHT I FIRST MET HER!*
I'VE CHIDED ALFRED FOR PLAYING HIS ROLE TOO BROADLY, BUT IT MAY BE MYSELF I HAVE TO WATCH! IT WON'T DO TO GET CARELESS WITH A LADY THIS SHARP!
AND SILVER ST. CLOUD KEEPS HER OWN COUNCIL!
*ON HIS YACHT IN DETECTIVE NO. 470! --Julie

SUNSET--

THE POLICE HAVEN'T FOUND DEADSHOT YET, AND THEY'RE NOT LIKELY TO! HE CLAIMED TO BE MY SUPERIOR, AND HE WASN'T WRONG BY MUCH!
I CAN SEE HIM AS IF IT WERE YESTERDAY! HE'S NOT THE KIND YOU FORGET!

"FLOYD LAWTON COULD HAVE BEEN ME-- TWISTED! A RICH YOUNG PLAYBOY WITH TIME ON HIS HANDS, WHO FANCIED HE SHOULD COMPETE WITH THE BATMAN!"
"HE DONNED HIS WHITE TIE AND TAILS, PLUS A BLACK VELVET MASK, AND SET OUT TO TRACK DOWN CROOKS!"
11

KPOW
KPOW
"HE WAS A DEAD SHOT -- BUT HE ALWAYS AIMED TO DISARM, NOT TO KILL--"

"-- SO HE GAINED A CONSIDERABLE FOLLOWING AS A CRIMEFIGHTER! BUT ALL THE WHILE, HE WAS SCHEMING TO USE HIS NEW CLOUT TO TAKE OVER THE CITY'S RACKETS!!!
"THEN ROBIN AND I TRIED TO PROVE IT--"

"-- IT LOOKED LIKE I WAS CRYING SOUR GRAPES! HE CAME CLOSE TO RUNNING ME OUT OF OWN TOWN -- OR MURDERING ME!"
"BUT I FOUND OUT WHO HE WAS -- SNEAKED IN AND ALTERED HIS GUNSIGHTS -- SO WHEN HE TRIED TO KILL ME -- HE MISSED!"

HE WAS JUST LIKE BOSS THORNE! THE MORE THINGS CHANGE, ETC.--!
NOBODY LIKES A LONE BAT -- IF THEY'VE GOT SOMETHING TO HIDE!

PKOW

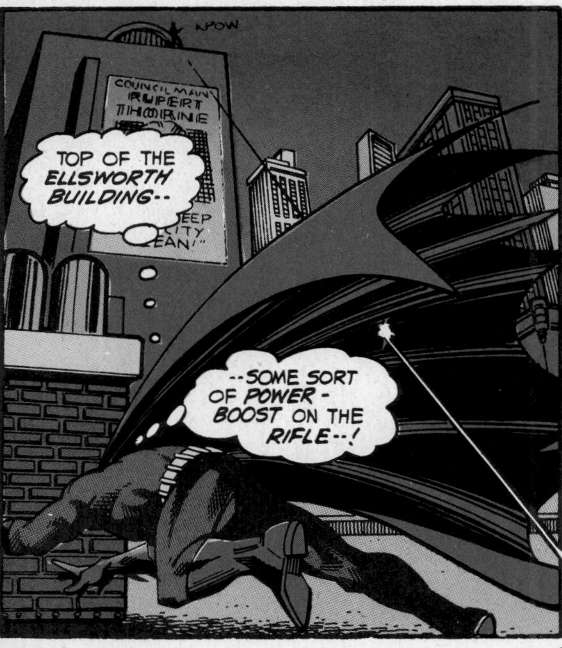
KPOW
COUNCILMAN RUPERT THORNE
TOP OF THE ELLSWORTH BUILDING--
--SOME SORT OF POWER-BOOST ON THE RIFLE--!

BATMAN! I KNOW YOU CAN HEAR ME! THIS IS DEADSHOT!
KPOW
DEADSHOT!
12

I TRIED YOU ONCE THE CLEVER WAY-- THE RICH MAN'S WAY! I TRIED TO SIMPLY DISCREDIT YOU-- BUT THAT FAILED, SO I PLANNED A "SHOOTING ACCIDENT"!
AND YOU OUTSMARTED ME! I WAS A WEALTHY MAN--I WAS SOMEBODY-- TILL YOU PUT ME IN A CELL-- MADE ME JUST ANOTHER CON--
--BUT I LEARNED SOMETHING IN THERE!

I LEARNED TO RELY ON POWER, NOT BRAINS! I LEARNED NOT TO PLAY THOSE FANCY GAMES!

MY NEW BLASTERS ARE LIKE PARTS OF MY ARMS! EVERY MAGNUM CHARGE I FIRE COMES STRAIGHT FROM ME-- FROM MY HATE--
--NOT FROM SOME FANCY SPORTING GUN! NOW--I TOUCH MY MIDDLE FINGER TO THE FIRING BUTTON IN MY PALM AND--

WOK

MY SUDDEN APPEARANCE DIDN'T EVEN FAZE HIM!
HE'S UP AS FAST AS I AM!

I WORKED OUT EVERY DAY IN PRISON, BATMAN! I HAD NO SUPER-POWER-- NO ESCAPE GIMMICKS--
--BUT I KNEW, SOMEDAY, I'D GET MY CHANCE!

WHAT A WASTE OF ALL THAT TIME!
WASTE? NO!
COUNCILMAN RUPERT THORNE
SAYS:-"HELP KEEP GOTHAM CITY CLEAN!"

NOT WHEN I CAN BE THE MAN WHO KILLED THE BATMAN!

THAT'S BEEN TRIED BY EXPERTS--
--AND I'M STILL HERE!
13

BUT NO SOONER HAS DEADSHOT TOPPLED, THAN HE LAUNCHES A NEW DEVICE FROM HIS RIGHT BLASTER!
THOK
COME ON, CHAMP--
--CATCH ME IF YOU CAN!
MY PLEASURE!

HA HAHAHAHA
THAT LAUGH -- FAMILIAR?

HA HA HAHA

WHAT IS THE HARLEQUIN OF HATE UP TO? SORRY, THAT MUST WAIT TILL NEXT ISSUE!
AHA HA HAHAHAHA

MY GOD! DEADSHOT'S LANDED ON TOP OF SILVER'S CONVENTION HALL!

KRASH
14

ELCOME WEISINGER OF
HOLY--! THE BATMAN!

OUTA THE WAY, SILVER! I'M CALLIN' THE COPS!
NO, BILL! IF YOU CALL ANYBODY, CALL THE PRESS!
BUT THE BATMAN'S BEEN ORDERED TO LEAVE TOWN! WE'RE SUPPOSED TO--
-- REPORT---
BILL, WE ARE NOT TURNING THAT MAN OVER TO THE FREAKIN' AUTHORITIES!
THAT'S AN ORDER!

DC
GIVE IT UP, DEADSHOT! THIS ISN'T BETWEEN JUST US TWO ANY MORE!
POK

YOU THINK I CARE ABOUT THESE BYSTANDERS, BATMAN? MAYBE ONCE, I WOULD HAVE -- BUT NOT NOW!
THIS AIN'T THE OLD DAYS! I DON'T PLAY BY RULES ANY MORE!

PEOPLE GOTTA TAKE THEIR CHANCES NOW, 'CAUSE ANYTHING GOES!
I WANT WHAT I WANT, AND DON'T CARE HOW I GET IT!
15

WELL, I CARE, DEADSHOT!
YOU'LL GET ME, ALL RIGHT--BUT NOT THE WAY YOU THINK!

AN ELOQUENT ANSWER, THE MASTER MARKSMAN CATAPULTS A CHARGE INTO THE CARRIAGE RETURN!
DIDN'T EXPECT THAT, HUH? THOUGHT MY AIM HADN'T HELD UP!
BACK SPACE
CHUK

WHA--?!

I'VE BEEN FOOLING YOU, BATMAN--LEADING YOU ON! I'VE WAITED SO LONG FOR THIS, I HAD TO MAKE IT LAST!

CREEP! I PRACTICED SIGHTING A HUNDRED TIMES A DAY-- WITH MY COMB, MY FINGER--!
I MIGHT ADD--I CAN SEE THROUGH THE MASK!
PKOW

I HAD--
HUH?
16

NOW'S THE TIME TO GIVE IT UP, DEADSHOT-- OR I'LL JUMP DOWN AND WRITE YOU A LETTER!
OKAY! OKAY! YOU WIN!
FOR NOW!

EEEEEEEE
HERE COME GOTHAM'S FINEST! THEY'LL TAKE CARE OF YOU, LAWTON!
SORRY I CAN'T STICK AROUND!

EEEEEEEEEEEEEEEEE
BATMAN!

IT WAS BRUCE!

I KNOW IT!
IT WAS BRUCE!

NEXT: AT LAST! THE JOKER!
AND MORE ON THE GIRL AND THE GHOST! DETECTIVE #475-- ON SALE THE LAST WEEK IN NOV.

PROLOGUE
IN THE NEW YORK OFFICES OF DC COMICS, ARTIST/ EDITOR ALLEN MILGROM BURNS THE MIDNIGHT OIL TO MEET A DEADLINE...
" FIRESTORM BOUNCES BADDY AGAINST WALL!"
MAYBE HE COULD JUST PUNCH HIM-- THAT WOULD BE A LOT EASIER TO DRAW!
PRETZELS
EENEX

EITHER I'M CRAZY OR SOMEBODY'S USING MY TYPEWRITER!
CLAKATACLAKATA!

UH-HUH! I'M CRAZY--
--WAITA-MINNIT!

AWRIGHT, WHO'S THE WISE GUY?
we want bat-mite!

SKREEEE
POOM
POOM

I'M DEFINITELY CRAZY!
WE WANT BAT-MITE

WE WANT
WE WANT BAT-MITE
WE WANT BAT-MITE!
WE WANT BAT-MITE!
BAT-MITE!
NO--I'M NOT CRAZY--EVERY-BODY ELSE IS!
EVERYBODY ELSE WANTS BAT-MITE!
1

Coloring by Anthony Tollin

YOU RANG?
HUNH?!? BAT-MITE... IN MY OFFICE... SITTING ON MY TELEPHONE?
SURE THING! I'D SIT ON SOMEBODY ELSE'S TELEPHONE, BUT THERE'S NOBODY ELSE AROUND-- JUST YOU!
THERE ARE DEFINITE DISADVANTAGES TO WORKING LATE! THERE ARE ALSO EIGHT MILLION STORIES IN THE NAKED CITY! THIS IS ONE OF EACH!
BAT-MITE'S NEW YORK ADVENTURE!
BOB ROZAKIS WRITER • MICHAEL GOLDEN ARTIST • BOB SMITH INKER • MILT SNAPINN LETTERER • ANTHONY TOLLIN COLORIST • TODD KLEIN PRODUCTION • ALLEN MILGROM EDITOR
WELL, SORRY I CAN'T TALK TO YOU RIGHT NOW-- BUT I'VE GOT A DEADLINE TO MEET!
MAYBE IF I IGNORE HIM, HE'LL DISAPPEAR! THIS HAS GOT TO BE WHAT HAPPENS WHEN YOU EAT PRETZELS AND SODA FOR DINNER AFTER 3 DAYS WITHOUT SLEEP!
DEADLINES? I CAN HELP WITH THAT!
WHAT--?!
PUFF!
2

CUTE... CUTE! BUT I DON'T THINK JACK C. HARRIS IS GONNA LIKE YOUR VERSION OF FIRESTORM!
THEN LET'S ASK HIM...
POOF!
HUNH?!? WHAT AM I DOING HERE? A SECOND AGO I WAS CHANGING STACY'S DIAPER--
DON'T WORRY! YOU CAN GO BACK TO THAT EXCITING CHORE AS SOON AS YOU TELL AL HOW MUCH YOU LIKE THIS ARTWORK!
BUT I DON'T LIKE IT--
--IN FACT, I THINK IT...
POOOOF!
AHHH, WHO ASKED YOU, ANYWAY!
ALL RIGHT, BAT-MITE! ASSUMING THAT YOU REALLY ARE HERE--
--WHAT ARE YOU HERE FOR?
I WANT WHAT I DESERVE...
...MY PLACE IN THE SUN... MY JUST DESSERTS...
...MY OWN FEATURE IN BATMAN FAMILY!
Dollar Comics
BATMAN FAMILY
B-BUT WE CAN'T JUST SAY OKAY AND YOU'VE GOT IT!
--WE'LL NEED A WRITER!
BATMAN
3

YOU MAKE THAT SOUND TOUGH! PRESTO --ONE BOB ROZAKIS!
POOF!
BRRINNG
MAYBE IT'S SOMEBODY CALLING TO WAKE ME UP--!

NICE TRICK, AL--BUT I'VE SPENT THE LAST FOUR HOURS ON THE LONG ISLAND RAILROAD, TRYING TO GET HOME! NOW I'VE GOT TO START ALL OVER AGAIN!
YES, JACK, YOU WERE!... THE WHAT?... HOLD ON!
YOU SEE A DIAPER?
YOU MEAN THIS?

YEAH, JACK...IT'S HERE! ...OKAY, I'LL HOLD IT FOR YOU!...'BYE!
HEEHEE! THIS IS SO MUCH FUN!

UH...AL! IS THAT WHO I THINK IT IS?
OF COURSE, SILLY! AND YOU'VE BEEN CHOSEN TO CHRONICLE MY ADVENTURES IN BATMAN FAMILY!
BEAR WITH IT, BOB! THIS IS MY HALLUCINATION, AFTER ALL!

HERE'S A TYPEWRITER-- YOU JUST TYPE WHAT I TELL YOU!
LISTEN, BAT-MITE! WE'RE GONNA NEED AN ARTIST...

COME ON AN' HURRY UP -- I AIN'T GOT ALL NI--
POOF!
4

"...AN INKER..."

"...A LETTERER..."

"...A COLORIST..."
Shadow

"...A PRODUCTION MAN..."

WHAT'S GOING ON? YOU INTERRUPTED MY *BRIDGE GAME!*
I WAS FILING MY *SHADOW* PULPS WHEN...
HEY! DON'T STEP ON THE DOG--!
GETTING A LITTLE *COZY* IN HERE!
AL--DO US ALL A FAVOR--*DON'T* TELL HIM WE NEED A *PRINTING PLANT!*
IS THIS WHAT *DC* DOES WHEN YOU'RE LATE ON AN ASSIGNMENT?
NO, IF YOU'RE *LATE*, THEY SEND *VINNIE* AFTER YOU--
DO WE GET OVERTIME FOR *THIS?*
PRETZELS
HOLD IT... *HOLD IT...* HOLD IT!!

5

SO... WHY DON'T YOU GET STARTED? YOU'VE GOT EVERYBODY YOU NEED!
LOOK... SUPPOSE I PROMISE TO DO A STORY ABOUT YOU FOR BATMAN FAMILY?
AND SUPPOSE I GET ALL OF THEM TO DO IT UP REALLY NICE?
WALT GIBSON KNOWS A TRICK LIKE THIS!
WHO CARES?
I DON'T SEE ANY WIRES--!
POOF!
YEAH... AND--?
WELL, IF WE PROMISE TO PUT IT IN BATMAN FAMILY... WILL YOU GO HOME ... AND NOT BOTHER US ANYMORE?
NOW?
NOW!
WELL, I GUESS I CAN TAKE YOUR WORD FOR IT!
OH YEAH! RIGHT, GUYS?
RI!GHT!
OKAY, BUT YOU BETTER! OR I'LL COME BACK...
...AND NEXT TIME I'LL BRING MXYZPTLK WITH ME!
POOOF!
CRASH!
ANYBODY WANT TO ORDER A PIZZA?
THE END (WE HOPE)
6

Coloring by Petra Scotese

WEDNESDAY IS NAMED FOR WODEN -- OR ODIN -- THE NORSE GOD OF WISDOM!
SO I WOULDN'T BE TRUE TO MY ROLE IF I WASN'T SMART ENOUGH TO KNOW WHEN TO TAKE MY LEAVE!
SEE YOU TOMORROW, ALL!

CALENDAR MAN IS PLAYING THIS FARCE TO THE HILT!
HIS CYCLE EVEN HAS EIGHT WHEELS TO EMULATE ODIN'S EIGHT-LEGGED HORSE, SLEIPNIR!
ONCE HE ENTERS THAT UNDERPASS, I'LL NEVER NAB HIM --

-- SO I'D BETTER MAKE SURE HE DOESN'T REACH IT!
WUMP!
WUMP!

WITH UNERRING ACCURACY, THE WHIRLY-BAT'S SMOKE-BOMBS STRIKE THE STREET IN FRONT OF THE NARROW UNDERPASS --
WHOOM!
WHOOM!
-- OBSCURING IT COMPLETELY --

-- AND FORCING THE VIKING-CLAD CALENDAR MAN TO TURN ASIDE, OR RISK A SHATTERING COLLISION!
WELL DONE, BATMAN!
YOU'VE IMPROVED YOUR BAG OF TRICKS SINCE LAST WE MET!*
* WAY BACK IN DETECTIVE #259. -- PAUL

UNFORTUNATELY, SO HAVE I!
ODIN SACRIFICED AN EYE TO GAIN KNOWLEDGE --

-- BUT I SACRIFICED MINE TO GAIN POWER!!
2

CALENDAR MAN'S COVERED ALL HIS BETS! THE LASER-BLAST THAT TOTALLED THE WHIRLY-BAT MISSED ME--
--BUT I'LL STILL BE SPLATTERED ALL OVER THE SIDEWALK--
SKWA-WHOOM!

--UNLESS I CAN TURN MY CAPE INTO A MAKESHIFT GLIDER--

--AND TRY A LITTLE FANCY MANEUVERING!

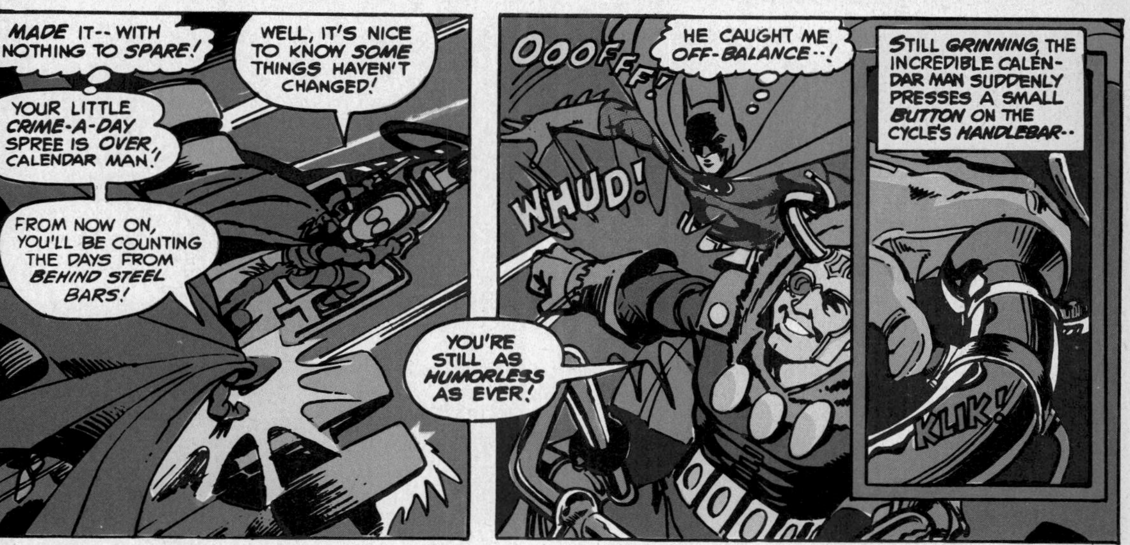
MADE IT-- WITH NOTHING TO SPARE!
YOUR LITTLE CRIME-A-DAY SPREE IS OVER, CALENDAR MAN!
WELL, IT'S NICE TO KNOW SOME THINGS HAVEN'T CHANGED!
FROM NOW ON, YOU'LL BE COUNTING THE DAYS FROM BEHIND STEEL BARS!
YOU'RE STILL AS HUMORLESS AS EVER!
OOOFFFF!
WHUD!
HE CAUGHT ME OFF-BALANCE--!
STILL GRINNING, THE INCREDIBLE CALENDAR MAN SUDDENLY PRESSES A SMALL BUTTON ON THE CYCLE'S HANDLEBAR--
KLIK!

--DETONATING A SERIES OF SPECIALLY-PREPARED EXPLOSIVE BOLTS--
POK!
POK!
--CUTTING FREE THE VEHICLE'S MASSIVE FRAME!

NO! THE CYCLE'S BECOME A REGULAR TWO-WHEELER-- LEAVING ME TRAPPED ON THIS RUNAWAY CHASSIS!

HAVE A NICE TRIP, BATMAN! HOPE YOU GET A BANG OUT OF IT!

CAREENING OUT OF CONTROL, THE SIX-WHEELED JUGGERNAUT ABRUPTLY VEERS TO ONE SIDE--

--AND DESTROYS ITSELF AGAINST A SOLID BRICK WALL!

3

PLAYS FOR *KEEPS*, DOESN'T HE?
IF THIS *LAMPPOST* HADN'T BEEN HERE, I'D BE *CHOPPED MEAT* RIGHT NOW!

THAT'S *THREE* CRIMES HE'S GOTTEN AWAY WITH--BUT I SWEAR IT'S THE *LAST!*

"CALENDAR MAN FIRST HIT TOWN ON *MONDAY* NIGHT, SMASHING INTO THE *GOTHAM PLANETARIUM* IN SUITABLY *APPROPRIATE* FASHION--
"--SINCE *MONDAY* IS NAMED FOR THE *MOON!*

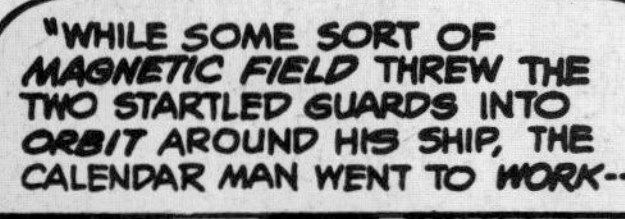
"WHILE SOME SORT OF *MAGNETIC FIELD* THREW THE TWO STARTLED GUARDS INTO *ORBIT* AROUND HIS SHIP, THE CALENDAR MAN WENT TO *WORK*--

"--SNATCHING UP HANDFULS OF THE PRICELESS *STAMPS* WHICH HAD BEEN ON DISPLAY THERE--
"--STAMPS WHICH HAD BEEN HAND-CANCELLED BY THE *ASTRONAUTS* DURING ONE OF THE LUNAR *VISITS!*

"BEFORE THE POLICE COULD *RESPOND* TO THE VIOLATED *BURGLAR ALARMS*, CALENDAR MAN WAS *GONE!*
MARCH
"--BUT HE LEFT HIS *CALLING CARD* BEHIND HIM!"

THE FIRST TIME WE FOUGHT, CALENDAR MAN COMMITTED FOUR CRIMES, EACH ONE BASED ON A DIFFERENT SEASON--
--BUT IT LOOKS LIKE HE'S BECOME A LOT MORE AMBITIOUS SINCE THEN!
THIS TIME HE'S PLANNING SEVEN CRIMES--ONE FOR EACH DAY OF THE WEEK!

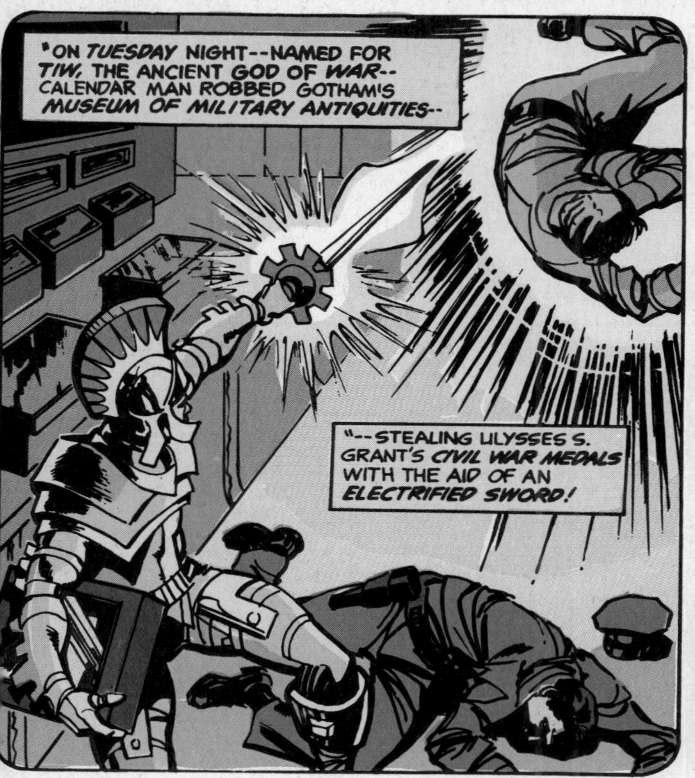
"ON TUESDAY NIGHT--NAMED FOR TIW, THE ANCIENT GOD OF WAR--CALENDAR MAN ROBBED GOTHAM'S MUSEUM OF MILITARY ANTIQUITIES--
"--STEALING ULYSSES S. GRANT'S CIVIL WAR MEDALS WITH THE AID OF AN ELECTRIFIED SWORD!

"I REACHED THE MUSEUM WITHIN MINUTES OF THE CRIME--BUT THE TRAIL WAS ALREADY STONE COLD!
MARC
"ALL I FOUND WAS ANOTHER CALENDAR PAGE--

"--WHICH WAS NOT SO MUCH A CLUE AS AN INVITATION!"
SEE YOU TOMORROW--
SOME TIME--
SOME PLACE!!

WELL, I CAME CLOSE TO THE CALENDAR MAN TONIGHT--
--JUST NOT CLOSE ENOUGH!
BUT IN ELUDING ME, HE MADE HIS FIRST BIG MISTAKE!

CALENDAR MAN HAS MANAGED TO COST ME MY NEW EXPERIMENTAL WHIRLY-BAT--
--AND THAT MAKES THIS LITTLE GAME PERSONAL!
5

THURSDAY, 8:23 PM-- AS A NIGHT-CLAD GUARDIAN STANDS VIGIL OVER THE CITY THAT HE LOVES...
I'VE WIRED EVERY SPOT IN GOTHAM THAT MIGHT BE A TARGET FOR A THURSDAY-INSPIRED CRIME!
IF CALENDAR MAN IS CRAZY ENOUGH TO STRIKE AGAIN TONIGHT--
--I'LL KNOW WHERE!

HOW'S IT GOING, BATMAN?
NOTHING YET, COMMISSIONER GORDON -- BUT IT'S ONLY A MATTER OF TIME!
WE'RE GOING TO NAIL THE CALENDAR MAN TONIGHT!

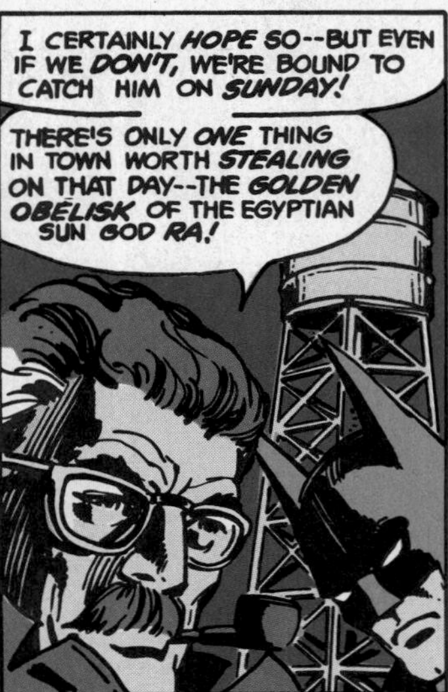
I CERTAINLY HOPE SO--BUT EVEN IF WE DON'T, WE'RE BOUND TO CATCH HIM ON SUNDAY!
THERE'S ONLY ONE THING IN TOWN WORTH STEALING ON THAT DAY--THE GOLDEN OBELISK OF THE EGYPTIAN SUN GOD RA!

WHEN CALENDAR MAN TRIES TO SNATCH IT, WE'LL BE WAITING FOR HIM WITH OPEN --
--EH?
BEEP BEEP BEEP
THAT'S IT, COMMISSIONER-- HE'S STRUCK!

AND WITH A RUSTLE OF VELVET AND AN UNCOILING OF STEEL-SPRING LEGS, THE BATMAN IS GONE--
--SWALLOWED BY THE DARKNESS THAT IS HIS NATURAL ELEMENT!
6

THURSDAY, 8:51 PM-- AS THE WELL-APPOINTED HALLS OF THE VAN DYKE ART GALLERY ON GOTHAM'S UPPER EAST SIDE RESOUND WITH THE ARMORED TREAD OF AN INCREDIBLY-CLAD INTRUDER...
SOFTLY WHISTLING TO HIMSELF, THE CALENDAR MAN CAREFULLY STUDIES EVERY PAINTING THAT HE PASSES--PAUSING AT LAST BEFORE A PRICELESS ABSTRACT CALLED "THE STORM KING"--

--AND WITH A FEW SWIFT STROKES OF A MINIATURE LASER BLADE--

--HE MAKES THE PAINTING HIS!

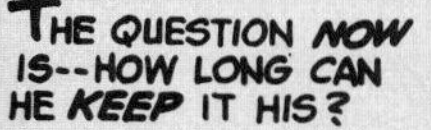
THE QUESTION NOW IS--HOW LONG CAN HE KEEP IT HIS?

IT'S ABOUT TIME, PUNK! I WAS GETTING TIRED OF WAITING OUT HERE!
WHO--?!?

DO I REALLY HAVE TO ANSWER THAT?

YOU MIGHT AS WELL, BATMAN--SINCE IT'S THE LAST THING YOU'RE EVER GOING TO SAY!
THURSDAY, YOU'LL RECALL, WAS NAMED FOR THE NORSE GOD OF THUNDER--
-- SO I'VE ARMED MYSELF WITH THE HAMMER OF THOR!

SKRAK-KOOOM!
YOU COULD ARM YOURSELF WITH A NUCLEAR WARHEAD --BUT IT STILL WOULDN'T HELP YOU!
YOU OWE A DEBT TO SOCIETY, CALENDAR MAN--
7

--AND I INTEND TO COLLECT IT!!
UUNNHH!!

SO WHO APPOINTED YOU SERVANT OF THE PEOPLE ANYWAY? YOU'RE JUST ANOTHER GUY IN A CRAZY COSTUME--
--LIKE ME!
YOU'RE WRONG, PUNK!

I'M NOTHING LIKE YOU--
POW!
-NOTHING!!

HIT A SORE SPOT, HUH? WELL, DON'T LET IT BOTHER YOU, BATMAN!
ANOTHER FEW SECONDS-- AND IT'LL ALL BE ACADEMIC!

AAWHOOOOOO
EH? HE TOUCHED HIS EAR-PHONES AND THAT STRAY DOG SUDDENLY STARTED HOWLING LIKE--
OF COURSE!

HAVE TO GET THAT HELMET OFF OF HIM BEFORE--
AARGGHH
CLOSE, HERO-- BUT A SECOND TOO LATE!

BLAST... I SHOULD'VE REALIZED... THOR WAS GOD OF THUNDER...
...SO CALENDAR MAN... IS USING ULTRASONIC THUNDER... TO DESTROY ME...
8

SIGNAL IS *BEYOND* THE RANGE OF HUMAN *HEARING*... BUT I CAN STILL *FEEL* IT...

IT'LL TURN MY *BRAIN* TO *JELLY*... UNLESS...

...I CAN SHUT THE SIGNAL... *OFF!*

SKRANG!

MY *HELMET*--! HE'S *SHATTERED* IT--!

BUT I *CAN* STILL *FINISH* THE JOB IT *STARTED!*

JUST *LIE* THERE, BATMAN! IN A FEW MORE SECONDS, YOUR SUFFERING WILL BE *OVER*--

--*PERMANENTLY!*

NO! GOTTA *MOVE*-- GOTTA *GET UP*--!

WEEEOWEEOWEEO

POLICE SIRENS--?!?

BATMAN, YOUR LUCK IS *INCREDIBLE!*

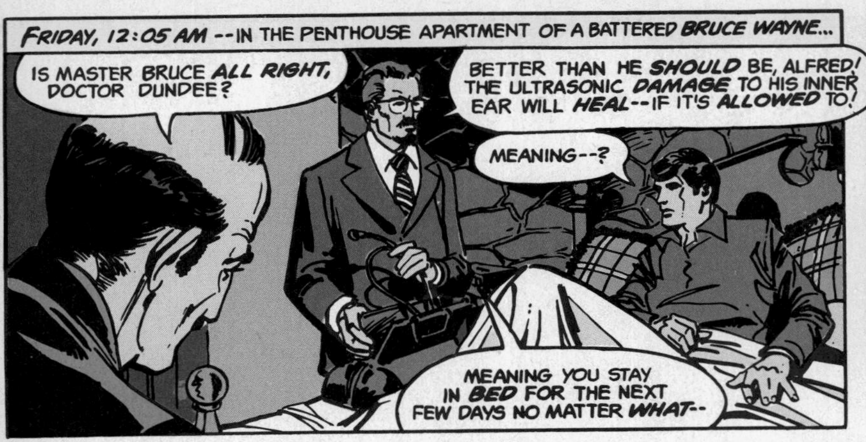
FRIDAY, 12:05 AM --IN THE PENTHOUSE APARTMENT OF A BATTERED BRUCE WAYNE...
IS MASTER BRUCE ALL RIGHT, DOCTOR DUNDEE?
BETTER THAN HE SHOULD BE, ALFRED! THE ULTRASONIC DAMAGE TO HIS INNER EAR WILL HEAL--IF IT'S ALLOWED TO!
MEANING--?
MEANING YOU STAY IN BED FOR THE NEXT FEW DAYS NO MATTER WHAT--

--OR YOU MAY MAKE THAT DAMAGE PERMANENT!
ALFRED, I LEAVE HIM IN YOUR HANDS!

DUNDEE'S A GOOD MAN--BUT HE WORRIES TOO MUCH!
NOW I'D BETTER GET DOWN TO THE BAT-CAVE AND START CHECKING ON--

YOU'LL DO NOTHING OF THE KIND, SIR!
BUT THERE'S WORK TO BE DONE, ALFRED!
THEN I'M AFRAID SOMEONE ELSE WILL HAVE TO DO IT!
YOU ARE STAYING IN BED, MASTER BRUCE--IF I'M FORCED TO SIT ON YOU TO KEEP YOU THERE!

ALFRED, HAS ANYONE EVER TOLD YOU YOU'D MAKE A GREAT MOTHER?

FRIDAY, 9:28 PM--
--DRESSED TO HONOR FRIGGA, GODDESS OF LOVE AND THE FUTURE, THE CALENDAR MAN ARRIVES UNINVITED AT A SOCIETY WEDDING, AND MAKES OFF WITH A FORTUNE IN JEWELS AND SILVER...
10

SATURDAY, 11:43 AM-- AS A BEDRIDDEN BRUCE WAYNE CONFERS WITH HIS FRIEND AND ASSOCIATE, LUCIUS FOX...
--AND THAT ABOUT COVERS EVERYTHING WE HAVE TO DISCUSS, BRUCE.
THE ONLY REALLY PRESSING BIT OF WAYNE ENTERPRISES BUSINESS IS THE DENNISON MERGER!
AND THAT'S LIABLE TO BE A TOUGH ONE, LUCIUS.

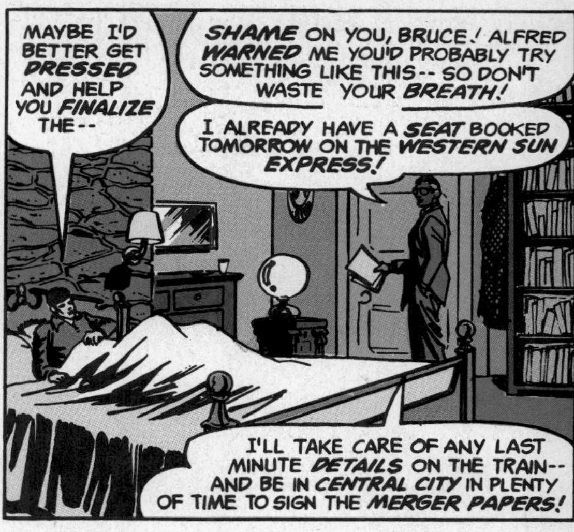
MAYBE I'D BETTER GET DRESSED AND HELP YOU FINALIZE THE--
SHAME ON YOU, BRUCE! ALFRED WARNED ME YOU'D PROBABLY TRY SOMETHING LIKE THIS-- SO DON'T WASTE YOUR BREATH!
I ALREADY HAVE A SEAT BOOKED TOMORROW ON THE WESTERN SUN EXPRESS!
I'LL TAKE CARE OF ANY LAST MINUTE DETAILS ON THE TRAIN-- AND BE IN CENTRAL CITY IN PLENTY OF TIME TO SIGN THE MERGER PAPERS!

WELL, YOU CAN'T BLAME A GUY FOR TRYING, CAN YOU?
CAN'T I?
YOU JUST STAY IN BED AND GET OVER THAT FLU, BRUCE--AND LEAVE THE BUSINESS TO ME!
THAT'S WHY YOU FIRST HIRED ME, REMEMBER?
I'LL CALL YOU FROM CENTRAL CITY AND LET YOU KNOW HOW EVERYTHING WENT!
ALFRED, YOU'D BETTER KEEP A CLOSE EYE ON YOUR BOSS--HE'S A TRICKY ONE.

BELIEVE ME, MASTER FOX-- I KNOW THAT BETTER THAN ANYONE.
YOUR CHICKEN SOUP, MASTER BRUCE!
WHOOPEE!

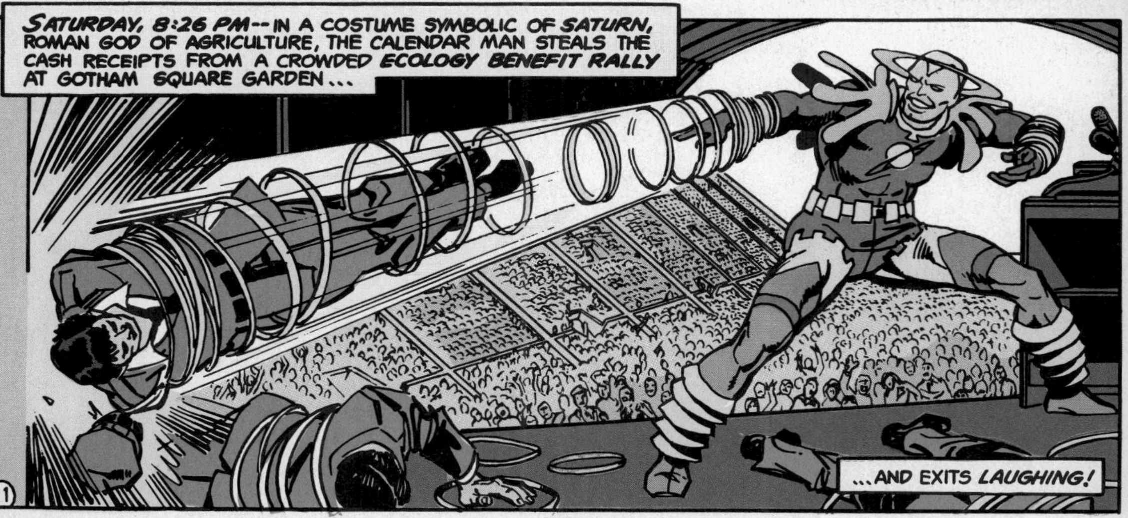
SATURDAY, 8:26 PM-- IN A COSTUME SYMBOLIC OF SATURN, ROMAN GOD OF AGRICULTURE, THE CALENDAR MAN STEALS THE CASH RECEIPTS FROM A CROWDED ECOLOGY BENEFIT RALLY AT GOTHAM SQUARE GARDEN...
...AND EXITS LAUGHING!
11

SUNDAY, 12:14 PM--
GET BACK IN BED THIS MINUTE, SIR!
SORRY, ALFRED--BUT I HAVE THINGS TO DO!
SUCH AS WHAT, SIR?
COMMISSIONER GORDON IS ALREADY WAITING TO APPREHEND THE CALENDAR MAN--

--AND MASTER FOX WILL BE LEAVING ON THE WESTERN SUN EXPRESS IN FIFTEEN MINUTES!
THERE'S REALLY NOTHING FOR YOU TO DO, SIR!
MAYBE YOU'RE RIGHT, ALFRED. MAYBE I--

HEY-- WAITAMINNIT!
HOW COULD WE ALL HAVE BEEN SO BLIND?

ER--AH--ALFRED, WOULD YOU MIND CALLING SELINA KYLE FOR ME?
IF I'M STAYING IN BED, I'D BETTER BREAK OUR DATE FOR TONIGHT.
WITH PLEASURE, MASTER BRUCE.
I REALIZE I MAY SEEM A TRIFLE HARSH ON YOU, SIR--

--BUT YOU KNOW I'M ONLY DOING IT FOR YOUR OWN GOOD.
MASTER BRUCE?
M-MASTER BRUCE?
OH NO!

SUNDAY, 12:23 PM--AND THE SPRAWLING RAILROAD TERMINAL THAT IS GOTHAM CENTRAL STATION BUSTLES WITH ACTIVITY...
12

ON TRACK 14, THE WESTERN SUN EXPRESS COMPLETES ITS FINAL LOADING AND PREPARES TO GET UNDER WAY--
--MUCH TO THE RELIEF OF ONE OF ITS PASSENGERS...
PLEASE BE CAREFUL WITH THAT TRUNK, PORTER. IT'S GOING A LONG WAY!
WESTERN SUN

WHICH IS A LOT MORE THAN ITS OWNER CAN SAY!
OH NO.
HOLY SMOKES, IT'S--

YOU DON'T HAVE TO TELL HIM, PORTER! I THINK HE ALREADY KNOWS!
THE BATMAN BUT HOW--?
HOW DID YOU FIND ME HERE?

WHERE ELSE WOULD YOU BE, CALENDAR MAN?
YOU'RE FAR TOO SMART TO PULL YOUR OBVIOUS SUNDAY CRIME WHEN YOU KNEW THE POLICE WOULD BE WAITING FOR YOU--
--SO THERE WAS ONLY ONE LOGICAL ALTERNATIVE!

SUNDAY IS ALSO A DAY OF REST--THE PERFECT TIME FOR YOU TO SKIP TOWN WITH WHAT YOU'D STOLEN--
--AND WHAT MORE APPROPRIATE MEANS OF TRANSPORTATION THAN THE WESTERN SUN EXPRESS?

IT WAS ALL REALLY QUITE SIMPLE-- IF ONE JUST THOUGHT ABOUT IT!
AND YOU'RE SIMPLE, BUSTER--

--IF YOU THINK FINDING ME IS THE SAME THING AS CATCHING ME!!
EH? HIS BOOK WAS RIGGED!
DOZENS OF CALENDAR PAGES SWIRLING ALL AROUND ME--LIKE A MINIATURE HURRICANE!

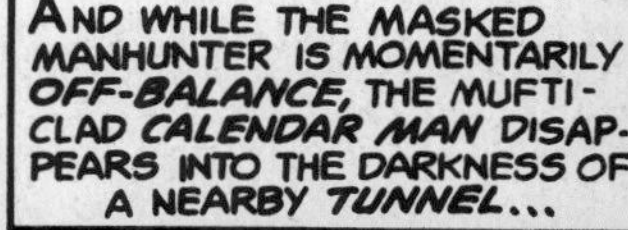
AND WHILE THE MASKED MANHUNTER IS MOMENTARILY OFF-BALANCE, THE MUFTI-CLAD CALENDAR MAN DISAPPEARS INTO THE DARKNESS OF A NEARBY TUNNEL...

13

...BUT THE HEAD-START IT GIVES HIM IS A SLIM ONE!
FOUND ITEMS OF CALENDAR MAN'S CLOTHING STREWN ALL ALONG THE TUNNEL--!
AND I CAN GUESS WHY!

" CALENDAR MAN ACTUALLY TOOK THE TIME TO CHANGE INTO A NEW COSTUME!"
ALL THE BETTER TO BEAT YOU WITH, BATMAN!
OR IS IT ILLEGAL THESE DAYS TO BE FASHIONABLE?
BAD TASTE IN CLOTHING IS THE LEAST OF YOUR CRIMES, MISTER--

--BUT IT'S REALLY A VERY MOOT POINT!

WHERE YOU'RE GOING, EVERYTHING YOU WEAR FROM NOW ON WILL HAVE STRIPES!
HHUUNNFF!!

FOR BOTH OUR SAKES, YOU'D BETTER SURRENDER QUICKLY, CALENDAR MAN--
--BEFORE THAT APPROACHING TRAIN TURNS US INTO HAMBURGER!

WHOK!
IN THE IMMORTAL WORDS OF TONTO--
--WHAT YOU MEAN US, BATMAN?

YOU WANT TO STAY AND GET SLAUGHTERED, GO RIGHT AHEAD--
--BUT I'M GETTING OUT OF HERE!
GOT TO GO AFTER HIM BEFORE--
--HUH?

I DON'T BELIEVE IT! MY FOOT IS CAUGHT BETWEEN THE TRACKS--!
14

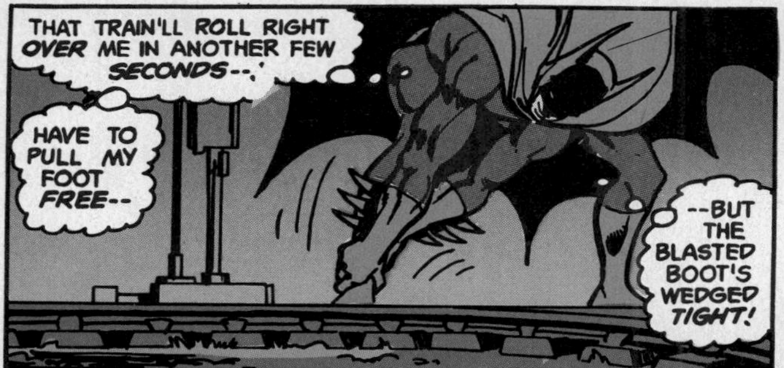
THAT TRAIN'LL ROLL RIGHT OVER ME IN ANOTHER FEW SECONDS--,
HAVE TO PULL MY FOOT FREE--
--BUT THE BLASTED BOOT'S WEDGED TIGHT!

--IT CAN HAVE--
NO MORE TIME TO WASTE! IF THIS TRACK WANTS MY BOOT--

CHAKATACHAKATACHAKATACHAKATACHA

BLAST--! THE STUPID TRAIN MISSED THAT POINTY-EARED PEST BY A HAIR!
BUT IT STILL HELD HIM UP LONG ENOUGH FOR ME TO PUT A LOT OF DISTANCE BETWEEN US!

CALENDAR MAN IS TOO FAR AHEAD OF ME-- I'LL NEVER CATCH UP!
ONLY ONE OTHER CHANCE--!

YOU'RE SLIPPING, BATMAN!
THAT BATARANG DIDN'T EVEN COME CLOSE!

BUT PERHAPS IT WAS NOT INTENDED TO--
--FOR, WITH SNAKE-LIKE AGILITY, THE SILKEN LINE ATTACHED TO THE BATARANG COILS AROUND THE HANDLE OF A SWITCHING SIGNAL IN CALENDAR MAN'S PATH--

--AND AS THE FLEEING FELON RUSHES PAST--

--THE DARKNIGHT DETECTIVE PULLS HIS BAT-LINE TAUT!
BLANG!

AND THAT, DARE I SAY IT, SIGNALS THE END OF THIS CASE!
CALENDAR MAN, YOU'VE HAD A BUSY WEEK-- BUT YOU'LL HAVE 20 YEARS TO LIFE TO RECOVER FROM IT!
END

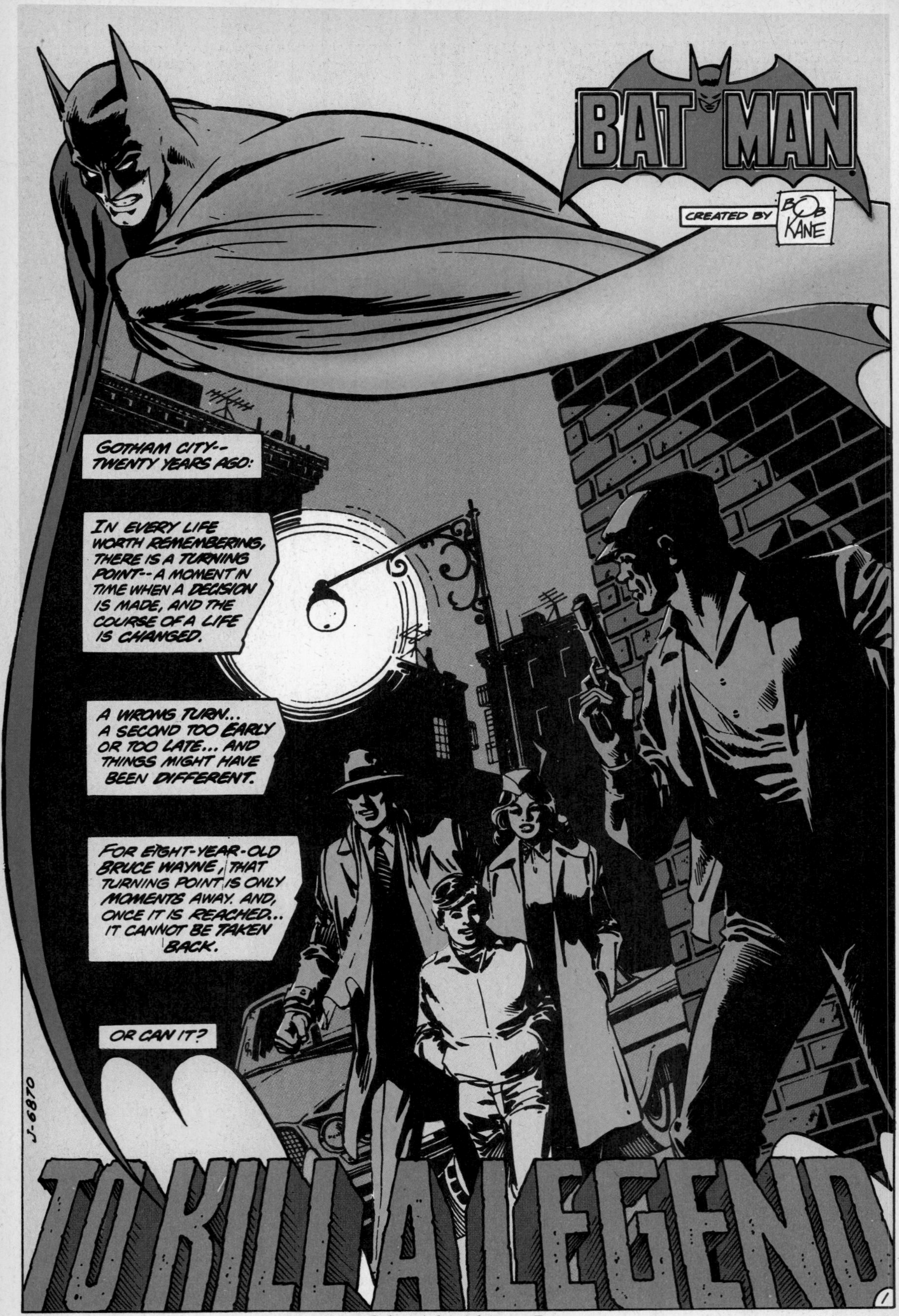

Coloring by Adrienne Roy

GOOD MOVIE, EH, MARTHA? THAT MARLON BRANDO SURE IS--
WHAT--WHAT IS THIS--?!
IT'S CALLED A STICK-UP, BUDDY! I'LL TAKE THAT NECKLACE THE LADY'S WEARIN'!
YOU HOODLUM! DON'T YOU DARE PUT YOUR HAND ON MY WIFE--!
UNNNHHH!!
MAYBE NOW YOU'LL KEEP QUIET!
BLAM
THOMAS!!
HELP! POLICE--HELP!!
CLICK!
AN' THIS--
--WILL SHUT YOU UP, LADY!
BLAM!
F-FATHER... MOTHER...
THEY'RE DEAD! YOU KILLED THEM!
S-STOP LOOKIN' AT ME LIKE THAT, KID! STOP LOOKIN' AT ME!
THE KILLER-- A MAN NAMED JOE CHILL-- FLEES. BRUCE'S PARENTS DO NOT MOVE.
THEY WILL NEVER MOVE AGAIN. THEY WILL NEVER HOLD HIM... NEVER COMFORT HIM AFTER A BAD DREAM... NEVER KNOW HOW MUCH HE REALLY LOVED THEM.
BRUCE STARTS TO SCREAM--
2

NO!!

-- AND FINISHES TWENTY YEARS LATER!

WHEW! FEEL LIKE I SPENT THE NIGHT IN A DISHWASHER! WHAT'S WRONG WITH ME, ANYWAY?

I HAVEN'T HAD THAT DREAM IN YEARS-- NOT SINCE I CAUGHT UP WITH JOE CHILL!

WHY SHOULD IT START AGAIN NOW?

WELL, I CERTAINLY CAN'T GO BACK TO SLEEP NOW!

I GUESS I'M LUCKY, IN A WAY. WHENEVER IT GETS TOO PAINFUL BEING BRUCE WAYNE--

-- I CAN ALWAYS BECOME THE BATMAN!

I WONDER HOW NORMAL PEOPLE MANAGE TO COPE?

THE ANSWER TO THAT IS: SOMETIMES THEY DON'T.
PLEASE... NO... I DON'T HAVE MUCH MONEY...
HEY-- THAT'S COOL! WE DON'T NEED MUCH!
NOW-- YOU GONNA LET GO OF THAT PURSE OR DO I REMOVE IT SURGICALLY?

NONE OF THE ABOVE, FRIEND!
OH NO.
OH YES. HEADS UP, MA'AM!
THWACK
3

ONE DOWN-- ONE TO GO...!
CRIPES! HOW'D I GET INTO THIS?!
GOTTA GET OUTTA HERE--!!

RUNNING INTO THAT FOG BANK--? HE'S SO PANICKED HE DOESN'T REALIZE THE ALLEY DEAD-ENDS UP AHEAD!
I SHOULD HAVE THIS WRAPPED UP IN A MATTER OF--

NO! IT ISN'T POSSIBLE! WE WERE NOWHERE NEAR HERE!
HE'S RUNNING STRAIGHT INTO--

CRIME ALLEY!

MY PARENTS DIED HERE TWENTY YEARS AGO! BUT IT'S CLEAR ON THE OTHER SIDE OF TOWN! WHAT THE DEVIL--?
UH OH-- I'M LOSING HIM! BETTER POUR ON THE SPEED BEFORE HE--

SUDDENLY...
HEY! LOOK! IT'S THE GOODRICH BLIMP!
WHAT--?!

DUMMY.
GOODRICH DOESN'T HAVE A BLIMP!
THOK!
UNHH!
ROBIN!
4

DICK! WHAT ARE YOU DOING HERE? I PUT YOU ON A PLANE TO EUROPE THIS MORNING!
PLANE...? EUROPE?
YES...OF COURSE. WHAT AM I DOING HERE?!
YOU ARE HERE... BECAUSE YOU MUST BE HERE!

PHANTOM STRANGER?!
SO YOU PULLED THAT TRICK WITH THE FOG! BUT WHAT BRINGS YOU TO GOTHAM? WHAT'S WRONG?
THE WRONG, MY FRIEND, HAS YET TO BE DONE... AND, GIVEN YOUR HELP, IT MAY NEVER BE DONE.

UH, WE'VE NEVER MET BEFORE, STRANGER, BUT I TAKE IT YOU'RE HEAVILY INTO CRYPTIC.
CARE TO TRANSLATE THAT?
OF COURSE. THERE ARE WORLDS BEYOND WORLDS, DICK GRAYSON...
...HUNDREDS OF EARTHS LIKE YOUR OWN, EXISTING IN AS MANY DIFFERENT DIMENSIONS.

ON ONE SUCH EARTH, BATMAN, FORTY YEARS AGO, ANOTHER BRUCE WAYNE SAW HIS PARENTS MURDERED... AND VOWED TO AVENGE THEIR DEATHS.
TWENTY YEARS LATER, ON THIS EARTH, YOU WATCHED YOUR PARENTS DIE... AND BECAME, LIKE YOUR PREDECESSOR, THE BATMAN.

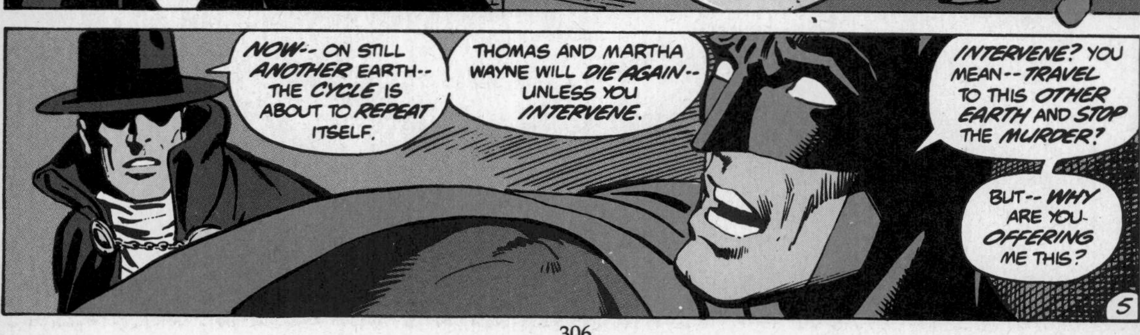
NOW-- ON STILL ANOTHER EARTH-- THE CYCLE IS ABOUT TO REPEAT ITSELF.
THOMAS AND MARTHA WAYNE WILL DIE AGAIN-- UNLESS YOU INTERVENE.
INTERVENE? YOU MEAN--TRAVEL TO THIS OTHER EARTH AND STOP THE MURDER?
BUT-- WHY ARE YOU OFFERING ME THIS?
5

YOU'RE A BRAVE MAN, BRUCE WAYNE... BUT DESPITE ALL YOUR COURAGE, ALL THE GOOD YOU'VE DONE...
...YOU STILL FEEL YOU FAILED THE ONES YOU LOVED THE MOST.

THIS IS YOUR SECOND CHANCE, BRUCE WAYNE--AND I OFFER IT TO YOU AS A FRIEND AND A COMRADE.
DO YOU CHOOSE TO TAKE IT?

BEHIND THE BATMAN'S MASK, BRUCE WAYNE CONSIDERS FOR LONG MOMENTS --UNTIL--
I'LL GO.
SO WILL I.
NO, DICK. I... APPRECIATE THE OFFER, BUT... I HAVE TO DO THIS ALONE.

SO BE IT.
ENTER THE FOG, BATMAN...
I DON'T LIKE THIS! BRUCE WON'T ADMIT IT, BUT WHEN IT COMES TO HIS PARENTS' DEATHS HE JUST CAN'T BE OBJECTIVE!
HE MAY NEED ME WHEREVER HE'S GOING...

...OR WHY ELSE WOULD I BE HERE?
ROBIN-- NO--!!
SAFE JOURNEY, MY FRIENDS-- AND GOOD LUCK TO YOU!

FOR A SPLIT-SECOND, THE TWO TRAVELLERS LOSE CONSCIOUSNESS AS THE FOG SWIRLS AROUND THEM...
AND WHEN IT FINALLY CLEARS, THEY FIND THEMSELVES AT--
6

GOTHAM HARBOR?! IS THIS REALLY ANOTHER WORLD--
--OR JUST ONE OF THE STRANGER'S ILLUSIONS? GOOD QUESTION. LET'S SEE IF WE CAN--
WHAT THE--
THA-BOOMM!
IT CAME FROM THE CARGO HOLD OF THAT SHIP! LET'S GO!

LOOK AT THIS STUFF! THOSE ANCIENT INCAS SURE KNEW HOW TO LIVE!
MY FENCE IS GONNA HAVE A HEART ATTACK WHEN HE SEES THIS!
THEN WE'LL JUST HAVE TO SPARE HIM THE SHOCK, WON'T WE?
WHA--?

WHAT IN THE NAME OF--WHAT IS IT?!
SOME KINDA GIANT BAT--SOME THING--!!
NO! IT'S COMIN' RIGHT AT ME--!!

NO! PLEASE! STAY AWAY FROM ME! STAY AWAY!!
OHHHH--
THIS IS BIZARRE! I BARELY TOUCHED HIM, AND HE FAINTED DEAD AWAY!

INCREDIBLE!
THEY PUT UP NO FIGHT AT ALL--ACTED LIKE THEY'VE NEVER SEEN ANYTHING LIKE US!
MAYBE THEY HAVEN'T!
WHOOP WHOOP WHOOP
SIRENS! LET'S GO TOPSIDE!

HEY! WHAT'S GOING--
ALL RIGHT! HOLD IT RIGHT THERE--WHOEVER YOU ARE!
I DON'T BELIEVE IT--!
7

--COMMISSIONER GORDON?!
LIEUTENANT GORDON--AND NOW THAT WE'VE AGREED ON WHO I AM--
--WHY DON'T WE START WITH WHO YOU ARE, AND HOW YOU BROKE INTO THIS SHIP!
UH, DON'T LOOK NOW, TOTO, BUT WE ARE DEFINITELY NOT IN KANSAS ANYMORE.
THIS CERTAINLY PROVES WE'RE ON ANOTHER EARTH! BUT SINCE WE'LL NEVER CONVINCE THE GOOD LIEU-TENANT OF THAT, WE'D BETTER--
--MOVE!
--THIS HURTS ME, OFFICER--
--ALMOST AS MUCH AS IT DOES YOU!
YOW!
FREEZE OR I'LL--
OWWW!
SORRY ABOUT THIS, LIEUTENANT--
--BUT IF WE TOLD YOU THE TRUTH--
--YOU'D HAVE US COMMITTED INSTANTLY!

MORNING IN GOTHAM-- AND TWO VISITORS WALK A FAMILIAR YET ALIEN CITY...
SO MANY SMALL DIFFERENCES! CRIME ALLEY IS STILL PARK ROW... BASIN STREET IS BASIN AVENUE...
HOW DO WE KNOW WHERE THE WAYNES LIVE ON THIS EARTH?
WE DON'T!
WHICH IS WHY WE USE THE SOCIAL REGISTER-- IN HERE!

I CAN'T HELP FEELING EXPOSED! WE ARE WANTED CRIMINALS NOW!
WE'RE ALSO CIPHERS-- WE DON'T EXIST IN THIS WORLD, SO HOW COULD ANYONE, EVEN THE POLICE, RECOG-NIZE US?
DR. WAYNE! IS THAT YOU?

BARBARA KEAN, REMEMBER--DETEC-TIVE GORDON'S FIANCÉE? YOU ARE THOMAS WAYNE, AREN'T YOU?
UH-- YES. OF COURSE. HOW ARE YOU, MISS KEAN?
PERIODIC
I WONDER-- COULD YOU SHOW ME WHERE THE SOCIAL REGISTER IS? I SEEM TO HAVE FORGOTTEN...

WHAT A STRANGE WORLD! PLENTY OF CRIME, TERRORISM, WAR-- BUT NOT A SINGLE COSTUMED HERO!
OF COURSE, THERE WEREN'T ANY COSTUMED HEROES ON OUR EARTH TILL A FEW DECADES AGO--BUT--
SPECIAL
GOTHAM NE
DOWNTOWN SNIPER KILLS FIVE
CONFLICT CONTINUES IN

--THERE DOESN'T SEEM TO BE ANY HEROIC MYTHOLOGY ON THIS WORLD, EITHER!
NO ROBIN HOOD-- NO CAMELOT-- NO HERCULES, ODYSSEUS, GILGAMESH--

EVEN THAT WOULDN'T BOTHER ME, THOUGH, IF IT WEREN'T FOR THIS!
ACCORDING TO THIS STAR ATLAS, THE RED STAR AROUND WHICH KRYPTON IS SUPPOSED TO ORBIT--

--DOESN'T EXIST!
IF THERE'S NO KRYPTON IN THIS DIMENSION, THEN THERE'LL BE NO SUPERMAN-- PERHAPS NO SUPER-POWERED HEROES AT ALL!
AND WITH NO LITERA-TURE TO INSPIRE THEM--
9

--THIS MIGHT BE A WORLD WITHOUT HEROES-- EXCEPT FOR ITS BATMAN!
THAT'S SUPPOSITION, DICK--NOT DEDUCTION! DIDN'T I TEACH YOU BETTER THAN THAT?
COME ON--LET'S GO SEE MY PAR-- UH, I MEAN THE WAYNES!

GREAT! WHENEVER BRUCE DOESN'T WANT TO HEAR WHAT I HAVE TO SAY, HE PULLS THE OLD MENTOR/PUPIL BIT!
WELL, THIS TIME I'M GOING TO HAVE TO MAKE HIM LISTEN--
--BEFORE IT'S TOO LATE!

AND, ABOARD A TRAIN THREE HOURS NORTH OF GOTHAM CITY...
OH, CRIPES! THEY BUSTED CHARLIE! I KNEW WE SHOULD'VE WASTED THAT GUARD BEFORE HE TALKED!
GOTTA STAY CALM! CHARLIE'S CONTACTS IN GOTHAM'LL TAKE CARE OF ME!
CLEVELAND FIRST NATIONAL ROBBED-- TWO ARRESTED

YEAH... SURE. WITH COPS IN THREE STATES LOOKIN' FOR ME... STAY CALM.
HIS NAME IS JOE CHILL. HE'S A SMALL, SCARED, MEAN LITTLE MAN... AND HIS TROUBLES ARE JUST BEGINNING.

MEANWHILE, AT A FAMILIAR SUBURBAN MANOR HOUSE OUTSIDE GOTHAM...
NO! I DON'T WANT IT! TAKE IT BACK!

YOUR MOTHER WENT TO A LOT OF TROUBLE TO GET THAT, BRUCE! I SWEAR, I'VE HALF A MIND TO--
THOMAS, NO! IT'S JUST A PHASE HE'S GOING THROUGH!
OH, I SUPPOSE...

DEAR LORD... IT'S AS IF THEY'VE COME ALIVE AGAIN! AS IF I COULD... REACH OUT AND TOUCH THEM AGAIN...
FATHER... MOTHER... I SWEAR BY ALL THAT'S DEAR TO ME... I WON'T LET YOU DIE AGAIN!
10

THIS BRUCE WAYNE IS A SPOILED LITTLE BRAT!
I WONDER... IF WE STOP HIS PARENTS' MURDER, WILL HE GROW UP TO BECOME THE BORED PLAYBOY THAT BATMAN ONLY PRETENDS TO BE?

SHORTLY, OUTSIDE POLICE HEADQUARTERS...
I KNOW WE NEED INFORMATION ON JOE CHILL'S WHEREABOUTS, BATMAN, BUT ISN'T IT RISKY BREAKING INTO POLICE HEADQUARTERS?
GOTHAM POLICE
NOT "BREAK IN"--WALK IN! AFTER ALL, WHO'D SUSPECT ANYTHING OF--

--DETECTIVE LIEUTENANT JAMES GORDON?

AND SO, TEN MINUTES LATER...
BLAST! CHILL DOESN'T EVEN HAVE A FILE! HE MUST'VE BEEN CAGEY ENOUGH TO KEEP RELATIVELY CLEAN!
ALL I CAN DO NOW IS OPERATE ON WHAT I KNOW ABOUT THE CHILL OF MY EARTH, WHO WORKED FOR--
CRIMINAL RECORDS
LOCAL

--LEW MOXON! HE HIRED CHILL TO KILL MY FATHER FOR TESTIFYING AGAINST HIM!
I CHECKED THE FILES--MOXON'S COUNTER-PART ON THIS EARTH RUNS A TRUCKING COMPANY ON CANAL STREET!
WELL, SINCE WE'RE SO CLOSE--
"--WHY DON'T WE JUST DROP OVER?"
WHAT IN THE--
11

WATCH CLOSELY NOW, GANG--AND TAKE NOTE THAT AT NO TIME--
--DO MY TOES EVER LEAVE MY FEET!
BLAM! BLAM! BLAM!
VROOOMM!
GOT TO MANEUEVER THIS JUST RIGHT--
--SO THEY DON'T HIT ME--
THA-BOOOMM!
--BUT THE GAS TANK!
12

WHILE THE THUGS ARE TEMPORARILY STUNNED BY THE BLAST--
GOING SOMEWHERE, MOXON?
OOF!
WHO--WHO ARE YOU?! HOW D'YOU KNOW MY NAME?

I'M ASKING THE QUESTIONS, MOXON! WHERE'S JOE CHILL-- THE THUG YOU'VE HIRED TO KILL THOMAS WAYNE?
I DUNNO WHAT YOU'RE TALKIN' ABOUT! SO HELP ME! I NEVER HEARD OF ANY CHILL!

LISTEN TO ME, MOXON! IF ANY HARM COMES TO THE WAYNES-- I'LL BE BACK! AND THIS TIME--
--I'LL DO A LOT MORE THAN BLOW UP ONE OF YOUR TRUCKS!

THOSE MANIACS KNOW ABOUT MY PLANS FOR WAYNE! GONNA HAVE TO MOVE UP MY TIMETABLE... BEFORE THEY GO TO THE COPS!
GOTTA FIND SOMEBODY TO KILL THOMAS WAYNE-- AS SOON AS I CAN!

TIME'S RUNNING OUT! IT'S THE 21ST OF THE MONTH--MY PARENTS WERE KILLED ON THE 26TH!
GOTHAM CENTRAL STATION
IF WE CAN'T FIND CHILL IN FIVE DAYS-- THEN WE FOLLOW THE WAYNES' EVERY MOVE...
...AND WAIT FOR CHILL TO MAKE HIS!

WHILE, JUST A HUNDRED FEET BELOW...
MADE IT! NOW TO LOOK UP-- WHAT'S HIS NAME...?
LEW MOXON! YEAH! CHARLIE SAID MOXON'S ALWAYS GOT WORK FOR A GUY!
SHOOT, RIGHT ABOUT NOW I'D BE WILLIN' TO DO ANYTHING...
13

HOURS LATER, AT WAYNE MANOR...
BRUCE, WE DON'T BELONG HERE! WE HAVE NO RIGHT TO INTERFERE! MAYBE EVERY WORLD NEEDS A BATMAN!
AND WHAT ABOUT YOUNG BRUCE? YOU SAW YOUR PARENTS MUR-DERED TOO, DICK--
--CAN YOU PUT SOMEONE ELSE THROUGH THAT?
I AM THINKING ABOUT YOUNG BRUCE! WE COULD BE CONDEMNING HIM TO A LIFE AS A SPOILED PLAYBOY...
...AND DENYING THIS EARTH ITS ONLY HERO!
I CAN APPRECIATE YOUR CONCERNS, ROBIN... BUT I CAN'T SHARE THEM. LIVES ARE AT STAKE HERE...
...INCLUDING A LITTLE BOY'S LIFE...

... A BOY WHO'LL SEE HIS FAMILY DIE BEFORE HIS EYES.
HE'LL NEVER FORGET THAT... NEVER LOSE THE ANGER OR THE ANGUISH.
NO ONE SHOULD BE ANGRY ALL HIS LIFE, DICK. NO ONE...

I... KNOW. BUT IT SEEMS SO IMPOSSIBLE. CHILL COULD BE ANYWHERE... PHOENIX, TORONTO, MIAMI...
WHA--? OF COURSE! HOW COULD I HAVE BEEN SO BLIND?

I JUST ASSUMED THAT THIS CHILL, LIKE THE ONE ON OUR EARTH, WAS FROM GOTHAM CITY!
I DIDN'T BOTHER TO CHECK THE INTERSTATE COMPUTER RECORDS AT POLICE HQ--
--UNTIL NOW, THAT IS!
14

BUT ONLY MINUTES AFTER THE BATMAN LEAVES...
GET YOUR COAT, BRUCE-- YOUR FATHER'S TAKING US TO A MOVIE!
BUT I WAS PLAYING WITH MY TRAINS--!
YOU CAN DO THAT LATER, SON.

LEAVING FOR A MOVIE? BUT BATMAN'S PARENTS WERE KILLED COMING HOME FROM A MOVIE!
OF ALL THE TIMES FOR BATMAN TO SPLIT! SOMETHING TELLS ME I'D BETTER STICK CLOSE TO THE WAYNES--
--AND PRAY!

MEANWHILE, IN POLICE HEADQUARTERS...
BINGO! ACCORDING TO THIS, THERE'S AN INTER-STATE BULLETIN OUT ON CHILL... AND IT'S BELIEVED HE'S HEADED FOR GOTHAM!
NOW TO SEE IF I CAN--
GOOD EVENING. ENJOYING YOURSELF?

DON'T MOVE, PLEASE.
I ASSURE YOU... I'M QUITE A GOOD SHOT.

AND IN THE STREETS OF GOTHAM...
BRUCE SAID THE MURDER WASN'T SUPPOSED TO HAPPEN FOR FIVE MORE DAYS, BUT--HE MAY HAVE BEEN WRONG!
IT MAY BE UP TO ME TO STOP THIS-- AND I STILL DON'T KNOW IF I SHOULD!
BATMAN, WHERE ARE YOU?!
EMA
DIANE KEATON
NIE HALL
Patti fashions
JOH

I CAN'T EXPLAIN IT ALL, BUT I'M TRYING TO STOP A MURDERER FROM KILLING TWO INNOCENT PEOPLE!
LIEUTENANT... IN ANOTHER WORLD, ANOTHER TIME... WE'RE FRIENDS. IF YOU CAN FEEL EVEN A HINT OF THAT... TRUST ME. LET ME GO. PLEASE!

GORDON CONSIDERS... AND SOMETHING IN HIM RESPONDS TO THIS STRANGER'S VOICE. HE CAN'T SAY WHY...

...BUT HE DECIDES TO TRUST HIM.
15

MINUTES LATER, IN A HOTEL ON DUMONT STREET...
GORDON'S INFORMANTS SAID CHILL TOOK A ROOM IN THIS--
GOOD LORD!
CHILL?!

CHILL! WHAT HAPPENED? WHO DID THIS?
M-MOXON! WENT TO SEE HIM... TOLD HIM MY NAME... HE THREW ME OUT... SAID SOME MANIAC WAS AFTER ME...
I GOT BACK... AN' ONE OF HIS GOONS WAS WAITING... ON HIS WAY TO ANOTHER HIT...

ANOTHER HIT?!
YEH... SOME DOCTOR... FUNNY, AIN'T IT... ALL MY LIFE... PART OF SOMEBODY ELSE'S GANG... SOMEBODY ELSE'S ORDERS...
AN' NOW I GET OFFED... ON THE WAY TO SOMEBODY ELSE'S FUNERAL...

MONDAY
21
CHILL ISN'T THE KILLER! SOMEONE ELSE IS-- AND IT'S GOING TO HAPPEN TONIGHT!
BUT HOW? TODAY'S THE 21ST-- IT'S NOT SUPPOSED TO HAPPEN FOR FIVE--
OH NO! OF COURSE! I SHOULD HAVE REALIZED!

MY PARENTS DIED TWENTY YEARS AGO! IN THAT TIME, THERE HAVE BEEN FIVE LEAP YEARS--

--FIVE EXTRA DAYS...

...THE CALENDAR DOESN'T RECORD!

FOR ALL PURPOSES, TONIGHT IS--

--THE NIGHT OF THE 26TH--

--AND HEAVEN HELP ME... IT'S HAPPENING ALL OVER AGAIN!

16

AND, AT THAT MOMENT ON PARK ROW..
REAL GOOD! WE CAME ALL THE WAY INTO TOWN JUST TO FIND THE MOVIE'S BEEN SOLD OUT!
BRUCE, THERE WAS NO WAY WE COULD HAVE KNOWN...

IT'S UP TO ME NOW! SHOULD I RESPECT BRUCE'S WISHES, AND INTERFERE--
--OR FOLLOW MY INSTINCTS, AND LET DESTINY TAKE ITS COURSE?
WHATEVER I DO--SOMEONE WILL SUFFER!

SUDDENLY...
WHAT--WHAT IS THIS--?!
IT'S CALLED A STICK-UP, BUDDY! I'LL TAKE THAT NECKLACE THE LADY'S WEARIN'!

YOU HOODLUM! DON'T YOU DARE PUT A HAND ON MY WIFE--!
TO BLAZES WITH DESTINY! BRUCE WAS RIGHT! I CAN'T LET INNOCENT PEOPLE DIE!
I ONLY PRAY I'M NOT TOO--
WAIT! WHAT THE--

BLAM
MAYBE THIS'LL SHUT YOU UP!
NO!!

NOT THIS TIME--YOU HEAR ME? THIS TIME YOU'RE NOT GOING TO WIN!
17

THIS TIME...

...I DIDN'T FAIL THEM...

BRUCE! WHAT HAPPENED? THAT ISN'T CHILL.

CHILL'S DEAD. THE POLICE SHOULD'VE FOUND HIM BY NOW... AND THEY'LL FOLLOW THE TRAIL RIGHT TO MOXON. THE WAYNES ARE SAFE.

AND SO YOUR TASK IS ENDED.

YOU MUST LEAVE NOW. YOU ARE STRANGERS HERE... AS MUCH A STRANGER AS I.

WILL WE EVER KNOW WHAT'LL HAPPEN--TO YOUNG BRUCE, HIS LIFE?

PERHAPS. BUT FOR NOW, ALL YOU NEED KNOW...

...IS THAT YOU SAVED TWO LIVES... AND ALTERED FOREVER A THIRD.
AMEN TO THAT.
THE FOG STARTS TO CLOSE IN AROUND THEM...

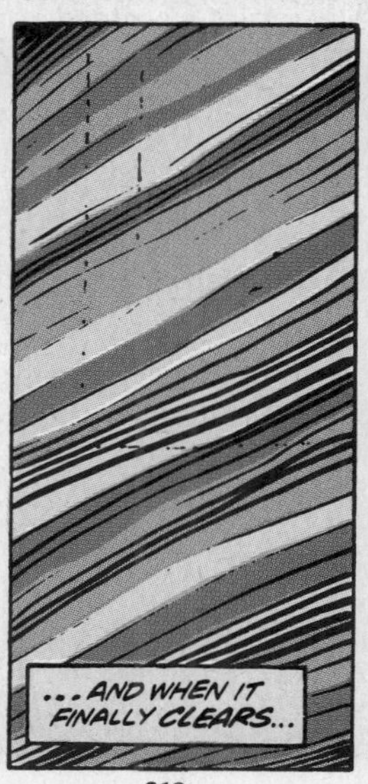

...AND WHEN IT FINALLY CLEARS...

...THREE STRANGERS HAVE RETURNED HOME.
18

EPILOGUE

THREE WEEKS LATER:
BRUCE? HOW'D YOU LIKE TO GO SHOPPING FOR SOME NEW TRAINS?
NO THANKS, MOM! GOT SOME THINGS TO DO--COUPLA BOOKS TO READ!
'SCUSE ME!

MARTHA WAYNE LOOKS AT THE NEW BOOKS THAT LINE BRUCE'S WALLS...THE NEW INTERESTS THAT FILL HIS LIFE...
CONAN DOYLE SHERLOCK HOLMES
THE PSYCHOLOGY of CRIME
THE CRIMINAL MIND
...AND DOESN'T QUITE KNOW WHAT TO MAKE OF IT ALL.

THOMAS, HAVE YOU NOTICED HOW... DIFFERENT BRUCE SEEMS SINCE THAT AWFUL ROBBERY?
IF BY DIFFERENT YOU MEAN QUIETER... MORE STUDIOUS... I THINK IT'S AN IMPROVEMENT.
MAYBE WE OUGHT TO GET MUGGED MORE OFTEN.

FOR AS LONG AS HE LIVES BRUCE WAYNE WILL REMEMBER THAT NIGHT, THREE WEEKS AGO...
...AND THE BAT-WINGED CREATURE THAT SWOOPED DOWN FROM THE SKY, SAVING THE LIVES OF HIMSELF AND HIS FAMILY.

THAT NIGHT, BRUCE WAYNE LEARNED WHAT DEATH WAS... AND HE LEARNED IT COULD BE AVERTED... AT LEAST TEMPORARILY.
YEARS FROM NOW, HE WILL MAKE A DECISION... CHOOSE A DIRECTION FOR HIS LIFE...

AND WHEN HE DOES, IT WILL NOT BE A DECISION BORN OF GRIEF, OR GUILT, OR VENGEANCE...
...BUT OF AWE... AND MYSTERY... AND GRATITUDE.
"TO KILL A LEGEND" by: ALAN BRENNERT writer DICK GIORDANO artist ADRIENNE ROY colorist JOHN COSTANZA letterer PAUL LEVITZ editor
END

Coloring by Lovern Kindzierski

...and became my wife.
The Autobiography of BRUCE WAYNE!
A VERY SPECIAL TALE OF THE GOLDEN AGE BATMAN, PRESENTED BY:
ALAN BRENNERT · writer
JOE STATON & GEORGE FREEMAN · artists
JOHN COSTANZA · letterer
LEN WEIN · editor
It was 1955, and police commissioner James Gordon was waiting--as he had so many nights before--on the roof of police headquarters.
I think I was more than a friend to Jim Gordon; I was his secret self, the adventurer he might have been had he not taken other paths.
He once told me he lived in dread of the night he would light the bat-signal... and no one would answer. Because the day I died, part of him would die, too.
2

That night, it all came true for him.
GOD IN HEAVEN! NO!!
RATATATATATATAT
PEDO
COMMISSIONER--NO--!
HAINER, LET ME GO! HE--HE MAY STILL BE ALIVE! HE MAY NEED HELP--!
EASY, JIM. YOU'RE THE ONE WHO NEEDS HELP.
I DON'T KNOW WHAT YOU THINK YOU SAW, COMMISSIONER, BUT IF THAT CHEMICAL ODOR IS ANY CLUE, I KNOW WHY YOU SAW IT.
IS THAT BOX YOU'RE HOLDING FOR ME, BY ANY CHANCE?
IT ARRIVED TODAY... THE POSTMARK COINCIDES WITH THE PAROLE DATE OF--
--JONATHAN CRANE, a.k.a. THE SCARECROW! OBVIOUSLY IT CONTAINED A TIMED-RELEASE GAS... DESIGNED TO CAUSE HALLUCINATIONS.
Y-YES... OF ONE'S... GREATEST FEAR...
PAROLED. THEY GO IN BAD... AND COME OUT WORSE. WHAT ARE WE DOING BUT... DETAINING THEM, TEMPORARILY?
WE DO WHAT WE'VE ALWAYS DONE, JIM-- WHAT WE HAVE TO DO.
GET SOME SLEEP. I'LL CHECK THIS IN THE BATCAVE.
3

THE YEAR'S NOT HALF OVER AND ALREADY I'VE HAD TO ROUND UP THE JOKER, THE PENGUIN, TWO-FACE... ALL EITHER PAROLED OR ESCAPED.
THIS ALL SEEMED A LOT EASIER, FIFTEEN YEARS AGO.
AND EVER SINCE THE JUSTICE SOCIETY DISBANDED...
...IT'S JUST BEEN ME, ROBIN, SUPERMAN AND WONDER WOMAN OUT HERE, TRYING TO HOLD THINGS TOGETHER.
FUNNY, THOUGH. I'M NOT NEARLY AS CONCERNED ABOUT THE SCARECROW BEING AT LARGE...
...AS I AM ABOUT ATTENDING LINDA PAGE'S WEDDING TOMORROW!
FIRST CLARK AND LOIS... THEN JAY GARRICK AND JOAN WILLIAMS...
LORD, HAS IT REALLY BEEN FIFTEEN YEARS?
It was the Batman who drove into the night...
...but, as usual, it was Bruce Wayne who had to face the DAY, at the estate of Linda's industrialist father.
WHAT THE-- BRUCE? WHAT ARE YOU DOING--
WELL, ACCORDING TO TRADITION IT'S BAD LUCK FOR THE GROOM TO SEE THE BRIDE--
-- BUT TRADITION DOESN'T SAY A THING ABOUT OLD BOYFRIENDS!
SAME OLD BRUCE. I'M SO GLAD YOU CAME. I WAS A LITTLE AFRAID YOU WOULDN'T WANT TO.
LINDA, IT'S BEEN TEN YEARS.
I KNOW, BUT THE THINGS I SAID BACK THEN...
4

...I HAD NO RIGHT TO TRY AND CHANGE YOU. I JUST COULDN'T FIGURE OUT WHY SOMEONE WITH YOUR INTELLIGENCE WOULD WANT TO SPEND HIS LIFE... PLAYING POLO.
IS THAT... STILL HOW YOU WANT TO BE REMEMBERED, BRUCE? AS JUST ANOTHER NAME ON THE SOCIAL REGISTER?
THERE'S...NO WAY I CAN EXPLAIN MYSELF TO YOU, LINDA.
MAYBE NOT. BUT I WISH YOU'D TRIED.
I DON'T KNOW WHAT SECRET PAIN YOU'RE HIDING, BRUCE...BUT WHATEVER IT IS...
...I DO HOPE YOU MAKE YOUR PEACE WITH IT.

DAMN THIS PLAYBOY POSE! I LOST JULIE MADISON BECAUSE OF IT...I LOST LINDA...
IT BEGAN AS A LARK--AMUSING TO PLAY AT BEING A RICH IDLER, WHILE PUMPING ACQUAINTANCES LIKE JIM GORDON FOR INFORMATION THE BATMAN COULD USE...
LATER, IT WAS NECESSARY TO ESTABLISH BATMAN AND WAYNE AS TWO DISTINCT PERSONALITIES, SINCE BOTH TRAVELED IN THE SAME CIRCLES...
...AND SOMEWHERE ALONG THE WAY, BRUCE WAYNE BECAME FROZEN INTO SOMEONE I'D NEVER INTENDED HIM TO BE!

LOOK AT THEM ALL. SHALLOW, STATUS-SEEKING HYPOCRITES... YET I HAVE TO PRETEND TO BE ONE OF THEM, SYMPATHIZE WITH THEM WHEN THEIR STOCKS DROP HALF A POINT!
MY ONLY REAL FRIENDS KNOW ME AS BATMAN... DICK, ALFRED, KATHY KANE...

EXCEPT...WHAT DO I DO WHEN DICK GRADUATES COLLEGE... AND ALFRED RETIRES...AND KATHY GIVES UP BEING BATWOMAN?
WHAT DO I DO... WHEN I'M FINALLY ALONE?
5

It was the first time I'd admitted to myself what I had made of my life.
The ceremony began...
And so did the nightmare.
OH MY LORD--!
EEEEEEEEEE
GET IT OFF ME! PLEASE, SOMEONE, GET IT OFF--!
BRUCE-- WHAT--
I'LL EXPLAIN ON THE RUN, DICK. LET'S GO.
CRANE!
WHEW! LUCKY FOR ME I HUNG OUT WITH THE SNAKE CHARMER AT THE CIRCUS.
IT'S GOING TO BITE ME--!
BETTER FIND SOME PLACE TO SWITCH TO BATWOMAN-- TRY TO QUELL THE PANIC!
6

MY, WHAT AN IDEAL CROSS-SECTION OF HUMANITY! HARD TO FIND A CROWD IN WHICH SOMEONE DOESN'T SUFFER FROM ARACHNOPHOBIA...OPHIOPHOBIA...HELMINTHOPHOBIA...
OR, RESPECTIVELY, FEAR OF SPIDERS, SNAKES, AND WORMS!
STILL THE SCHOOLTEACHER AT HEART, EH, CRANE? ALWAYS LECTURING.
NO WONDER HE BECAME A PSYCHOPATH. PROBABLY TOO BORING TO GET TENURE.
WHAPP!
YOU'RE LATE TO CLASS, BATMAN. I THOUGHT I MIGHT DRAW YOU INTO THE OPEN AT THIS AFFAIR-- MISS PAGE IS KNOWN TO BE ONE OF YOUR FRIENDS!
CAN I CRASH THIS COURSE, TOO?
:SIGH: THAT'S RIGHT-- DRIVE IT INTO THE GROUND, WHY DON'T YOU.
YOU PEOPLE DON'T KNOW WHEN TO LEAVE A GOOD METAPHOR ALONE, DO YOU?
GOOD LORD, CRANE--
--AREN'T WE BOTH GETTING A LITTLE OLD FOR--
ARGGHHH!
I thought it was just a flare-bomb designed to slow me down...
...but in the next instant I watched in horror as Robin--Dick--
--literally VANISHED into thin air!
BATMAN, ARE YOU ALL...
ROBIN!
7

For me, the nightmare had begun--

BATWOMAN, WHAT--WHAT HAPPENED? WHAT HAPPENED TO ROBIN?

ROBIN...?

But for everyone else--

BATMAN, CAN YOU HEAR--

ROBIN'S RIGHT HERE BESIDE ME!

WHAT ARE YOU TALKING ABOUT? HE JUST VANISHED INTO THIN--

OH NO--NO--NOT YOU, TOO--!

BATWOMAN! BATWOMAN!

BATMAN, ARE YOU ALL RIGHT? WHAT'S GOING ON?

LINDA, STAY BACK! YOU COULD BE--

...NEXT...!
NOOOOO...!
I DON'T UNDERSTAAA...

SCARECROW! YOU DID THIS, SOMEHOW! I'LL FIND YOU IF IT'S THE LAST THING I DO-- YOU UNDERSTAND?!
ROBIN, IT'S NO USE. HE CAN'T SEE, HEAR, EVEN FEEL US!
BATMAN, WE'RE OKAY, WE'RE HERE--
8

CRANE'S BOMB... IT MUST HAVE TRIGGERED HIS DEEPEST SUBCONSCIOUS FEAR...
THE FEAR... OF BEING ALONE...
THERE MUST BE SOMETHING WE CAN DO FOR HIM, ROBIN--
SO, BATMAN--YOUR DEMON, YOUR ROOM 101, IS AUTOPHOBIA, IS IT?
I WISH THERE WERE.
CRANE DIDN'T CREATE THE FEAR... JUST AGGRAVATED IT. ALL WE CAN HOPE...
...IS THAT HE COMES TO GRIPS WITH IT... BEFORE IT COMES TO GRIPS WITH HIM.
INTERESTING. THE MORE YOU SEARCH FOR YOUR FRIENDS, THE MORE HOPELESS IT WILL SEEM...
...AND THE DEEPER INTO DELUSION YOU WILL SINK--SO DEEP YOU SHALL NEVER ESCAPE!
I was alone, truly alone, for the first time since my parents had been killed.
I needed an ALLY--someone, anyone, to help me find Dick and Kathy and Linda.
I went to police HQ, but Gordon was nowhere to be seen.
I went to Wayne Manor, but Alfred, too, was missing.
I called Metropolis, but at the other end of the Kents' line there was only silence.
HELLO? HELLO?
There were no FRIENDS to turn to...
9

...but what about--
an old ENEMY?

After an accident had freed her from the amnesia which plagued her for over a decade-- during which time she had first become the Catwoman--

--Selina Kyle surrendered to serve her prison term, peacefully. There had always been an attraction between us--

--but would she help me now?

BATMAN, I--I BARELY REMEMBER WHAT I DID AS THE CATWOMAN! I DON'T WANT TO. DON'T ASK ME TO PUT ON THAT DAMNED COSTUME AGAIN.

IT COULD MEAN PAROLE, SELINA. AND YOU SEE, I...

...I DON'T HAVE ANYONE ELSE I CAN TURN TO. TOO MUCH OF MY WORLD SEEMS TO BE... SHRINKING. DEAD ENDS AND LOCKED DOORS.

SHRINKING... YES.

I... KNOW THAT FEELING.

WILL YOU HELP ME, SELINA?

10

Two hours later...
GOTHAM UNIVERSITY? WHY WOULD CRANE BE HERE?
HE TAUGHT HERE BEFORE HE TURNED TO CRIME-- AND THAT DOLL HE SENT WAS WRAPPED IN PIECES OF THE COLLEGE NEWSPAPER.
LIKE THE JOKER, HE NEEDS TO CONFRONT ME, DELIBERATELY PROVIDING ME WITH CLUES TO FIND HIM.
HE MUST BE CRAZY. ALL I EVER WANTED WAS TO AVOID YOU LONG ENOUGH TO GET AWAY WITH THE LOOT!
I KNOW. AFTER PSYCHOTICS LIKE THE JOKER AND THE SCARECROW, YOU HAVE NO IDEA HOW REFRESHING IT WAS TO DEAL WITH SOMEONE WHO WAS JUST IN IT FOR THE MONEY.
I'LL TAKE THAT AS A--
ROARRR
BATMAN!
SNAPP
NO TIME TO USE MY CAT-NIP-- I HAVE TO DRAW ITS ATTENTION!
SORRY, LEO. IT ONLY HURTS FOR A SECOND.
CAN'T BLAME YOU FOR BEING ANGRY, LEO--I'D BE, TOO, IF SOMEONE PAINTED ME WHITE!
STILL--
11

--I HOPE YOU DON'T MIND A LITTLE TRANQUILIZING POWDER IN YOUR FACE!

OF ALL THE INHUMAN--! CRANE MUST'VE DRUGGED HIM, RENDERING HIM RELATIVELY IMMOBILE ON THAT PEDESTAL--

--THEN ACTIVATED THIS ELECTRIC SHOCK STIMULUS BY REMOTE CONTROL, SENDING THE POOR THING INTO A RAGE JUST AS WE APPROACHED!

YOU REALLY LOVE THOSE ANIMALS, DON'T YOU?

THEY'RE BETTER THAN MOST PEOPLE.

I'LL REMOVE SOME OF THIS GREASEPAINT SO HE WON'T SUFFOCATE...

...AND WHEN I GET MY HANDS ON THE MANIAC WHO DID THIS, I'LL PLUCK THE STRAW OFF HIM WITH MY CAT-O'-NINE-TAILS!

Entering the main hall, we found...
...TODAY'S CLASS WILL FOCUS ON SOME OF THE MORE ESOTERIC PHOBIAS HUMAN BEINGS ARE PREY TO...
...I'M SPEAKING, OF COURSE, OF THE FEAR OF NATURAL PHENOMENA... THINGS OVER WHICH WE HAVE NO CONTROL...
FEARS SUCH AS HELIOPHOBIA, OR AN ABNORMAL DREAD OF THE SUN...
...SIDEROPHOBIA, A FEAR OF STARS...
...EVEN COMETOPHOBIA, WHICH IS, I SHOULD THINK, RATHER SELF-EXPLANATORY!
13

MORE COMMON IS ASTRAPHOBIA, FEAR OF LIGHTNING...
Van der Graaf generator

... AND PYROPHOBIA, THE TERROR, OF COURSE, OF--
SELINA!!
CROSSBOW
ANEROMETER

--FIRE!
AAAAGHHHH!
BATMAN!

LOST SEVERAL SECONDS GETTING MY CAPE OFF... DEAR GOD, LET HIM BE ALL--
...A RELATED PHOBIA...
THAT CAN'T BE THE SAME RECORDER! WHERE--
RADIO

...IS KNOWN AS--
SQUAWWK
OH, SHUT UP!
MY GOD, WAS I THE ONLY ARCH-CRIMINAL AROUND WHO DIDN'T DELIVER LECTURES?
19

SHORTLY, IN THE CAMPUS MEDICAL CENTER...
I THOUGHT THAT OUTFIT OF YOURS WAS FLAME-RETARDANT.
RETARDANT, YES; INDESTRUCTIBLE, NO.
IF YOU HADN'T SMOTHERED THE FLAMES IN TIME--

WELL, YOU SAVED ME FROM THAT HAIL OF--
GOOD... LORD...
BAD BURN?
NO, IT'S JUST... ALL THIS... SCAR TISSUE ON YOUR BACK...

OH. THAT. OCCUPATIONAL HAZARD. FIFTEEN YEARS OF FIGHTING WILL DO THAT TO A PERSON.
DOES IT... HURT?
SOMETIMES. YOU LEARN TO LIVE WITH IT.

NO ONE... SHOULD HAVE TO LIVE WITH THIS MUCH HURT.

WHY DO YOU DO IT? WHY DID YOU START?
I don't know why I answered-- but I did.

MY... PARENTS... WERE KILLED BY A PETTY THIEF. WHEN I WAS TEN.
FOR SOME, THE MEMORY OF THAT WOULD FADE IN TIME. FOR ME, IT JUST GOT MORE VIVID.
I HAD TO DO SOMETHING... TO MAKE LIVING WITH IT EASIER. TO GET THE ANGER OUT.

ANGER... MAKES YOU DO STRANGE THINGS, DOESN'T IT?
SO YOU BECAME THE BATMAN... AND YOU'VE SPENT YOUR LIFE... AVENGING THEIR DEATHS?

YES. AND I WON'T LOSE ROBIN AND THE OTHERS... THE WAY I LOST MY PARENTS.
I'LL FIND THEM... IF IT TAKES MY LIFE TO DO IT!
15

And, unknown to us at the time...
TIME TO MOVE ON TO ADVANCED STUDIES, BATMAN! HA HA
MY FIRST GAS-BOMB AWAKENED YOUR SUBCONSCIOUS FEARS...
THE GAS HAS THE SAME RELATIVE DENSITY AS AIR ITSELF, SO IT WILL LINGER... CREATING POCKETS OF FEAR ALL OVER THE CAMPUS!
YOU'RE BOUND TO PASS THROUGH A FEW OF THEM IN YOUR SEARCH.
...BUT THESE CAN TRIGGER SPECIFIC PHOBIAS OF MY CHOOSING!
OF COURSE, THE EFFECTS ARE ONLY TEMPORARY...BUT COMBINED WITH YOUR ANXIETY OVER YOUR "MISSING" FRIENDS...
...I THINK WE CAN LOOK FORWARD TO A COMPLETE EMOTIONAL BREAKDOWN BEFORE THE NIGHT IS DONE!
YOU KNOW, BATMAN... IF THE SCARECROW MADE GORDON SEE WHAT HE DID LAST NIGHT... PERHAPS YOUR FRIENDS' DIS-APPEARANCE WAS ALSO SOME KIND OF--
ILLUSION?
I THOUGHT OF THAT. AND DISMISSED IT. IT WAS REAL, SELINA. REAL AS THIS ROPE I'M HOLDING!
EMOTIONALLY REAL, PERHAPS, BUT--
I'M TELLING YOU, IT WAS NO TRICK! I KNOW REALITY FROM ILLUSION!
THE SUBJECT IS CLOSED!
:WHEW: THAT CUTS IT. HE'S DEFINITELY NOT HIMSELF...UNDER SOME KIND OF SPELL.
EXCEPT HOW DO I CONVINCE HIM OF--
16

OH MY...LORD... WHAT...
SELINA! WHAT'S WRONG?
SO...HIGH UP! WHAT AM I...DOING UP HERE?
OH GOD, THE GROUND, IT'S SO FAR AWAY! HOW--HOW DO I GET DOWN?
HOW DO I--
NO!!
SELINA!
EASY. I'VE GOT YOU!
THIS IS...ABSURD! I'VE NEVER BEEN AFRAID OF... HEIGHTS BEFORE...!
IT'S GONE NOW. THE SCARECROW... HE MUST BE--
SELINA! DO YOU--DO YOU FEEL IT? THE DARKNESS? CLOSING IN?
IT'S GOING TO CRUSH US... KILL US, IF WE DON'T--
NO... NOT THE DARKNESS...
LOOK WHERE WE ARE, BATMAN! LOOK AROUND US!
Sudden AGORAPHOBIA sent us running to the nearest building--
SO MUCH OPEN SPACE! WHAT FOOLS WE ARE--CRANE COULD PICK US OFF LIKE FLIES!
YOU'RE RIGHT! WE--WE'VE GOT TO FIND COVER!
17

-- THE UNIVERSITY LIBRARY!
I FEEL LIKE A FOOL! RUNNING LIKE A--
I HATE FEELING SO-- SO HELPLESS! I BECAME THE CATWOMAN SO I'D NEVER HAVE TO BE AT ANYONE'S MERCY EVER AGAIN, AND NOW LOOK AT ME!
"BECAME THE..."?

I THOUGHT AS MUCH.
THAT STORY YOU TOLD ME, SELINA... HOW A PLANE CRASH GAVE YOU AMNESIA...
IT WAS ALL A LIE, WASN'T IT?

DAMN.
I'M SORRY, BATMAN. I DIDN'T WANT TO LIE TO YOU, BUT... I JUST DIDN'T SEE ANY OTHER WAY OUT.
OUT? OUT OF WHAT?
YOU FIRST KNEW ME AS A JEWEL THIEF CALLED THE CAT. LORD, IT SEEMS A MILLION YEARS AWAY, DOESN'T IT?

WHAT YOU DIDN'T KNOW... WAS THAT I HAD BEEN THE CAT FOR OVER TWO YEARS... SINCE THE END OF MY... MARRIAGE.

YOUR--?

I'D BEEN VERY YOUNG-- IT WAS A MISTAKE, A BAD ONE. MY HUSBAND WAS VERY WEALTHY.

HE ALSO LIKED TO BEAT ME.

WHEN I DIVORCED HIM, HE RESPONDED... BY USING HIS CONNECTIONS TO TRY AND RUIN ME FINANCIALLY, PROFESSIONALLY, EMOTIONALLY!

18

I HATED HIM, WANTED TO GET BACK AT HIM. BUT THE ONLY LOSS HE UNDERSTOOD WAS MATERIAL LOSS, SO...
ONE NIGHT, WHEN HE WAS OUT OF TOWN, I SNEAKED ONTO HIS ESTATE... RANSACKED HIS OFFICE, HIS SAFE, THE JEWELS HE'D BOUGHT ME AND THEN KEPT...
IT FELT SO GOOD! TOO GOOD. IT WAS SO EASY TO CONTINUE... TO CONVINCE MYSELF THAT I DESERVED THE THINGS I STOLE, BECAUSE OF ALL THE PAIN I'D BEEN THROUGH!
"BUT... WHY THE CHARADE, THE AMNESIA--?"
BECAUSE I WAS TRAPPED! I WASN'T SELINA KYLE ANYMORE, I WAS THE CATWOMAN! BECAUSE I WAS THIRTY YEARS OLD AND I DIDN'T WANT TO DIE WITHOUT LOVE, WITHOUT CHILDREN--
I WANTED TO START OVER AGAIN. IS THERE SOMETHING WRONG WITH THAT?
NO.
FUNNY. WE BOTH CHOSE OUR PATHS OUT OF ANGER... AND WE BOTH FOUND OURSELVES TRAPPED. YOU LOST SELINA KYLE, AND I LOST... SOMEONE ELSE.
BUT YOU FOUND A WAY OUT, AND I... I DON'T KNOW HOW TO GET OUT.
DON'T YOU?
19

I never wanted to hold on to someone as much in my life...but...

SELINA, THIS ISN'T RIGHT. NOT WHILE ROBIN AND THE OTHERS ARE STILL MISSING. WE HAVE TO FIND THEM!

BATMAN, LISTEN TO ME--

--THE SCARECROW, HE'S AFFECTED YOUR MIND-- THEY'RE NOT REALLY--

LOOK! THERE HE IS! COME ON!

IF THEY WERE GONE, WOULDN'T IT BE IN THE PAPERS? WOULDN'T THE POLICE BE HERE? WOULDN'T--
CRANE! CRANE, YOU DEMENTED JACKAL, WHERE ARE THEY?!
OH GOD--HE'S GOING OVER THE EDGE...

BLAST YOU, CRANE, WHERE ARE--
WHAT--NO! NO! IT CAN'T-- YOU CAN'T--

BLAST YOU! BLAST YOU, WHERE ARE THEY?!
ROBIN! KATHY! LINDA!--
BATMAN, PLEASE--
I turned to face her...
20

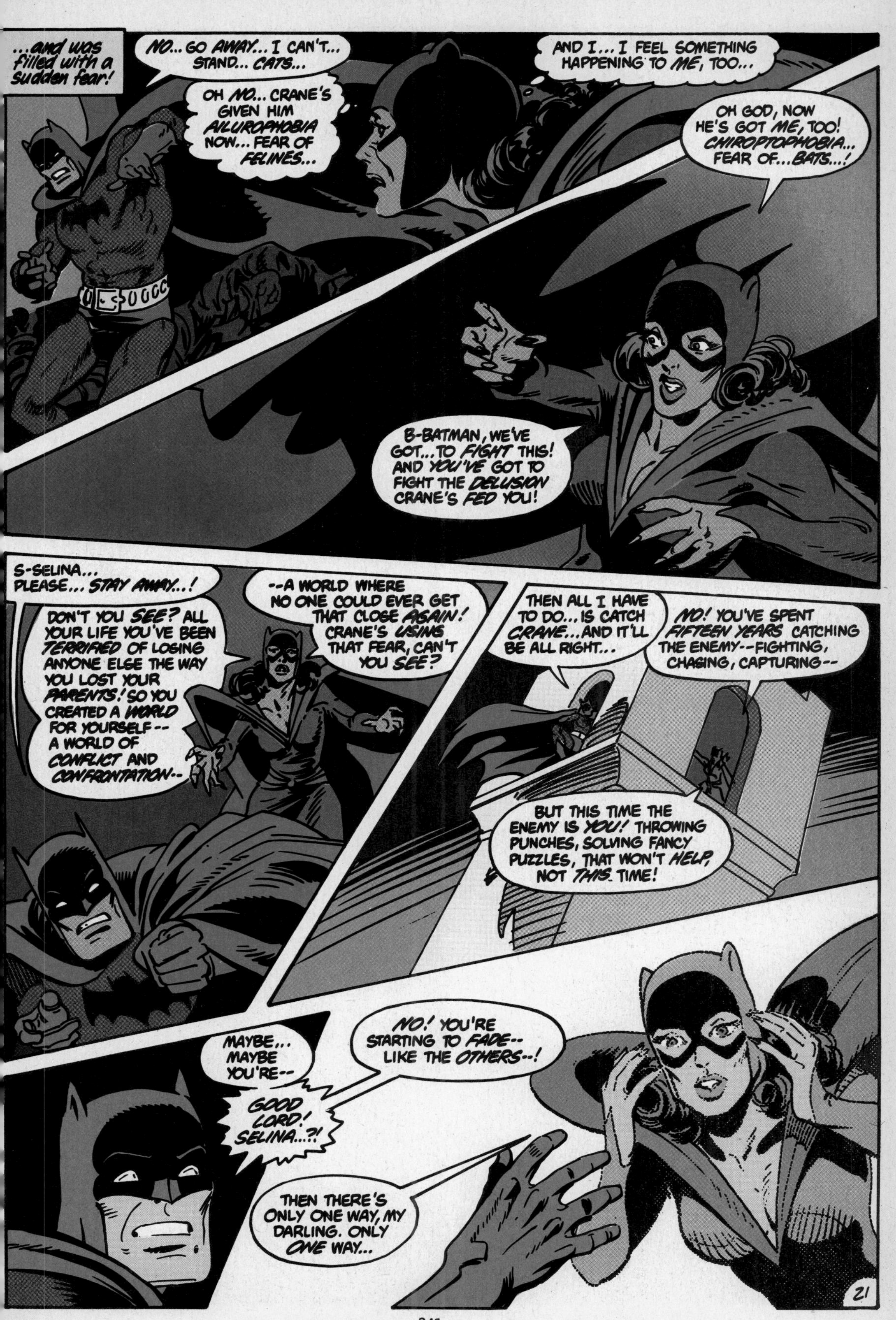
...and was filled with a sudden fear!
NO... GO AWAY... I CAN'T... STAND... CATS...
OH NO... CRANE'S GIVEN HIM AILUROPHOBIA NOW... FEAR OF FELINES...
AND I... I FEEL SOMETHING HAPPENING TO ME, TOO...
OH GOD, NOW HE'S GOT ME, TOO! CHIROPTOPHOBIA... FEAR OF... BATS...!
B-BATMAN, WE'VE GOT... TO FIGHT THIS! AND YOU'VE GOT TO FIGHT THE DELUSION CRANE'S FED YOU!
S-SELINA... PLEASE... STAY AWAY...!
DON'T YOU SEE? ALL YOUR LIFE YOU'VE BEEN TERRIFIED OF LOSING ANYONE ELSE THE WAY YOU LOST YOUR PARENTS! SO YOU CREATED A WORLD FOR YOURSELF-- A WORLD OF CONFLICT AND CONFRONTATION--
--A WORLD WHERE NO ONE COULD EVER GET THAT CLOSE AGAIN! CRANE'S USING THAT FEAR, CAN'T YOU SEE?
THEN ALL I HAVE TO DO... IS CATCH CRANE... AND IT'LL BE ALL RIGHT...
NO! YOU'VE SPENT FIFTEEN YEARS CATCHING THE ENEMY--FIGHTING, CHASING, CAPTURING--
BUT THIS TIME THE ENEMY IS YOU! THROWING PUNCHES, SOLVING FANCY PUZZLES, THAT WON'T HELP, NOT THIS TIME!
MAYBE... MAYBE YOU'RE--
NO! YOU'RE STARTING TO FADE-- LIKE THE OTHERS--!
GOOD LORD! SELINA...?!
THEN THERE'S ONLY ONE WAY, MY DARLING. ONLY ONE WAY...
21

LOOK! THE CAT IS GONE. THERE'S NOTHING TO BE AFRAID OF ANYMORE.
NOW...IT'S YOUR TURN, MY DARLING. TO TAKE AWAY MY FEAR...
I knew what had to be done...but a lifetime of inhibition stayed my hand.
I couldn't--

I COULDN'T--

I HAD TO.

SELINA! OH GOD, SELINA, I ALMOST LOST YOU...!
BUT CRANE... HE'S STILL OUT THERE... I SHOULD CATCH HIM--
DON'T YOU ALWAYS? IT CAN WAIT.

YES...I SUPPOSE IT CAN.
22

I found and captured the scarecrow, of course... but more important... that night I found Bruce Wayne.
And I found the woman who would share my life for the next twenty years.

She's been gone, now, for many months, but it still seems impossible to me.
Her death was pointless, tragic...

...but I have long since given up trying to find meaning in death.
The meaning is in life; not death...

...and Selina's life was as full of meaning as it was of love, and spirit, and courage.

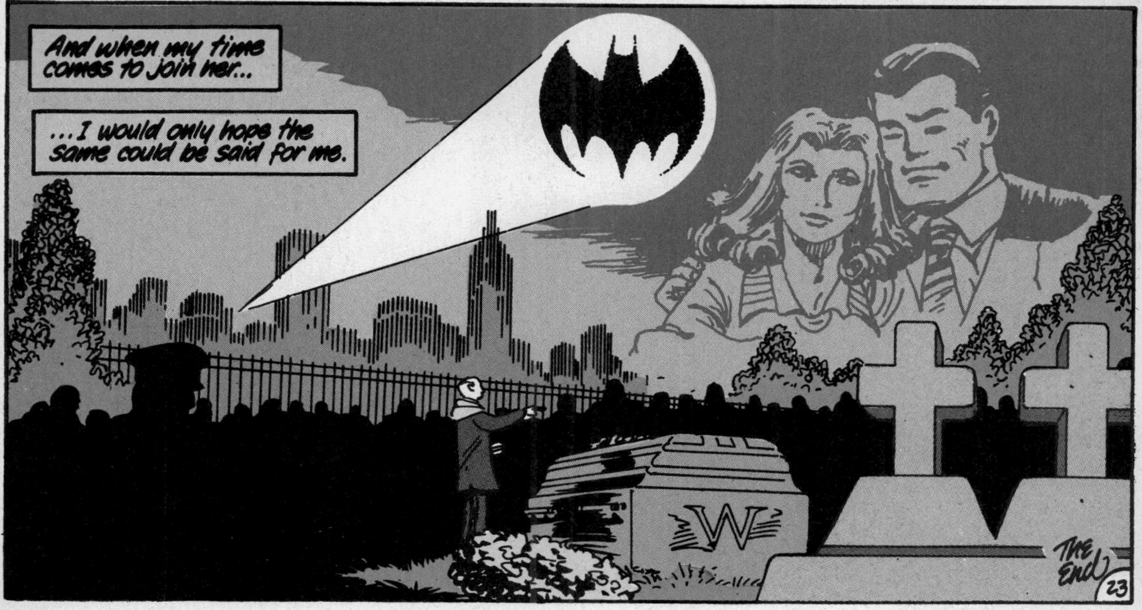
And when my time comes to join her...
...I would only hope the same could be said for me.
THE END
23

ENDNOTES

BY ROBERT GREENBERGER

He's been called the Caped Crusader, the Darknight Detective, the World's Greatest Detective and, most to the point, The Batman.

Over the past fifty years, his image has been dark and foreboding: the giant cape and bat-eared cowl, inspiring fear in criminals around the world. His is a night world, populated by the bizarre and deranged, where light is rarely seen and evil lurks in many guises. And for five decades, Batman has been an internationally acclaimed hero of mythic proportions.

It's not surprising, then, that Batman remains so popular, more so today than at almost any other time in his career. Batman represents the opposite of his predecessor, Superman. Whereas Superman has always been a light, positive hero, Batman has been grim and possessed. Their worlds rarely mesh but they have, together, thrilled readers for decades.

The nominations for this volume shows the breadth and depth of stories created over the years for Batman and two different kids named Robin. While the stories ultimately chosen best represent the Batman since his debut in 1939, the others remaining on the runner-up list show an amazing variety and versatility many never would imagine for The Darknight Detective.

One of Batman's greatest strengths has been his large and colorful rogues' gallery. His collection of foes includes, obviously, the Joker, Riddler, Catwoman, Penguin, and Two-Face; it also includes such lesser known villains as Clayface, Killer Moth, the Cavalier, Tweedledum and Tweedledee, Professor Hugo Strange and Mr. Freeze. Suffice to say that when it comes to oddball opponents, The Batman has given Dick Tracy a run for his money.

The Joker remains Batman's greatest nemesis and so many excellent stories were nominated, it became obvious to our publisher, Jenette Kahn—herself a Batman fan of some renown—that a separate volume was the only way to do him justice. In that volume are many of the nominated Joker sagas, including the first two such stories, his triumphant return in the 1970's in "The Joker's Five-Way Revenge," and the classic two-part story from the late 1970's by Steve Englehart, Marshall Rogers, and Terry Austin. While his brief appearance in this volume may confuse some, don't forget that whenever the Joker and Batman face off, the battle is classic.

When Batman returned to his roots in the early 1970's under editor Julius Schwartz and writers Dennis O'Neil and Frank Robbins, it was felt that the rogues' gallery needed "freshening." Denny invented Ra's al Ghul, who quickly became one of the top villains for The Batman. The story in which he was introduced, "Daughter of the Demon," is also one of the most often *reprinted*, leading to its exclusion this time around.

Ra's' daughter, Talia, has appeared in numerous stories, several of which were nominated, including her introductory tale and one in which Talia, following her religious beliefs, weds Batman. To date, Batman has never acknowledged the wedding but cannot deny his attraction to her.

Many nominated adventures have been reprinted frequently over the last few years, given the continuing appetite for classic and new Batman material. For that reason, seminal stories such as the first appearances of Batman and Robin were not included here. They remain available in other publications for the interested reader. The entire Ra's al Ghul saga was reprinted on high-quality Baxter paper just a few years ago.

After the Joker and Ra's al Ghul, tales of the Penguin, Catwoman, and Two-Face were the next most often nominated. "The Umbrella Man" introduced us to Chester Oswald Cobblebot, the Penguin, and we have been enchanted by him ever since, all the more so after Burgess Meredith's delightful rendition of the character during the 1960's. Again, the Englehart-Rogers-Austin team received multiple nods for their use of the Penguin.

Catwoman was Batman's first *femme fatale* and many consider her his best. As a result, her introductory tale from BATMAN #1 was voted for often and others, including Bob Kane and Jack Schiff, suggested her second appearance from BATMAN #4 where she donned a cat mask for the first time.

Poor Harvey Dent was the crusading district attorney who was first physically and then psychologically scarred into becoming Two-Face. His reliance on the "two" motif for his crimes and reliance upon a double-headed coin (one side scarred, the other clean) has made him one of the more popular Batman foes. His first few stories, starting with "The Crimes of Two-Face" and continuing into the 1950's, received votes. Two-Face is still a popular foe with today's writers who can't resist bringing him back every now and then.

There were other foes, most of them one-shot adversaries, but a few were memorable enough for nominations. Cited most often was "The Strange Case of Professor Radium" from BATMAN #8. This one featured a scientist who explored radium as a possible "cure" for death. His experiments worked on dogs but no one believed his results. Upset, the professor was accidentally exposed to pure radium waves and transformed into a living radium being. His very touch could kill. It fell to the Dynamic Duo to stop the deranged man, but he brought about his own death.

When the Batman television series made him the most popular comics character of the 1960's, management felt it wise to give him as much exposure as often as possible. For better than 100 issues of THE BRAVE AND THE BOLD, Batman was teamed with virtually every member of the DC Universe. Several of those stories were nominated for this volume, ranging from the odd meeting with the House of Mystery to his more obvious pairing with the villainous Eclipso. One of the other stories, "The Senator Has Been Shot," is an important tale, but more for co-star Green Arrow than for The Batman. Here, artist Neal Adams visually redesigned Green Arrow, moving him away from being a simple Batman clone and making him someone distinctive. It was also one of Adams's earlier art jobs with Batman, and the vitality shows.

Batman's very existence brought him into thematic confrontation with many unusual types. During the 1970's, the Denny O'Neil-Neal Adams team was remaking Batman into a creature

Opposite, top: DETECTIVE #38, April, 1940—the debut of Robin, the Boy Wonder.

Opposite, center, Berni Wrightson's vision of the Batman (from SWAMP THING, #7, 1973—"The Night of the Bat.")

Opposite, bottom: Joe Staton and Bob Layton capture one of the Masked Manhunter's most tragic moments (from DC SUPER-STARS #17, 1977—"From Each Ending—a Beginning"

to be feared, producing many excellent tales along the way. Most of these stories received at least one nomination—one story in particular, "Night of the Reaper," had Batman deal with racial prejudice set against a festive Halloween backdrop. It was a gripping story with effective artwork that most recall fondly today.

But it is not just the rogues' gallery that made the Batman stories wonderful. There were also the elements that made up the Batman's defense system: his equipment. While Superman may have retreated to his Fortress of Solitude for a rest, Batman practically *lived* in his Batcave, directly beneath stately Wayne Manor. Inside were wonderful machines, housing for the Bat-vehicles and a neat trophy room dominated by a giant penny and a life-size dinosaur. "1001 Secrets of the Batcave" and "10,000 Secrets of Batman" were solid stories that surveyed this aspect of the Caped Crimefighter's arsenal.

In fact, Batman's gimmicks allowed the writers in the 1950's to come up with variations on the theme, turning Batman's costume into a mold for fashion exploration. He had literally dozens of outfits during that decade: a zebra suit, a paper-thin one, a submersible outfit, a rainbow design, a pure white one for snow fighting, and a pure black one for stealth. Some of these variations, such as "The Mirror Batman," resulted in nominations.

While Superman spent a large part of the 1960's involved in "imaginary stories," tackling such issues as the consequences of marrying Lana Lang, Batman was spared most imaginary business. Instead, it was a decade later that people began to play around with Batman's mythos. As explored in "The Autobiography of Bruce Wayne," the Batman of an alternate Earth had a life rich beyond anyone's dreams. In the 1950's he married Selina Kyle (a.k.a. The Catwoman) and sometime later they had a daughter, Helena. Helena grew up to become a superhero in her own right, a popular crimefighter called The Huntress.

Her origin tale, by Paul Levitz and Joe Staton, showed us the tragic results of life in a world of costumed characters. Selina was

conned into becoming Catwoman one final time and the crime resulted in her death—and the birth of another person making a graveside pledge to fight crime. The Huntress was popular enough to join the fabled Justice Society of America and even had her own back-up series for a time. The origin's poignancy brought in a number of votes.

The gadgets and hardware aided The Batman, but his most useful tool was his very image. To the citizens of Gotham he was someone to be both cheered and shunned. Wherever he went, danger was sure to follow and many stories played with that concept. Sal Amendola, Steve Englehart, and Dick Giordano gave us "The Night of the Stalker" from the early 1970's—a touching story in which The Batman said not a word as he tracked down thugs who committed a crime which left a young boy orphaned.

Or witness the issue of the original SWAMP THING in which that muck-monster ended up in Gotham and had to confront its champion. The oft-reprinted "Night of the Bat" by Len Wein and Berni Wrightson did much to foster the restoration of Batman's dark qualities.

The Batman series has offered unique Christmas tales since the 1940's, and they bring out the best in the character and his creators. "The Silent Night of Batman", a seven page Christmas tale by Mike Friedrich and Neal Adams, was the most often nominated of these stories, but it had already been selected for use in a special Christmas collection coming at the same time as this volume.

Of course, there are numerous stories that don't neatly fit into a niche, once again bespeaking Batman's versatility. There was the one and only Batman story written by famed author Leigh Brackett, "Murder at Mystery Castle."

Many stories were personal favorites of the creators involved and are worth noting here. Jack Schiff offered "Brothers-in-Law" from WORLD'S FINEST COMICS #8, a human interest story that was one of the earliest Batman stories he wrote. Denny O'Neil mentioned "Vow from the Grave" being his technically best Batman collaboration with Neal Adams and the best detective story he has written for comics.

Interestingly, Bob Kane noted a large number of stories from the early, establishing years and wrote, "...the stories listed here are prime examples of the fertile and imaginative mind of my old friend, Bill Finger. He was the best darned Batman writer of them all." Unfortunately, negatives did not exist for the majority of Bob's suggestions, but we did include the Hugo Strange story from BATMAN #1 and the Gardner Fox-written two-part "Batman versus the Vampire" from DETECTIVE COMICS #31–32.

From time to time, Batman was made to follow in Superman's footsteps, given female counterparts and even a dog and a magical imp. He was also saddled with fighting aliens and appearing in time travel or "imaginary" stories throughout the 1950's into the early 1960's. These years were seen by most as low points for Batman, and the lack of significant voting in that era bears that out.

When Julius Schwartz took over editorship of the Caped Crusader, he added the yellow oval to Batman's chest, improved the quality of the artwork and went back to the crime-solving basics. The "new look" succeeded and that first story from DETECTIVE COMICS #327 received several nods. As stories go, however, it was an okay start but marred by Batman's use of a gun, something he has refused to do since his origin. Schwartz quickly learned his lesson and a vital rebirth period was under way.

While we might enjoy the concept of flying high with Superman, we also thrill to the scent of danger provided by following Batman into Gotham's darkest corners, knowing that it is by skill and wits that the enemy will be overcome. It is that element that remains in the stories and is one of the key reasons Batman has survived to year fifty.

As long as there is crime, there will always be a Batman. And as long as there is Batman, people will find that he brings out the best in their writing or art.

(Robert Greenberger is an editor at DC Comics and a member of its editorial development group.)

Opposite: Wrightson's Batman, redux.

CREATING THE GREATEST
BY MARK WAID

Jerry Robinson (1943).

NEAL ADAMS ["Ghost of the Killer Skies," "Half an Evil"]
Neal Adams began his comics career at the age of 18, drawing various features for Archie Comics and later working on the *Bat Masterson* and *Ben Casey* newspaper strips. From there, Adams picked up substantial commercial advertising assignments, where he learned to draw in an unusual *non*-comics manner. Bringing that point of view to DC, he single-handedly created an artistic revolution with his highly realistic style of illustration and dynamic page layouts. When in 1970, together with Dennis O'Neil, Adams was given the opportunity to take the then-super-heroic Batman back to being a dark, brooding "creature of the night," Adams changed The Batman forever. Though he went on to make his mark on other comics series, and other artists have come before and since to handle the Darknight Detective, many fans will always consider Neal Adams *the* Batman artist.

JIM APARO ["Deathmask"]
In 1966, advertising artist Jim Aparo was hired by Dick Giordano, then editor at Charlton Comics, to pencil and ink a variety of features. When Giordano came to DC in 1968, he brought Aparo over as well. Here, Aparo picked up more substantial long-running assignments on AQUAMAN, PHANTOM STRANGER—and THE BRAVE AND THE BOLD, where he drew the adventures of The Batman for nearly ten years. Aparo is currently the penciller on BATMAN.

TERRY AUSTIN ["The Deadshot Ricochet"]
Having gotten his break inking backgrounds for Dick Giordano, Terry Austin quickly came into his own in the comics field. Consistently voted as fandom's favorite inker, Austin has worked with many of the industry's best pencillers, including John Byrne on Marvel Comics' *X-Men* and Marshall Rogers on DETECTIVE COMICS. Recently, Austin has turned his talents toward scripting and writes *Cloak and Dagger* for Marvel.

ALAN BRENNERT ["To Kill A Legend," "The Autobiography of Bruce Wayne"]
Alan Brennert, a successful television and science-fiction writer, has always had a special fondness for super-heroes. Having been peripherally involved with DC as the story editor on the *Wonder Woman* TV series, Brennert was subsequently invited by DC editors to script whatever handful of stories his time allowed. It is a tribute to Brennert's talent that, of the five Batman tales written by Brennert, *two* have been chosen for inclusion in this book.

Jim Mooney (1951).

JACK BURNLEY ["The Penguin"]
Jack Burnley, a syndicated sports cartoonist in his teens, became part of the Joe Shuster studio and one of the many men to "ghost" the Superman feature during the early 1940's. Burnley's more illustrative style led to other DC assignments: not only was he one of the artists for the Justice Society of America, he was co-creator, with Gardner Fox, of the Golden Age Starman. Burnley drew many Superman and Batman covers for DC during the '40s, and pencilled all of the *Batman* Sunday strips and several of the dailies.

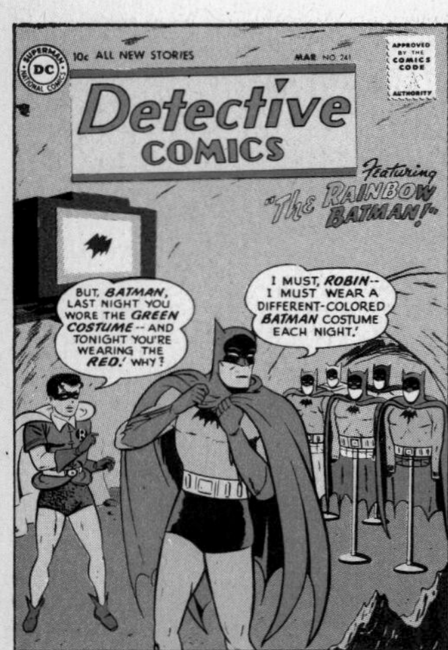

Sheldon Moldoff (1957).

STEVE ENGLEHART ["The Deadshot Ricochet"]
Writer Steve Englehart's comic-book credits are legion; he has worked extensively for both Marvel and DC over the past two decades. Englehart's major contribution to the Batman mythos remains his mid-'70s run on DETECTIVE COMICS with artists Walt Simonson, Marshall Rogers, and Terry Austin. In those issues, Englehart reintroduced Hugo Strange and Deadshot; gave new dimension to the Penguin and the Joker; and introduced Silver St. Cloud, with whom The Batman shared an intense but unconsummated love and who many fans consider to be *the* woman in The Batman's life.

BILL FINGER ["Dr. Hugo Strange and the Mutant Monsters"]
"Bill is the unsung hero of Batman," Bob Kane has said of Bill Finger, his collaborator on the Darknight Detective. Finger scripted the first and many of the best Batman stories during the Golden Age of Comics and beyond, writing for BATMAN and DETECTIVE through the 1960's. Finger created or co-created Catwoman, The Penguin, Riddler, Two-Face, and a host of other elements important to the Batman legend; he is probably best known for

his predilection for including giant-sized props of everyday items in his stories—mammoth working typewriters, building-sized cigarette lighters, and the like. Though Finger produced some material for the Timely, Quality, and Fawcett groups during the mid-1940's, most of his work, most notably Green Lantern and Wildcat, was for DC. Finger passed away in 1974.

Curt Swan and Stan Kaye (1959).

GARDNER FOX ["Batman vs. The Vampire," "The Blockbuster Invasion of Gotham City"]

One of the most innovative and prolific writers in comic books, Gardner Fox worked in the field almost from its birth, creating Starman, Dr. Fate, the original Flash, Hawkman, the Justice Society, the Justice League, the modern-day Atom, Adam Strange, and literally hundreds more heroes and villains. Fox was, after Bill Finger, the second scripter of the adventures of The Batman. Though he did not write an overwhelming number of scripts for the character during Batman's first 25 years, concentrating on assignments for other DC characters and for other companies instead, Fox returned with a vengeance in 1964 and penned some of the best and most fondly remembered Batman tales of that period until his retirement from DC in 1968. Until his death in late 1986, Gardner Fox continued to write comics and novels, scripting over 100 books of all genres under the pen names "Jefferson Cooper" and "Bart Sommers," as well as a number of fantasy titles under his own name.

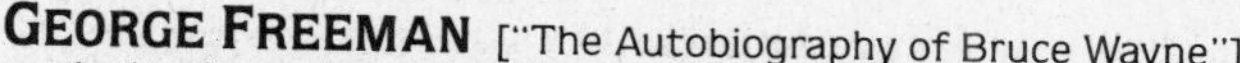

GEORGE FREEMAN ["The Autobiography of Bruce Wayne"]

Artist George Freeman first gained attention in 1977 by working on *Captain Canuck*, a Canadian comic book distributed in the U.S. Since that time, Freeman has worked for every major comics company in one capacity or another, be it as penciller, inker, illustrator, or colorist. His most recent credits include First Comics' *Eiric* and DC's WASTELAND.

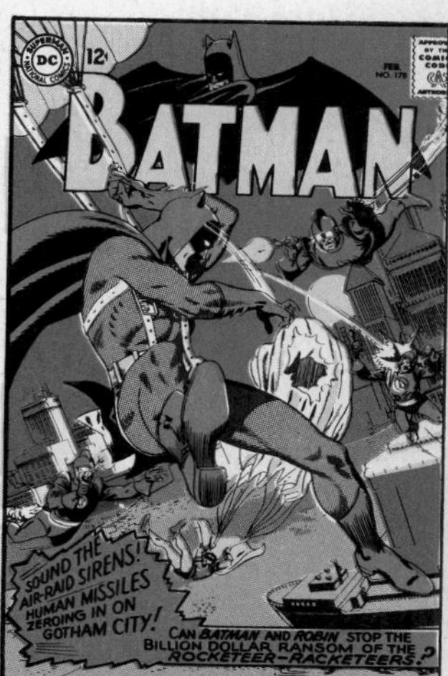

Gil Kane and Murphy Anderson (1966).

JOE GIELLA ["The Blockbuster Invasion of Gotham City"]

Joe Giella began his inking career in the 1940's, working at Hillman Publications and at Timely, the company that was to become Marvel Comics. Giella came to DC in 1951 and, until his retirement in the early 1980's, worked on every major DC character and inked the work of many of DC's best pencillers. Giella also pencilled and inked a string of Batman syndicated comic strips during the 1960's.

DICK GIORDANO ["Ghost of the Killer Skies," "Half an Evil," "The Batman Nobody Knows," "No Hope In Crime Alley," "A Caper a Day Keeps The Batman Away," "To Kill A Legend"]

Dick Giordano's formative professional years were forged at Charlton Comics, where he freelanced as an artist beginning in 1952. In 1965, Giordano was made editor-in-chief of the Charlton line and introduced a tremendous amount of new talent into the comics field, working with Jim Aparo, Dennis O'Neil, Steve Skeates, and many others, all of whom came with him to DC in 1967 for his three-year editorial tenure at that time. Giordano's artistic skills earned him many accolades and industry awards. During the early 1970's, as the perfect inker to Neal Adams' pencils, Giordano helped return The Batman to his roots as an avenging vigilante. Giordano continues to be instrumental in shaping the legend of The Batman to this day, though playing a different role—as DC's Vice President-Executive Editor.

Carmine Infantino and Joe Giella (1966).

MICHAEL GOLDEN ["Bat-Mite's New York Adventure"]

Artist Michael Golden made his mark on comics in the 1970's as the initial penciller of Marvel's *Micronauts*. Among his other assignments, Golden pencilled a number of stories featuring Batman and his supporting cast in the pages of BATMAN FAMILY, one of which is included here. Golden's other works include Marvel's *The 'Nam* and Continuity's *Bucky O'Hare*.

ARCHIE GOODWIN ["Deathmask," "Death Haunts the Skies"]

Archie Goodwin, a former art director for *Redbook*, began his involvement in comics by assisting Leonard Starr on the *On Stage* comic strip in 1959. Goodwin spent the 1960's as an associate editor/writer for the Warren line of magazines and as the writer of the *Secret Agent Corrigan* newspaper strip. Before joining the Marvel editorial staff in 1975, Goodwin spent several years at DC and enjoyed a brief tenure as the editor of DETECTIVE COMICS, where he penned several Batman tales and co-created with Walt Simonson the industry award-winning Manhunter feature. Goodwin is currently editor-in-chief of Marvel's Epic Comics.

CARMINE INFANTINO ["The Blockbuster Invasion of Gotham City"]

Though Carmine Infantino had been pencilling all types and genres of features for DC since his debut in the late 1940's, including Flash and Adam

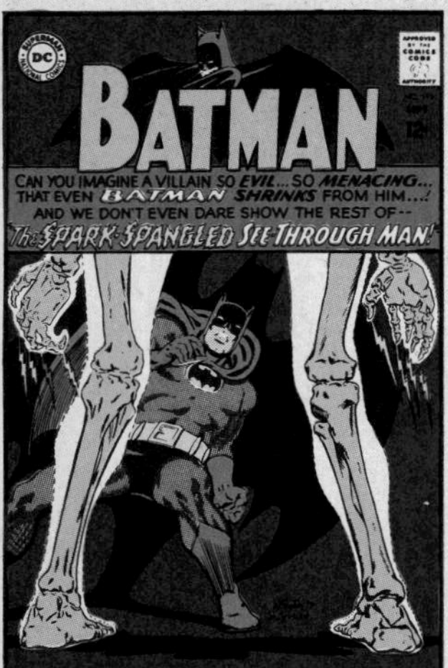

Carmine Infantino and Murphy Anderson (1967).

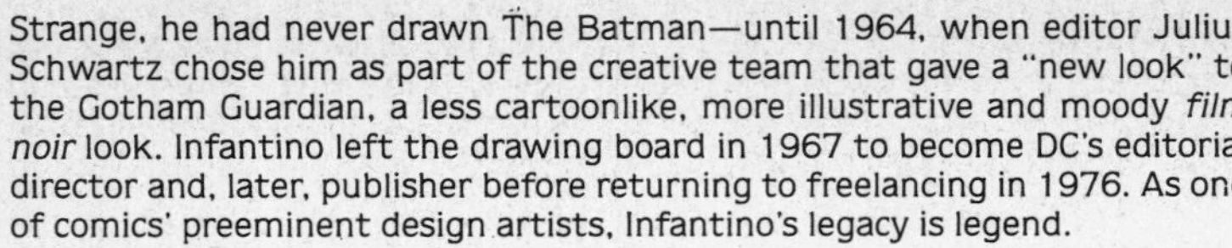

Strange, he had never drawn The Batman—until 1964, when editor Julius Schwartz chose him as part of the creative team that gave a "new look" to the Gotham Guardian, a less cartoonlike, more illustrative and moody *film noir* look. Infantino left the drawing board in 1967 to become DC's editorial director and, later, publisher before returning to freelancing in 1976. As one of comics' preeminent design artists, Infantino's legacy is legend.

BOB KANE ["Batman vs. The Vampire"]

Bob Kane, of course, is the man who started it all. Though Bill Finger scripted the Caped Crusader's first story, The Batman began with Kane and his crude sketches of a masked man in a bat-winged costume inspired by sources as diverse as Zorro, the 1931 movie *The Bat Whispers*, and the drawings of Leonardo da Vinci. Having already established a working relationship with DC Comics, Kane and Finger brought them the cover-featured star of the May, 1939 issue of DETECTIVE COMICS—and the rest was history. Along with Finger, Jerry Robinson, Gardner Fox, and a host of others, Kane quickly made The Batman into one of the most popular comic book characters ever. Though he eventually retired from comic books to devote his energies to animation, painting, and other creative endeavors, with his creation Kane left his mark permanently on popular culture.

STAN KAYE ["The Origin of the Superman-Batman Team"]

Stan Kaye was one of the finest inkers of the Golden Age of Comics. During the early 1940's, he was the illustrator of Alfred Bester's Genius Jones for DC; in the early to mid-1950's, his smooth pen graced many of DC's best pencillers, including Curt Swan on JIMMY OLSEN and Dick Sprang on WORLD'S FINEST COMICS.

Irv Novick (1968).

SHELDON MOLDOFF ["Robin Dies At Dawn"]

An artist originally influenced heavily by Alex Raymond and Hal Foster, Sheldon Moldoff is probably best known for his work on Hawkman from late 1940 to early 1945. During that time, he became a mainstay of the early DC, pencilling several features. His work began appearing more and more frequently in BATMAN and DETECTIVE during the 1950's, to the point where his style virtually defined Batman during the late '50s and early '60s.

JIM MOONEY ["Operation: Escape"]

Now in semi-retirement, Jim Mooney has enjoyed a long career as a comics artist, having worked at one time or another for every major publishing company. Though he is best known for his work on DC's Supergirl and Tommy Tomorrow, Mooney was first recognized for his work on some of the better Batman stories of the early 1940's. His contribution to the Batman legend included the artistic chores on dozens of Batman tales, many Batman/Superman team-ups in WORLD'S FINEST, and a long run of Robin solo stories in STAR-SPANGLED COMICS.

DENNIS O'NEIL ["Ghost of the Killer Skies," "Half an Evil," "No Hope In Crime Alley," "Death Strikes at Midnight and Three"]

Dennis O'Neil began his career as a comic book writer in 1965 at Charlton, where then-editor Dick Giordano assigned him to several features and later brought him to DC. There, O'Neil scripted several series for Giordano and for Julius Schwartz and quickly became one of the most respected writers in comics. O'Neil earned a reputation for being able to "revamp" stale characters such as Superman, Green Lantern, Captain Marvel—and The Batman, whom O'Neil, with the help of Neal Adams and Dick Giordano, brought back to his roots as a dark, mysterious, gothic avenger. Besides being the most important Batman writer of the 1970's, O'Neil has served as an editor at both Marvel and DC. Fittingly, he is currently the editor of the Batman line of comics.

Neal Adams (1970).

CHARLES PARIS ["The Penguin," "The Birth of Batplane II," "Jungle Cat-Queen," "Robin Dies At Dawn"]

Charles Paris, one of the more versatile inkers and finishers working during the 1940's and 1950's, is best known for having been the main inker on Dick Sprang's Batman work, giving Sprang's manic pencils an extra degree of depth and fullness. Paris also inked Jack Burnley's pencils on many of the *Batman* Sunday strips.

FRANK ROBBINS ["Man-Bat Over Vegas," "The Batman Nobody Knows"]

Frank Robbins, an internationally celebrated comics creator, began his career in 1939 by taking over the *Scorchy Smith* comic strip for the King Features Syndicate. Five years later, he created for them the long-running *Johnny Hazard* strip. From 1968 to 1976, Robbins entered the field of comic books full-time as a writer, working almost exclusively for DC on hundreds of stories for FLASH, SUPERBOY, THE SHADOW, THE UNKNOWN SOLDIER, and BATMAN—on the latter two occasionally as both writer and artist. In addition to his comics work, Robbins has done illustrations for such publications as *Life, Look,* and *The Saturday Evening Post* and has had his paintings exhibited at the Corcoran Gallery, the Whitney Museum, and the Metropolitan Museum.

Berni Wrightson (1980).

JERRY ROBINSON ["Knights of Knavery"]

Jerry Robinson is one of the giants of the comics industry. Not only is he a prolific writer, artist, political cartoonist, and comics historian, but he has received more industry awards than anyone working in the comics field. In 1939, at age 17, he started assisting Bob Kane on Batman and, in a very short time, graduated to pencilling and inking the feature as well as contributing most of the classic Batman covers of the early 1940's. It was Robinson who took Kane's crude style of moodiness and angularity and perfected it, defining the look of the '40s Batman. That was one of his two lasting contributions; the other was the naming of Robin, the Boy Wonder.

MARSHALL ROGERS ["Death Strikes at Midnight and Three," "The Deadshot Ricochet"]

One of DC's fastest-rising stars in the late 1970's, Marshall Rogers, a former architecture student, pencilled but a handful of short mystery and super-hero stories before being teamed by editor Julius Schwartz with writer Steve Englehart and inker Terry Austin for a six-issue run of DETECTIVE COMICS that many comics fans to this day consider to be the *definitive* portrayal of the Dark Knight. Since that time, Rogers has worked on a number of DC titles and is currently the artist on Marvel's *G.I. Joe*.

GEORGE ROUSSOS ["Knights of Knavery"]

In 1940, having answered an ad run by Bob Kane for an art assistant, George Roussos got a job as background man and letterer for the Batman series on the recommendation of Bill Finger. Roussos eventually began inking over several Batman pencillers, including Jerry Robinson, and illustrated many stories for other DC features, such as Air Wave. Roussos' major contribution to comics was in his innovative coloring techniques; his were always among DC's best-colored stories. In 1972, Roussos left DC for Marvel, where he currently works as cover colorist.

Ed Hannigan and Dick Giordano (1983).

BOB ROZAKIS ["Bat-Mite's New York Adventure"]

A comics fan well-known to the DC staff of the 1960's, Bob Rozakis began his professional career in the early 1970's as an assistant editor to Julius Schwartz. Since that time, Rozakis has shifted his focus away from the editorial side of comics and currently handles one of the most important jobs at DC, that of Production Director. Over the years, Rozakis has scripted dozens of stories for DC as well, including a string of Robin tales.

WALTER SIMONSON ["A Caper a Day Keeps The Batman Away"]

Current writer/artist of Marvel's *X-Factor*, Walter Simonson has made a number of important contributions to DC Comics over the years, including the award-winning Manhunter series he produced with Archie Goodwin as the back-up feature in DETECTIVE COMICS during 1973–74. When the Manhunter series came to an end in the pages of the Batman feature, readers were treated to the first—but not the last—depiction of the Darknight Detective *à la* Simonson.

BOB SMITH ["Bat-Mite's New York Adventure"]

Inker Bob Smith first became a comics fan in college and, after graduation, sent art samples to various companies. In 1974, Smith got his start illustrating features for *Crazy*, Marvel Comics' humor magazine. Shortly thereafter, Smith became the regular inker on DC's PLASTIC MAN and SUPER FRIENDS, eventually graduating to the Batman stories in BATMAN FAMILY. Smith is currently the regular inker of DC's CAPTAIN ATOM and STARMAN.

DICK SPRANG ["The Birth of Batplane II," "Jungle Cat-Queen," "The Origin of the Superman-Batman Team"]

When DC began asking for more Batman material than Bob Kane and Jerry Robinson could produce, Dick Sprang was one of the earliest artists hired to help draw the strip anonymously in the Kane style. But from the first, Sprang exhibited an exciting, dynamic style that, by the mid-'40s, could never have been mistaken for Kane's or anyone else's. While Robinson's Batman was dark and brooding, Sprang's was full of life and energy. Sprang's barrel-chested Dark Knight, who had a square jaw sharp enough to cut leather, constantly battled the most visually interesting criminals of the 1950's. Sprang was unquestionably one of the Batman masters and defined

Pat Broderick (1985).

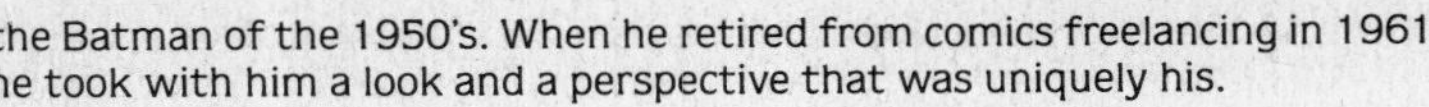

the Batman of the 1950's. When he retired from comics freelancing in 1961, he took with him a look and a perspective that was uniquely his.

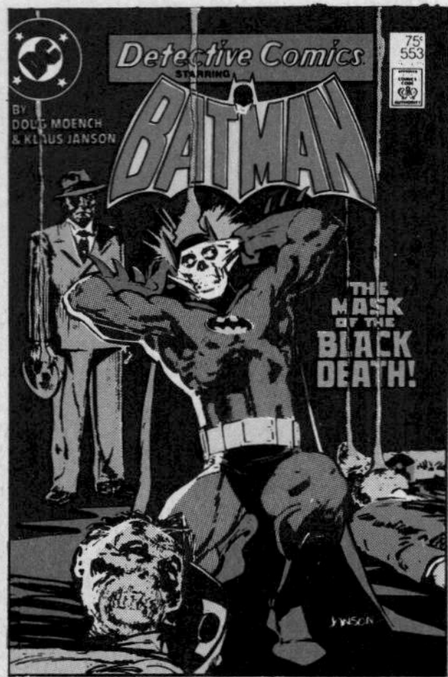

Klaus Janson (1985).

JOE STATON ["The Autobiography of Bruce Wayne"]

Joe Staton began his career at Charlton, co-creating a fondly-remembered book called *E-Man*. From there, his next stop was Marvel, where he inked several titles before coming to DC in the mid-1970's. Since then, Staton—equally adept at pencilling and inking—has drawn nearly every single DC character and, with writer/DC Vice President Paul Levitz, co-created a Batman spin-off character called The Huntress, the daughter of the Batman of another dimension.

ALEX TOTH ["Death Haunts the Skies"]

Illustrator Alex Toth began working for DC in 1947, drawing Dr. Mid-Nite, Green Lantern, Johnny Thunder, and a large number of western and science-fiction tales. Toth, whose style was highly influenced by strip illustrators such as Noel Sickles, quickly earned the admiration of his peers and is today known as one of the masters in the field. Though he left comics in 1964 for a long stint at the Hanna-Barbera animation studio, where he designed such cartoon characters as Space Ghost and the Super Friends, Toth returns to the drawing board from time to time to lend his unique approach to storytelling. During his lengthy career, Toth has illustrated but one Batman story—the one included in this volume.

LEN WEIN ["A Caper a Day Keeps The Batman Away"]

Len Wein is a mainstay of the comics field, having created dozens of characters and having held numerous editorial positions both at DC and at Marvel. As a Batman writer in the 1970's and early 1980's, Wein's trademark was to bring more of a Golden Age sense of fun and wonder back to the Gotham Guardian. Wein's Batman fought colorful costumed villains more often than not, and while he was not a "super-hero," he was more costumed crimefighter than terrifying vigilante. Like Dennis O'Neil and Dick Giordano, Len Wein has enjoyed a dual role in shaping Batman's career—as a writer until 1982, and, from 1982 to 1986, as the editor of BATMAN and DETECTIVE.

(Mark Waid is an associate editor at DC Comics, and a member of its development group.)

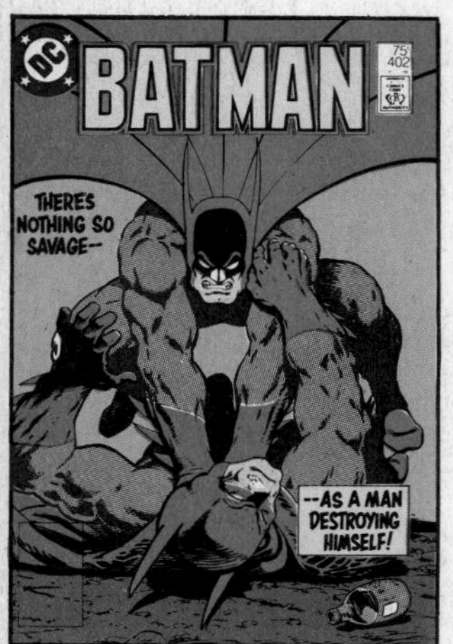

Jim Starlin (1986).

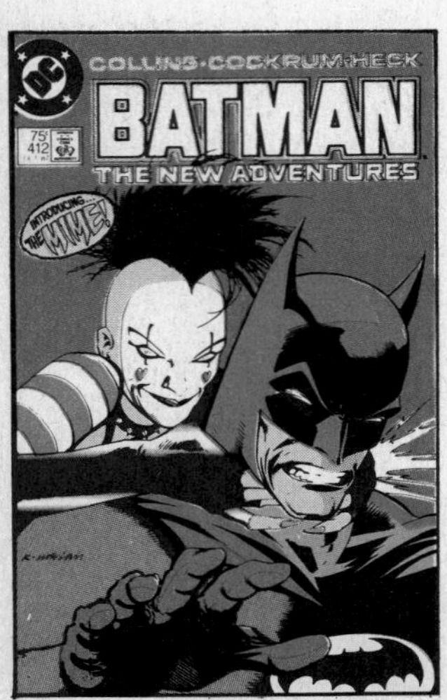

Kevin Nowlan (1987).